THE *A*DVENT HOPE IN SCRIPTURE AND HISTORY

Editor
V. NORSKOV OLSEN

CONTRIBUTORS

Godfrey T. Anderson, Niels-Erik Andreasen, Bryan W. Ball, Richard K. Emmerson, Harold E. Fagal, Fritz Guy, Paul J. Landa, V. Norskov Olsen, Norval F. Pease, Richard Rice.

REVIEW AND HERALD PUBLISHING ASSOCIATION
Washington, DC 20039-0555
Hagerstown, MD 21740

Copyright © 1987 by
Review and Herald Publishing Association

Printed in U.S.A.

Bible texts credited to Phillips are from J. B. Phillips: *The New Testament in Modern English,* Revised Edition. © J. B. Phillips 1958, 1960, 1972. Used by permission of Macmillan Publishing Co., Inc.

Bible texts credited to RSV are from the Revised Standard Version of the Bible, copyrighted 1946, 1952 © 1971, 1973.

Library of Congress Cataloging in Publication Data

The Advent hope in Scripture and history.

Includes bibliographies and indexes.
Contents: The Advent hope in the Old Testament; The Advent hope in apocalyptic literature/Niles-Erik Andreasen—The Advent hope in the New Testament/Harold E. Fagal—The Advent hope in early Christianity/Paul J. Landa—[etc.].
1. Second Advent—History of doctrines. 2. Hope—Religious aspects—Christianity—History of doctrines. 3. Seventh-day Adventists—Doctrines. 4. Adventists—Doctrines. I. Olsen, V. Norskov (Viggo Norskov).
II. Anderson, Godfrey Tryggve, 1909-
BT886.A36 1987 236'.9 86-22088
ISBN 0-8280-0311-4

THE *A*DVENT
HOPE
IN SCRIPTURE
AND
HISTORY

Table of Contents

About the Authors

Godfrey **T. Anderson** was research professor of American history and university archivist at Loma Linda University, Loma Linda, California. He served in many educational posts, including president of La Sierra College from 1946 to 1954 and Loma Linda University from 1954 to 1967. He received his Master's degree in education from Northwestern University, Evanston, Illinois, in 1934, and earned a Ph.D. degree in history from the University of Chicago in 1944. He was awarded the Doctor of Laws degree by Walla Walla College, College Place, Washington, in 1961. His published writings include *Walk God's Battlefield* (1971); *Outrider of the Apocalypse: Life and Times of Joseph Bates* (1972); *The Past Is Always Present* (1977); and *Spicer: Leader With the Common Touch* (1983).

Niels-Erik Andreasen is associate dean of the Division of Religion and professor of Old Testament at Loma Linda University, having also taught in the religion departments of Pacific Union College, Angwin, California, and Avondale College, Cooranbong, New South Wales, Australia. He received his undergraduate degree in religion and history from Newbold College, Bracknell, Berkshire, England, in 1963; the M.A. degree in Old Testament in 1965 and the B.D. degree in 1966 from Andrews University, Berrien Springs, Michigan; and the Ph.D. degree in 1971 from Vanderbilt University, Nashville, Tennessee. He has authored three books—*The Old Testament Sabbath* (1972), *Rest and Redemption* (1978), and *The Christian Use of Time* (1978)—along with numerous articles, essays, and reviews.

Bryan W. Ball is president of Avondale College, Australia. Prior to this present post he chaired the department of theology and Christian philosophy, Graduate School of Theology, Newbold College, England. His earlier experience included service as a church administrator. He holds an M.A. degree from Andrews University (1966) and a Ph.D. degree from the University of London, England

7

(1971). He has authored two books: *A Great Expectation: Eschatological Thought in English Protestantism to 1660* (1975), and *The English Connection: The Puritan Roots of Seventh-day Adventist Belief* (1981).

Richard K. Emmerson is professor of English in the department of English, Walla Walla College, having joined the faculty there in 1971. He holds an M.A. degree in English from Andrews University (1971) and a Ph.D. degree from Stanford University (1977). His publications include *Antichrist in the Middle Ages: A Study of Medieval Apocalypticism, Art, and Literature* (1981); *Homo, Memento Finis: The Iconography of Just Judgment in Medieval Art and Drama; Census and Bibliography of Medieval Manuscripts Containing Apocalypse Illustrations, c. 800-1500;* and a large number of contributions to professional journals.

Harold E. Fagal is professor of New Testament in the Division of Religion, Loma Linda University, having joined its faculty in 1964. His earlier experience included services as a pastor and church departmental leader for nineteen years. He holds the M.A. degree (1954) and M.Div. degree (1964) from the Seventh-day Adventist Theological Seminary, Andrews University; and an M.Th. degree (1969) and Ph.D. degree (1975) from Fuller Theological Seminary, Pasadena, California. Publications include "John and the Synoptic Tradition," in *Scripture, Tradition, and Interpretation* (1978); and several articles in the newly revised *International Standard Bible Encyclopedia,* vol. 3.

Fritz Guy is associate pastor of the University Church of Seventh-day Adventists in Loma Linda. From 1977 to 1984 he was professor of theology in the Department of Theology and Christian Philosophy, Seventh-day Adventist Theological Seminary, Andrews University. His earlier service included dean of the College of Arts and Sciences, Loma Linda University, where he also served as associate dean and professor of theology. Prior to this he served as assistant editor of *The Youth's Instructor,* Washington, D.C., and as a pastor of the Seventh-day Adventist Church in the Southeastern California Conference. He earned an M.A. degree (1955) and a B.D. degree (1961) from the Seventh-day Adventist Theological Seminary, Andrews University, and an M.A. degree (1966) and Ph.D. degree (1971) from the University of Chicago. His writings include *Man and His Time: Three Contemporary Theological Interpretations* (1971) and articles in the *Seventh-day Adventist Encyclopedia,* the *Westminster Dictionary of Church History,* and numerous other magazines and journals. He was coeditor of *Meeting the Secular Mind: Some Adventist Perspectives* (1985).

Paul J. Landa is professor of church history and chairman of the Department of Historical Studies in the Division of Religion, Loma Linda University, having joined the faculty in 1971. He received his undergraduate degree from Avondale College. He earned an M.A. degree from Andrews University (1967), and an M.A. degree (1968) and the Ph.D. degree (1976) from Vanderbilt University. He is managing editor of the journal *Adventist Heritage* and has contributed to two books: *The Sanctuary and the Atonement* (1981) and *Colloque Guillaume Farel* (1982).

V. Norskov Olsen, professor of church history, retired in 1984 as president of Loma Linda University. Before joining the faculty of Loma Linda University, he was chairman of the department of religion and academic dean of Newbold College, England, where he became president in 1960. He joined the faculty of Loma Linda University in 1968 as professor of church history; he became chairman of the Department of Religion in 1970, dean of the College of Arts and Sciences and provost of the La Sierra campus of Loma Linda University in 1972, and president of the university in 1974. He holds an M.A. degree (1950) and B.D. degree (1951) from the Seventh-day Adventist Theological Seminary, Andrews University; a M.Th. degree (1960) from Princeton Theological Seminary; a Ph.D. degree (1966) from the University of London; and a Th.D. degree (1968) from the University of Basel, Switzerland. He has authored two books—*The New Testament Logia on Divorce* (1971) and *John Foxe and the Elizabethan Church* (1973)—along with numerous articles and reviews.

Norval F. Pease is emeritus professor of applied theology at Loma Linda University. His early service included pastoral work and academy teaching. He served as president of La Sierra College, Arlington, California, from 1954 to 1960; as chairman of the Department of Applied Theology of the Seventh-day Adventist Theological Seminary, Andrews University; and as chairman of the Department of Religion on the Loma Linda campus of Loma Linda University and also on the La Sierra campus of the same institution. He holds the degrees of M.A. in religion and B.D. from the Seventh-day Adventist Theological Seminary, and the Ph.D. degree from the School of Communication Arts, Michigan State University, East Lansing, Michigan. His writings include *By Faith Alone* (1962), *"And Worship Him"* (1967), *The Faith That Saves* (1969), *Think on These Things* (1969), *Heal the Sick* (1972), *Saint Under Stress* (1980), and *The Good News* (1982).

Richard Rice is professor of theology in the Division of Religion, Loma Linda University. His earlier service included pastoral ministry in southeastern California. He received his M.Div. degree (1969) from the Seventh-day Adventist Theological Seminary, Andrews University, and his M.A. degree and Ph.D. degree (1974) from the University of Chicago Divinity School. He assumed his teaching position at Loma Linda University in 1974. He has written numerous articles and is the author of the books *The Openness of God* (1980), *When Bad Things Happen to God's People* (1985), and *The Reign of God* (1985).

Preface

THE Christian evaluation of the conditions, meaning, and purpose of life is conceived within the framework of a great conflict between good and evil. This controversy, with its theological issues, is centered in three great events: (1) the primeval temptation and fall of man; (2) the incarnation of Christ, with correlative events of the crucifixion, the resurrection, and the ascension; and (3) the second advent of Christ. God's promise of redemption, after the original fall of man, and the redemptive effects of the incarnation of Christ, as well as the assurance of the glorification of the saved at His second coming and the Edenic restoration of the earth, make the message of the Bible one of hope.

In the ancient world man had little concept of history, and what understanding he had was conceived as a circular movement of historical events. The uniqueness of the Hebrew prophets' idea of history was a specific linear concept climaxing in the appearance of the Son of man.

A landscape painter may in the same painting portray in the foreground a village, with its houses and people, and in the background a valley and hills, sky and sun, even though some are a very great distance away. Likewise, the Old Testament writers, in describing the future, depicted the first and second advents of Christ, the first as the foreground and the latter as the background of salvation history.

The Biblical hope with its many facets does not move in a circuit, with one center, around the first or the second advents of Christ; it moves in an ellipse, which has two foci, around both advents, inseparably. The New Testament writers expressed strong faith in a fully realized hope at the second advent on account of the redemptive accomplishments at Christ's first advent. In the great conflict between good and evil, the first advent is the D-day, when the decisive battle was won; but Christ's return will be the V-day—the final victory of the righteous will then take place.

The present volume has as its title *The Advent Hope in Scripture and History*.

11

Accordingly, the advent hope is examined both in the Old and New Testaments (chapters 1 and 3). The intertestamental period was rich in apocalyptic literature, which sought to disclose future events. This literature is significant for an evaluation of both the Old and New Testament apocalyptic material (chapter 2).

During the history of the Christian church, with Christ's first advent in the past, the study of the advent hope was focused on the second advent of Christ. The understanding, role, and significance of the second advent in the lives of the believers and in the teaching of the church during the most significant periods of church history have been analyzed (chapters 4 to 7).

For a clearer understanding of the events leading to the creation of the Seventh-day Adventist Church, the story of the great second advent awakening prior to 1844 has been retold (chapter 8). The theological place of the doctrine of the second advent in the history and life of the Seventh-day Adventist Church has been reviewed (chapter 9). The advent hope in contemporary Christian thought is presented (chapter 10), and after the various authors have evaluated the Biblical and historical material, the volume, most appropriately, closes with a presentation of the total theological meaning of the advent hope. Such is the scope and outline of the present study.

In order to aid the general reader with many technical words, a glossary has been provided. The extensive Scripture index and a general index will be found useful. The student who is interested in pursuing further study of a given topic will find the comprehensive notes furnished at the close of each chapter to be most valuable.

The present work is a symposium, each author responsible for the content of his respective chapter. There was, however, a joint effort of the ten scholars, who are specialists in their specific areas of writing, to make their individual contribution a unified part of the total work. A number of these are professors in Biblical and theological studies at Loma Linda University, California. Each writer sought, within the space limitations, to bring together the most distinctive aspects of his topic.

The idea and initiative for this book came from Raymond F. Cottrell, former head book editor of the Review and Herald Publishing Association. He not only conceived the idea but suggested the scope and outline of the work and was of inestimable help in its beginning stages. In retirement he has followed the development of the project with interest and counsel. Raymond H. Woolsey, one of the Review book editors, has patiently brought this many-authored work through the multifaceted editorial and publishing stages.

The book is a companion volume to *The Sabbath in Scripture and History*. The purpose was to publish a two-volume work dealing with the two doctrines that gave birth to the name Seventh-day Adventist.

The Advent Hope in Scripture and History was long in writing. Now that it is ready to go to press, I wish to express my deep appreciation to my colleagues—the authors—and to the publisher and its staffs. In editing a multiauthored book, much correspondence and detailed work takes place. I do wish to acknowledge the continued assistance of my secretary, Antoinette Yakush. These and others deserve sincere gratitude.

Christ is the goal of history. While He was on earth He knew that He had a function in the great drama of history pictured in the Old Testament. The apostles and the early church lived, preached, and worked within the charged atmosphere of the latter days. They considered their own time an apocalyptic age. They lived in a historical tension between the first advent and the second advent, between the now and then. In spite of the delayed second advent, world history and salvation history are constantly moving toward this climax. The apostle Paul states it in these words:

"Praise be to God and Father of our Lord Jesus Christ for giving us through Christ every spiritual benefit as citizens of Heaven! For consider what he has done—before the foundation of the world he chose us to be, in Christ, his children, holy and blameless in his sight. He planned, in his love, that we should be adopted as his own children through Jesus Christ—this was his will and pleasure that we might praise that glorious generosity of his which he granted to us in his Beloved. It is through him, at the cost of his own blood, that we are redeemed, freely forgiven through that free and generous grace which has overflowed into our lives and given us wisdom and insight. For God has allowed us to know the secret of his plan, and it is this: he purposed long ago in his sovereign will that all human history should be consummated in Christ, that everything that exists in Heaven or earth should find its perfection and fulfilment in him. In Christ we have been given an inheritance, since we were destined for this, by the One who works out all his purposes according to the design of his own will. So that we, in due time, as the first to put our hope in Christ, may bring praise to his glory! And you too trusted him, when you had heard the message of truth, the gospel of your salvation. And after you gave your confidence to him you were, so to speak, stamped with the promised Holy Spirit as a pledge of our inheritance, until the day when God completes the redemption of what is his own; and that will again be to the praise of his glory" (Eph. 1:3-14, Phillips).

Here the apostle Paul presents the "Christ alone" of history as well as Adventism at its best. The "Christ alone" of history is a living person, and His redemptive deeds—past, present, and future—should be proclaimed in all their historical and eschatological realism as an answer to all our human needs.

Yours in the "blessed hope,"

Viggo Norskov Olsen
Editor

CHAPTER 1

The Advent Hope
in the Old Testament

Niels-Erik Andreasen

T HE expression "advent hope" is associated both with Christ's first coming, notably during the weeks of advent leading up to Christmas, and especially with His second coming in the end of the world. This hope has been a firm conviction and constant companion of many Christians since New Testament times. But also God's people in Old Testament times shared the advent hope, and we find it expressed in the pages of the Bible from Genesis to Malachi. The Old Testament advent hope was based upon the promises of a coming Redeemer—the same promises that the early Christians applied to Jesus Christ, according to the New Testament. But whereas the New Testament hope focuses exclusively upon the return of Christ, the Old Testament hope has two foci—the nearer first advent and the more distant second advent. Frequently, both foci come to expression in a single picture. This chapter will examine the advent hope in the Old Testament: its basic meaning, its object, its two foci, and its fulfillments.

Hope in the Old Testament

Before turning to the specific Old Testament promises of the advent hope, let us consider the meaning of hope itself. This becomes helpful when we realize that hope occupies an important place in the Old Testament and is associated with many objects.[1] Among the more common Hebrew terms with the meaning "hope," the following stand out: 1. *qwh* is a Hebrew root that forms both verbs and nouns and expresses the idea of "cord," "stretching out," and hence "tension."[2] When referring to hope, it therefore indicates a strained expectation. For example, Zechariah 9:12 speaks about "prisoners of hope," and in Isaiah 5:2 God looked, hoped strenuously, but, as it turned out, in vain, for His vineyard to yield fruit. 2. *hkh*, with a basic meaning of "wait for," also expresses hope, but in this case a hope characterized by waiting or lingering (Isa. 8:17), perhaps patiently (Dan. 12:12). 3. *sbr* has the meaning of "think," "examine," or "inspect," but it also expresses hope that watches out for or anticipates something (Ps. 104:27; 145:15).

Its corresponding noun *sêber* is also translated "hope" (Ps. 146:5). 4. *yhl*, with two derivatives *tohelet* and *yahil*, indicates hope that expects, waits, even endures, perhaps in the face of opposition or discouragement (Isa. 42:4; Job 6:11).

Taken together, these terms weave a rich tapestry of the Old Testament concept of hope. It involves tense waiting, patient longing, watchful expectation, and enduring longing. All of these, in turn, contribute to our understanding of the meaning and experience of the advent hope in the Old Testament: It is a very intense and deeply personal concept.

What is the object of such hope within the Old Testament? For what did ancient Israel hope? To answer this question in detail would be nearly impossible here, but it is worth noting that the pages of the Old Testament hold out hope for many different things. The patriarchs hoped for a new land and for posterity (Gen. 12:1-3; 48:21); the Hebrew slaves in Egypt hoped for deliverance (Ex. 2:23-25). Moses and his fellow wanderers in the wilderness hoped for the Promised Land (Deut. 34). Israel under the judges and kings hoped for rest (1 Kings 8:56) and peace (1 Chron. 22:9). Job hoped for personal restoration in a meeting with his redeemer (Job 19:25-27), the psalmist looked hopefully to Jerusalem (Psalm 122). In the prophets we read of hope for a new earth (Eze. 36:34, 35), and for a return from Babylon to the homeland (Isa. 51:9-11; Dan. 9:1, 2; Zech. 14:16-21). And these are but some of the objects of hope within the Old Testament.

Where did this hope originate? What is its fountain and inspiration? Some have suggested that it goes back to the early history of the patriarchs, who always looked forward to green pastures, a new land, a city made by God (Heb. 11:10).[3] Others think that Israel's exodus from Egypt, the forty years of wandering, the conquest and settlement, played a major role, for here she experienced anew the hope for a land with rest and peace.[4] More likely, no historical experience should be singled out as the source of this hope, for it is in reality a fundamental element of faith in God. Through revelation, God makes certain promises. To believe in Him means to hope.[5] This explains why hope persists throughout the Old Testament. Where there is faith in God, hope reigns; but where there is doubt, despair overrules.[6] Thus, all hope—whether for a land, freedom, rest, peace, restoration, Jerusalem, or a new earth—is really hope in God (Ps. 39:7; 130:7; Isa. 25:9; Jer. 17:7).

Here lies the crux of the matter. All Old Testament hope ultimately is hope in God. Therefore, the fulfillment of the Old Testament hope can never be assured by Israel, even when she may put forward her best efforts. Only God can fulfill this hope, and that happens not when Israel finally succeeds in coming to God, but when God comes to His people.[7] Consequently, all Old Testament hope ultimately is an advent hope: namely, the hope that God will come to His people.

The Immanuel prophecy in Isaiah 7:14 demonstrates this understanding of hope very forcefully. The story is familiar. Young king Ahaz (732-716 B.C.) came under attack by two enemy kings, Pekah of Israel and Rezin of Syria, and the situation turned desperate for him. We know from verse 3 that he attended to the fortification systems of Jerusalem, and 2 Kings 16:10-16 informs us that he even went so far as to make an alliance with the dangerous Assyrian military power to secure help with his immediate problem. Worst of all, he burned his own son as a sacrifice to foreign gods (verse 3). After these desperate and regrettable efforts to seek peace, the king was met by the prophet Isaiah and received a promise from God, a promise that God Himself would deliver Jerusalem, but a promise Ahaz refused (Isa. 7:12).

Then Isaiah returned with a sign from God that no king could refuse, the Immanuel sign, meaning "God with us" (verse 14). Through this sign, the deliverance and security of Jerusalem was taken out of the hands of King Ahaz, and all his plans—whether the child sacrifice, the alliance with Assyria, or the repaired defenses of Jerusalem—were rejected as useless. Nothing he or his subjects had accomplished could give hope. Only God Himself became that hope. He would be with them to deliver them, as indicated by the birth of the Immanuel child.

This promise, though given to King Ahaz in Old Testament times, did not meet its fulfillment until nearly eight centuries later, when God was born in Jesus Christ to be with us (Matt. 1:23). Thus, the Old Testament hope in the Immanuel child becomes an advent hope, fulfilled in the first coming of Christ.

Therefore, though it takes many forms, Old Testament hope is in the final analysis an advent hope, a hope in God, and specifically a hope that God will come to His people: "God with us." "The prophetic promise proclaims at its deepest level not a coming *something,* after the manner of the fortunetellers, but *He* who comes."[8] For this advent the people of God in the Old Testament waited anxiously, lingered patiently, watched expectantly, longed for with endurance. All the emotions of hope focused upon Him who comes.[9] We will now examine some of the ways whereby the Old Testament presents the advent hope.

He Who Comes

Most readers of the Old Testament are familiar with the great Messianic prophecies in Isaiah 9 and 11 and Micah 4 and 5, and readily associate these with the Old Testament advent hope. In fact, these constitute only a small portion of the texts and images that portray this hope, leaving us with this question: Through what miltifaceted presentations does the Old Testament portray the advent hope?

The victor.—Genesis 3:15 has traditionally been interpreted as the earliest gospel *(protevangelium)* by both Jewish and Christian exegetes,[10] for it promises one who will come and defeat the enemy of mankind. Nevertheless, this interpretation has been challenged in recent years. For example, some have argued that the protagonists in Genesis 3:15 are not two individuals but a long line of descendants from two progenitors, the woman and the serpent;[11] or that the serpent does not represent the devil or even an evil principle, but that it is merely a snake;[12] or that no victory, such as that achieved by the Messiah, is promised here, but merely continuous confrontation in which man has the advantage over the snake but remains threatened;[13] or that Genesis 3:15 doesn't really contain a promise to the seed of the woman, but merely a curse upon the serpent.[14]

How shall we respond to these objections? First of all, we need not limit the prophecy exclusively to Mary the mother of Christ (the woman), as some have done, and her Son (the seed), for it does seem to imply a continuous conflict between two sets of descendants (seeds) as well.[15] However, this conflict will not continue forever, for one of the inflicted wounds is mortal. The struggle may be long and painful, but its outcome will be final victory when the head of the serpent will be crushed.

Second, the serpent of Genesis 3:15 is a real enemy, not just a symbolic, impersonal demonic power.[16] It was one of God's creations (verse 1), a fact that underscores the inexplicable mystery of sin but also its reality.[16] The serpent, then, is an evil being in God's world. Moreover, the text identifies the protagonists as the seed of the woman and the serpent. The word *seed* (*zr'*) is singular, and that could be understood collectively, in the sense of two lines of descendants (cf. Gen. 12:7). But it also implies individuality, for the text speaks of *your* head, *his* heel (chap. 3:15b). Thus, the conflict is very personal and carried out by individuals.

Does this text really contain a promise, or only a curse, as some have charged? Notice that the serpent is condemned to the dust of the earth, a symbol of humiliation and death.[17] From this same dust man himself had been taken (chap. 2:7) and raised up to sonship of God. Thus, the conflict is fought over the position of sonship of God in this world. In order to bring man down into the dust of humiliation and defeat, the serpent strikes at his heel, but in the process exposes its head to be mortally crushed.[18] Here lies the promise. Someone will crush the head of this deadly enemy and bring it low into the dust. The result is death (2 Sam. 22:37-43). But in the process someone else will be raised up from the dust to receive honor and life. The result is victory (1 Kings 16:2). Who will fulfill this promise of victory over evil but the One whose seed endures forever (2 Sam. 7:12; Ps. 89:4), God's Messiah? [19] This victor was promised in the Old Testament, and His victory was fulfilled in the New Testament by the first advent of Christ, born of a woman. And yet as we focus on this fulfillment, a second emerges before our eyes when He will come again a second time and "reign until he has put all his enemies under his feet" (1 Cor. 15:25, RSV).

Here, then, we find the first Old Testament reference to the advent hope. Notice that it is a hope in God, specifically that God will come to His people, and that it has two parts. First, the promise of the seed of a woman born into enmity with the seed of the devil met its fulfillment in the first advent. Second, the promise of victory, where the seed will put the enemy under his feet once and for all, looks forward to the second advent. The Old Testament frequently portrays these two advent hopes in the same breath, as it were, whereas the New Testament sorts out the two foci for us.

The prophet.—Readers of the New Testament know of a Messianic expectation associated with a prophet to come.[20] Jewish and early Christian writings give evidence of the same hope.[21] Also, the Old Testament speaks of a prophet who will come (Deut. 18:15; Joel 2:28, 29; Zech. 12:10; 13:2-6; Mal. 4:5). What do these passages tell us about the Old Testament advent hope?

Deuteronomy 18:15 falls in a section of that book dealing with three appointed leaders: the king (chap. 17:14-20), the priests (chap. 18:1-8), and the prophet (verses 15-22). In connection with the latter, assurance is given us that God Himself will raise up a prophet to speak His word to the people. This prophet will be like Moses, who also was charged to announce God's word to the people from Mount Sinai (Ex. 20:18-20; Deut. 5:22-27). In fact, Moses serves as a model for the promised prophet, particularly with reference to his role as spokesman. But who is this prophet to come?

Many interpreters have understood this promise simply as an assurance of a continuing prophetic office in Israel,[22] arguing that "prophet" (singular in this case) is really to be understood collectively as also is the case with the king (chap.

17:14).[23] But chapter 18:15 clearly promises more than merely a sequence of prophets. Notice that whereas king, priest, and prophet receive instruction in this passage, only the role of the prophet is further expanded by a reference to the model prophet, Moses (verse 15), who will stand before any subsequent prophet as an ideal. And moreover, as a second Moses, the prophet to come as lawgiver and mediator between God and man belongs to the future. He is the eschatological prophet.[24] That hope was fulfilled by Jesus Christ when He stood on the Mount of Blessing and announced the word of God, the law, and the promises, to His people (Matt. 5-7). Here a second facet of the Old Testament hope emerges, a hope for a prophet who will come to mediate between God and people, teach them God's law, and proclaim His word.[25] It was fulfilled during the first advent.

Zechariah 12:10, in conjunction with 13:6, refers to a prophet to come, but he will be rejected and martyred by his own people, despite the fact that he set out to help them.[26] When they see what they have done, the people will mourn bitterly for him (chap. 12:10). This promise of a prophet to come and suffer also met its fulfillment in the first advent, particularly in the treatment of Jesus Christ by the hand of His own people, according to His words: " 'A prophet is not without honor except in his own country and in his own house' " (Matt. 13:57).

In Isaiah 40:3-8 a prophetic word announces the coming of God to redeem His people, a promise fulfilled in the New Testament by John the Baptist, who announced the first advent of Christ (John 1:23). A number of other Old Testament passages speak of a coming prophet who will prepare the way for the advent, both the first advent and the second (eschatological) advent. Joel 2:28, 29 speaks of the existence of prophets at the time of the end.[27] (Acts 2:17-21). Malachi 4:5 promises an Elijahlike prophet who will be a messenger assigned to prepare the way for Christ's coming (Mal. 3:1; Matt. 27:46, 47; Mark 9:12). This expectation of a prophetic forerunner of the advent was widely held among Jews and Christians in the New Testament period.

Thus the Old Testament teaching regarding the advent hope speaks about a prophet to come before both the first and the second advent. A prophet will announce the event, but furthermore, the one who comes will himself be a prophet like Moses, a mediator, a spokesman for God, and like so many other prophets, he will be rejected by his own people.

The priest.—Both Jews and Christians of New Testament times looked for a special priest, a high priest, or a royal priest to come.[28] What are the Old Testament roots of this aspect of the advent hope?

The most important Old Testament passage is Psalm 110: Here God announces His ruler in Zion (verse 2), and designates him "a priest for ever after the order of Melchizedek" (verse 4). Some interpreters view this as a coronation psalm used for the crowning of Israel's kings in Old Testament times,[29] and all agree that it is related to the ancient story of Melchizedek, priest and king of Salem (Jerusalem), whom Abraham visited after he delivered Lot from captivity (Gen. 14:17-20).[30] However, the connection with Genesis 14 indicates that our psalm must not be reduced merely to a coronation psalm for the kings of Jerusalem, for it points to a very ancient and important relationship between king and priest. Elsewhere in the Old Testament kings are warned not to usurp the office of the Levitical priest in Jerusalem (cf. 2 Chron. 26:16-21), but that is another matter. Here the two offices are combined by one person, for Psalm 110: 1, 4, 5 points to a special ruler, sitting at the right hand of God, who, like ancient Melchizedek, serves as both priest and king. He executes God's rule on earth in a unique way,[31] a rule whose fulfillment Christ secured when He sat down at the right hand of God, indicating His appointment to priestly office (Heb. 1:3; 5:6). This hope for a ruler who is both king and priest is an advent hope. No king or priest in Israel enjoyed such a joint designation. Only God's anointed could, like Melchizedek of old, hold both offices. In other words, the Old Testament roots of Christ's priesthood are sunk not only in the Levitical office of the Temple but also in the royal priesthood of Melchizedek. Consequently, His priestly services are not limited in aspect as are those of the Jerusalem sanctuary, as the letter to the Hebrews points out. Rather, as reality is to shadow, so He enlarges upon both the Levitical and the Melchizedekian types (Hebrews 7-9). Thus Psalm 110:4 announces the promise of Christ's royal priesthood into which He was inaugurated after His resurrection and ascension (see Heb. 5:5, 6; Acts 13:33).

Zechariah 6:9-14 reports upon the role of the priest in postexilic Judaism (c. 520 B.C.) by speaking about crowns[32] to be placed upon Joshua the high priest (verse 11) while "the Branch," the political leader, Zerubbabel, "shall bear royal honor, and shall sit and rule upon his throne" (verse 13). Here two leaders, a priest and a prince, will share the government in "peaceful understanding" (verse 13), each apparently wearing a crown.[33] Do they represent the Messiah, as in the case of the two anointed (literally, sons of oil) in the vision of the lampstand (chap. 4:14)? It would appear to be the case[34] so that the office of priest, together with the office of ruler, tells us about the coming Messiah, who will not only rule but also serve, intercede, mediate, and offer sacrifice (Heb. 8:1-7).

Thus the Old Testament advent hope looks for a coming priest who will minister to the people of God. He will be an intermediary royal priest who will perform such service as Israel was called to perform (Ex. 19:6) but failed to carry out. Having been born a son of God (Ps. 2:7; Acts 13:33), seated at the right hand of God (Heb. 8:1) and having obtained a "better" ministry (verse 6), He will come a second time to judge and "to save those who are eagerly waiting for him" (chap. 9:26-28). The Old Testament promise of a special priesthood was fulfilled in the first advent, but the hope of this promise continues until the second advent.

The servant.—The term *servant* is widely used in the Old Testament,[35] sometimes with a very honorable connotation,[36] but its best known occurrences are in the passages in Isaiah, particularly chapters 42:1-4; 49:1-6; 50:4-10; 52:13; 53:12, which consequently sometimes are referred to as the servant songs.[37] In them we read about the coming and the activity of someone called the servant of God. Who is this servant, and what can we learn about the Old Testament advent hope from these passages?

The scholarly studies dealing with these passages are legion, and many of them have focused upon the question of the identity of the servant. According to Isaiah 42:1-4, the servant will bring justice to Israel and to the nations around her. In chapter 49:1-6, he will give light to the nations. Chapter 50:4-11 promises a prophet who will teach God's word to Israel, despite opposition. And finally in chapters 52:13-53:12 we meet one who suffers vicariously for others. Who is this servant?

Some have held that he should be identified with Israel collectively[38] or with an individual of the past, present, or future.[39] Others have proposed that though the servant is an individual, he cannot be identified with any one single historical person, past or present, but that he is an ideal individual who encompasses in his personality all that is best and ideal in God's people—a sort of corporate personality.[40] However, none of these suggestions suffices, for no fitting single individual can be located in Israel's history. No priest, prophet, or king, past or present, adequately fulfills the servant's role. No period in Israel's history produced a people able to fill the servant role. Therefore, he is an individual to come, ultimately, not from the ranks of the people of Israel, but from God himself. "The servant stands at the eschaton." [41] He must be identified as the "coming one." [42] Hence, the servant songs belong to the Old Testament advent hope, but what do they say about the one who is to come?

He is a chosen, anointed ruler, like a king or judge, not one who draws attention to himself, but one who is selflessly dedicated to his task (chap. 42:1-4). Second, he is a national leader, like Moses, who gathers his people into a nation and establishes them in the world, but not without deep personal cost and suffering (chap. 49:1-6). Third, he is God's faithful teacher and spokesman to the people, like the prophet to come. He obediently hears God's instruction to them, even though they ignore his word and make sport of it (chap. 50:4-11). Fourth, he suffers and dies for others, thus fulfilling and completing all Israel's sacrifices in his own person (chap. 52:13-53:12; John 1:29; 1 Peter 2:24).

In every instance, whether fulfilling the role of ruler, leader, prophet, or priest, this individual to come is characterized by the concept of service, such service as Israel long had been called to perform but so far had neglected, for in one instance (Isa. 49:3) Israel is actually called "my servant." But in this the people failed, so that the burden of all the unfulfilled service will fall upon one single individual to come. Who is he?

Jesus Christ adopted the title and role of servant for Himself when He said, " 'A servant is not greater than his master; nor is he who is sent greater than he who sent him' " (John 13:16). By these words Jesus attempted to instruct His disciples in the purpose of His whole life on earth. His miracles, His parables, His instruction, His kindness—all were designed to show that He had come to serve, and at last He bent down to wash His disciples' feet to impress this upon their minds, especially upon Peter's (John 13:6-10). Years later the apostle Paul explained the purpose of the Incarnation as service with these words: "But [He] emptied himself, taking the form of a servant" (Phil. 2:7). Here in the Incarnation, in the life and death of Jesus Christ, the advent hope of the servant songs met their fulfillment.

The Messiah.—*Messiah* comes from a Hebrew word *māshiah,* meaning "anointed," and like its Greek equivalent, *christos* (christ), it is understood by all Christians as a name for the second person of the Godhead. We must now momentarily set aside that familiar identification to ask about the specific facets of the Old Testament advent hope that comes to expression in it. In an effort to do this, we may wish to distinguish between the general meaning of *messiah* (anointed) and the special meaning of *Messiah* (the coming redeemer, Christ).[43]

The Old Testament associates anointing with various individuals, including prophets (1 Kings 19:16), priests (Ex. 29:21), kings (1 Sam. 16:13f), and even a foreign king (Isa. 45:1), but more than any other official of Israel, it is used about the king. Consequently, when referring to the advent hope of the Messiah, the

Old Testament focuses upon a royal person. The Messiah is a king, in the line of David, a prince in Jerusalem, and a ruler over Israel (Isa. 9:6; 11:1; Jer. 23:5; Micah 5:2; Matt. 2:5, 6; Luke 2:4).

To be sure, some interpreters have become accustomed to name all Old Testament references to a coming redeemer *Messianic*, including Genesis 3:15, Deuteronomy 18:15, Isaiah 53, etc.[44] However, it would seem appropriate, at least from this perspective, to distinguish between a variety of ways whereby the advent hope comes to expression in the Old Testament. We have found that the promised victor, priest, prophet, servant, all express this hope and that the New Testament announced the fulfillment of all these in one person, Jesus Christ.

Now we come to the role of the royal messiah in expressing this hope, and as we shall see, it is a very important role indeed. The key passages associated with the royal messiah are Genesis 49:10-12; Numbers 24:17; 2 Samuel 7; Psalms 2, 45, 110; Isaiah 7:14; 9; 11; Jeremiah 23:5, 6; Ezekiel 34:20-24; Micah 4:8; 5:2-4; Zechariah 9:9; Daniel 9:24-27. All of them make use of royal concepts, reminding us that the Old Testament hope for the Messiah indeed looks for a coming king.[45] What can we say about this hope?

Some interpreters have suggested that since Israel became a kingdom rather late in history, during the time of Saul and David, the Messiah concept must also be late. In fact, the idea of kingship is much earlier and reaches back to the very beginnings of Israel's history (Ex. 19:6),[46] and so does the hope for a royal messiah. Already Genesis 49:10, 11 announces that the tribe of Judah will be a royal tribe and that it will provide a future ruler over all the people, both in war and in peace. A similar glimpse of the future king (scepter), who will arise in Israel as a star rises on the horizon, occurs in Balaam's prophecy in Numbers 24:17. Here a seed is planted that will grow into a full-fledged Messianic hope, but the chief characteristics of the Messiah are already clear. He will arise from Israel, in the tribe of Judah; he will rule the people, both in war and also in peace; and the shadows of this promise will reach down to the second advent.

The next important passage is 2 Samuel 7:12-14. It is a promise to David from Nathan the prophet after he had denied David the request to build a house for God. God, explained Nathan, will build a house for David instead, meaning that God would establish David's throne forever. How could later generations have kept faith in that promise when they saw David's line falter, the nation become divided, and its kings eventually killed or taken prisoner (1 Kings 12:16; 2 Kings 17:5, 6; 25:6, 7)? The answer comes from several psalms and many prophecies, namely, that God will fulfill His promise by sending a Messiah king in the line of David, a promise that was fulfilled in the birth of Jesus Christ in David's line and in David's city (Matt. 2:5, 6; Luke 2:4).[47] Yet the fulfillment of this hope reaches far beyond the first advent.

Three psalms call for special attention here, Psalms 2, 45, and 110. They are typically referred to as royal psalms because they all speak of the king, his strength, his glory, his rule, and his justice.[48] But this characterization of the psalms is inadequate, for no Israelite king in Jerusalem or Samaria ever lived up to the expectations of these psalms. Therefore, we have here prophecies of God's royal Messiah, who is to come in the future. He will be God's victorious Son (Ps. 2:7; Acts 4:25-29; 13:33); His throne will endure forever (Ps. 45:6; Heb. 1.8), and He will rule at the right hand of God as priest and king, in justice and peace (Ps. 110; Matt.

22:44; Acts 2:34; 1 Cor. 15:25; Eph. 1:20; Heb. 1:3, 13). Thus the prophecy of Nathan, enlarged in the Psalms, becomes an important aspect of the Old Testament advent hope, the hope for a royal messiah, a king and ruler, which was fulfilled by Jesus Christ during His first advent (Matt. 27:11; Mark 15:2-5; Luke 23:2-5), but it reaches forward to His second advent as well (Rev. 19:16).

However, Jesus Christ accepted the role of king only with serious qualifications, as indicated in these words: "Jesus answered, 'My kingship is not of this world'" (John 18:36). That is to say, the royal messiah whom God will send is unlike any ordinary historical king of ancient Israel. Therefore, no direct line of development exists between the role of Israel's king, even the best of these kings, and the Messiah. The Messianic hope does not derive or develop from an expectation of Israel's ideal king, so that the advent hope would be merely a projection from the hope of a good king in the near future.[49] Rather, the Messiah is someone new, sent from God. In short, the Old Testament advent hope does not speculate about what may come out of Jerusalem, but looks expectantly for what God will bring about. The great Messianic prophecies in Isaiah, Jeremiah, Ezekiel, Daniel, Micah, et cetera emphasize this point.

First, from where would the Messiah appear? According to Micah 5:2, He will come from Bethlehem in Ephrathah, south of Jerusalem; that is to say, He will not come a naturally born son from David's royal family in Jerusalem.[50] Rather, born in Bethlehem, He will come forth a scion of Jesse, the father of king David (Isa. 11:1; Amos 9:11). The natural family tree of Jesse has been cut down, and only the stump remains; yet from this nearly extinct root God will miraculously produce the Messiah. But this is not all. The Messiah has a double origin. He comes not only from the family tree of David, but also from eternity, from God Himself (Isa. 9:6; Eze. 34:23; Micah 5:2). This double origin of the Messianic hope (David's royal family and God Himself) corresponds with a double fulfillment of it in the first advent of Jesus Christ. Thus Matthew and Luke repeat the birth of Christ in Bethlehem (Matt. 2:1; Luke 2:4-6), whereas John reminds us that Christ was with God from the beginning, indeed, is Himself God (John 1:1). In this way the Old Testament advent hope affirms the mystery of incarnation (1 Peter 1:10), that the Messiah king would come as both man and God.

In light of the concrete, historical nature of the Messianic hope, we should not be surprised that the Old Testament advent hope looked to a specific time for its fulfillment. In Isaiah 9:1, 2, we read of the Messianic appearance as a great light in a time of great darkness among the people of Zebulon, Naphtali, and Galilee. Jeremiah 23:5 anticipates days to "come" when the Messiah will save Judah and Israel. And Daniel 9:24-27 announces seventy weeks of years (490 years) as the time interval between the rebuilding of Jerusalem and the coming Messiah.[51] Thus the Messianic hope is both historical and temporal in nature, but also final, eschatological, and eternal. Consequently, we observe that the Messiah's rule will have no end, but will last from this time and forevermore (Isa. 9:7), that He shall be priest forever (Ps. 110:4), and that He will bring about everlasting righteousness (Dan. 9:24).

Second, what kind of kingship will the Messiah introduce when He comes? The Old Testament portrayals of the Messianic rule employs expressions typical of the royal rule in Israel, but qualifies them in important ways. For example, Ezekiel 34:20-24 and Micah 5:4 describe that rule as the work of a shepherd who saves, protects, and feeds his sheep, in distinction from other shepherds who feed upon the sheep, an illustration applied to Jesus Christ in John 10:1-6. Elsewhere the Old Testament employs terms such as *justice, righteousness,* and *peace* to describe the Messiah's rule (Jer. 23:6; Isa. 9:7). A most detailed description is given in Isaiah 11:2-5. The Messiah, like David of old (2 Sam. 23:2) is filled by the Spirit of God, giving him wisdom and understanding, counsel and might, knowledge and fear of God. That same Spirit was given to Christ symbolically upon His baptism (Matt. 3:16; Luke 4:1; John 1:32). Provided with this gift, the Messiah will judge fairly, not on the basis of externals or hearsay (Isa. 11:3), but with equity, in righteousness and faithfulness (verses 4, 5). In consequence of His judgments, a distinction is made between right and wrong, as when a shepherd distinguishes between "sheep and sheep, rams and he-goats" (Eze. 34:17), whereupon his kingdom is established and a covenant confirmed with its citizens (Dan. 9:27).

The hope for such a ruler might be frightening, for it includes a judgment. Yet the Old Testament Messianic prophecies make it clear that, unlike ordinary rulers who judge, punish, and oppress, the Messianic ruler will not govern for his own sake but for the sake of his subjects. He will bring good news to the poor, lift up the brokenhearted, grant liberty to the captives, proclaim God's favor, and fill the mourners with joy (Isa. 61:1-4). Jesus called this promise of a Messianic rule into existence at the inauguration of His public ministry (Luke 4:16-21), and proceeded to carry it out in some very concrete ways (Matt. 11:5; Luke 7:22). Here we must also recall the servant prophecies in Isaiah. "A bruised reed he will not break, and a dimly burning wick he will not quench" (chap. 42:3). Here also belong Zechariah 9:9: "Lo, your king comes to you; triumphant and victorious is he, humble and riding on an ass, on a colt the foal of an ass." Thus Christ came to His city, in triumph, but humble (Matt. 21:5; John 12:14, 15). Is it possible for the Messiah to triumph through service and humility? The prophet answers, "Surely he has borne our griefs and carried our sorrows. . . . He was wounded for our transgressions, he was bruised for our iniquities; upon him was the chastisement that made us whole, and with his stripes we are healed" (Isa. 53:4, 5). The Old Testament advent hope of a Messiah looks for a victorious ruler, but one who, unlike other kings, will bear the brunt and pay the price of his victory in his own person. That hope was fulfilled in the first advent of Jesus Christ.

Third, what is the final outcome of the Messianic rule? The most vivid pictures of it appear in Isaiah 11:6-16, though they are confirmed in many other places. Here a new world is portrayed, as though restored to the pristine conditions of paradise. To achieve this, the very physical laws of nature must change, so that lamb and lion, child and poisonous snake, will live together in harmony (verses 6, 7). This peaceful condition will not be brought about through force but will come about naturally, as it were, founded upon the knowledge of God, which will cover the whole world (verse 9).

Consequently, this peaceful Messianic kingdom will be neither isolated nor localized, but universal in scope. All nations shall seek it (verse 10), remnants from the far corners of the world will join in and receive citizenship in it (verse 11) as they travel toward the kingdom on a way especially prepared for them (verse 16).

Has this hope of a Messianic kingdom been fulfilled? Some have thought that a measure of fulfillment of it has occurred in the life of the church,[52] but even such a limited fulfillment only foreshadows a still future fulfillment, perhaps as a foretaste, for no present or past achievement in this world has produced such a kingdom of peace. Rather, we have here an Old Testament advent hope still waiting for its fulfillment at the time of the second advent.

The Old Testament hope for a coming Messiah enriches our advent hope in several ways. It is the hope for a second son of David, born in Bethlehem, at a specific time, who in this present world will reestablish the principles of the kingdom of God: justice, righteousness, peace. Its fulfillment occurred in the first advent of Jesus Christ, born in Bethlehem, in the family of David, who in His life and death finished transgression, put an end to sin, atoned for iniquity, and brought in everlasting righteousness (Dan. 9:24). But this same promise also looks to the second advent of the Son of God, who comes from eternity and who will again restore the earth to its original state and establish His eternal kingdom of peace.

The Son of Man.—The second, eternal aspect of the promised Messiah receives further emphasis in the hope for a coming Son of man. This expression occurs repeatedly in the book of Ezekiel (e.g., chaps. 2:1; 3:4; 4:1) with the ordinary meaning "man" and refers merely to the prophet. However, in one place (Dan. 7:9-14) the expression "son of man" has a special meaning of importance to the Old Testament advent hope. The verse in question reads: "I saw in the night visions, and behold, with the clouds of heaven there came one like a son of man, and he came to the Ancient of Days and was presented before him" (verse 13). Several aspects of this coming Son of man call for our attention.

First, He does not come to earth. Consequently, we are not dealing with the first advent hope. Rather, He comes to the Ancient of Days, another name for God, in the clouds of heaven. There He receives dominion over all the peoples of the earth, an "everlasting dominion" over an eternal kingdom (verse 14). Second, His dominion and kingdom follow upon the heels of the kingdoms of this earth. They are judged (verse 10), and the enemies of God (the beasts) are slain (verses 11, 12). Consequently, the hope of a coming Son of man occurs in the end of earth's history, in the time of the final judgment and the restoration of all things. It is the second advent hope, associated with the prophecy of Daniel 8:14 and pertaining to "many days hence" (chap. 8:26) when God will decide the fate of mankind in His heavenly court.

In this connection it is interesting to note that Jesus Christ cherished the title "Son of man" for Himself and preferred not to use the title "Messiah" (Matt. 12:8; 26:63, 64; Mark 2:28; 8:31; 9:9; 14:61, 62; Luke 22:67-70). This situation calls for a number of observations. First, we know that the title "Messiah" was misunderstood in the time of the New Testament to mean a political deliverer who would drive out the Roman forces and restore a political nation, Israel (cf. Acts 21:38).[53] This narrow view stood in sharp distinction from the Old Testament Messianic hope, and Jesus Christ distanced Himself from it and generally did not employ the term *Messiah* for Himself. Second, the term *Son of man* was well known in New Testament times, for example in the pseudepigraphical book of 1 Enoch,[54] and it had the same general meaning that we have found in Daniel 7:13.[55] Hence, when using the expression *Son of man* about Himself, Jesus employed a commonly understood term, and one that would ultimately draw attention to the book of Daniel. Third, Jesus Christ would have wished to direct the attention of those who experienced the first advent to the second advent of the Son of man in the clouds of heaven, without which the advent hope would not be complete.

Thus, the Old Testament advent hope looks for a coming Son of man in the end of the world who will receive dominion from God after the judgment has sat and who will establish an everlasting kingdom. When Jesus Christ accepted that title for Himself, He affirmed that this hope has two foci, one in the near foreground of His first advent, and another in the distant background of His second advent.

Redeemer and judge.—Most people think of hope especially during times of trouble. Old Testament hope also comes to clearest expression during such times. Thus, Abraham hoped when he had no heir. Israel hoped during her servitude in Egypt. The prophets brought messages of hope in times of distress and oppression. In fact, hope in general is the Bible's response to trouble, whereas the advent hope in particular is the Bible's strongest response to the greatest trouble. That greatest trouble is sometimes referred to as "the day of the Lord."

Many suggestions have been made regarding the origin of this expression,[56] but one thing is quite clear. It designates the time of trouble when God will intervene in the experience and history of His people. In places it refers to known past events in Israel's history during Old Testament times (Isa. 22:1-14; Jer. 46:2-12; Lam. 1:12; Eze. 30:1-4). Elsewhere, it represents momentous future divine interventions in the experience of ancient Israel (Isa. 10:20; 13:1-22; Hosea 2:15, 16; Eze. 7:1-27). But, most important, this expression describes the final, eschatological worldwide turmoil in the end (Joel 2:10, 11; Mal. 4:1-6; Eze. 38, 39; Zech. 14).

Generally speaking, the day of the Lord is the day of judgment upon the people and upon the world, and therefore a day to be feared (Amos 5:18-20). However, it also is a time for the preparation and purification of a repentant remnant (Isa. 10:20; Zeph. 3:8-13; Jer. 31:31-34). How does the advent hope relate to this terrible day?

First, the Old Testament advent hope expects a coming judgment. God will judge the world from His heavenly sanctuary (Micah 1:2, 3), and He will begin with His own people (Eze. 9:6). Therefore, the coming judgment has two parts: It inquires about God's people, seeking out those who are loyal (verse 4; Jer. 5:1-5), and it brings judgment upon the enemies of God whose disloyalty to Him stands exposed (Joel 3:1-3; Zech. 14:1-15; Eze. 38, 39).

Second, the advent hope in the Old Testament waits for a coming redemption that is God's ultimate response to the terror of judgment on the day of the Lord. Thus, even the judgment of God contributes to the accomplishment of redemption, as portrayed, for example, in Isaiah 63:1-6. In this picture from the watchtower a lone warrior returns from battle. He has fought, he is strong and victorious, and has judged and defeated his foes. But more important, he brings salvation (verse 1) and redemption to those who wait for him (verse 4). Thus, judgment and redemption belong together in this passage, and they occur in the end of time.[57]

The Old Testament word for redeemer (goel) in Isaiah 63:4 means kinsman[58] (Ruth 4:6; Job 19:25), which indicates that the hope for redemption is both very strong and very personal. As Ruth sought redemption from her kinsman, Boaz, so the people of the Old Testament sought redemption from their God in a personal experience of deliverance (Isa. 25:9), which, like the coming judgment, has two facets. First, it liberates from the burdens of life, oppression, and sin, according to the prophecy of Isaiah 61:1-3, which met its fulfillment during the ministry of Jesus Christ in the first advent (Luke 4:16-20). Second, it liberates from death, annihilation, the last enemy and oppressor, as we found in Isaiah 63:1-6. This final deliverance is the second advent redemption, to which the Old Testament bears witness with the words: "For I know that my Redeemer lives, and at last he will stand upon the earth; and after my skin has been thus destroyed, then from my flesh I shall see God" (Job 19:25, 26). Here the Old Testament advent hope anticipates the destruction of death when God comes to restore His people in the end:[59] "He will swallow up death for ever, and the Lord God will wipe away tears from all faces, and the reproach of his people he will take away from all the earth" (Isa. 25:8; cf. Dan. 12:1-4). And finally, the advent hope culminates in the announcement: " 'For behold, I create new heavens and a new earth; and the former things shall not be remembered or come into mind' " (Isa. 65:17; cf. Rev. 21:1-5). This hope is waiting its fulfillment in the second advent, when it will be said, " 'Lo, this is our God; we have waited for him, that he might save us. This is the Lord; we have waited for him; let us be glad and rejoice in his salvation' " (Isa. 25:9).

Summary and Conclusion

Summary.—Hope, we discovered, is an integral part of Old Testament faith. To believe in the God of the Old Testament means to hope, hope in Him who comes. To be sure, Israel hoped for many things—land, freedom, rest, peace, et cetera—but these hopes never depended upon that which Israel could accomplish for herself. Rather, their hope depended upon God, specifically that God Himself would come to fulfill His promises to them. Hence, Old Testament hope is ultimately an advent hope.

How will all the promises of God be fulfilled and how will the Old Testament advent hope be honored? The answer to this question has many facets, like a cut jewel. God will send a victor to defeat the enemy; He will send a prophet to teach the people, a priest to mediate and minister, a servant who will lay down His own life for the sake of His people, a royal messiah to rule in righteousness, justice, and peace forever, a Son of man to hold dominion over the whole world at the end of time when the judgment will sit, and God will come to redeem His own. This advent hope persists throughout the pages of the Old Testament. Beginning in Genesis and rising to a crescendo in the Psalms, it shouts from the pages of the prophets and echoes down through coming centuries.

Hundreds of years later Jesus Christ came and assembled in His own unique person the fulfillment of all the facets composing the Old Testament advent hope. He is that victor who defeated the enemy by treading him underfoot. He is the prophet to come, God's Word to us, He is the faithful high priest who brought His own sacrifice for many. He is the servant who laid down His life for others. He is God's Messiah, whose kingdom of justice and peace is not of this world. He is the Son of man, our judge, and our redeemer. This Old Testament advent hope was fulfilled in the first advent as reported in the New Testament. However, although Christ fulfilled all these promises, the advent hope itself was not consummated in New Testament times, for Christ was rejected by His own people, crucified, and

He died.

Consequently, the New Testament, like the Old Testament, becomes a book of promise and hope. It begins with a promise of one born, to be named Jesus, " 'for he will save his people from their sins,' " (Matt. 1:21), and of Immanuel, which is "God with us" (Matt. 1:23), and like the Old Testament it too ends with a promise: "He who testifies to these things says, 'Surely I am coming soon.' Amen. Come, Lord Jesus!" (Rev. 22:20).

Conclusion.—Although the Old Testament advent hope focuses primarily upon the first coming of Christ to establish His kingdom, it foresaw His suffering and death and so bears witness to the fact that the kingdom of God will be rejected at first, yet it will ultimatey succeed when God comes a second time. Accordingly, the Old Testament looks forward to a second coming as well, and it keeps on inspiring our advent hope as it inspired the hope of the first followers of Jesus Christ. To them it meant that Jesus is, indeed, the one who "will come." To us it means that this Christ has come as promised and will come again a second time in order to fulfill at last all the promises that God has ever made.

NOTES

[1] See the surveys by W. Zimmerli, *Man and His Hope in the Old Testament*, SBT II/20 (London, 1971), pp. 4-9; H. W. Wolff, *Anthropology of the Old Testament* (Philadelphia, 1974), pp. 149f.

[2] Koehler-Baumgartner, *Lexicon in Veteris Testamenti Libros* (Leiden, 1958), pp. 559, 830, 1038f.

[3] See V. Maag, "Malkut Jhwh," *SVT* 7 (1960): 129-153.

[4] E.g., G. von Rad, "The Form-critical Problem of the Hexateuch," in *The Problem of the Hexateuch and Other Essays* (New York, 1966), pp. 1-78.

[5] H. D. Preuss, *Jahweglaube und Zukunfterwartung*, BWANT 7 (Stuttgart, 1968), p. 207.

[6] Wolff, *Anthropology*, pp. 154f.

[7] See Zimmerli, *Man and His Hope*, p. 24.

[8] W. Zimmerli, "Promise and Fulfillment," in C. Westermann and J. L. Mays, eds., *Essays in Old Testament Hermeneutics* (Richmond, 1963), p. 105.

[9] See, for example, the study by S. Mowinckel, *He That Cometh* (Nashville, 1956).

[10] For a Jewish Messianic interpretation of Genesis 3:15 see J. Skinner, *Genesis*, ICC 1 (New York, 1910), pp. 80f. The pre-Christian Greek translation of the Old Testament (LXX) apparently understood the verse in a Messianic sense. Thus R. A. Martin, "The Earliest Messianic Interpretation of Genesis 3:15," *JBL* 84 (1965): 425-427. Irenaeus, among the early Church Fathers (second century A.D.), developed this interpretation. *Against Heresies* 21. 1 *(ANF* 1:548).

[11] Thus C. Westermann, *Genesis* 1 (Neukirchen, 1982), book 1, p. 354; G. von Rad, *Genesis* (Philadelphia, 1972), p. 90; E. A. Speiser, *Genesis*, AB 1 (Garden City, N.Y., 1964), p. 22; Skinner, *Genesis*, p. 81.

[12] Skinner, *Genesis*, p. 81; cf. Von Rad, *Genesis*, p. 90.

[13] Skinner, *Genesis*, p. 81.

[14] Some interpreters have seen a relationship between verse 14 and verse 15. Cf. Westermann, *Genesis*, p. 354.

[15] Relying upon the Vulgate (Latin) translation: *"Ipsa conteret caput tuum"* ("she shall bruise your head"), many medieval exegetes applied the verse directly to the virgin Mary (Skinner, *Genesis*, p. 81). Luther corrected the translation to "it [the seed] shall bruise," and referred the promise to Jesus Christ. J. Pelikan, ed., *Lectures on Genesis*, Vol I of *Luther's Works* (St. Louis, 1969), pp. 191-198. Also, Calvin strenuously objected to the Vulgate translation, arguing that it confuses the mother of Christ with her seed. Moreover, he understood the seed collectively, but did concede that its victory was ultimately achieved by Christ. *Commentary on the Book of Genesis* (Edinburgh, 1847), Vol. I, p. 170. On this point see also E. G. White, *Patriarchs and Prophets* (Mountain View, Calif., 1958), p. 66. For a discussion of the history of the Vulgate translation and the interpretation of the promise in Genesis 3:15, see also B. Vawter, *On Genesis* (Garden City, N.Y., 1977), p. 83.

[16] Westermann, *Genesis*, p. 355.

[17] For the significance of being in the dust, see W. Brueggemann, "From Dust to Kingship," *ZAW* 84 (1972): 1-18.

[18] The translation of the verbs "bruise" (Heb. *šup*) is difficult. Perhaps two different roots are used here, one meaning "to tread underfoot," the other "to snap after" (Koehler-Baumgartner, *Lexicon*, p. 956). Or the second verb meaning "to seek after," "to overpower," and the like should serve to describe both activities. Or the first verb, of Akkadian origin with the meaning "to step upon with the foot," may through wordplay be given the meaning "to grasp," as with talons. For the latter hypothesis, see W. Wifall, "Gen. 3:15—A Protevangelium?" *CBQ* 36 (1974): 364. However, though the verbs may have the same meaning, the objects do not, and the outcomes of the respective actions are radically different.

[19] See Brueggemann, "From Dust to Kingship," pp. 8-11.

[20] This prophet is generally identified with John the Baptist (Mark 9:9-13; Matt. 11:11-15), but also Jesus was believed to be the prophet by some of His contemporaries (Luke 7:16; Mark 6:14f.; John 7:40; Acts 3:22).

[21] For the Jewish expectation see 1 Maccabees 14:41; Ecclesiasticus 48:1-10. In most instances this prophet represents a return of an Old Testament prophet, e.g., Moses, Elijah, Enoch, who will prepare the advent of the Messiah, but he himself was also considered to be a prophet by the Qumranites (1 QS 9:11; 4 QT). See O. Cullmann,

The Christology of the New Testament, rev. ed. (Philadelphia, 1963), pp. 14-23; H. M. Teeple, *The Mosaic Eschatological Prophet,* SBLM 10 (Philadelphia, 1957); F. M. Cross, *The Ancient Library of Qumran* (Garden City, N.Y., 1961), p. 219.

[22] See G. E. Wright, "Deuteronomy," *IB,* vol. 2, p. 448; Keil and Delitzsch, *The Pentateuch* (Grand Rapids, 1949), Vol. III, p. 394; S. R. Driver, *Deuteronomy, ICC* 5 (New York, 1909), p. 227. W. L. Holladay has suggested that Jeremiah saw himself as standing in the line of the Mosaic prophets: "The Background of Jeremiah's Self-understanding," *JBL* 83 (1964): 153-164; "Jeremiah and Moses: Further Observations," *JBL* 85 (1966): 17-27. This would indicate that the expectation of a prophet like Moses was kept alive in Old Testament times.

[23] P. C. Craigie, *The Book of Deuteronomy* (Grand Rapids, 1976), p. 262.

[24] G. von Rad, *Deuteronomy* (Philadelphia, 1966), p. 123; *Old Testament Theology* (New York, 1965), Vol. II, p. 261.

[25] Craigie, *Deuteronomy,* pp. 262f.; Keil and Delitzsch, *The Pentateuch,* Vol. III, p. 395.

[26] See D. Winton Thomas, "Zechariah," *IB,* vol. 6, p. 1108; W. Rudolf, *Haggai-Sacharja-Malachi,* KAT XIII/4 (Gerd Mohn, 1976), pp. 223f. The reference is clearly to the martyrdom of a coming deliverer. Whether or not he should be designated a prophet is debated by the interpreters. Cf. Keil and Delitzsch, *The Twelve Minor Prophets* II (Grand Rapids, 1949), p. 388.

[27] H. W. Wolff, *Joel and Amos* (Philadelphia, 1977), p. 66.

[28] See below, chapter 2. Additional references from the rabbinic literature are accumulated in Strack-Billerbeck, *Kommentar zum Neuen Testament,* Vol. IV, pp. 452-465. For a brief assessment of the whole problem see Cullmann, *Christology of the New Testament,* pp. 83-87. The Christian expectation of a priest or high priest comes to expression in the letter to the Hebrews and elsewhere (cf. John 17:1-26). See Cullmann, *Christology of the New Testament,* pp. 89-107.

[29] Thus A. Weiser, *The Psalms* (Philadelphia, 1962), p. 693; M. Dahood, *Psalms* III, AB 17c (Garden City, N.Y., 1970), p. 117; H.-J. Kraus, *Psalmen* (Neukirchen, 1966), Book XV/2, pp. 757f. For a contrary view, see S. Schreiner, "Psalm cs und die Investitur des Hohenpriesters," *VT* 27 (1977): 216-222.

[30] See J. G. Gammie, "Loci of the Melchizedek Tradition of Genesis 14:18-20," *JBL* 90 (1971): 385-396.

[31] Weiser, *The Psalms,* p. 693.

[32] Thus W. Harrelson, *Interpreting the Old Testament* (New York, 1964), pp. 396f.

[33] For an alternative interpretation, see D. Winton Thomas, "Zechariah," *IB,* vol. 6, p. 1080. According to it only one crown was made, and it was originally placed upon the head of Zerubbabel, not Joshua. However, this interpretation requires textual emendations that in our view are unwarranted.

[34] See E. G. White, *Prophets and Kings* (Mountain View, Calif., 1943), pp. 593-597.

[35] See Zimmerli, *The Servant of God* (London, 1957), pp. 9-34.

[36] Thus Joshua 1:2 (about Moses) and Ps. 89:3 (about David). *Servant* is here a title of distinction.

[37] In addition to these so-called servant songs, the servant theme appears prominently in the surrounding chapters of Isaiah (40-48). See J. Muilenburg, "Isaiah 40-66," *IB,* Vol. 5, p. 406. Cf. H. Ringgren, *The Messiah in the Old Testament* (London, 1956), pp. 54-64. Clearly the servant concept occupies a prominent place in the Old Testament.

[38] Isaiah 49:3 identifies the servant as Israel.

[39] Among the suggested identifications by interpreters are: a prophet-teacher; Isaiah; Zerubbabel; Jehoiachin; Moses; Uzziah; Hezekiah; Josiah, the king; a new Moses; an unknown martyr; Jeremiah; Meshullam; Onias, the priest of Maccabean times; and the city of Jerusalem.

[40] See H. H. Rowley, "The Servant of the Lord in the Light of Three Decades of Criticism," in *The Servant of the Lord and Other Essays on the Old Testament,* 2d ed., revised (Oxford, 1965), pp. 51-60; J. L. McKenzie, *Second Isaiah,* AB 20 (Garden City, N.Y., 1968), pp. I-IV; C. Westermann, *Isaiah 40-66* (Philadelphia, 1969), pp. 92f. Cf. Muilenburg, "Isaiah 40-66," pp. 408-410.

[41] Muilenburg, "Isaiah 40-66," p. 413.

[42] *Ibid.*

[43] Among the studies of the Old Testament Messiah are: S. Mowinckel, *He That Cometh* (Nashville, 1956); H. Ringgren, *The Messiah in the Old Testament* (London, 1956); J. Klausner, *The Messianic Idea in Israel* (New York, 1955); J. Loppens, *Le messianisme et sa relève prophétique* (Gembloux, 1974); *Le messianisme royal* (Paris, 1968); J. Becker, *Messianic Expectation in the Old Testament* (Philadelphia, 1980).

[44] See E. H. Hingstenberg, *Christology of the Old Testament* (Grand Rapids, 1956), vols. 1-4.

[45] However, it must be remembered that the Messianic king is not simply a by-product of the royal office in Israel and the ancient Near East but is someone new and unique whose roots anteceded the royal office. See W. Harrelson, "Nonroyal Motifs in the Royal Eschatology," in B. W. Anderson and W. Harrelson, eds., *Israel's Prophetic Heritage* (New York, 1962), pp. 147-165.

[46] For the antiquity of the concept of God's kingship, see M. Buber, *Moses* (New York, 1958), pp. 78, 104.

[47] Although this passage has reference to Solomon, David's immediate successor, it also takes a longer view to the promised Messianic successor of David (Acts 2:30). See Francis D. Nichol, ed., *The Seventh-day Adventist Bible Commentary* (Washington, D.C., 1953-1957), vol. 2, p. 631.

[48] Contemporary commentaries have minimized the Messianic elements in these psalms, focusing instead upon the testimony they give to Israel's historical kings. See Weiser, *The Psalms,* p. 63; S. Mowinckel, *The Psalms in Israel's Worship* (Nashville, 1962), pp. 46-50.

[49] Some interpreters speak of an ideal kingship as a forerunner of the Old Testament Messianic hope, meaning a hope for a king who is far better than any known king but still not the Messiah. As for the origin of the ideals in the hoped-for king, some interpreters locate these among Israel's neighbors, e.g., Mowinckel, *He That Cometh,* pp. 21-95; H. Ringgren, *Israelite Religion* (Philadelphia, 1966), pp. 220-238. Others locate them within the Old Testament itself. E.g., W. Harrelson, "Nonroyal Motifs in the Royal Eschatology," pp. 147-165; M. Noth, "God, King, and Nation," in *The Laws of the Pentateuch and Other Studies* (Philadelphia, 1966), pp. 145-178; J.J.M. Roberts, "The Davidic Origin of the Zion Tradition," *JBL* 92 (1972): 329-344. The position of this chapter is that the Messianic concept is distinct from the concept of the ideal kingship, and not a development from it.

[50] R. E. Wolfe, "Micah," *IB,* vol. 6, p. 931.

[51] For details regarding this prophecy see *The Seventh-day Adventist Bible Commentary,* vol. 4, pp. 851-855, and chapter 8 in this volume.

[52] For example, the Reformers saw its fulfillment both in the first advent of Christ and in the life and work of the church. J. Pelikan, ed., *Lectures on Isaiah, 1-39,* Vol. XVI of *Luther's Works* (St. Louis, 1969), pp. 117-123; J. Calvin, *Commentary on the Prophet Isaiah* (Grand Rapids, 1958), Vol. I, pp. 370-387.

[53] See chapters 2 and 3 in this volume.

[54] See chapter 2.

[55] See, for example, the discussion in Cullmann, *Christology of the New Testament*, pp. 137-152.

[56] S. Mowinckel suggested that it originated in the religious practices of Jerusalem (*He That Cometh*, p. 132). G. von Rad looked to the holy war experience in early Israel (*Old Testament Theology*, Vol. II, pp. 119-125). F. M. Cross has suggested that the views of Mowinckel and Von Rad complement each other by referring to different periods of Israel's history. *Canaanite Myth and Hebrew Epic* (Cambridge, Mass., 1973), pp. 91-111. The Old Testament itself presents it throughout as the "day" on which God acts in the world.

[57] Although Bible readers have associated the prophecy in Isaiah 63:1-6 with the death of Christ, the context of the passage places it in the eschaton. Thus the final judgment and the final eschaton come together in the second advent. See C. Westermann, *Isaiah 40-66*, p. 384.

[58] Koehler-Baumgartner, *Lexicon*, pp. 162f.

[59] See G. F. Hasel, "Resurrection in the Theology of Old Testament Apocalyptic," *ZAW* 92 (1980): 267-284.

CHAPTER 2

The Advent Hope

in Apocalyptic Literature

Niels-Erik Andreasen

APOCALYPSE, from which *apocalyptic* is derived, means "revelation" or "disclosure." [1] It is a word that generally serves to characterize certain Jewish and Christian religious literature from approximately the years 200 B.C. to A.D. 100. True to its name, apocalyptic literature is preoccupied with the revelation, or disclosure, of future events taking place in the world. Prominent among these events are the arrival of the Messiah and the establishment of the kingdom of God. Consequently, a symposium volume dealing with the advent hope in Scripture and history must take account of the apocalyptic literature.

The Time, Place, and Characteristics of Apocalyptic Literature

Many Bible readers assume that the New Testament follows after the Old Testament both theologically and historically. Little do they realize how many events and ideas are crowded onto the one blank page that in most Bibles separate the two testaments. The time, place, and characteristics of apocalyptic literature belong for the most part on this page as well, i.e., in the intertestamental period.

The intertestamental period began sometime during the Persian Empire, or around 400 B.C.[2] In the succeeding seventy years the Middle East was dominated by the placid Persian Empire. The Jews, who at this time lived not only in the province of Judea but also in the Diaspora,[3] enjoyed political, economic, and religious freedom.[4]

To be sure, the canonical books of Daniel, Esther, Ezra, Nehemiah, and the apocryphal books of Judith and Tobit, both of which presume to describe Jewish communities under Persian rule, mention some oppression of the Jews, but they also intimate the high position that Jews could acquire at the Persian court.[5]

In 332 B.C. Palestine was conquered by Alexander the Great, and Judea came under Hellenistic rule. Whereas the Persian Empire appears to have supported a policy of tolerance toward the indigenous cultures of its many provinces, Alexander and Hellenism actively supported a policy of merging Eastern culture and Greek civilization.[6] Ultimately this merging of East and West would have serious and lasting consequences for Judaism, but for the first one hundred years or so, Judea remained a relatively peaceful province of Egypt ruled by the Ptolemies.[7]

During these years Judea was apparently left as a "temple land" entrusted to the priestly authorities in Jerusalem, with a minimium of Hellenistic ideas forced upon it.[8]

By 200 B.C. Judea fell under the control of Syria and remained thus for about thirty-five years. At first the Syrian rulers respected Judaism, but under Antiochus IV (175-164 B.C.) a program of religious oppression was forced upon Jerusalem and Judea.[9] This led directly to the Maccabean rebellion (167-142 B.C.) and to the Hasmonaean rule (142-63 B.C.).[10] The Hasmonaean kings and high priests kept Judea free of foreign political domination, but they were unable to save the nation from internal strife.

During this period the parties of Pharisees and Essenes were chiseled out of the Hasidim (pious ones) who had once supported the Maccabean revolt but who now opposed the Hasmonaean leaders. Also, the Sadducean party became clearly defined at this time.

Though the question as to the precise nature and origin of these parties is not fully settled, it is well known that they were actively and sometimes violently involved in the affairs of their day and that they contributed to the general turmoil that finally led to Roman interference in and ultimate control over the affairs of Judea.[11] From the year 63 B.C., when the Roman general Pompey entered Jerusalem (and the Holy of Holies in the Temple), until A.D. 70, when Jerusalem fell to another Roman general, Titus, Judea was controlled by Roman procurators and by such Herodian princes as Rome would designate rulers over this territory.[12]

Meanwhile, the Diaspora grew so that large Jewish communities existed in Alexandria, in Syria, in the provinces of Asia Minor, in Greece, and in Rome itself.[13] Generally speaking, the Jews in the Diaspora maintained organized communities that enjoyed some autonomy and civic privileges, and though these communities experienced both internal and external conflicts,[14] they not only remained distinct but also in a remarkable way retained their Jewish heritage.

Our knowledge of Judaism during this period is gained from a large amount of source material that for the sake of convenience is commonly grouped into the following divisions: (1) rabbinic writings, (2) Apocrypha, (3) pseudepigrapha, (4) Qumran library, (5) Josephus, (6) Philo. This is not an entirely satisfactory classification, for the six divisions are not made according to any one principle, such as uniformity of content, provenance, or literary type. However, it is a much used and broadly accepted classification. Within these divisions we find many types of literature; among them are religious law, homiletical commentary, wisdom teaching, historical narrative, oracle, hymn, quasi-philosophical treatise, and of course apocalypse.

It is a testimony to the vitality of Judaism during this trying period that, although geographically scattered, politically and religiously divided, and oppressed both at home and abroad, it produced such a startling amount of religious literature. Moreover, it is a testimony to the restlessness and tensions within Judaism of this time that it produced such divergent types of religious literature. Finally, it is a testimony to the hegemony of Judaism during this time that all this literature still can (and ought to) be considered "Jewish."

One of the most fascinating types of this literature is the apocalypse. The Jewish apocalypses with which we are concerned in this chapter are found in the Apocrypha, the pseudepigrapha, and the Qumran library.[15] Since these apocalypses are unusual, it may be well to sketch their distinct features.[16]

1. Apocalyptic, which is often compared to prophecy, distinguishes itself from the latter by frequently taking the form of a testimony from some ancient worthy, or of a record of a vision, or of a programmatic writing such as the War Scroll from Qumran. At times it assumes the form of a lengthy discourse, perhaps involving an interpreting angel.

2. Apocalyptic is often characterized as "esoteric," i.e., it presents knowledge that is ordinarily hidden. This knowledge may have been revealed to an ancient patriarch, e.g., Noah, Enoch, Moses, or all the sons of Jacob. Elsewhere it is revealed through an angelic interpreter, or on heavenly tablets whose content is disclosed to a worthy person.

3. In view of its esoteric nature, it is not surprising that apocalyptic literature should employ symbolic language. This undoubtedly served well, both to create a vivid kaleidoscopic presentation of past and future events and also to protect the apocalyptists when describing sensitive contemporary events or hostile personages. Animals (often composite creatures), numbers, colors, stars, branches, crowns, horns, and water are among the commonly used symbols.

4. Generally speaking, the apocalyptic literature is pseudonymous, i.e., its authors are not known. Instead, the apocalyptic writings are frequently attributed to various ancient worthies. A number of explanations of this pseudonymity have been offered, among them that the apocalyptic author simply wished to deceive his readers.[17] But more plausible explanations exist, e.g., that the apocalyptist used an alias to avoid persecution for his writing,[18] or in order to give more authority to his writing at a time when a scriptural canon was already in existence, or because of his infatuation with the "glamor of antiquity."[19] Perhaps H.H. Rowley and D.S. Russell are closest to the truth when they propose that by attributing his writing to an ancient worthy the author indicated his identity with the personality whose name he borrowed.[20]

5. Apocalyptic literature is characterized by the word "urgency." It is crisis literature, written at a time when Judaism was scattered and subject to extraordinary pressures from within and without. Its primary intention was undoubtedly to be a "living source of strength" to people who lived in a time "which to them was the extreme moment of destiny."[21] Thus we find in this literature expectations that in the immediate future the present age will be overthrown in a cosmic catastrophy, and this takes us directly to the subject of the advent hope.

The Present Age and the Age to Come

Anyone who seeks to investigate the advent hope in the apocalyptic literature will quickly be caught in the seeming confusion and inconsistency with which this theme is presented. One often looks helplessly for some concrete conceptual structures into which the apocalyptists fitted their advent expectations. Therefore it may be well at the outset to consider in a schematic way some models according to which these expectations can be ordered.

The model of a terrestial restoration.—

E
The present age N The age to come
D

This model lies behind some Old Testament passages,[22] and, according to Russell, it fits the earlier apocalyptic writings.[23] The present age is dominated by the Gentiles—the kingdoms of this world—[24]and by evil cosmic powers.[25] It is characterized by lawlessness and oppression,[26] and it will be terminated by a series of events, among which are arrival of a deliverer,[27] destruction of all earthly powers,[28] wars,[29] judgments,[30] cosmic shakings,[31] and a resurrection of the dead.[32] So far, general agreement prevails in the various presentations of the advent hope. It is the introduction of the age to come, which calls for different models. According to our first model, the end of the present age will lead directly into the age to come, which will be established on a purified and productive earth.[33] It will embrace all people,[34] have its center in Jerusalem with a rebuilt Temple,[35] require high ethical standards,[36] and be everlasting.[37]

The model of a cosmic restoration.—

E The age to come
N
The present age D

As in the first model, the present age is wearing old and will terminate at the arrival of a deliverer and its concomitant events. However, the age to come is now a cosmic age, not limited to the earth but including the whole universe. The parables of Enoch (1 Enoch 37-71) approach such a cosmic view of the age to come. Here both heaven and earth will be transformed by the Elect, who is in the presence of God (chaps. 45:4, 5; 48:2; 49:2). The judgment extends to angels as well as to men (chaps. 54:1-6; 56:1-4). In the end the redeemed will live in a re-created world (chap. 45:5), but apparently also in the presence of the Elect and of the Lord of Spirits (chap. 49:2; 61:4).

Likewise, the Assumption of Moses portrays a cosmic redemption extending "throughout all His creation" (chap. 10:1). All enemies, including Satan, will be destroyed, and Israel will approach the starry heaven in her redemption (verse 10).

The model of a temporary Messianic Kingdom.—

E   E The age to come
The present age N Messianic age N
D (temporary) D

According to this model, the present age, which is again characterized as in the previous models, will be followed by a temporary Messianic kingdom. While this kingdom belongs to the present age, it also participates in the future age, because it opens the way for the glorious climax inaugurating that age to come. According to Russell, this model fits the later apocalyptic writers.[38]

The so-called apocalypse of weeks, according to which the world is divided into ten weeks, is contained in chapters 93 and 91 of 1 Enoch. The first seven, especially the seventh, are periods of unrighteousness. At the conclusion of the seventh week righteousness will appear and will dominate the eighth and ninth weeks, leading to a universal judgment in the tenth week (chap. 91:15). These last three weeks belong to the interim period of the Messianic kingdom, which is followed by the age to come with the creation of a new heaven and with the establishment of eternal bliss for all (verses 16, 17).

The writer of 2 Enoch appears to know of the so-called world week. Seven days of Creation represent seven thousand years of world history, of which the seventh thousand, corresponding to the Sabbath, is the interim period of the Messianic kingdom. That is followed by an eighth thousand years—"a time of not-counting, endless, with neither years nor months nor weeks nor days nor hours" (chap. 33:2). However, no Messiah is mentioned here, and the Messianic interim kingdom is not explicitly referred to.

In a similar way 2 Baruch assumes the arrival of a temporary Messianic kingdom at the end of the present age and after the twelve woes have fallen (chap. 27:1-15). "The Messiah shall then begin to be revealed" (chap. 29:4). Evil will be extinct, and the earth will be fruitful (verses 5-8). At this point the Messiah returns, i.e., "when the time of the advent of the Messiah is fulfilled" (chap. 30:1). It is not entirely clear whether he returns to heaven or earth,[39] but a resurrection takes place, and the age to come is inaugurated. In 2 Baruch 39 and 40 the Messiah is revealed after the last of four kingdoms, whereupon he will establish his principate "until the world of corruption is at an end" (chap. 40:3). Again the Messianic kingdom belongs to this age, but it will inaugurate the age to come. Finally (2 Baruch 70-73), the Messiah will destroy the last black waters (final evil age), consuming some nations and sparing others (chap. 72:2, 3). Thereafter he will establish his kingdom in peace, and then "joy shall then be revealed, and rest shall appear" (chap. 73:1).

According to 2 Esdras 7:27-29, the Messiah will appear at the end of this age in order to establish his kingdom in joy for four hundred years, after which he will die, together with all of mankind.[40] This thrusts the world into seven days of primeval silence (verse 30). Then follows the resurrection, judgment, and the dawn of the age to come.

The general concept of a temporary Messianic kingdom came to occupy an important place in New Testament eschatology, either in the form of the present reign of Christ or in the form of a millennium.[41] Also, rabbinic eschatology was acquainted with such a temporary Messianic kingdom of varying durations.[42]

The Present Age Is Wearing Old

Different views have been advanced to explain the rise and profusion of apocalyptic literature.[43] Most of them take account of the critical period through which Judaism passed between the years 200 B.C. and A.D. 100. During these years Judaism found itself in the maelstrom of world empires with their shifting religious, cultural, and economic values. The pressing question was how Judaism could survive. In addressing themselves to this problem, the apocalyptists took their bearing in the redemptive history of ancient Israel, especially the early period from Adam to Moses. Yet they were convinced that this history could not maintain its course much longer in the present critical time. A solution that offered itself to the apocalyptists as a way out of this impasse was the dualistic worldview.[44] According to this view, the present world would indeed end very soon, at which point the course of Israel's history would be resumed in a new and eternal world, as we have just seen. Coupled with this temporal dualism is an ethical dualism that associates immorality and evil with the present age, and moral perfection with the age to come. It is precisely the ethical dualism that energizes the apocalyptic preoccupation with the temporal dualism, for not only is the present world evil, but it is getting increasingly worse, and this increase in evil determines the fast-approaching end of the present age.

With this in mind, the apocalyptists are offering concrete evidence that the present age is indeed wearing old and are providing calculations whereby the end may be determined chronologically. Let us consider some of these.

The present age is rapidly approaching its end, even within the lifetime of the apocalyptists.[45] "The youth of the world is past, and the strength of the creation already exhausted, and the advent of the times is very short . . .; and the pitcher is near the cistern, and the ship to the port, and the course of the journey to the city, and life to (its) consummation." [46] This general tiredness of the earth is reflected in a lack of productivity. The very natural processes of rain, light, and seasons will become upset.[47] Among people the last generation will be apostate, under the influence of evil forces,[48] and, as a consequence, will experience untold sorrow, sickness, and tribulation.[49] The writer of 2 Baruch 27 enumerates these tribulations into twelve plagues leading up to the end of the age. The final world crisis will be further intensified by a new and uncompromising conflict between Israel and her enemies. The latter are identified as an external military power, such as Syria,[50] or Rome,[51] a person like the wicked priest, or some anonymous oppressor.[52]

With the expectation of such an imminent end to the present age questions naturally arose as to the exact time of its end. To accomplish that, various chronological calculations were employed. One was the seven-thousand-year world week, according to which the present evil age would end six thousand years after Creation, at the arrival of the Redeemer, and be followed by a thousand-year Messianic reign. Such calculations were well known in rabbinic Judaism,[53] and they appear to have entered apocalyptic Judaism, too.[54] Using a different system of reckoning, the Assumption of Moses calculates 4,250 years, or 85 jubilees, from Creation to the end of the age (chaps. 1:2; 10:12).

A system of ten weeks is employed by 1 Enoch. The sixth week ends with the destruction of the first Temple (chap. 93:8), then follows a week of apostasy (verse 9), after which the Messianic age will arrive (verse 10; chap. 91:12, 13). Nine and a half parts have passed, and two and a half remain.[55] Additional numerical systems based on a five-thousand-year world history and on the seventy-year captivity were also used, but these cannot detain us here.[56]

Finally, attempts were undertaken to determine the final course of history by tracing the sequence of kingdoms on earth. For example, the well-known eagle vision in 2 Esdras 11-13 is given as an extensive elaboration on the circumstances surrounding the last of four world kingdoms (chap. 12:10-13). The purpose of this would be to specify with more precision the arrival time of the Messiah, here symbolized as a lion (chap. 11:37). In a similar way, 2 Baruch 39 also portrays the existence of four kingdoms, the fourth being the most powerful, after which the Messiah will set up his principate. It would seem that both 2 Esdras and 2 Baruch are here borrowing from the book of Daniel.

Although it is generally difficult to extract any precise evidence, at least some of the apocalyptists apparently identified the last earthly kingdom with specific contemporary powers, such as a nation or a dominating personality. It is important to note that whatever system of calculation the apocalyptists used, they expected the end of the present evil age to dawn in the immediate future. The chronological schemes generally end at the time of their authors.

Nevertheless, the time of the end is ultimately in God's hand, according to 2 Esdras 4:33-44. "He has weighed the age in the balance, and with measure has measured the times, and by number has numbered the seasons: neither will he move nor stir things, till the measure appointed be fulfilled" (verses 36, 37). The measure to be completed refers to the number of the saints (verses 36, 39, 41, 42). From the New Testament point of view it is surely a weakness that the apocalyptists could not leave the determination of the end with God, but that they felt compelled to pursue this issue relentlessly. "Show me this also: whether there be more to come than is past, or whether the more part is already gone by us?" (verse 45).

Signs of the End

The imminent end of the present age will be announced by a series of specific signs. Some of these simply indicate that the present age is reaching its end, others are part of the general disarray into which the world is falling due to the reign of evil, while still others may serve to test and sift the people of the last days.

One sign of the end will be general moral degeneracy. "When the time of the end has ripened, . . . the Mighty One will bring upon the earth and its inhabitants and upon its rulers perturbation of spirit and stupor of heart. And they shall hate one another, and provoke one another to fight, and the mean shall rule over the honourable, and those of low degree shall be extolled above the famous."[57]

A second group of signs involves disarray in the normal processes of life. The agricultural seasons will be suddenly upset[58] and, according to 1 Enoch, will be reversed. "Their seed will be tardy. . . . The fruits of the earth shall be backward, and shall not grow in their time" (chap. 80:2, 3). This will of course produce famines.[59] The book of 2 Esdras extends these disorders to man and animal. "Women [shall] bear monsters . . . [and have] untimely births at three and four months, and these shall live and dance" (chap. 5:8). "The wild beasts shall desert their haunts" (verse 8), "the sea shall cast forth its fish" (verse 7), "and the birds shall take to general flight" (verse 6). In the material world "blood shall trickle forth from wood, and the stone utter its voice" (verse 5),[60] and "the earth o'er wide regions shall open, and fire burst forth for a long period" (verse 8).[61] The water of the earth shall fail,[62] and the earth shall quake,[63] while the mountains are displaced and the earth wasted.[64]

A third group of signs involve the sun, moon, and stars. According to 1 Enoch, sun, moon, and stars will change their ordinary positions (chap. 80:4-6). Apparently the stars in their normal courses serve to guide the righteous people, for "the whole order of the stars shall be concealed from the sinners" (verse 7), presumably so that they will not discern the end. More specifically, the sun will shine at night and the moon by day, or they will not shine at all. This is caused by breaking the "horns of the sun," and by turning the moon into blood.[65] However, even the resultant darkness will be penetrated by still other heavenly signs. The Sibylline Oracles speak of "swords in the star-lit heaven" at dusk and dawn (3. 798, 799). These swords, painted by sun and clouds, are symbols of war,[66] more precisely, of the heavenly participation in the final battle (5. 512-517). Then, as the heavenly battle touches the earth "a sign comes from the rocks with dripping streams of blood" (3. 798-807).

Partly as a result of these frightful signs and partly as a consequence of the final throes of the age, a fourth sign will issue in a frightening time of trouble. The twelve woes in 2 Baruch are signs of the end to those who have understanding (chap. 27-28:1). The last of these woes are most perplexing: "And in the twelfth part confusion from the mingling together of all those things aforesaid" (chap. 27:13). Apparently the woes reach a climax of confusion and disarray that only the wise shall be able to withstand. This final accumulation of trouble will be so severe that it will cause the breakdown of the very fabric of human integrity. Parents will abandon their children, and children will take the lives of their parents.[67] The Qumran Hodayot (book of hymns) compares the trouble of the end to a woman in childbirth (3.6-18). Her pain will end only with the birth of a man-child, "that marvel of mind and might," a reference to the one who is wonderful in counsel, a mighty God (Isa. 9:5), i.e., the end of the trouble coincides with the coming of the Messiah.[68]

He Who Comes

The apocalyptic writers identify the expected deliverer by means of two important figures, Messiah and Son of man, as well as by several titles, such as Elect One, Righteous One, Shepherd, Blessed Man, Heavenly One, and Son. The Messiah and Son of man are of special importance because of their wide usage in Jewish and Christian literature.

The Messiah.—Messiah (annointed) is an Old Testament term that is applied to priest (Ex. 28:41) and prophet (1 Kings 19:16), but most notably to the king (1 Sam. 9:16; 16:13).[69] In the Old Testament this royal title applied not only to Israel's kings but also to the future eschatological ruler.[70] According to one interpretation, the Messiah "is the future, eschatological realization" of the ideal king.[71] This fact may account for the royal terminology so often employed to describe the Messianic figure.

Since apocalyptic literature is eschatological, we often assume that it must also be thoroughly Messianic in nature, but such is not the case. In fact, "Messiah" is entirely missing from some of our documents.[72] Second, following our general definition of the title Messiah, we should expect it to be filled by someone in the royal line of David, from the tribe of Judah, a king who will fufill the expectations of a true king of the Old Testament. Although our texts reveal just such a figure, they also present what appears to be a priestly Messiah from the tribe of Levi.

The Levitical Messiah.—The suggestion has been made that with the establishment of the priestly Hasmonaean dynasty the Messianic hope was temporarily transferred from the house of David to the house of Levi.[73] The crucial texts in question are found in the Testaments of the Twelve Patriarchs. The Testament of Reuben 6:5-12 attributes sovereignty to Levi, while Reuben must harken to Levi, who knows the law, gives judgment, and offers sacrifice "as the anointed High Priest." The Lord has chosen him to be king over all the nation, and Reuben must "bow down before his seed," who "will be among you an eternal king." According to the Testament of Levi 18:1-11, the Lord will "raise up a new priest" to whom the words of the Lord are revealed and who shall execute righteous judgment. "His star shall arise in heaven as of a king." He shall be magnified, shine as the sun, remove all darkness, and there shall be peace. "The spirit of understanding and sanctification shall rest upon him," and in his priesthood shall sin come to an end. Lawlessness shall cease, and he shall open the gates of paradise, whereupon he shall give the saints to eat from the tree of life. Finally, in Jubilees 31:13-15, Isaac, when blessing Judah and Levi, gives preeminence to the latter.

Whether the Hasmonaean king-priests inspired such an expectation of a Levitical Messiah is a question that cannot detain us here. It is noteworthy, however, that immediately after the return from Babylonian captivity the high priest appears prominently by the side of the political leader (cf. Zechariah 3-6). Later Ben Sira (Ecclesaiasticus 50) described Simon the high priest in terms that would generally befit a king.

It would be natural if, in the absence of a strong political leader, the high priest came to occupy the center of the Messianic hope. To this end he is capable of marshaling all the glory and splendor of the royal Messiah, though perhaps not quite the power required for destroying the enemies of Israel and of God. That task would still fall upon the royal leader, or at least a layperson.

Such an explanation, rather than textual interpolations, may account for the fact that even in the Testaments of the Twelve Patriarchs the Levitical Messiah is sometimes joined by the royal Messiah from the tribe of Judah. Thus, "there shall arise unto you from the tribe of [Judah and of] Levi the salvation of the Lord; and he shall make war against Beliar" (Test. Dan. 5:10).[74] And again, "be united to Levi and to Judah; for through them shall salvation arise unto Israel" (Test. Naphtali 8:2). Finally, the Testament of Judah 24:1-6 may, according to Charles, expect a Levitical and royal Messiah, though here certainly combined in one person. However, this last passage is difficult and may have received Christian editing.[75]

The royal Messiah.—Since the Messiah is a royal figure, in the line of David, he belongs to this present age and will appear, not in the age to come, but toward the end of this age. Thus, according to 2 Baruch, after the twelve woes, "the Messiah shall then begin to be revealed" (chap. 29:3). The most complete description of this royal Messiah is found in the Psalms of Solomon 17, 18. Here we read that he will "reign over Israel," "shatter the unrighteous rulers," "purge Jerusalem," and destroy all sin and godlessness "with the word of his mouth" (chap. 17:23-27). Then he will "gather together a holy people," lead them in righteousness, and resettle them in the land (verses 28-31). The heathen nations will be subject to him and will fear him (verses 32-38). He, however, shall reign in a purifed and holy Jerusalem. He neither trusts in weapons nor multiplies silver or gold, but "the Lord Himself is his king" (verses 37-44). God will make him mighty and wise, and he will shepherd the flock "faithfully and righteously" in the spirit of wisdom. None shall stumble, none shall be proud, for he will judge and instruct them with words "like the words of the holy ones" (verses 45-51; chap. 18:8-10).

Throughout, the royal Messiah takes an active part in the judgment upon all evil, both terrestrial and celestial, at the end of the present age. To that end he is not only a descendant of David,[76] a prince,[77] but also a celestial man, a star from the east, sent from God.[78] Thus, the Messiah figure blends with the Son of man figure, who is a heavenly Redeemer. The man from the sea is "he whom the Most High is keeping many ages, [(and) through whom he will deliver his creation]" (2 Esdras 13:26, 27). Yet he shall stand on Mount Zion (verse 36), reprove the nations (verse 37), gather in the tribes of Israel (verses 40-47), and establish them in peace (verse 47). In short, he is the royal Messiah as well as the heavenly Son of man, or "blessed man."[79]

Dual messianism.—The Testaments of the Twelve Patriarchs advance not only the Levitical character of the Messiah but appear, as already noted, to also announce two Messianic figures. "And now, my children, obey Levi and Judah, and be not lifted up against these two tribes, for from them shall arise unto you the salvation of God. For the Lord shall raise up from Levi as it were a High-priest, and from Judah as it were a King [God and man]. He shall save all [the Gentiles and] the race of Israel."[80] Although this reference to two Messiahs has been considered a Christian interpolation, with the original text referring only to the *tribes* of Levi and Judah,[81] such a dual Messiahship occurs also in the Qumran literature and so cannot be swept aside too easily. Interestingly, fragments of a testament of Levi and of Naphtali have been found at Qumran.

Messianism in Qumran is not easy to evaluate, for it has been subject to many divergent opinions.[82] However, the following pattern seems to have distilled. Two Messiahs (of Aaron and of Israel) appear in the Manual of Discipline. Their respective functions are not delineated, but this document instructs that the community must abide by its rules until the coming of these Messiahs.[83] Elsewhere, in the additions to the community rule (for the future congregation), the priestly leader appears to take precedence over the royal leader (Messiah) at the banquet.[84] More puzzling are the references in the Damascus Document that speak of a Messiah from Aaron and Israel (2. 1 [ms. B]; 12.—13. 1 [ms. A]; 13. 21; 14. 19). The main difficulty is that though these references would suggest an expectation of two Messiahs, a priestly and a royal, the word "Messiah" is singular. K. G. Kuhn has suggested that a later scribe emended the plural to singular on theological grounds, but that is an unhappy solution to the problem.[85] A better approach would be to ask if the document elsewhere speaks of two redemptive figures.[86] This does, in fact, happen in 7. 18-21, where in a commentary on Numbers 24:17 the star is interpreted to be a priestly leader and the sceptre a royal leader. However, we cannot be certain that this reference must be understood eschatologically. It would seem, nevertheless, that if not two Messiahs, at least a dual understanding of the Messiahship is present in the Damascus Document.

Elsewhere in the Qumran writings the dual Messiah appears in the Testimonia,[87] the Messianic Florilegium,[88] and the Isaiah commentary.[89] The War Scroll gives a prominent position to the chief priest, but also to the prince, presumably as a leader in battle.[90]

Thus, though the precise nature of the Messianic expectations among the Qumranites is difficult to determine, it would seem that they did expect both a priestly and a royal eschatological leader. Their expectation is closely molded by the character of the community itself. It was strictly religious, founded by a priest, and yet it was also militant.[91] This may explain the dual Messianic hope. It was a

Messianic hope suited for a community that nourished none of the universal Messianism of 2 Esdras and the Psalms of Solomon. Qumran eschatology is narrowly conceived. The Messiahs of Aaron and Israel are Qumranites—one a priest who heads the community, the other a prince who executes its warfare. The apparent subordination of the royal Messiah (of Israel) to the priestly Messiah (of Aaron) corresponds with Jesus' own evaluation of the political Messiah,[92] although in Qumran it was probably arrived at through deep reverence for the priestly leader, not through mistrust of the political and military leader.

The Son of Man.—The common Old Testament expression "son of man," meaning simply "man" (e.g., Ps. 8:4; Eze. 2:1) received a special eschatological meaning already in the book of Daniel (chap. 7:13). Here it makes reference to a heavenly being who in the last days will appear in the presence of God to execute judgment. In the opinion of scholarship the Son of man title was in time influenced by the ideal man figure that is known in Near Eastern thought, especially since Persian times,[93] but of that we cannot be certain.

When we come to Jewish apocalyptic, the Son of man figure appears prominently in the so-called parables of Enoch (1 Enoch 37-71). Here the Son of man is strictly a heavenly being who is in the presence of God (chaps. 46:1-3; 48:2; 69:29). He is preexistent (48:3), was kept hidden with God from the beginning (verse 6; chap. 62:7), but will be revealed in the end of time (chap. 48:2). Two characteristics of the Son of man stand out. One is his proximity to God ("the Lord of Spirits"). He is chosen by the Lord of Spirits (chaps. 46:3; 48:6), and in fact bears the title "Elect" (chaps. 45:3-5; 49:2; 51:3; 52:6; 53:6; 61:4, 5; 62:1). He stands before the Lord of Spirits (chap. 48:2), or sits on a throne (chaps. 51:2, 3; 61:8; 69:29). Consequently he receives worship (chaps. 48:5; 61:7; 62:9). A second characteristic is his close proximity to the causes of man. He has the appearance of man (chap. 46:1), and of course is revealed to man at the eschaton (chap. 69:26) when He makes the cause of righteous man his own (chap. 46:4-7).

Three functions are attributed to the Son of man at his appearance. He will reveal righteousness, secrets, and wisdom treasures to the elect (chaps. 46:3; 49:3; 51:3). He will judge the kings and other agents who oppress the righteous (chaps. 46:5-8; 48:9, 10; 52:6, 7; 62:2, 3; 63:11). He will bring salvation and peace to the elect (chaps. 45:3, 4; 48:7; 51:3-5; 62:13-16). A resurrection precedes this latter function (chaps. 51:1; 61:5).

Elsewhere in our literature the redeemer appears in the Sibylline Oracles 5. 414 as the "blessed man" from heaven, and in 2 Esdras 13 as the Man from the sea. The latter has the same functions of judgment and redemption as the Son of man (verses 6-16, 33-38), and he too brings a revelation of God's mysteries in the end (verses 52, 53). However, he also bears the title "my Son," a Messianic appellative (verses 32, 52).

This raises the question of the identification of the Son of man in relationship to the Messiah. First Enoch 71:12-17 poses a strange problem, for this passage identifies the Son of man with Enoch.[94] Various views have been forwarded in an attempt to clarify this unusual identification, among them that the Son of man is a collective symbol,[95] a corporate personality,[96] or a heavenly archtype who incorporates even Enoch,[97] but these are not likely solutions. More important is the relationship between Son of man and Messiah. Although it may appear on the surface that Messiah and Son of man are simply two names for essentially one eschatological figure, all interpreters agree, and our survey of texts supports this, that the Son of man concept not only has a different origin from that of the Messiah, but also fills a somewhat different role. Essentially Messiah emphasizes the human, earthly, historical quality of the eschatological redeemer. He is revealed among men and executes his task upon the earth at the conclusion of the present age, whereupon he hands over the final judgment and restoration of all things to God. Son of man, on the other hand, emphasizes the divine, heavenly, cosmic quality of the eschatological redeemer. He is revealed in heaven by God, executes his task from a heavenly throne, and acts as God's deputy in the final judgment and restoration.

Nevertheless, the two figures overlap. According to Rowley they did not merge until the time of Jesus, who preferred the term Son of man to that of Messiah (cf. Mark 14:61, 62).[98] But this merging probably occurred earlier, as seems evident in our literature. Thus the parables of Enoch, which, according to Rowley, make no mention of the Messiah,[99] attribute qualities to the Son of man normally reserved for the Messiah, e.g., his righteousness, wisdom, election by God, lordship over the kings of the world who offer him homage. He is a light to the Gentiles (chap. 48:4), and is called the anointed of God (chaps. 48:10; 52:4). Similarly, the Messiah, especially in 2 Esdras, seems to blend with the Son of man (the Man from the sea), both of whom are called "my Son" (chaps. 7:28, 29; 13:32, 52). In fact, the very introduction of a temporary Messianic kingdom before the inauguration of the age to come, as in 2 Esdras 7:27-35, points to a merging of the Messiah and the Son of man eschatologies; Messiah would correspond to the Messianic age, Son of man to the age to come. Presumably some merging of these two eschatological figures occurred prior to the time of Jesus.[100]

Finally, it may be asked if any relationship exists in our literature between either Messiah or Son of man and suffering servant. This question is of some importance since Jesus (Mark 8:30, 31) identified His Messiahship by associating Son of man with suffering servant, an association that caused a violent reaction from His disciples. Indeed, little support exists for this association in our sources. To be sure, suffering is a common feature in the eschatological redemption, especially on the part of the saints, and, in at least one instance, on the part of the Messiah who, according to 2 Esdras 7:29, together with all mankind will die after a four-hundred-year-long Messianic age.[101] However, no evidence exists that this suffering is vicarious or in any way furthers the work of redemption. On the contrary, it should be attributed to the this-worldy nature of the Messianic age.

In summary, the following sketch of the apocalyptic advent hope emerges: The present age can no longer continue. Its rulers may exert great energies of dominance and oppression, but their efforts will ultimately fail—in fact, the very powers and dominions in the world constitute signs of its imminent end. The apocalyptic advent hope is thus spiteful of all earthly conditions and adverse circumstances. What is the foundation of such a hope? The answer is found in the concept of dualism that enabled the apocalyptists confidently to announce the end of the present age in the face of the most powerful and unsympathetic forces at work in the world.

The apocalyptic advent hope has two foci. First, it announces the advent of a Messiah figure who has both priestly and royal features. He will redeem the present age and secure the Messianic kingdom amid the ruins of a crumbling world. This is an "earthly" kingdom with its center in Jerusalem, and it is, at least in some of our sources, of a temporary nature. Second, this hope looks for the advent of a Son of man figure who will inaugurate the age to come. He is a heavenly figure whose redemptive work is cosmic in scope. He appears at the side of God, executes the final judgment, and inaugurates the eternal age to come.

These two figures who constitute the advent hope in apocalyptic literature are not entirely distinct but merge in important aspects, so that it is even possible to speak of one two-faceted advent hope. Nevertheless, a clear distinction must be maintained between the (temporary) Messianic age and the eternal age to come, a distinction that flows over into the New Testament and the early Christian advent hope.

NOTES

[1] The English word *apocalypse* comes from a common Greek word *apokalupsis* with the same meaning.

[2] Nehemiah, the last political leader of Judea mentioned in the Old Testament, began his second term as governor during the latter reign of the Persian king Artaxerxes (465/4-424/3), according to Nehemiah 13:6.

[3] *Diaspora* refers to the dispersion of the Jews, at first in Babylon (2 Kings 25:11), Persia (Esther 2:5, 6), and in far-off Media (Tobit 1:14). A small colony lived in Elephantine, in Egypt, and others perhaps in Asia Minor (Joel 3:6). Thus B. Reicke, *The New Testament Era* (Philadelphia, 1968), pp. 24f. See also S. Safrai and M. Stern, eds., *The Jewish People in the First Century* (Assen, 1974), Vol. I, pp. 117-183.

[4] Testimonies to this are offered by the Murashi and Sons banking firm in Babylon (G. Cardascia, *Les archives de Murasu* [Paris, 1951]) and by the independence of the Jewish colony at Elephantine (B. Porten, *Archives from Elephantine* [Berkeley, 1968]).

[5] Thus Dan. 1; 6:1f.; Esther 2:15-18; Tobit 1:13, 21f.; Judith 10ff.; Ezra 7:6; Nehemiah 1, 2. On the historical setting of Judith, see Reicke, *The New Testament Era*, pp. 24, 31.

[6] V. Tcherikover, *Hellenistic Civilization and the Jews* (New York, 1970), p. 7.

[7] Ptolemy I (Soter) gained control of Judea after his victory at Gaza in 312 B.C. Ptolemy V lost this territory to Antiochus III (of Syria) after the battle of Panias in 200 B.C.

[8] Cf. Reicke, *the New Testament Era*, pp. 47f.; Tcherikover, *Hellenistic Civilization*, pp. 59ff.

[9] 1 Maccabees 1; 2 Macc. 4:13-15; 5-7.

[10] 1 Macc. 2:23-28. Cf. Josephus *Antiquities* 12. 6.

[11] The precise process whereby Jewish society fragmented into Pharisees, Essenes, and Sadducees is not known. Some would attribute the development of the Pharisee party to socioeconomic factors, others to strictly religious concerns. Cf. L. Finkelstein, *The Pharisees* (Philadelphia, 1938), Vol. II, pp. 570-625; "The Origin of the Pharisees," in *Pharisaism in the Making: Selected Essays* (New York, 1972), pp. 175-186; L. Baeck, *The Pharisees and Other Essays* (New York, 1947), pp. 3-50; G. F. Moore, *Judaism*, (New York, 1958), Vol. I, pp. 56-71; Reicke, *The New Testament Era*, pp. 71-75.

[12] Herod I, 37 B.C.-4 B.C.; Archelaus (Judea and Samaria), 4 B.C.-A.D. 6; Herod Antipas (Galilee and Perea), 4 B.C.-A.D. 39; Philip (Transjordan), 4 B.C.-A.D. 34; Agrippa I, A.D. 37-44.

[13] See R. H. Pfeiffer, *History of New Testament Times* (New York, 1949), pp. 166-181; Tcherikover, *Hellenistic Civilization*, pp. 269-295; Safrai and Stern, eds., *The Jewish People*, pp. 117-183.

[14] The best-known such incident occurred in the Jewish community of Alexandria in the time of Caligula (A.D. 37-41). Cf. Philo, *C. Flaccus* and *Embassy to Gaius;* Josephus *Antiquities* 18. 1. 1. See Safrai and Stern, eds., *The Jewish People*, pp. 464-503.

[15] In the Apocrypha 2 Esdras (4 Ezra) (c. A.D. 100) is apocalyptic, in the Pseudepigrapha Jubilees (c. 100 B.C.), 1 Enoch (c. second to first century B.C.), The Testaments of the Twelve Patriarchs (c. first century B.C. to first century A.D.), the Sibylline Oracles (c. second century B.C. to first century A.D.), The Assumption of Moses (c. first century A.D.), 2 Enoch (c. first century A.D.), 2 Baruch (c. A.D. 100), 3 Baruch (c. second century A.D.), The Psalms of Solomon (c. first century A.D.), and in the Qumran library, especially the War Scroll (c. second to first century B.C.). The standard translation is R. H. Charles, *The Apocrypha and the Pseudepigrapha of the Old Testament* (London, 1913), Vol. II. For the Qumran library (Dead Sea scrolls) see G. Vermes, *The Dead Sea Scrolls in English* (Baltimore, 1962); T. H. Gaster, *The Dead Sea Scriptures*, 3d. rev. ed. (New York, 1976); A. Dupont-Sommer, *The Essene Writings From Qumran* (New York, 1973). For a general introductory treatment of all the apocalyptic literature see D. S. Russell, *The Method and Message of Jewish Apocalyptic* (London, 1964), pp. 36-69.

[16] Cf. Russell, *Method and Message*, pp. 104-139; K. Koch, *The Rediscovery of Apocalyptic*, SBT II/22 (London, 1972), pp. 18-33.

[17] H. R. Balz, "Anonymität und Pseudonymität in Unchristentum," *ZTK* 66 (1969): 403-436.

[18] See the discussions by Russell, *Method and Message*, pp. 127-139, and Koch, *Rediscovery of Apocalyptic*, p. 26, n. 21.

[19] Cf. Russell, *Method and Message*, p. 130.

[20] H. H. Rowley, *The Relevance of Apocalyptic*, new and rev. ed. (London, 1963). pp. 39ff.; Russell, *Between the Testaments* (London, 1960), pp. 114ff.; *Method and Message*, pp. 131-139.

[21] Rowley, *Relevance of Apocalyptic*, p. 52.

[22] E.g., Isa. 2:1-4; (Micah 4:1-5); Zech. 14:1-21; cf. Dan. 2:34f., 44f.

[23] *Method and Message*, p. 286; cf. S. Mowinckel, *He That Cometh* (Oxford, 1956), pp. 267-279.

[24] Cf. 1 Enoch 46:5-8; 48:8f.; 53:5; 62:9-12. Cf. Dan. 2:44; 7:12ff.; 2 Esdras 11-13.

[25] Named variously "Satan" (1 Enoch 54:6), "Satanail" (prince of the Grigori) (2 Enoch 18:3), "Watchers" (1 Enoch 1:5), "devil" (the evil spirit of the lower places), "Sotona," "Satomail" (2 Enoch 31:3-5), "Adversary" (Books

of Adam and Eve 17:1), "Azazel," "Semjaza" (1 Enoch 9:6f.), "Mastema" (Jubilees 10:8), "Beliar" (chap. 1:20).
26 The problem of the present evil age is pondered by 2 Baruch 14-19 and by 2 Esdras 3-5; 6:35-7:25.
27 E.g., 1 Enoch 1:9 (cf. Jude 14, 15); Test. Levi 18; Test. Judah 24; Sibyl. Or. 3. 652-656; 5. 414f.; 2 Baruch 29:1-4; 40:lf.; 70:9-73:7; 2 Esdras 7:26-30; Pss. Sol. 17:23; 18:8; Manual of Discipline 9. 11; War Scroll 12. 1ff.
28 See number 24.
29 E.g., Sibyl. Or. 3. 689-701.
30 E.g., 1 Enoch 1:9; 22:10f.; 45:3f.; 62:1-5. Cf. Habakkuk Commentary 5. 1-7.
31 E.g., Test. Judah 23; Sibyl. Or. 3. 689-701; 2 Baruch 70:2f.
32 E.g., 1 Enoch 51; 90:33; 91:10-92:3; Test. Simeon 6:7; Test. Zebulon 10:2; Test. Benjamin 10:8; Sibyl. Or. 4. 179-182; 2 Baruch 30; 49-51.
33 E.g., 1 Enoch 10:17f., 19ff.; 25:6; Sibyl. Or. 3. 741-759, 788-795.
34 E.g., 1 Enoch 90:30; Test. Dan 5:10-13.
35 E.g., 1 Enoch 90:28f.; Test. Dan 5:12; Sibyl. Or. 3. 702-709.
36 E.g., Sibyl. Or. 3. 710-731; Jubilees 23:26.
37 Sibyl. Or. 3. 767; Test. Joseph 19:12.
38 *Method and Message*, p. 291.
39 R. H. Charles (*The Apocrypha and Pseudepigrapha*, Vol. II, p. 498) understands this as a return to heaven. However, Rowley (*Relevance of Apocalyptic*, p. 120) leans toward an understanding which associates the "return of the Messiah" (2 Baruch 30:1) with the "revelation of the Messiah" (2 Baruch 29:3), meaning his arrival on earth. Cf. B. Violet, *Die Apokalypsen des Ezra und des Baruch in deutcher Gestalt* (Leipzig, 1924), p. 246. It is possible that a temporary Messianic departure is to be understood between 2 Baruch 29:3 and 30:1.
40 So the Latin and Arabic texts. The Syriac reads "thirty years" and a later Arabic manuscript has "one thousand years." Other manuscripts (Ethiopic and Armenian) omit any reference to a time period. The thirty-year period is probably a Christian tradition introduced to conform with the lifetime of Jesus. The thousand-year Messianic kingdom may also be a Christian interpolation. Cf. Rev. 20:3. The four hundred years are generally associated with Genesis 15:13 and Psalm 90:15 and can be traced into rabbinic teachings. Cf. Charles, *Apocrypha and Pseudepigrapha*, Vol. II, p. 582. See also J. W. Bailey, "The Temporary Messianic Reign in the Literature of Early Judaism," *JBL* (1934): 170-187.
41 Cf. E. Schweizer, *Jesus* (Atlanta, 1971), pp. 52-64; O. Cullmann, "The Return of Christ," in *The Early Church* (Philadelphia, 1956), pp. 141-162; Bailey, "The Temporary Messianic Reign," p. 187.
42 F. Moore, *Judaism*, Vol. II, pp. 375f.; H. L. Strack and P. Billerbeck, *Kommentar zum Neuen Testament* (Munich, 1926), Vol. III, pp. 823-827.
43 Space limitations preclude discussion here.
44 The world consists of two periods, "this age," and "the age to come." See Mowinckel, *He That Cometh*, pp. 263-266; Russell, *Method and Message*, pp. 266-271; John G. Gammie, "Spatial and Ethical Dualism in Jewish Wisdom and Apocalyptic Literature," *JBL* 93 (1974): 356-385.
45 2 Esdras 4:26: "If thou livest long thou shalt marvel; for the age is hastening fast to its end." Cf. 2 Baruch 20:1; 83:1.
46 2 Baruch 85:10. Cf. 2 Esdras 14:10.
47 1 Enoch 80:2-8; 2 Esdras 5:3.
48 1 Enoch 10:15; 93:9; 104:10; Habakkuk Commentary 2. 1-10; 8. 16—9. 7; 10. 9-13.
49 2 Esdras 4:27-30; 5:1-7; 2 Enoch 66:6; Assumption of Moses 8:1.
50 1 Enoch 90:6-12; Assumption of Moses 8:1-5.
51 The kittim of the Habakkuk Commentary and the War Scroll are undoubtedly Romans. Thus F. M. Cross, Jr., *The Ancient Library of Qumran*, rev. ed. (New York, 1960), pp. 123f.
52 The wicked priest appears prominently in the Habakkuk Commentary. Elsewhere the enemy is termed "Gog and Magog" (Sibyl. Or. 3. 319, 512); "king of the kings" (Assmption of Moses 8:1); "dragon" (Pss. Sol. 2:29-31); "last leader" (2 Baruch 40:1); "one whom the dwellers upon the earth do not look for" (2 Esdras 5:6). The antichrist appears in the Ascension of Isaiah (4:2ff.), which is of Christian origin, but, according to Charles (Test. Dan 5:4-7), this title is anticipated by an identification of Dan with Satan. See, however, Rowley, *Relevance of Apocalyptic*, p. 73.
53 Strack and Billerbeck, *Kommentar*, Vol. IV, pp. 989-994.
54 Testament of Abraham 17, 19; 2 Enoch 33:1, 2. Cf. C. W. Rordorf, *Sunday* (Philadelphia, 1968), pp. 48-51.
55 2 Esdras 14:11, 12. Cf. the vision of the twelve waters (2 Baruch 53, 54). Here the eleventh black water represents the present calamities, while the twelfth white water represents the restoration of Israel after which follows the judgment and the age to come (chapters 69, 70). Also 2 Esdras 14:11 makes brief reference to a twelve-part division of the world history. Nine and one half parts have passed already.
56 Cf. Strack and Billerbeck, *Kommentar*, Vol. IV, pp. 986-1015.
57 2 Baruch 70:2, 3. Cf. 2 Esdras 5:1, 2; 9:3; 1 Enoch 99:5; Jubilees 23:19-21.
58 2 Esdras 6:22; Sibyl. Or. 3. 539-542.
59 "God shall make the great heaven above brazen, and draught over the whole earth, and it of iron" (Sibyl. Or. 3. 539, 540). Cf. 2 Baruch 27:6; 70:8; Jubilees 23:18; 2 Esdras 6:22.
60 See also Sibyl. Or. 3. 804.
61 See also 2 Baruch 27:10; 70:8.
62 Assumption of Moses 10:6; 2 Esdras 6:24.
63 2 Esdras 9:3; 2 Baruch 27:7.
64 2 Esdras 5:3.
65 2 Esdras 5:4; Assumption of Moses 10:5; Sibyl. Or. 3. 802, 803.
66 Cf. 2 Macc. 5:1-4.
67 1 Enoch 99:4, 5; 100:1, 2.
68 Literally "one who is wonderful in counsel, a mighty God." Cf. Isa. 9:5. See Gaster, *The Dead Sea Scriptures*, p. 143, n. 8. Cf. War Scroll 1. 12; Assmption of Moses 8:1; Jubilees 23:13.
69 Cf. Mowinckel, *He That Cometh*, pp. 155ff.
70 *Ibid.*, p. 123. Cf. A. Bentzen, *King and Messiah* (London, 1955), p. 37; H. Ringgren, *The Messiah in the Old Testament*, SBT I/18 (London, 1956), pp. 23f.
71 Mowinckel, *He That Cometh*, p. 156.

[72] Jubilees; 1 Enoch 1-36; 91-104; Assumption of Moses; 1 Baruch; 2 Baruch. See Russell, *Method and Message*, p. 309.

[73] Thus Charles, *Apocrypha and Pseudepigrapha*, Vol. II, p. 294. Cf. Rowley, *Relevance of Apocalyptic*, pp. 69f. For a fuller discussion of the complexities of the Levitical Messiah, see Russell, *Method and Message*, pp. 310-316.

[74] Charles (*Apocrypha and Pseudepigrapha*, Vol. II, p. 334, n. 10) considers the bracketed words an intrusion into the text in which "tribe" is in the singular. Similarly, the Damascus Document has a singular Messiah from Aaron and Israel. See below, p. 40.

[75] Cf. M. de Jonge, "Christian Influence in the Testaments of the Twelve Patriarchs," *NT* 4 (1960), 199-205.

[76] Pss. Sol. 17:23; 2 Esdras 12:32. Elsewhere he is the Son of God. 1 Enoch 105:2; 2 Esdras 7:28, 29; 13:32, 37, 52; 14:9. Cf. Ps. 2:7, where the royal son is adopted as God's son.

[77] Jubilees 31:18; Sibyl. Or. 3. 49.

[78] Sibyl. Or. 3. 652; 5. 108; Test. Judah 24:1.

[79] This expression is found in Sibyl. Or. 5. 414.

[80] Test. Simeon 7:1f. Cf. Test. Naphtali 5:3-5; 6:6; 8:2; Test. Simeon 5:5, 6; Test. Dan 5:4, 7.

[81] Thus De Jonge, "Christian Influences," pp. 213f. The purpose of the Christian additions with reference to the two Messiahs would be to indicate that Jesus Christ was both priest and king.

[82] See A. S. van der Woude, *Die messianischen Vorstellungen der Gemeinde von Qumran* (Assen, 1957); R. E. Brown, "The Messianiam of Qumran," *CBQ* 19 (1957): 53-82; K. G. Kuhn, "The Two Messiahs of Aaron and Israel," in K. Stendahl, ed., *The Scrolls and the New Testament* (New York, 1957), pp. 54-64; M. Black, *The Scrolls and Christian Origins* (New York, 1961), pp. 145-163.

[83] Manual of Discipline 9. 10f. They appear together with a prophet, perhaps a Messianic forerunner, but nevertheless an eschatological figure as well. This has led L. H. Silberman to view the triumvirate (prophet, priest, and king) as representing a muted eschatology. They are figures who will put to an end the present unsatisfactory situation of the community, but they are not strictly eschatological figures. "The Two Messiahs of the Manual of Discipline," *VT* 5 (1955): 77-82.

[84] Manual of Discipline for the Future Congregation 2. 11-22; Formulary of Blessings 2. 22-28; 5. 20-29.

[85] "The Two Messiahs of Aaron and Israel," pp. 59f. Cf. Russell, *Method and Message*, p. 321.

[86] See R. E. Brown, "The Teacher of Righteousness and the Messiah(s)," in M. Black, ed., *The Scrolls and Christianity* (London, 1969), p. 42.

[87] In addition to priest and Messiah (a star of Jacob), a prophet is also expected.

[88] The reference to the "Branch of David and the Interpreter of the Law" is a commentary on 2 Sam. 7:11-14.

[89] On Isa. 11:1-4 (fragment D, 1-8).

[90] War Scroll 2. 1; 15. 4ff.; 18. 3ff. Cf. 5.1.

[91] The Teacher of Righteousness (the community's founder) is now known to have been a priest (like his opponent, the Wicked Priest). Thus Cross, *The Ancient Library of Qumran*, p. 128. See Damascus Document 6. 2-11; Habakkuk Commentary 2. 1-10; 11. 4-8.

[92] O. Cullmann, *Christology of the New Testament*, rev. ed. (London, 1959), pp. 116-118.

[93] See Mowinckel, *He That Cometh*, pp. 427-431; F. H. Borsch, *The Son of Man in Myth and History* (London, 1967), pp. 55ff.

[94] The text reads "you are the Son of Man." Charles found this identification so difficult that he amended the text to read "this is the Son of Man" (*Apocrypha and Pseudepigrapha*, Vol. II, p. 237). Mowinckel (*He That Cometh*, p. 443) understands Enoch to be the Son of man in the ordinary sense of the term, i.e., meaning simply "man."

[95] Cf. T. W. Manson, *The Teaching of Jesus* (Cambridge, 1963), pp. 227f.; "The Son of Man in Daniel, Enoch, and the Gospels," *BJRL* 32 (1950): 171-193.

[96] See Russell, *Method and Message*, p. 352.

[97] Borsh, *Son of Man in Myth and History*, p. 152.

[98] *Relevance of Apocalyptic*, pp. 32, 33.

[99] *Ibid.*, pp. 61f.

[100] Cf. W. F. Albright, *From the Stone Age to Christianity* (New York, 1957), pp. 378-380; Russell, *Method and Message*, pp. 331-334; M. F. Stone, "The Concept of the Messiah in IV Ezra," in J. Neusner, ed., *Religions in Antiquity*, Numen Suppl. 14 (Leiden, 1968), pp. 295-312; B. Lindars, "Re-enter the Son of Man," *NTS* 22 (1976): 52-60.

[101] The Ethiopic manuscript of 2 Esdras has "my servant" for "my son," a possible reading. See Russell, *Method and Message*, p. 333; Stone, "The Concept of the Messiah in IV Ezra," p. 303.

CHAPTER 3

The Advent Hope
in the New Testament

Harold E. Fagal

WHEN the New Testament authors wrote they used a vocabulary that was familiar to them from the Old Testament, especially the Greek translation of the Hebrew Scriptures, the Septuagint. When the Old Testament prophets spoke of "the day of the Lord," they were referring to the time when God would intervene in human affairs and bring to an end this present age of evil and usher in the long-awaited age to come. At that time God would deliver His people from the hands of their oppressors, execute judgment upon those who had done wrong, and establish His people in their rightful dominion. Since the first or second century B.C. the Jews had expressed their eschatological hope in terms of two ages—this age and the age to come; the dividing point was the day of the Lord as described by certain of the Old Testament prophets.

The early church inherited this vocabulary from its Jewish background, but it did not take it over without change. The church had to take into account the rejection of the Messiah by the Jews and the subsequent changes that came about in the fulfillment of the plan of God through the church, the new Israel of God. In view of the fact that the promises of the Old Testament were given to the Israel of old and were to find their fulfillment in literal Israel, and that Israel had broken her covenant relationship with God, it was necessary for God to raise up a new people bound to Him by a new covenant. Therefore, the church reinterpreted the eschatology of the Old Testament, tied as it was for its fulfillment to the Jewish nation as the people of God, and understood it in a wider sense. The church saw the day of the Lord, not as the time when the Jewish nation would find deliverance from oppression and be established in her rightful dominion, but as the time when the new Israel of God, gathered from all the nations of the world, would see the consummation of her hopes in the return of Jesus to this earth. This would be the beginning of that glorious future age in the kingdom of God of which the prophets wrote.

As the church looked back upon the events that had recently transpired in the

46

life and ministry of Jesus of Nazareth, it realized that something decisive had happened. God had broken into history in the person of His Son. The Messianic Age had dawned. In the signs and mighty wonders Jesus performed, the people saw a demonstration of those powers that were thought to have been reserved for the age to come. He healed the sick, cast out demons, and even raised the dead—and all this before the time of consummation had come. This meant that in a sense the day of the Lord had come already, in spite of the fact that the day of final consummation was still future. Jesus would come again to establish God's reign over the nations, and this would be the beginning of the glorious age to come. The early church lived in a tension between the "already" and the "not yet." This present evil age of sin continued as it had since the entrance of sin into the world, but a decisive act of God had taken place in the coming of Jesus to this world that would soon lead to the fulfillment of all hopes in the glorious age to come.

This hope of future consummation was tied in with Jesus' promise to return to this earth at the end of the age. In expressing this hope, the New Testament writers used a variety of expressions. Four Greek words especially come to mind. The first is *erchesthai*, "to come," a word of common occurrence that is used with reference to the return of Jesus in such texts as Matthew 24:30, 42-44; 25:31; Luke 12:45; 15:5, 6; 19:23. The second word is *epiphaneia*, "appearing," "presence," which occurs once in 2 Thessalonians 2:8 and five times in the Pastoral Epistles (1 Tim. 6:14; 2 Tim. 1:10; 4:1, 8; Titus 2:13). The third word is *apokalupsis* (and the verb *apokaluptein),* "revelation," "unveiling," and is found in reference to Christ's second advent in such verses as Luke 17:30 and 1 Peter 1:13. The fourth and most unique word used for the coming of Christ in Messianic glory is *parousia*, a word that means "presence" but is also used in secular Greek of the arrival and subsequent visit of a king or emperor. In the New Testament it is never used of the first advent of Jesus but is used some fifteen to twenty times of the second "coming" (Matt. 24:3, 27, 37, 39; 1 Cor. 15:23; 1 Thess. 2:19; 3:13; 4:15; 5:23; 2 Thess. 2:1, 8, 9; James 5:7, 8; 2 Peter 1:16; 3:4, 12; 1 John 2:28). In addition to these words, there are references to "the day of the Lord" (Acts 2:20; 1 Cor. 1:8; 5:5; 2 Cor. 1:14; Phil. 1:6, 10; 2:16; 1 Thess. 5:2; 2 Thess. 2:2; 2 Peter 3:10, 12) and related expressions such as "the day of judgment" (Matt. 10:15; 11:22, 24; 12:36; 2 Peter 2:9; 1 John 4:17; Jude 6) and "that day" (Matt. 7:22; Luke 10: 12; 21:34; 2 Thess. 1:10; 2 Tim. 1:12; 4:8).

The phrase "second coming" is not found in the New Testament. The adjective "second" is, however, found once in Hebrews 9:28 with reference to Christ's coming in power and great glory ("Christ . . . will appear a second time").* But while neither Jesus Himself nor the early church used the term, it is true that belief in a second coming of Jesus permeated the thinking of both Jesus and the early church. In this chapter we will examine the New Testament eschatological hope as it is found in the various strata of the New Testament, specifically in the Synoptics, the Johannine literature, the Acts and General Epistles, and Paul's letters.

---

*Unless otherwise noted, Bible texts in this chapter are from the Revised Standard Version.

The Synoptic Gospels

The eschatology of Jesus as reported in the Synoptic Gospels is to a great extent tied in with the kingdom of God, which, according to the Synoptists, was the central theme of Jesus' teaching. Mark says that "after John was arrested, Jesus came into Galilee, preaching the gospel of God, and saying, 'The time is fulfilled, and the kingdom of God is at hand; repent, and believe in the gospel!'" (Mark 1:14, 15). This was the same message that His forerunner, John the Baptist, preached, for his message of repentance was based on the fact that "the kingdom of heaven is at hand" (Matt. 3:2).

This theme keeps recurring again and again throughout the teachings of Jesus. Mark 4 and Matthew 13 are parallel chapters that contain a number of Jesus' best-known and best-loved parables, and from them we learn that Jesus often began His parables with the same expression: "The kingdom of God is like . . ." (Matthew substitutes "heaven" for "God.") Mark records the parable of the mustard seed in these words: "And he said, 'With what can we compare the kingdom of God, or what parable shall we use for it? It is like a grain of mustard seed, which, when sown upon the ground, is the smallest of all the seeds of the earth; yet when it is sown it grows up and becomes the greatest of all shrubs, and puts forth large branches, so that the birds of the air can make nests in its shade'" (Mark 4:30-32). Jesus told this story, not to entertain His hearers, but to teach them something about the kingdom of God. The same is true of the other parables in these chapters. Not only is the kingdom of God an important theme in His teachings, but it is central to an understanding of His eschatology. What did Jesus mean by the kingdom of God, and how was this understanding related to His parousia?[1]

This expression has been studied so intensively in our present century that A. M. Hunter in 1951 referred to "the discovery of the true meaning of the kingdom of God."[2] No doubt he had in mind the growing consensus in New Testament scholarship that there are both present and future aspects to this teaching of Jesus. However, the exact relationship between these two aspects is still the subject of scholarly debate. A brief survey of the debate would be in order here.

The "old liberal" view[3] was that anything eschatological found in the teachings of Jesus in the New Testament had to be removed as one would remove the outer husk to get at the real kernel of Jesus' message that had to do with the fatherhood of God, the value of the human soul, and the ethic of love. But it was soon found that this noneschatological interpretation of Jesus resulted in removing Him from the setting of His own time and modernizing Him and His message. Johannes Weiss reacted against this view and broke new ground by interpreting Jesus' message about the kingdom, not by removing the eschatological and the apocalyptic, but in terms of first-century Jewish apocalyptic.[4] Albert Schweitzer used this same approach in the last part of his book *The Quest of the Historical Jesus*, in which he elaborated his own view of Jesus. Schweitzer saw Jesus as a Jewish apocalyptist and understood that the essential element in His message concerned the kingdom, which He thought was so close that it would come to reality in His lifetime. This made His message exclusively eschatological. Thus Schweitzer's interpretation of Jesus' teaching about the kingdom is called consistent eschatology. But such an interpretation confines any relevance in Jesus' message to the first century and led even Schweitzer himself to this pessimistic conclusion: "The historical knowledge of the personality and life of Jesus will not be a help, but perhaps even an offense to religion. . . . Jesus as a concrete historical personality remains a stranger to our time." [5]

C. H. Dodd reacted unfavorably to Schweitzer's views and introduced a concept of eschatology that has been called realized eschatology. He saw Jesus' proclamation that " 'the kingdom of heaven is at hand' " (Matt. 4:17) as synonymous with Matthew 12:28, " 'the kingdom of God has come upon you.' " The kingdom has come; the decisive moment was present in the ministry of Jesus. It is not something future but something present—something already realized. The heart of Jesus' teaching was that "the ultimate, the kingdom of God, has come into history. . . . The absolute, the 'wholly other,' has entered into time and space. . . . 'The Day of the Son of Man' stands for the timeless fact. So far as history can contain it, it is embodied in the historic crisis which the coming of Jesus brought about." [6]

Where Dodd saw eschatology as something already realized, others saw it as something yet to be realized in the future. R. H. Fuller believes that the kingdom is imminent but not realized. "The kingdom of God has not yet come, but it is near, so near that it is already operative in advance. . . . 'Realized eschatology' asserts that the decisive event has already occurred. The view outlined here on the other hand seeks to give full, though not exaggerated emphasis to what is already happening in the ministry of Jesus, yet at the same time to place the decisive event in the future." [7] This view has been called futuristic eschatology.

In response to this continuing debate George Eldon Ladd points out that "the most important factor in the entire study is the point of departure and the fundamental definition of the Kingdom." [8] The question for us is: What did Jesus teach (according to the Synoptic Gospels) regarding the kingdom of God, a concept that formed the heart of His message? Was He referring to something present or future? Is His teaching to be interpreted in the light of first-century Jewish apocalyptic, and therefore has no relevance for modern man? Is it to be interpreted as something wholly in the future, so that when Jesus referred to the "kingdom of God" it was to something that had not been realized yet? Or does it share aspects of both present and future?

In every language certain words have more than one meaning. Generally speaking, this causes us little trouble, for we are able to grasp the intended meaning from the context in which the word is used. In New Testament Greek the word for kingdom (basileia) has more than one meaning. It can refer to a domain or realm over which a king rules, or it can refer to the reign or rule of a king. In fact, when we examine how the word is used in the Synoptics we discover that it is used in at least three different ways. First, it is used of a future apocalyptic kingdom that would be established at the end of this present evil age. Here the "kingdom of God" is understood as "the age to come" (Mark 9:47; 10:23-25; 14:25; Matt. 8:11; Luke 13:28). Second, the "kingdom" is something that is already present among men—something that is to be received now (Mark 10:15), to be sought after now (Matt. 6:33; Luke 12:31), a power already active in the world (Matt. 11:12; 12:28), something within or among men now (Luke 17:21), and something into which men are entering now (Matt. 11:11, Luke 16:16; Matt. 21:31; 23:13). The third usage of "kingdom" reflects the abstract meaning of *basileia,* the reign or rule of a king. In John 18:36 the word is translated "kingship," and in Luke 19:12, 15; 23:42 the underlying idea is similarly "kingship" or "kingly power."

What did Jesus have in mind when He announced to His hearers that " 'the kingdom of God is at hand' " (Mark 1:15)? It is unlikely that He had only some far-off event in mind, the kingdom of glory that was not established in the lifetime of those who heard Him preach and has not been established yet. It is more likely that something was taking place before the very eyes of those who lived when He lived on earth that made it possible for Him to say that "the kingdom of God is at hand." God's saving sovereignty was seen in action in the signs and mighty wonders that Jesus did during His earthly ministry. It could be said that powers thought to be only of the age to come—power to heal the sick, cast out demons, cleanse lepers, and even to raise the dead—were being demonstrated at that very time in a new order of things never before seen by men. The future suddenly broke into the present. The things that men looked forward to in a future Messianic kingdom were now seen in the person and work of Jesus. There was a sense in which the future age of consummation had already begun, for those powers that were to be realized in the future kingdom of glory were now being realized in the midst of this present evil age.

When the seventy disciples returned from their mission and reported what they had accomplished in Jesus' name, that even demons were subject to them, Jesus said, " 'I saw Satan fall like lightning from heaven' " (Luke 10:18). This was evidence that Satan's power over men was broken by the power of God displayed not only in the ministry of Jesus but also now in the work He entrusted to His disciples. Jesus had invaded Satan's kingdom and released many who had been held in the power of the evil one. The world could never be the same again, for Jesus had come and brought with Him a demonstration of the powers of the age to come. Satan was seen to be a defeated foe, defeated in the very world in which his power had so long been in control.

Some of the people who witnessed the miracle of Jesus healing a man who was possessed with a demon (Matt. 12:22ff.) saw it as evidence that He was the expected Messiah, the Son of David. Others, such as many Pharisees, attempting to discredit the miracle, said that Jesus did what He did by the power of Beelzebul, the prince of demons. Jesus exposed the fallacy in their reasoning by showing how impossible it would be for a satanic demon to be exorcised by Satan, the prince of demons himself. Then He said, " 'But if it is by the Spirit of God that I cast out demons, then the kingdom of God has come upon you' " (Matt. 12:28). When Jesus broke the powers of evil and cast out satanic demons, He was giving a demonstration of the saving sovereignty of God in action. That is what He meant when He said that "the kingdom of God has come upon you." Satan's power was broken, and it would be only a matter of time until he would come to his end. Because of this Christ's followers are assured of victory over the enemy, not only when Jesus comes the second time, but even now while they are awaiting that great day.

In explaining the parable of the sower to His disciples, Jesus said: " 'To you has been given the secret of the kingdom of God, but for those outside everything is in parables' " (Mark 4:11). The word "secret" (*mustērion*) does not refer to something unexplained, but to something hidden from the understanding of men in past ages but now made known.[9] The secret of the kingdom to which Jesus referred is something that before the coming of Jesus, men did not understand; but now its meaning is made clear in the fuller revelation that came in Jesus' life and ministry. The secret of the kingdom is the understanding that the kingdom of God was to break into the world in a small way at first. In Jesus the powers of the age to come were to be demonstrated before the time of consummation came. Jesus invaded Satan's kingdom and left him a defeated foe. But although final victory was assured, the battle was not over yet. Many skirmishes would have to be fought with Satan. The Christian does not need only to wait for the final victory; he can enjoy the fruits of that victory through Christ in his own life right now.

The eschatology of Jesus, tied in as it is with His use of the phrase "kingdom of God," has in it elements of both realized and futuristic eschatology. There is a sense in which the kingdom is "realized" now as the believer seeks it, enters into it, finds it as something that is within him. The kingdom is truly "at hand" (Mark 1:15). But there is also a future aspect—the "not yet" aspect—that awaits the eschaton and the parousia. It is to this future aspect that we turn our attention now.

In the Synoptic Gospels the word *parousia* is found only in Matthew. Its four occurrences are found in the Olivet discourse (chap. 24:3, 27, 37, 39). When we take into account the fact that Jesus spoke Aramaic and the evangelists wrote in Greek, we understand that we cannot build too much on a particular Greek word placed on the lips of Jesus. Although the word *parousia* does not frequently occur, it is true that, regardless of the particular word used, the Synoptists show that, at least from the time of His visit to Caesarea Philippi, Jesus' thinking was permeated with ideas of His second coming.

When the word *parousia* is used in the New Testament it is a technical term for the second advent of Jesus. After Jesus foretold His death and subsequent resurrection (Mark 8:31ff.), He said, "For whoever is ashamed of me and of my words in this adulterous and sinful generation, of him will the Son of man also be ashamed, when he comes in the glory of his Father with the holy angels" (verse 38). Then follows an account of the Transfiguration, which is a miniature portrayal of what will take place at the second coming. On the mount Jesus was glorified, His divinity shown through His humanity, and He was seen communing with Moses (who is representative of those who will be resurrected from the dead at the second coming) and Elijah (who represents those who will be taken to heaven without experiencing death). Again, the parable of the pounds (Luke 19:11-27) is given in the setting of the false concept of the Messianic kingdom held by the disciples and the Jews generally. Apparently the "kingdom-fever" of the disciples had reached such a high point that they expected "the kingdom of God . . . to appear immediately" (verse 11), perhaps even at the coming celebration of the Passover in Jerusalem. In the "certain nobleman" who went into a far country to receive a kingdom and then returned, Jesus is portraying His own mission. The admonition, "'Trade with these till I come'" (verse 13), shows that, like the nobleman who expected to be away for an indefinite period of time, Jesus too expected a period of time to ensue before His return. In this parable the parousia is implied but not explained.

When Jesus appeared before Caiaphas, the high priest, during His arraignment before Jewish authorities, He was asked, "'Are you the Christ, the

Son of the Blessed?' " Jesus replied, " 'I am; and you will see the Son of man seated at the right hand of Power, and coming with the clouds of heaven' " (Mark 14:61, 62). The emphasis here is on Jesus' forthcoming enthronement at God's right hand, but the idea of the parousia is also present. In His lament over Jerusalem, Jesus concluded by saying, " 'For I tell you, you will not see me again, until you say, "Blessed is he who comes in the name of the Lord" ' " (Matt. 23:39). Jesus had just left the Temple for the last time, and with His departure God had also departed as the prophets had forewarned (Jer. 12:7; Eze. 8:6). Only at the parousia would these scribes and Pharisees He was addressing see Him again (cf. Rev. 1:7). That would be the time when " 'all the tribes of the earth will mourn, and they will see the Son of man coming on the clouds of heaven with power and great glory' " (Matt. 24:30).

The most detailed and extended discussion of the parousia in the Synoptics is found in Jesus' Olivet discourse (Mark 13; Matt. 24, 25; Luke 21). Here Matthew uses the word *parousia* in its New Testament technical sense of the second advent. In response to Jesus' referring to the time when not one stone of the Temple would be left one upon another (Matt. 24:2), the disciples asked Him, " 'When will this be, and what will be the sign of your coming [parousia] and of the close of the age?' " (verse 3). While the disciples framed their question in terms of their understanding of the setting up of the kingdom of God, which they believed to be as near even as the coming Passover festival, Jesus responded by blending together the events connected with the end of the Temple in Jerusalem and the end of the world at His parousia. Verses 4-14 of Matthew 24 seem to apply primarily to the destruction of Jerusalem, while verses 21 on seem to apply quite exclusively to the events that will take place leading up to the parousia.[10]

Jesus said that His coming would be preceded by the great tribulation (verses 21, 22), which will be shortened for the sake of the elect, and the deception of false Christs and false prophets who " 'will arise and show great signs and wonders, so as to lead astray, if possible, even the elect' " (verse 24). Then, to keep His true disciples from being deceived by these great deceptions, Jesus made clear what His parousia would be like. " 'For as the lightning comes from the east and shines as far as the west, so will be the coming [parousia] of the Son of man' " (verse 27). There would be nothing secret about His coming. It would be preceded by signs in the sun, moon, and stars (verse 29), which are described as the shaking of "the powers of the heavens," and " 'then will appear the sign of the Son of man in heaven, and then all the tribes of the earth will mourn, and they will see the Son of man coming on the clouds of heaven with power and great glory' " (verse 30). This will be the time when the resurrection of God's elect takes place, for " 'he will send out his angels with a loud trumpet call, and they will gather his elect from the four winds, from one end of heaven to the other' " (verse 31).

In the parable of the fig tree (verses 32-35) Jesus emphasized the need of knowing when the parousia is near. Just as the approach of summer is recognized by the sign of leaves appearing on the branches of the fig trees, so one could discern by the signs just enumerated when the parousia was near. In fact, " 'this generation [the generation that sees the last of these signs] will not pass away till all these things take place' " (verse 34). There will be no prolonged period of time between the fulfilling of the signs and the event they portend. Although it is possible to know when it is near, the exact time of the parousia is known only to the

Father (verse 36). The conditions prevailing among the men of Noah's day with regard to eating, drinking, and marrying, will be repeated in the days preceding the parousia of the Son of man (verses 37-39). An unconcern with what is about to happen will lead to a total lack of preparation and a perverting of those things that, under proper circumstances, are right but when carried to extreme and excess lead to evil.

When the parousia does take place a great separation will occur. " 'Then two men will be in the field; one is taken and one is left. Two women will be grinding at the mill; one is taken and one is left' " (verses 40, 41). The picture is that of Jesus "taking to himself" (Greek middle voice) those who are His at the parousia and "sending away" those who are not His. This great separation is further described in the description of the great judgment with which the discourse ends in Matthew 25:31-46. There the picture is of a shepherd separating the sheep from the goats. It will take place " 'when the Son of man comes in his glory, and all the holy angels with him' " (verse 31). The result will be that those who are on the King's right hand will receive the kingdom that was prepared for them from the foundation of the world, while those on the left are told to " " "depart from me, you cursed, into the eternal fire prepared for the devil and his angels" ' " (verse 41). The point upon which the decision of the judgment will hinge is the attitude that men have shown to Christ in the persons who are in physical and spiritual need: " " "as you did it to one of the least of these my brethren, you did it to me" ' " (verse 40; cf. verse 45). The separation that follows is eternal, for the wicked will " 'go away into eternal punishment, but the righteous into eternal life' " (verse 46). This same scene is described earlier in the discourse, in the picture of the one in the field and the one in the mill being taken while the other is left (chap. 24:40, 41). There follows a warning to be watchful, for the parousia will be as unexpected to the unconcerned and unprepared as the coming of a thief in the night. " 'Therefore you also must be ready; for the Son of man is coming at an hour you do not expect' " (verse 44).

The lesson of watchfulness is further illustrated by the parable of the ten maidens. The wise were concerned enough to be prepared even though the coming of the bridegroom was delayed. The foolish waited too long to make the necessary preparation. When the cry was heard, " " "Behold, the bridegroom! Come out to meet him!" ' " (Matt. 25:6), the foolish tried to borrow oil for their lamps from the wise, but it was too late. While they went to buy the needed oil, the door was shut, and when they returned they were refused admittance. To their knock came the reply, " " "I do not know you" ' " (verse 12). The parable concludes with the warning, " 'Watch therefore, for you know neither the day nor the hour' " (verse 13).

As we have seen, the eschatology of the Synoptic Gospels is closely connected with Jesus' proclamation about the kingdom of God. It has as its background the Jewish antithesis of the two ages—this age and the age to come—as well as the Old Testament concept of the day of the Lord that would bring the present evil age to an end and usher in the glorious future. This way of looking at time is everywhere assumed in the Synoptics, although it is not often expressed. However, within the framework of this horizontal dualism of present and future there is a new element introduced. The kingdom of God as proclaimed by Jesus is not only a future hope but a present reality. It is clear from the discussion Jesus had with His disciples after His talk with the rich young ruler that eternal life is indeed life in the future kingdom of God (Mark 10:17-31). But it is equally clear from Jesus' teachings on other occasions that the kingdom became present in the world through His person and ministry. There is a tension in the Synoptic Gospels between the "already" and the "not yet" aspects of the kingdom. In His parables Jesus stressed the "already," and in His Olivet discourse the "not yet." Those whom Jesus confronted in His person and who responded in faith to Him had already entered the kingdom, but they were also to prepare to enter the future kingdom at His parousia.

The Johannine Literature

When we turn from the Synoptics to the Johannine literature, especially the Fourth Gospel, we notice that different terms are used to express eschatological concepts. Where the Synoptic Jesus spoke about the kingdom of God, the Johannine Christ speaks of eternal life. The phrase "kingdom of God" is found only twice in the Fourth Gospel (chap. 3:3, 5), both times in connection with Jesus' interview with Nicodemus regarding the new birth. But the central message in John has to do with eternal life, which Christ offers to men now. The coming of the Son of man in the clouds of heaven, such as was prominent in the Synoptics, especially Matthew, is not found in the Fourth Gospel. John does not record the Olivet discourse, but he does record Jesus' discourse in the upper room (chapters 13-16) with its emphasis on the coming of the Paraclete as Christ's representative, a discourse that is not found in the Synoptics. This is not to imply that any reference to the second advent is lacking in John's writings, for John is the only evangelist to record Christ's promise to His disciples regarding His second coming (chap. 14:1-3); however, the eschatological emphasis in John is different from that which we have seen in the Synoptics.

One of John's characteristic words that he introduces early in his prologue is "life": "In him was life, and the life was the light of men" (chap. 1:4). Life is thus linked to Christ. John is using the word here at the beginning of his Gospel in order to prepare the way for the development of the thought that Christ has brought a new *quality* of life to the Christian. He uses the word "life" thirty-six times in his Gospel, thirteen times in 1 John, and fifteen times in Revelation. To him it characteristically refers to eternal life, which is God's gift to men through Christ. The adjective "eternal" *(aiōnios)*, which he always uses in connection with "life," means literally "pertaining to an age." The age to which it refers is the age to come, and so "eternal life" becomes an eschatological term meaning "the life proper to the age to come." [11]

John, however, uses the term not only to describe the everlasting duration of the age to come but also to describe the quality of life the Christian is able to enjoy here and now. Leon Morris describes John's concept in these words: "The notion of time is there. Eternal life will never cease. But there is something else there, too, and something more significant. The important thing about eternal life is not its quantity but its quality." [12] Westcott says, "It is not an endless duration of being in time, but being of which time is not a measure." [13] In His discourse with Nicodemus Jesus referred to the lifting up of the Son of man and said that the result would be " 'that whoever believes in him may have eternal life' " (chap. 3:15). Eternal life is a present possession that results from being " 'born anew' " (verse 3). The present tense of the verb is used in the phrase " 'may have eternal life' " (verse 15) and carries with it the force of continuous action in present time. It could be translated "may continue to have eternal life." The same is true in verse 36: "He who believes in the Son has [or, continues to have] eternal life." The thought is elaborated upon in chapter 5:24: "'He who hears my word and believes him who sent me, has eternal life; he does not come into judgment, but has passed from death to life.'" The eschatological experience of passing from death to life has already come to the believer who is united spiritually with his Lord. He shares that quality of life that belongs to the Lord, not only in the future life but here in this life. This does not do away with the hope of a future resurrection, for in the very next verse Jesus speaks of that event: "'Truly, truly, I say to you, the hour is coming, and now is, when the dead will hear the voice of the Son of God, and those who hear will live'" (verse 25). That which "is coming" is the future resurrection (see also verse 21), but the phrase "and now is" can only refer to the experience of passing "from death to life" now, about which Jesus has just commented. Such a transformation of life from that of being spiritually dead in sin to that of being alive in Christ can be described, not only as being "born anew," but also as being a sharer in the quality of life that Christ makes possible now. The eschatological hope of the future has broken into the present in the "eternal life" that is the present possession of those who are Christ's.

Although this concept is expressed in different terms, it is similar in many respects to the concept of the kingdom of God found in the Synoptics. That which was believed to be reserved for the age to come has broken into the present and is something to be enjoyed now. The future has, in a sense, become the present. But this is not the whole story, for there is something yet to come. In the Synoptics it is the parousia of the Son of man who will come on the clouds of heaven; in John it is the coming of Jesus to take His people to His Father's house where He has prepared a place for them (chap. 14:1-3). Thus there are elements of a realized eschatology as well as a futuristic eschatology in John as well as in the Synoptics. Of the relationship between the two in John, C.F.D. Moule has this to say: "The only 'realized eschatology' in the Fourth Gospel is on the individual level; and such a type of 'realized eschatology,' far from *replacing* a futuristic eschatology, need be only its correlative." [14]

The idea of a second coming of Jesus is present in the parting counsel Jesus gave His disciples just before His crucifixion (chaps. 13:31-16:33). He announced His departure by saying, "'Little children, yet a little while I am with you. You will seek me; and as I said to the Jews so now I say to you, "Where I am going you cannot come."'" (chap. 13:33). It was Peter who asked, "'"Lord, where are you going?" Jesus answered, "Where I am going you cannot follow me now; but you shall follow afterward"'" (verse 36). Then Jesus comforted His disciples with the promise of His coming again: "'Let not your hearts be troubled; believe in God, believe also in me. In my Father's house are many rooms; if it were not so, would I have told you that I go to prepare a place for you? And when I go and prepare a place for you, I will come again and will take you to myself, that where I am you may be also'" (chap. 14:1-3). Again in verse 18 He says, "I will not leave you desolate; I will come to you" (cf. verse 28; chap. 16:16). This coming of Christ is mentioned twice in the Johannine Epistles. The first mention uses the word *parousia* in its technical New Testament sense of the second advent: "'And now, little children, abide in him, so that when he appears we may have confidence and not shrink from him in shame at his coming [parousia]'" (1 John 2:28). The second uses the word "appearing": "Beloved, we are God's children now; it does not yet appear what we shall be, but we know that when he appears *[phaneroō]* we shall be like him, for we shall see him as he is" (chap 3:2). Other eschatological expressions used by John include "in that day" (John 14:20; 16:23, 26), and "at the last day" (chaps. 6:39, 40, 44, 54; 11:24; 12:48). Again we see the blending of the two aspects of the Christian life involving the present possession of eternal life and the future hope of resurrection life in the age to come "at the last day."

The book of Revelation is written in language that is similar to that found in Jewish apocalyptic literature. It deals with developments and sequences leading up to the eschaton. In its several lines of prophecy the major events of the last days and the culmination of the conflict that has been going on between Christ and Satan are revealed. It will be possible here to mention only briefly those eschatological passages that speak specifically of the coming of Christ.

The theme toward which the whole book moves is given at the beginning in these words: "Behold, he is coming with the clouds, and every eye will see him, every one who pierced him; and all tribes of the earth will wail on account of him" (chap. 1:7). In the vision of the seven trumpets the complete triumph of Christ is portrayed under the symbol of the seventh trumpet. A voice from heaven is heard saying, "'The kingdom of the world has become the kingdom of our Lord and of his Christ, and he shall reign for ever and ever'" (chap. 11:15). The word "kingdom" is used here in its abstract sense to refer to the authority, or rule, that men have exercised in the world, and this authority will pass into the hands of Christ whose rule will never end. The same thought is expressed by the loud voice from heaven that says, "'Now the salvation and the power and the kingdom of our God and the authority of his Christ have come, for the accuser of our brethren has been thrown down, who accuses them day and night before our God'" (chap. 12:10). The "coming" of this kingdom is the coming of the authority and rule of God that will usher in the new and glorious age to come.

In chapter 14 Christ at His coming is portrayed symbolically as a reaper with a sickle in hand who goes out to gather the harvest. The setting of the three angels' messages of verses 6-12 shows that they are sounded just before the coming of Christ and the harvest of the earth, and are therefore the last warning that God gives to the inhabitants of the earth before the end of this age. The harvest that is described in verses 15-20 will be accomplished in two phases. Verses 15 and 16 refer to the harvest of the righteous, described as the harvest of ripe grain, and verses 17-20 refer to the harvest of the wicked who are gathered for destruction, described under the symbol of ripe grapes. Certain events preceding the coming of Christ are given symbolically in the sixth of the seven bowls of the wrath of God that are poured out (chapter 16). Verse 14 speaks of "demonic spirits, performing signs, who go abroad to the kings of the whole world, to assemble them for battle on the great day of God the Almighty." This "day of God" is reminiscent of "the day of the Lord" of Old Testament eschatology, a day in which God would break into history both in judgment and for salvation (cf. Amos 5:18-20; Jer. 46:10; Eze. 7:19; 13:5; 30:2, 3; Obadiah 15). Following the mention of this battle of Armageddon (Rev. 16:16), the thought is added parenthetically, "'Lo, I am coming like a thief'" (verse 15). Here the imagery of the unexpectedness of Christ's coming is the same as that used in the Olivet discourse (Matt. 24:43) to encourage watchfulness for the parousia of the Son of man.

A somewhat extended vision of the second coming of Christ is given in Revelation 19:11-20:6. Heaven is opened, and Christ descends with the armies of heaven. He comes in power and majesty as King of kings and Lord of lords to defeat those who are bent on the destruction of His people and to deliver the righteous. Satan is bound so that he can deceive the nations no more, and the righteous reign with Christ for a thousand years as priests of God and Christ. The last two chapters of Revelation have to do with the glorious fulfillment of all the promises of God in the age to come. A new heaven and a new earth will take the place of this former, sin-cursed earth. To John came this assurance: " 'These words are trustworthy and true. And the Lord, the God of the spirits of the prophets, has sent his angel to show his servants what must soon take place. And behold, I am coming soon' " (chap. 22:6, 7). The phrase "I am coming soon" is repeated twice more (verses 12, 20), and the book closes with the promise, " 'Surely I am coming soon.' Amen. Come, Lord Jesus!" (verse 20).

A comparison of the way the advent hope is expressed in the Synoptics and the Johannine literature reveals certain differences; but these differences should not be overemphasized, for they are differences of vocabulary more than of concept. In both we find aspects of realized eschatology, the Synoptics with the emphasis on the present reality of the kingdom of God and John with the emphasis on eternal life as a quality of life one enjoys here; and in both we find aspects of futuristic eschatology, the Synoptics in the Olivet discourse and the parousia of the Son of man and John with the portrayal of the new heavens and new earth as well as the use of eschatological terms such as *parousia,* "that day," and "on [at] the last day." While the vocabulary and the way of presentation differ, the central message of the advent hope remains the same.

The Early Church

In order to find how the early church viewed eschatology we turn to the book of Acts and the letters of Peter and James. In Acts, Luke has described the development of the church from the ascenson of Jesus to the early sixties, the period during which the final break was made between the followers of "the Way" (Acts 9:2) and Judaism.

A study of the content of the primitive preaching of the apostolic period brings one inevitably to the work of C. H. Dodd and his book *The Apostolic Preaching and Its Developments.*[15] In his study Dodd has analyzed the early sermons in Acts, which he believes contain the type of material such as the Aramaic-speaking church at Jerusalem, of which Peter was the spokesman, used in public preaching following the resurrection and ascension of Jesus. The main theme of that preaching was the proclamation of Jesus as Lord and Messiah. This early apostolic proclamation, which Dodd calls the *kerygma (kērugma,* "proclamation," "preaching"), can be summarized in six points taken from Peter's four sermons recorded in Acts, chapters 2 to 4:

1. The age of fulfillment has dawned.

2. This fulfillment has taken place through the ministry, death, and resurrection of Jesus, of which a brief account is given, with proof from the Scriptures that all took place "according to the definite plan and foreknowledge of God" (chap. 2:23).

3. By virtue of the resurrection, Jesus has been exalted at the right hand of God, as Messianic head of the New Israel.

4. The Holy Spirit in the church is the sign of Christ's present power and glory.

5. The Messianic Age will shortly reach its consummation in the return of Christ.

6. The appeal for repentance, with which the kerygma always closes, is based on the offer of forgiveness and of the Holy Spirit, and the promise of "salvation," that is, "of the life of the age to come," to those who enter the elect community.[16]

It is interesting to note that the early church not only believed in but taught the return of Christ. It is also interesting that the central theme of Jesus' preaching—the kingdom of God—is not one of the central themes of the early apostolic preaching. However, it is not altogether absent, for Luke says that Philip "preached good news about the kingdom of God" (chap. 8:12), and Paul at Lystra spoke of the present aspect of the kingdom when he said that "through many tribulations we must enter the kingdom of God" (chap. 14:22; cf. chaps. 19:8; 28:23). Dodd points out that the apostolic kerygma follows the lines of the summary Mark gives of the preaching of Jesus: "Now after John was arrested, Jesus came into Galilee, preaching the gospel of God, and saying, 'The time is fulfilled, and the kingdom of God is at hand; repent, and believe in the gospel'" (Mark 1:14, 15).[17] It is within the framework of this preaching concerning Jesus that the early church carried on its mission of proclaiming Christ to the non-Christians around them.

The book of Acts begins with an account of the ascension just before which the disciples asked Jesus this question: "'Lord, will you at this time restore the kingdom to Israel?'" (Acts 1:6). By their question it is clear that the disciples were still looking for the establishment of Jewish national sovereignty such as they had enjoyed under David and Solomon. In His answer Jesus did not correct their mistaken view regarding what was going to take place and when. What He did say was "'It is not for you to know the times or seasons which the Father has fixed by his own authority'" (verse 7). It was not for them at that time to understand the full program of God with regard to the future. Their work was to be His witnesses "'in Jerusalem and in all Judea and Samaria and to the end of the earth'" (verse 8). F. F. Bruce says, "The question in verse 6 appears to have been the last flicker of their former burning expectation of an imminent political theocracy with themselves as its chief executives."[18]

Just after the ascension two men in white robes gave Jesus' disciples the promise of His return to earth: "'Men of Galilee, why do you stand looking into heaven? This Jesus, who was taken up from you into heaven, will come in the same way as you saw him go into heaven'" (chap. 1:11). It was not for the disciples to know when this would take place, but they had the assurance that it would take place and that Jesus' return would be in the same manner as His ascension—bodily and visible. In the meantime they were to be witnesses of what they had seen and experienced concerning Jesus and of His return to earth again.

That the disciples and the early church did witness concerning the return of their Lord is evidenced by the place that this belief occupied in the church's preaching and teaching. For example, in his sermon following the healing of the lame man by the Beautiful Gate of the Temple, Peter spoke of the time when God would "'send the Christ appointed for you, Jesus'" (chap. 3:20). Peter's teaching concerning the Advent hope is also found in his two canonical letters to the church. In his first letter, written to those Christians in northern Asia Minor who had already undergone some persecution and for whom further trials awaited, he encouraged his readers in the hope of the second coming, which he called "the revelation [apokalupsis] of Jesus Christ" (1 Peter 1:7, 13) and the time "when his glory is revealed [literally "in the revelation of the glory of him"]" (chap. 4:13). He calls Jesus "the chief Shepherd" and refers to His coming as the time when He "is manifested [phaneroō]" (chap. 5:4). In his second letter he writes to remind his readers of the truths of the gospel and warns them against the destructive heresies that certain false teachers were bringing in. In so doing, he uses the word parousia three times in its technical New Testament sense of the second coming of Christ (chaps. 1:16; 3:4, 12). He reminds them that "we did not follow cleverly devised myths when we made known to you the power and coming [parousia] of our Lord Jesus Christ, but we were eyewitnesses of his majesty" (chap. 1:16). Here he is reminding them of the divine power that he saw on the Mount of Transfiguration. Just as the transfiguration was a miniature representation of the glorification of Jesus that will take place at His coming, so is it a pledge that that great event will take place. The fact that Peter and his two companions were eyewitnesses of this is used as proof that the belief in a future parousia is not some cleverly devised myth.

Peter interprets the events that will take place at the parousia in the light of the Old Testament "day of the Lord": "But the day of the Lord will come like a thief, and then the heavens will pass away with a loud noise, and the elements will be dissolved with fire, and the earth and the works that are upon it will be burned up" (chap. 3:10). He uses the same imagery here of the unexpectedness of the parousia to those who are not prepared for it that Jesus did in the Olivet discourse (Matt. 24:43; cf. Luke 12:39). Those who know about the coming of the day of the Lord will live lives of "holiness and godliness" while they wait for and hasten "the coming [parousia] of the day of God, because of which the heavens will be kindled and dissolved, and the elements will melt with fire!" (2 Peter 3:11, 12). In his Pentecostal sermon Peter used the term "day of the Lord," which was familiar to the Jews from the Old Testament, to explain what was taking place at that time. He quoted from the prophet Joel to show that the day of the Lord would be accompanied by an outpouring of the Holy Spirit on young and old alike and by "wonders in the heaven above and signs on the earth beneath" (Acts 2:19). What was taking place before their eyes was this eschatological outpouring of the Spirit, which was thought to be reserved for the end-time but was already breaking into the present. The "mighty works and wonders and signs which God did through him [Jesus] in your midst" (verse 22) were another evidence that the promised future blessings of God were already being experienced. The "day of the Lord" was not only future but also present. The tension between the "already" and the "not yet," between present fulfillment and future consummation, focuses not only on the present but also on the future. This was the case, as we have seen, with Jesus' teaching regarding the kingdom of God. Peter does not use the same terminology of the kingdom that is prominent in the teachings of Jesus as found in the Synoptics, but the same idea is present in his writings. His eschatology is both realized and futuristic. The only explanation he can give for the Pentecostal outpouring of the Holy Spirit is that it is a fulfillment of what Joel prophesied would take place on the day of the Lord. But there is still a future consummation when an entrance is provided "into the eternal kingdom of our Lord and Savior Jesus Christ" (2 Peter 1:11). Fulfillment has come already, but consummation waits for "new heavens and a new earth in which righteousness dwells" (chap. 3:13).

The letter of James was written for very practical purposes. His Jewish Christian readers were suffering at the hands of other Jews, and he wrote to encourage them in their trials. The letter contains one passage admonishing patience while awaiting the coming of the Lord: "Be patient, therefore, brethren, until the coming [parousia] of the Lord. Behold, the farmer waits for the precious fruit of the earth, being patient over it until it receives the early and the late rain. You also be patient. Establish your hearts, for the coming [parousia] of the Lord is at hand" (chap. 5:7, 8). In the early verses of the chapter James spells out the dangers connected with fraudulent gain and the wrong use of riches, and he looks forward to the time when the righteous will be vindicated at the Lord's parousia. Just as the farmer must patiently wait for the early and late rains to produce a harvest, so must the Christian wait patiently for the time when the Lord at His coming will make all things right.

The eschatology of the early church contains the same concepts as those already noted in the Synoptic Gospels and the Johannine literature. The "day of the Lord" terminology is taken over from the Old Testament, but it is interpreted as both realized and futuristic. Although the church placed the greater emphasis upon the future consummation, yet the idea of present fulfillment is also present. The "last days" are here (Acts 2:17), but the final realization of the kingdom awaits the parousia. There is both a horizontal and a vertical dualism, horizontal with regard to this evil age and the glorious age to come, and vertical with regard to the world below and the world above. Jesus is the Lord of the church now, but at His parousia He will be revealed to the world for what He really is, the Lord of all creation.

Pauline Letters

The eschatology of Saul, the Jewish rabbi, who became Paul, the Christian apostle to the Gentiles, has as its background the Jewish Messianic hope such as is found in the Old Testament and in other Jewish writings. This hope envisioned a day of the Lord when God would step into human affairs and establish His reign on earth. It would be a day when the Messiah would destroy the enemies of God, redeem Israel from her oppressors, and establish the kingdom of God. Later apocalyptic and rabbinic Jewish literature developed the terminology of the two ages—this age and the age to come—to express the hope and goal for the future. Everywhere in his writings Paul reflects this idiom of the two ages, although he expresses it in its complete form only in Ephesians 1:21: "not only in this age but also in that which is to come." However, he does speak often of "this age" (1 Cor. 1:20; 2:6, 8; 3:18; cf. 2 Cor. 4:4), "the age of this world" (Eph. 2:2), and "the present evil age" (Gal. 1:4).

When Paul uses the terminology of the day of the Lord of the Old Testament (cf. Amos 5:18-20; Joel 2:1, 11), he interprets it in the light of the Lord Jesus Christ and His return to earth. Not only does he call it "the day of the Lord" (1 Thess. 5:2; 2 Thess. 2:2), but he also calls it "the day of our Lord Jesus Christ"

(1 Cor. 1:8; 2 Cor. 1:14) and "the day of Jesus Christ" (Phil. 1:6). It is a day yet to come (2 Thess. 2:2), whose coming will be sudden and unexpected "like a thief in the night" (1 Thess. 5:2). It will bring with it deliverance from "the present evil age" (Gal. 1:4) and usher in the glorious age to come (Eph. 1:21). Connected with it will be the parousia (1 Thess. 2:19; 3:13; 5:23; 2 Thess. 2:1, 8). Paul refers to the coming age by the term "kingdom of God," so familiar from the Synoptic Gospels. It is something the unrighteous will not inherit (1 Cor. 6:9; 15:50; Gal. 5:21; Eph. 5:5) but is reserved for the righteous (1 Thess. 2:12; 2 Tim. 4:18). Following the parousia Christ will deliver "the kingdom to God the Father after destroying every rule and every authority and power. . . . the last enemy to be destroyed is death" (1 Cor. 15:24-26). Then "the creation itself will be set free from its bondage to decay and obtain the glorious liberty of the children of God" (Rom. 8:21).

As a good Jew, Paul shared the apocalyptic dualism of "this age" and "the age to come" with the rabbinic writers of the first century, but he understood its meaning no longer in the light of the Old Testament perspective but in the light of the future coming and reign of Christ. The future aspect of this eschatological hope in Paul's writings is nowhere more clearly brought out than in his Thessalonian correspondence. In what may well be his first extant letter to one of his churches, he answered the question that had arisen there about the fate of those who had died before the parousia and whether there was any hope of a future for them in the plan of God. He described the resurrection that will take place at the parousia and shows that death will not be a barrier that will keep those who have fallen asleep in Christ from the future reward. "For the Lord himself will descend from heaven with a cry of command, with the archangel's call, and with the sound of the trumpet of God. And the dead in Christ will rise first; then we who are alive, who are left, shall be caught up together with them in the clouds to meet the Lord in the air; and so we shall always be with the Lord" (1 Thess. 4:16, 17). The unprepared will cry " 'peace and security' " (chap. 5:3), but the day of the Lord will come "like a thief in the night" (verse 2) with sudden destruction. The suddenness of this travail that will come upon the earth can only be compared with the suddenness of the onset of labor to a pregnant woman—"there will be no escape" (verse 3). Those who are "sons of light and sons of the day" (verse 5) will not be taken unawares, for they understand "the times and the seasons" (verse 1). They do not sleep as others do at this time but are awake and sober (verse 6).

Some in the Thessalonian church misunderstood what Paul had written. They understood the day of the Lord to involve a whole series of events and believed that these events were already unfolding—that the day of the Lord had come (2 Thess. 2:1, 2). It was necessary for Paul to explain that, while the day of the Lord was imminent, it had not come yet. First there would be a great rebellion during which time "the man of lawlessness" would carry out his nefarious work against God. A restraining power was holding him back, but the time would come when he would "be revealed, and the Lord Jesus will slay him with the breath of his mouth and destroy him by his appearing and his coming [parousia]" (verse 8).

There is a decided futuristic eschatology in Paul's letters. He looked for a glorious consummation that would take place at the end of the age when Christ returned. He called this "our blessed hope, the appearing of the glory of our great God and Savior Jesus Christ" (Titus 2:13). But Paul thought not only of the end-time as something future but as something present as well. There was a sense in which the future eschatological blessings to be realized in the age to come were already beginning to unfold within history. With the coming of Jesus, the Messianic Age began; and with His death and resurrection and the outpouring of the Holy Spirit, redemption had begun. The blessings of the age to come were being realized while the consummation was awaited. In this connection Ladd points out that Paul's eschatology is inseparable from his theological thought as a whole. "The death of Christ is an eschatological event. Because of Christ's death, the justified man stands already on the age-to-come side of the eschatological judgment, acquitted of all guilt. By virtue of the death of Christ, the believer has already been delivered from this present evil age (Gal. 1:4). He has been transferred from the rule of darkness and now knows the life of the Kingdom of Christ (Col. 1:13). In His cross, Christ has already defeated the powers of evil that have brought chaos into the world (chap. 2:14ff.)." [19]

Paul sees an eschatological aspect to the resurrection of Jesus. The final resurrection at the last day is a real hope because Jesus Himself was resurrected from the dead. His resurrection was the first act of the unfolding drama of which the final resurrection is the climax. By His death and resurrection Jesus demonstrated His power over death. "For as in Adam all die, so also in Christ shall all be made alive. But each in his own order: Christ the first fruits, then at his coming [parousia] those who belong to Christ" (1 Cor. 15:22, 23). To belong to Christ means, to Paul, to be "in Christ." "If any one is in Christ, he is a new creation; the old has passed away, behold, the new has come" (2 Cor. 5:17). The Christian belongs to the new age and is experiencing the life and power of that new age even while living in this present age. By his baptism he is baptized into Christ's death and rises to resurrection life in Him. "We were buried therefore with him by baptism into death, so that as Christ was raised from the dead by the glory of the Father, we too might walk in newness of life. For if we have been united with him in a death like his, we shall certainly be united with him in a resurrection like his" (Rom. 6:4, 5). In a spiritual sense the Christian has already experienced death and resurrection and is already living the life of the age to come. God has "made us alive together with Christ . . . , and raised us up with him, and made us sit with him in the heavenly places in Christ Jesus, that in the coming ages he might show the immeasurable riches of his grace in kindness toward us in Christ Jesus" (Eph. 2:5-7). Even now we are sharers with Christ in His resurrection life.

For Paul there is always the tension between the realized and the futuristic aspects of the eschatological hope. Life must still be lived in this present world even while being a sharer with Christ in His resurrection life. God has already "delivered us from the dominion of darkness and transferred us to the kingdom of his beloved Son" (Col. 1:13), but, on the other hand, "our commonwealth is in heaven, and from it we await a Savior, the Lord Jesus Christ, who will change our lowly body to be like his glorious body" (Phil. 3:20, 21). We have already been saved (Eph. 2:5), but we await our future salvation which "is nearer to us now than when we first believed" (Rom. 13:11). We have been resurrected to newness of life (chap. 6:4), and yet we long for that resurrection when "what is mortal may be swallowed up by life" (2 Cor. 5:4). The Christian lives, as it were, in two ages. He must live in this present evil world until the parousia; but as one who is truly "in Christ," he lives the life of the age to come. There is fulfillment but not consummation; the consummation awaits the return of Christ and the inauguration of the age to come.

Conclusion

The advent hope in the New Testament is closely tied in with the eschatology of the Old Testament reinterpreted in the light of the great events that transpired in the life and ministry of Jesus of Nazareth. The kingdom of God of future expectation had already come—and yet in another sense it was still to come. In each of the strata of the New Testament this tension between the "already" and the "not yet" is present. One cannot speak of the advent hope in the New Testament and refer only to the future aspect of this hope, for the two were inseparably entwined in the hope and belief of the church. The Christ who had come in great humility was coming again, this time in great power. At His first advent He brought with Him proleptically the powers of the age to come; at His second coming there will be the inbreaking of the age to come with the full realization of the powers reserved for that age of consummmation.

In his book *Christ and Time*, Oscar Cullmann discusses the different divisions of time as understood by Judaism and Christianity and their relationship to eschatology. The Jewish viewpoint of time was of two ages—this age and the age to come—with the dividing point being the coming of the Messiah. The midpoint (understood to be the dividing point between the two ages) was still future. The Christian viewpoint of time is also based (according to the New Testament) on the two ages, but with a different midpoint. In the light of what transpired in the life and ministry of Jesus, the church understood that the decisive point of time was not in the future but had already been reached. The event that would bring this present age to a close and usher in the glorious future age was yet to come, but the coming of Christ the first time marked a new intersection of the time line. The day of the Lord at the end of the age was understood to be the second coming of Christ, and that was still future. But in the light of Jesus' ministry to this world something decisive took place that could only mean that the decisive point in time had been reached before the end of the age.

Cullmann illustrates how Christ's first advent could be the decisive point of time even before the end of the present age by saying: *"The decisive battle in a war may already have occurred in a relatively early stage of the war, and yet the war still continues.* Although the decisive effect of that battle is perhaps not recognized by all, it nevertheless already means victory. But the war must still be carried on for an undefined time, until 'Victory Day.' Precisely this is the situation of which the New Testament is conscious, as a result of the recognition of the new division of time; the revelation consists precisely in the fact of the proclamation that *that event on the cross, together with the resurrection which followed, was the already concluded decisive battle."* [20]

Because the decisive battle is in the past, the end of the war against Satan is assured; Christ's victory over the forces of evil will one day be complete. Cullmann says, "The center of time is not in the object of hope but rather in an already occurred historical fact. This then means that the hope for the future can now be supported by faith in the past, faith in the already concluded decisive battle. That which has already happened offers the solid guarantee for that which will take place. *The hope of the final victory is so much the more vivid because of the unshakably firm conviction that the battle that decides the victory has already taken place."*[21]

This is the radically new element in the eschatology of the New Testament. That for which the Jews looked was entirely in the future; that for which the church hopes is still future, but it is based on a past historical event. When Jesus came the first time the decisive point in the time line of redemptive history was reached. He is the Lord of the church now, but one day He will be acknowledged for what He will be—"King of kings and Lord of lords" (Rev. 19:16). For this the church still waits in joyful anticipation.

NOTES

[1] The author wishes to acknowledge his indebtedness to the work of George Eldon Ladd on New Testament eschatology. Especially helpful have been *The Presence of the Future* (Grand Rapids, 1974), which is the revised edition of *Jesus and the Kingdom* (New York, 1964), and *A Theology of the New Testament* (Grand Rapids, 1974). Other works by Ladd on the same subject include *Crucial Questions About the Kingdom of God* (Grand Rapids, 1952), *The Blessed Hope* (Grand Rapids, 1956), *The Gospel of the Kingdom* (Grand Rapids, 1959), and *The Pattern of New Testament Truth* (Grand Rapids, 1968).

[2] Archibald M. Hunter, *Interpreting the New Testament, 1900-1950* (Philadelphia, 1952), p. 136.

[3] Representative of this view is Adolf von Harnack, *What Is Christianity?* (New York, 1956; original edition, 1901).

[4] Johannes Weiss, *Jesus' Proclamation of the Kingdom of God* (Philadelphia, 1971; English trans. of first German edition, 1892).

[5] Albert Schweitzer, *The Quest of the Historical Jesus* (New York, 1961; English trans. of first German edition, 1906), p. 401.

[6] C. H. Dodd, *The Parables of the Kingdom* (New York, 1961, rev. ed.), pp. 82, 83.

[7] Reginald H. Fuller, *The Mission and Achievement of Jesus* (London, 1954), p. 25.

[8] Ladd, *Presence of the Future,* p. 41.

[9] G. S. Hendry, "Mystery," in *A Theological Word Book of the Bible,* ed. Alan Richardson (New York, 1951), pp. 156, 157.

[10] Francis D. Nichol, ed., *The Seventh-day Adventist Bible Commentary,* (Washington, D.C., 1953-1957), vol. 5, p. 497.

[11] Leon Morris, *The Gospel According to John* (Grand Rapids, 1971), p. 227.

[12] *Ibid.*

[13] Brooke Foss Westcott, *Commentary on the Epistles of St. John* (Grand Rapids, 1966; first edition 1883), p. 215.

[14] C. F. D. Moule, "The Individualism of the Fourth Gospel," *New Testament,* vol. 5, p. 174.

[15] C. H. Dodd, *The Apostolic Preaching and Its Developments* (New York, 1964).

[16] *Ibid.,* pp. 21-23.

[17] *Ibid.,* p. 24.

[18] F. F. Bruce, *Commentary on the Book of Acts* (Grand Rapids, 1954), p. 38.

[19] Ladd, *A Theology of the New Testament,* p. 551.

[20] Oscar Cullmann, *Christ and Time* (London, 1962, rev. ed.; first German edition, 1946), p. 84.

[21] *Ibid.,* pp. 86, 87.

CHAPTER 4

The Advent Hope
in Early Christianity

Paul J. Landa

LIKE their immediate predecessors, the members of the Christian congregations of the postapostolic decades (A.D. 90-140) were conscious of standing in an intermediate period both of fulfillment and of expectation as they experienced the continuing tensions of living between the "already" and the "not yet." They were certain of the reality of their salvation, thanks to the decisive victory achieved by Jesus Christ over the forces of evil, sin, and death. Their participation in the rites of baptism and the Eucharist,[1] and their experience of the power of the Holy Spirit in their lives, convinced them not only that they were living in the last times foretold by the ancient prophets but that *already* they were sharing the blessings of eternal life. In baptism they had died to sin and risen again with Christ, thus receiving the guarantee of their inheritance; they had been sealed for the final redemption at the parousia—the second appearing of Christ.[2] In their frequent celebration of the Eucharist, they partook of "the medicine of immortality and the antidote against death"[3] as they looked forward with anticipation to the eschatological "marriage supper of the Lamb."[4] Through the empowering of the Holy Spirit, they were enjoying while still on earth the experience of the supernatural life.[5]

At the same time, all that they possessed of redemption and the new life in Christ seemed as a mere foretaste of the reality yet to come. It increased their longing for the completion and fulfillment of the divine plan of redemption, when evil, sin, and death would be eradicated forever and they would be able to receive their inheritance and enjoy fellowship with God, Christ, and the heavenly hosts. By His first advent Christ had opened a parenthesis in time, inaugurating the kingdom of God. It now remained for Him to close the parenthesis by actually establishing His kingdom. And this, they believed, would occur at the parousia, when He would appear in majesty and power, clothed in the garments of royalty.[6]

In expressing their eschatological hopes and longings, the Christians of the early second century used the ideas, expressions, and formulations found in the

New Testament writings that depict the final denouement in terms of (a) the soon return of Christ, (b) the resurrection of the dead, (c) the final judgment, and (d) the catastrophic end of the present world order.

The Soon Return of Christ.—While still committed to the concept of the imminence of their Lord's return, the early Christian authors known as the Apostolic Fathers[7] clearly show in their writings that the level of immediacy had subsided considerably.[8] The passage of time and the continuing delay of the parousia demanded that adjustments be made as to *when* the final scenario could be expected. No longer did the concept of imminence mean that it *had* to be close at hand, only that it *could* be and that it *could* overtake them unexpectedly.

This was the conviction of Ignatius, the Christian bishop of Antioch, who believed that he was living in "the last times," when "things [were] coming to an end,"[9] and who admonished his readers to "look for Him who is beyond all time."[10] A similar exhortation based on a similar conviction is found in the last chapter of the Didache: "Watch over your life—do not let your lamps be extinguished, nor your waist be ungirded. But be ready, for you do not know when our Lord is coming."[11] According to Hermas' vision, the tower that signified the church was nearing completion, clearly indicating the proximity of the end. But when he enquired whether the consummation had arrived yet, his visionary interlocutress brusquely responded: "Stupid man, do you not see that the tower is still being built? Whenever the building of the tower is completed, that will be the end. But, it will be built quickly. . . . Let this reminder and the renewal of your spirits be sufficient for you and the saints."[12]

In a similar vein the author of the Epistle of Barnabas, an Egyptian Christian, though satisfied that the day was near when all things would perish with the evil one,[13] felt, on the basis of his interpretation of the Creation story, in which each day was made to represent a thousand years, that the universe would last six thousand years, of which the greater portion had already expired. The parousia would thus occur at the end of the sixth millennium and would inaugurate the great cosmic Sabbath.[14]

Several expected that a period of fierce persecution would precede the second advent, during which time the faith of men and women would be tested by the great deceiver of souls, who was described in terms like those found in 2 Thessalonians 2:3-12. Only at the end of this time of tribulation would the world "see the Lord coming on the clouds of heaven."[15] Thus, while the advent hope remained strong among the postapostolic Christians, many were coming to the realization that their earthly pilgrimage would last longer than when they first believed and that they probably would not witness the second coming in their own lifetime. They were not dismayed by the prospect of their own death, however, because they also believed that their returning Saviour would call them out of their graves at the resurrection.

The Resurrection of the Dead.—Belief in the general resurrection of the dead, to be followed by the last judgment, was intimately linked with the parousia from the very start. Using Pauline arguments developed in 1 Corinthians 15, Christian believers looked upon the wondrous reality of Christ's resurrection as the strongest guarantee of their own resurrection, for just as "he was truly raised from the dead by the power of his Father, in like manner his Father, through Jesus Christ, will raise up those of us who believe in him."[16] Some, such as Clement of

Rome,[17] saw promises of the resurrection not only in the sacred writings of the Old Testament[18] but also in the pagan legends of the phoenix bird,[19] as well as in the natural order of God's creation as revealed by the cycle of the seasons, the sequence of days and nights, and the transformation of decaying seeds into vigorous plants.

And all Christians affirmed—against Docetists and Gnostics who rejected the possibility that bodies could be raised to eternal life—the resurrection of the flesh, arguing that, in Ignatius' words, "even after his resurrection," Christ "was in the flesh." This was incontrovertibly demonstrated when He came to the disciples and invited them to touch, handle, and hold Him, and "ate and drank with them like everyone else with a body, even though in his spirit, he was one with the Father." [20] Therefore, based in the clear evidence of His bodily resurrection, they too could look forward to sharing the same experience, and they were quick to silence their would-be detractors with the confident affirmation "Let not any one . . . say that this flesh is not judged and does not rise again." [21] They knew better.

The Final Judgment.—The Christian doctrine of the impending last judgment had antecedents in the Old Testament and the teachings of Judaism; it was deeply rooted in the message of Jesus and the apostolic *kerygma*.[22] A final judgment was viewed as indispensable in the sequence of eschatological events, for the simple reason that a world like this simply cannot continue forever; it must be brought to terms by the Lord of history. Moreover, the kingdom of God cannot be established without a judgment, for all that is evil contradicts the divine purposes for the world. Therefore, the author of sin and the perpetrators of evil, suffering, and death must be confronted and dealt with in a final and decisive manner.

It is true that at an individual level, the judgment is *already* being manifested, for wherever the gospel is being proclaimed, men and women are judging themselves according to their acceptance or rejection of the truth. But this ongoing process is anticipatory of the final verdict on "the last day" when Christ will appear in glory and power, sent by the Father "as a judge." [23]

All the nations and generations of earth will be gathered before this last, great assize.[24] None will escape it. The just will be separated from the wicked, each according to his works.[25] And each one, without respect of person, "will receive according to his deeds. If he be good, his goodness will lead him; if he be evil, the recompense of his evil is in store for him." [26] This translates into a death sentence and execution by "unquenchable fire" [27] for those who have rejected the gospel. The righteous, on the other hand, will be rewarded with the gift of "life in immortality" [28]—an endless, joyous experience of fellowship with the saints, the worthy heroes of the faith, the holy angels, and the Lord Himself.[29]

Some added certain distinctly materialistic and sensual enjoyments. Thus Papias, bishop of Hierapolis in the first half of the second century, whose theological ancestry was traced back by Irenaeus to certain "elders" and to the apostle John, taught that the saints would luxuriate in the delights of a transformed earth in which unprecedented fertility would yield vines with ten thousand branches, each with ten thousand twigs, each with ten thousand shoots, each with ten thousand clusters, each with ten thousand grapes, each yielding enormous quantities of wine! Wheat and other plants would produce in similar proportions.[30] While it is uncertain whether Papias' idyllic tableau was intended to depict Christ's earthly millennial kingdom only or whether it also was meant to describe the eternal abode of the redeemed, it is certain that Papias' materialistic chiliasm reflected the hopes and longings of some Asian Christians when they thought about the second coming of Christ and the establishment of the divine kingdom.[31]

The End of the World.—The execution of the last judgment, leading to the extermination of the wicked and resulting in the eradication of evil from God's creation, would entail the catastrophic end of the present world order, according to the early Christians. Consistent with the apostolic preaching, the author of 2 Clement declared that " 'the powers of heaven shall dissolve'; and the whole earth shall be as lead melting in the fire." [32] Similar predictions were made by Hermas, who declared that "this world must be destroyed in fire and blood," in order that a new earth might be made ready for the righteous. Indeed, God is already at work, "moving away the heavens, the mountains, the hills, and seas, and all is becoming level for his elect to fulfill the promise he made in fulness of glory and joy." [33]

Such was the early Christian proclamation regarding the imminent parousia, the resurrection of the dead, the last judgment, and the catastrophic end of the world. It represented a new and radical set of concepts in the Greco-Roman world—too radical in fact to be credible.[34]

The Christian Eschatological Hope and Hellenism

The very nature of eschatology was quite foreign to Greek philosophy, which was dominated by the ideas of permanence and recurrence. Despite some major differences in the various schools of thought, the concept of an "eternal" cosmos remained as the one constant factor. This was based upon the premise that everything that is worthy of existence had to have actually existed in the most perfect manner through all eternity. Nothing can really be added to this perfection, no fundamental change is possible, and nothing "novel" can ever emerge in the future, since the true, perfect reality is always *behind (from* eternity) and never *ahead* (in the sense of *to* eternity).[35] This being the case, the only movement possible—and desirable—is circular, since it involves a return to what was and *is* perfect and real. Only the circle depicts accurately and perfectly the fact that in time there is no "progress," but only eternal "returns," a "cyclophoria." [36] "The consequence," as Georges Florovsky wrote, is that "there was no room for any real 'eschatology' in such a scheme. Greek philosophy indeed was always concerned rather with the *'first* principles' than with the *'last* things.' " [37]

In addition to this basic conceptual problem, the very components making up the Christian eschatological proclamation were offensive to the classical mind. Given the radical ontological dualism between the "spiritual" (uncreated) and the "material" (created) espoused by pagan thinkers, they could no more grasp the idea of the second advent of Christ than they could the first. For God to enter the world would mean a change in His being; He would in fact cease to be God, which is impossible![38] Even more offensive to them was the concept of bodily resurrection, since the body was viewed as the prison of the immortal soul, from which it was finally liberated by death. The thought of resurrecting the body was, accordingly, outrageous and dismissed as belonging to "old women's fables." [39] "For what sort of human soul . . . would still long for a body that had been subject to corruption?" asked the pagan Celsus. The whole notion was "exceedingly vile, and loathsome, and impossible." Not even God could make a body of flesh "to exist for ever." Therefore, "such a hope is simply one which might be cherished by worms." [40] The doctrine of the last judgment and of rewards and punishment was dismissed with equal derision, as having been conjured up "to excite the astonishment of the ignorant" [41] and flatter the vanity of the proud. As to the fiery end of the present world order, not only did it contradict the universally accepted view of the permanence of the cosmos, but it also presented an insurmountable problem, according to Celsus. He is quoted as saying, "It is folly . . . to suppose that when God, as if He were a cook, introduces the fire (which is to consume the world), all the rest of the human race will be burnt up, while they alone [the Christians] will remain." [42]

This outright rejection of the Christian eschatological scenario by Hellenistic thinkers was also the response of the various Gnostic groups who, while deeply concerned with eschatological doctrines, as evidenced by the systems of Basilides and Valentinus and by the Apocryphon of John, nevertheless rejected all religious traditions that involved or tied the supreme God to the material world in any way at all. This was the result of their uncompromising dualism in which God and matter were thought to be radically opposed to each other, and in which salvation consisted in the complete severing of the spiritual part of man from all connections with the material world. Such an outlook inevitably led to a docetic understanding of Christ, negated the need for a second advent, and made ridicule of the Christian doctrines of the resurrection of the body and the transformation of the world into the eternal home of the righteous. [43] Indeed, Gnosticism represents the final religious expression of Hellenistic soteriology set over against the original Christian eschatological *kerygma*. [44]

The Delay of the Parousia

Complicating the whole situation for the Christians of the second century was the increasing embarrassment and problem caused by the delay of the supposedly "imminent" parousia. The obvious contradiction between their eschatological proclamation and the actual course of history led to a major crisis for the followers of Christ. [45] This crisis, added to the pressures resulting from the overt challenges of Hellenism and Gnosticism, forced them into a reassessment of their beliefs about the second advent, which came to be expressed more carefully than before and with new emphases and fresh lines of thought, partly for apologetic reasons and partly to answer the profound disillusionment that was increasingly being experienced by the rank and file. This was the beginning of what Albert Schweitzer called the "de-eschatologising" of Christianity, [46] that gradual, progressive doctrinal and ethical reorientation marked by a clearly discernible shift from proclamation to preservation, from prophetism to ecclesiasticism, from the charismatic to the traditional, and from eschatological to Christological concerns. As part of this shift, the advent hope gradually receded into the background. Christians still looked forward to the second coming, but they no longer prayed, "Maranatha"—"Lord, come." Instead, they petitioned God on behalf of "the emperors, . . . their deputies, and all in authority, for the welfare of the world, for the prevalence of peace, and for the *delay* of the final consummation." [47]

Initially, the fact of the delay was answered by arguments that did not affect the advent message itself, but only the primitive spirit of urgency relating to it.

1. By postponing the parousia, the gracious God was giving an opportunity for more people to repent. This line of reasoning had already appeared in 2 Peter 3, where the "forbearance" of the Lord is viewed in salvific terms. God's desire is "that all should reach repentance." And Christians are exhorted to lead "lives of holiness and godliness, waiting for and hastening the coming of the day of God."[48] A parallel passage is found in the so-called Second Letter of Clement to the Corinthians, where sexual relations—presumably marriage among Christians—are explicitly singled out as the sin yet to be renounced; for when "a brother seeing a sister has no thought of her as female, nor she of him as male," then, says Jesus, "the Kingdom of my Father shall come."[49] According to Clement, then, it would appear that it is the sins of the Christians that are delaying the parousia.

2. Related to the first argument was the explanation that the end would come only after the gospel had been proclaimed in all the world. This would tend to make the incredulity and hard-heartedness of the pagans the primary cause for the nonoccurrence of the advent. The original idea of the universal proclamation of the gospel before the eschaton goes back to Jesus Himself[50] and is echoed in Christian literature well into the third century.[51] As to the pagans' response to the gospel, Origen of Alexandria promoted the idea that God has postponed the parousia and the day of wrath so that the full consequences of the evil actions of men might be revealed and the divine judgment vindicated.[52]

A variant of this general concept suggests that the end will come when the *number* of the elect, which has been predetermined by God, has been reached. Originally found in Jewish apocalyptic literature,[53] this notion was developed by Clement of Rome[54] and later by the Christian apologist Justin Martyr, who took the gospel commission seriously and spoke of witnessing " 'daily some . . . becoming disciples in the name of Christ, and quitting the path of error.' "[55] It was his firm conviction that God would continue to keep the Son in heaven "until the number of those who are foreknown by Him as good and virtuous is complete, on whose account He has still delayed the consummation."[56] Indeed, he believed that among the elect were some who had not yet been born.[57] Similar concepts are found again in the third-century *Syriac Didascalia Apostolorum* and the fourth-century Apostolic Constitutions.[58]

3. Still another explanation for the delay of the parousia tended to take the responsibility away from humankind altogether by suggesting that the divine prophetic timetable had not yet been fulfilled. This argument also had antecedents in Judaism and rested on two not unrelated attempts, found in rabbinic literature, to calculate the time of the coming of the Messiah and the establishment of the kingdom of God from an exegesis of the prophecies of Daniel and using a millennial-age theory approach.[59] According to the latter, the six days of Creation prefigured six thousand years of history, since, for God, one day is as a thousand years (Ps. 90:4). Thus some rabbis reasoned that the end would come at the expiration of the sixth thousand-year period. Others thought that the history of the world was to be divided into three periods: two thousand years without the Torah, two thousand years under the Torah, and two thousand years of Messianic time—meaning that the age appointed for the Messiah had, in fact, already started.[60] The millennial periodization scheme entered Christian eschatology

probably through the influence of the apocalyptic book of Enoch[61] and made its first appearance in the Epistle of Barnabas, as previously noted. This work tried to promote the idea of an imminent end of the world, quoting loosely from the book of Enoch (" 'The Lord has shortened the seasons and the days' ")[62] and giving an even looser exegesis of Daniel 7, at the end of whch the author admonished, "So, let us be on watch in the last days."[63] At the same time, the work relied on the chiliastic scheme to show that six thousand years must first elapse before "everything will be ended."[64] Only then will the Son "come and destroy the time of the lawless one and judge the godless," and "he shall indeed rest on the seventh day."[65] This approach, based on a selective interpretation of Daniel and a chiliastic world view, became a salient feature of early Christian eschatology from the middle of the second century onward, as evidenced by a wide sampling of writings from such writers as Justin Martyr, Irenaeus, Hippolytus of Rome, Lactantius, Victorinus of Pettau, and others.[66]

Thus, faced by the crisis occasioned by the delay of the parousia, the members of the second-century Christian congregations reassessed their position in the light of an already firmly established Jewish apocalyptic tradition and found ways of successfully reducing the enormous tensions stemming from the apparent disconfirmation of their fondest hope, while maintaining the core of their eschatological doctrine inviolate.

Openly challenged by Jews and pagans, the followers of Jesus developed a sense of corporate identity as they began to realize that they constituted an institution in society with a past behind it and, quite obviously, a future before it. Forced by external pressures into an apologetic posture, their sometimes divergent voices gradually united in a reaffirmation of the reality of the mighty acts of God in Christ, expressed in historical events. These events pointed forward to a future hope, glimpses of which they were experiencing weekly—if not daily—in the liturgy and the celebration of the sacraments.[67] Moreover, the increasing hostility and overt persecution that they experienced throughout the third century and into the fourth always made the eschatological embers glow brighter, for in such adverse circumstances the forces of evil proved too strong for believers to rest content with any notion of "realized eschatology." Such times never failed to revive the reassuring hope that God would soon intervene and bring about the final, decisive victory.[68] In addition, the fact that the Christian message continued to draw large numbers of converts could not help confirming the believers in their faith in Jesus and their hope of His eventual return, spurring them on to evangelize with continuing fervor.[69]

But this fervor, which is very evident in the works of the Christian apologists and theologians of the second and third centuries, was now channeled in a somewhat different direction. The chief concern was to provide an effective defense of Christianity against the prevailing misunderstanding, intolerance, and persecution of the Roman authorities. Rather than stress the approaching end of all things—including the Roman Empire—Christian leaders sought to obtain the official recognition of Christianity as a religious philosophy of "superior" quality, with the right to exist *in* the world *for* the good of the world. Their new thesis was that Christianity worked beneficially for the development of human culture in general and for the stability of the empire in particular. As Aristides of Athens had proclaimed, "Christianity preserves the world"![70]

This new orientation inevitably led some to a devaluation of the apostolic eschatological message. While attempting to cling to the advent hope, they tried to "personalize" the delayed parousia and retreated into mysticism, stressing the need for the all-important experience of the Holy Spirit through which the human soul becomes spiritual and immortal, thus experiencing even now God's heavenly rewards.[71] This was the first step toward the Origenistic concept of the deification of the soul, a course that ended up negating the hope of the second coming, the future resurrection, the final judgment, and the renewal of creation altogether. Others went in the opposite direction and lapsed into what Lampe has called "a pedestrian and somewhat Judaistic moralism," [72] in which heaven came to be viewed as the ultimate prize to be won as the reward for endurance and right behavior while on earth. This approach tended to promote a religious activism that smacked of spiritual "atheticism," with people preoccupied by fear of the judgment and of God, the exacting judge and rewarder.[73] Such people usually hoped for the continuing delay of the parousia, trying to put off the final day of reckoning as far into the future as possible. So did those who feared the catastrophes that, according to Scripture and tradition, would coincide with the second advent.[74]

Yet, in spite of these influences that tended to reshape the apostolic eschatology, Christian thinkers on the whole still remained faithful to the traditional teachings about the second advent. While their *emphasis* was different, their general understanding of the sequence of events surrounding the parousia remained essentially unaltered. The point of departure was the Creation story, which prefigured the duration of the history of the world for six thousand years. "Since . . . in six days God made all things, it follows that 6,000 years must be fulfilled. And they are not yet fulfilled, as John says." But all things "will come to an end at the sixth thousand year." [75] The second half of the sixth millennium was interpreted as the period of the church that had its beginning with the first advent of Christ, which "took place in Bethlehem, under Augustus, in the year 5500. . . . From the birth of Christ, then, we must reckon the 500 years that remain to make up the 6000, and thus the end shall be." [76]

The era of the church was expected to be a time of increasing tribulation for God's elect as the devil, working though the Roman state, would persecute the followers of Christ, for "Babylon . . . in our (St.) John is a figure of the city of Rome, . . . great and proud in royal power, and warring down the saints of God." [77] The end of the tribulation will be marked by the personal appearance of the mysterious antichrist, who will be a descendant of the tribe of Dan, whose number will be 666, quite likely meaning *Lateinos*—an obvious reference to the Roman state and emperor. He will tyrannize the world for three and a half years, during which time " 'he shall speak words against the most high God, and wear out the saints of the most high God, and shall purpose to change times and laws; and [everything] shall be given into his hand until a time of times and a half time,' that is, for three years and six months, during which time, when he comes, he shall reign over the earth." [78]

Then, at the divinely appointed time, the parousia will occur, accompanied by the resurrection of the righteous dead, "that the indissoluble and everlasting kingdom of the saints may be brought to view, and the heavenly King manifested to all, no longer in figure, like one seen in vision, or revealed in a pillar of cloud upon the top of a mountain, but amid the powers and armies of angels, as God incarnate and man, Son of God and Son of man—coming from heaven as the world's judge." [79] The conquered Satan will be bound for a thousand years, during which time Christ will reign with the righteous in a renewed land of Canaan. " 'And hence all men everywhere, whether bond or free, who believe in Christ, and recognize the truth in His own words and those of His prophets, know that they shall be with Him in that land, and inherit everlasting and incorruptible good.' " [80]

At the end of the millennium, all the dead will be raised to appear before the final judgment of Christ. The wicked will then be cast into a lake of fire, the whole earth will be transformed, and the righteous will receive their eternal reward. "Those who are deemed worthy of an abode in heaven shall go there, others shall enjoy the delights of paradise, and others shall possess the splendor of the city; for everywhere the Saviour shall be seen according as they who see Him shall be worthy." [81]

Such was, in broad outline, the eschatological scenario envisioned by the Christian writers of the period A.D. 140-230. Despite individual differences, they shared a common outlook on several important issues:

1. In marked contrast with the Gnostic myth of the soul's upward ascent and reabsorption into the divine pleroma (the spiritual realm of light), which negated totally the doctrine of the second advent, the Christians emphasized the *literal return* of Christ to the earth, in power and glory. Justin Martyr went so far as to suggest that the returning Lord would appear in the city of Jerusalem, where He would be seen and recognized by the very Jews who put Him to death; He would also eat and drink with His disciples during the millennial reign in the Holy City. [82]

2. Although their views indicate a significant degree of confusion, it appears that the early Christian Fathers rejected the Platonic theory that the soul is "immortal by nature." As Justin declared: "It is not the property of the soul to have life in itself as it is the property of God." [83] This was also the view of Tatian; he unequivocally added, "The soul is not in itself immortal, O Greeks, but mortal." [84] They vigorously affirmed against Platonists, Epicureans, and Gnostics the biblical doctrine of the resurrection of the body, in which both body and soul are granted immortality by an act of God's will. And since man is a composite being, made up of body and soul, and since salvation affects the entire man—body as well as soul [85] (as evidenced by the fact that in the Incarnation, the Word became flesh in order to save our flesh) [86]—it is reasonable to expect that both will be conjoined in the experience of reward [87] or punishment. And to all skeptics, they quoted Jesus' words "What is impossible with men is possible with God." [88] Therefore, it is not logically absurd to expect such a miraculous happening on the great "Day of the Lord."

3. In varying degrees, all were exponents of the millenarian, or chiliastic, doctrine. Not only did the millennial-age theory serve to explain the delay of the parousia, but it was also used to reinforce the idea of the objective nature of God's eternal kingdom by making it palpable, material, and earthly. Christ will dwell with His people in a restored city of Jerusalem, on a renovated earth, for a thousand years. " 'I and others who see right-minded," declares Justin, "are assured that there will be a resurrection of the dead, and a thousand years in

Jerusalem, which will then be built, adorned, and enlarged.' " [89] The saints, adds Irenaeus, quoting Ezekiel 28:26, " 'shall dwell in it in peace; and they shall build houses, and plant vineyards, and dwell in hope.' . . . The whole creation shall, according to God's will, obtain a vast increase, that it may bring forth and sustain fruits." And "the righteous shall reign in the earth, waxing stronger by the sight of the Lord: and through Him they shall become accustomed to partake in the glory of God the Father." [90] Such were the chiliastic dreams of the majority in the Christian congregations. J.N.D. Kelly is correct, however, in recognizing that opposition to millenarian ideas "was gathering force" throughout this period,[91] especially in the urban churches of Rome and Alexandria.

4. Rejecting the prevalent concept of fatalism, the Greek and Latin Christian apologists insisted on the principles of free will and responsibility, deducing from them the idea of a final judgment and the reasonableness of a system of rewards and punishments. While the wicked will ultimately experience annihilation,[92] the righteous will experience "deification," or participation in the divine nature, and share God's immortality, having been "deemed worthy of becoming 'gods,' and . . . sons of the Highest." [93] They will see the Father "face to face" and will be transformed "like unto Him." Thus, mankind's original image and likeness to the Creator, which were lost at the time of the Fall, will be restored. "Men therefore shall see God, that they may live, being made immortal by that sight, and attaining even unto God." [94]

5. The fate of the faithful who died during the ever-extending interval caused by the delay of the parousia became a matter of increased concern and speculation during this period. In opposition to the Gnostics who taught that all souls begin the heavenly ascent immediately after death, Christians, pointing to the experience of Christ, who descended to Hades (the place of the departed) for three days, speculated that "every soul is detained in safekeeping in Hades until the day of the Lord." [95] "They go to an invisible place designated by God, and there remain until the resurrection, . . . then, receiving their bodies, and rising again perfectly, that is bodily, just as the Lord arose, they shall come . . . into the presence of God." [96] Hippolytus speculated further about the condition of the souls in the underworld, the "guardhouse for souls": The souls of the righteous dwell in a locality full of light called Abraham's bosom, where they enjoy "the contemplation of the blessings which are in their view, and [delight] themselves with the expectation of others ever new, . . . deeming those ever better than these." [97] A vast abyss separates them from the souls of the wicked, who are consigned to "the confines of hell" where they can hear constant cries and feel the hot smoke. And "as they see the terrible and excessively glowing spectacle of the fire, they shudder in horror at the expectation of the future judgment, [as if they were] already feeling the power of their punishment." [98] At the parousia each soul will be reunited with its proper body. The souls of the just will be clothed with new, pure, and incorruptible ones, to enjoy God's eternity. "But the unrighteous will receive their bodies unchanged, and unransomed from suffering and disease, and unglorified, and still with all the ills in which they died." [99] In those bodies they shall be tormented throughout eternity.

Concern and speculation over an intermediate state between death and the second advent provided a connecting link for the development of an "individual eschatology" that increasingly tended to compete with the cosmic-oriented eschatology of the earliest Christian Scriptures. For with the continuing postponement of the parousia, the question of the final destiny of an individual became more important than that of the ultimate fate of the world, in what seemed to be an ever more distant future.[100]

The preoccupation with the intermediate state, and the growing interest over individual eschatology, underscores the fact of the increasing slackening of the expectation of the end. It was inevitable that the longer the nonfulfillment of the parousia of Christ and the final events connected with it continued, the weaker became the conviction that the end of the world would come soon. It should be noted, however, that the disappearance of the sense of expectancy did not take place without some turmoil and a crisis.

This crisis, over the question of the second advent, came to a head in the Montanist movement during the second half of the second century.[101] Nathanael Bonwetsch accurately summarized the ethos of Montanism as "an effort to shape the entire life of the church in keeping with the expectation of the return of Christ, immediately at hand; to define the essence of Christianity from this point of view; and to oppose everything by which conditions in the church were to acquire a permanent form for the purpose of entering upon a longer historical development." [102]

It is worth noting again that the movement arose at a time when the apocalyptic vision was becoming less vivid and confidence in the *imminent* second coming of Christ had all but vanished. Thus, Montanism represented a serious attempt to check the decline of the advent hope by reviving the apostolic persuasion that the Lord's return was near at hand. This was done through a veritable "explosion of prophesying" [103] on the part of the movement's founders, Montanus and his two women associates, Maximilla and Priscilla. They claimed to be the instruments of the Paraclete (the Advocate), promised by Christ to His disciples at the Last Supper, and to be gifted with visions and special revelations.[104] The content of these revelations was essentially eschatological: The end was nearer than ever, since the last sign before the final denouement—the manifestation of the Paraclete—had occurred among them. "After me," declared the prophetess Maximilla, "no other prophet will come, but only the final end." [105] Moreover, the dreadful years of epidemics and the distress occasioned by the wars of Emperor Marcus Aurelius were seen as the fulfillment of divine prophecy about the end of the world, and heightened the feeling of expectancy.[106]

Thoroughly immersed as they were in the apocalyptic message of the book of Revelation, the Montanists believed they would live to see the New Jerusalem descend from heaven and settle on the site of Pepuza, a small country town in the Asian province of Phrygia. Here Christ in the form of a shining female figure had appeared to Priscilla in a dream and "caused wisdom to sink into her heart and had revealed to her that this was a holy place, and here would Jerusalem descend out of heaven." [107] Tertullian, who became the best known and most influential convert to Montanism, added that the coming of the New Jerusalem would inaugurate the millennium, at the end of which the last judgment would take place.[108]

On the basis of these clear eschatological expectations, the new prophecy led to a very rigorous ethical code. Marriage was discouraged, being viewed as an earthly bond that prevented full consecration to God.[109] The rapid approach of the end also called for greater strictness in the practice of fasting, which was interpreted as "standing on guard duty," watching for the advent.[110] These questions, together with issues such as flight from martyrdom and penitential discipline,[111] formed the principal moral emphases of the Montanist prophecy, which was intended to call the church to repentance, for the kingdom of God was now finally at hand.

From the very beginning the Phrygian prophetic movement greatly stirred the minds of those believers who were uncomfortable with the loss of expectancy and the growing complacency and moral laxity evident in many Christian congregations. The movement spread rapidly not only throughout Asia Minor but to Western Europe, as well. "Whole cities . . . went over to the reformers, and very soon people spoke currently of the churches of the prophets, that is, of communities wholly won over to the prophecy."[112] In places where Christianity was already well established, however, there was initial hesitation followed by overwhelming, concerted opposition, even though, for quite some time, no one knew how to refute what appeared to be a perfectly orthodox revival movement.[113]

Nevertheless, in the end Montanism was condemned as an aberration because its prophetic claims appeared to supercede the revelation contained in the Gospels, because its doctrine of the Holy Spirit seemed extravagant, because it was a disruptive force at a time when there was a desperate need for unity, and because belief in the nearness of the end of the world already had ceased to play a central role in the mainstream of Christian development.[114] To be sure, eschatological enthusiasm was never formally condemned as heretical, but it no longer seemed to fit in a period when Christians were seeking recognition from the state as they were becoming adjusted to the reality that the church might have to live in the world for a considerable time. As John Gager put it: "The reaction to the apocalyptic fervor of Montanism clearly reveals that it [Christianity] had come to regard eschatological movements as a serious threat" to its contemporary aspirations.[115]

Further Decline of the Eschatological Hope: The Speculative Views of Origen

Further proof of this new orientation is provided by the eschatological speculations coming from the school of Alexandria and its most famous representative, Origen. Claiming for himself the widest liberty to drink from all the fountains of Greek rationalism, Origen was the first Christian thinker "to enter into the genuine tradition of the Platonic school, and both his intake and his output fully reflect the Platonic heritage which was alive in his day."[116] He was also profoundly attached throughout his life to the Bible, which he interpreted allegorically, despite long years of painstaking labor seeking to establish a reliable original text.[117] Approaching the corpus of Christian doctrines with Neoplatonic presuppositions and a commitment to spiritualizing the Biblical witness, Origen's penetrating and creative mind offered new insights and radical reinterpretations of most Christian beliefs, including eschatology.

Perceiving that the traditional end-of-the-world scenario handed down from apostolic times bristled with an assortment of difficulties for the Greek mind, the Alexandrian doctor dismissed the popular views regarding the second advent, the literal, physical resurrection of the body, the earthly millennium with its sensate pleasures, and the final judgment with its attendant phenomena—including the assignment of rewards and punishments. Yet he did not reject the Biblical *language* upon which the advent hope rested. Instead of criticizing the Scriptures, he rejected the literal interpretations of his Christian predecessors, thereby attempting to escape what he regarded as the utter absurdities of Judeo-Christian millenarianism.

Thus Origen could maintain the ideas that Christ was coming again, that the dead would be raised, and that the present world would end, though not in the expected manner. For behind all the catastrophic imagery of the New Testament, he found a "spiritual meaning," which seemed to him to be substantiated by other Scripture, indicated clearly the change from the old order to the new would be a gradual process[118] effected through the religious development of individuals and humanity in a long succession of worlds, each populated by rational beings passing through different phases of existence, higher and lower, depending upon their willingness to choose good or evil.[119]

To use Origen's own language, it was not the first time that God did "begin to work when He made this visible world; but as, after its destruction, there will be another world, so also we believe that others existed before the present came into being." According to his Biblical exegesis, "it is established both that there were ages before our own, and that there will be others after it. It is not, however, to be supposed that several worlds existed at once, but that, after the end of this present world, others will take their beginning." [120] That there would ultimately be an end to this successive cycle of worlds, Origen was quite certain.[121] There will come an age, he believed, when the creatures, having reached the end of their evolutions, will be perfect, when they will be divested of all corporeality as pure, ethereal essences, when they will be subject to Christ and God, and when "God will be all and in all." [122]

Given this elaborate theory of the "spiritual evolutions" of humanity, it was inevitable that the doctrine of the second advent should be entirely recast, in order to fit into the new "Alexandrian" plan of salvation. Despite Origen's claim that he had no intention of "rejecting . . . the second coming of the Son of God understood in its simpler form," [123] he ended up doing just that, as the vivid imagery of the New Testament was spiritualized away into symbolism. For him the parousia will not occur at a given time, in a given place, in the future. Instead, he saw Christ already making Himself known everywhere as the Lord and Saviour of mankind. In the light of this divine self-disclosure, men and women are coming to see themselves as they really are, while at the same time coming to a realization of who Christ really is. This is leading many to present themselves before His throne in the sense that they recognize His divine nature and authority and accept Him as their Redeemer. For them the end of the sinful world has already come, and so has the parousia.

In this sense the second advent is equated with the spread of the gospel and the expansion of the Christian church throughout the world: "The second advent of Christ, however, is with mature men, concerning whom a dispenser of His word says: 'However we speak wisdom among the perfect.' In addition, these mature ones . . . praise the beauty and comeliness of the Word; and to His second advent is joined the end of the world in the man who comes to perfection and says, 'Far be it from me that I should glory except in the cross of our Lord Jesus Christ, through whom the world is crucified to me and I to the world.' for if the world is crucified to the righteous, it has become the end of the age for those to whom the world is crucified. Of necessity, therefore, let those who have the faith to come individually to Christ, if they wish to learn the sign of the advent of Christ and of the end of the world, show themselves worthy to see His second advent and the second end of the world which we have taught to you." [124]

At a more personal level, Origen sees the parousia occurring through the study of the Scriptures, which often results in a glorious union of Christ with the believer. In this sense the second advent is equated with the experience of spiritual enlightenment: "With much power, however, there comes *daily*, to the soul of every believer, the second advent of the Word in the prophetic clouds, that is, in the writings of the prophets and apostles, which reveal Him and who in all their words disclose the light of truth, and declare Him as coming forth in their explanations which are divine and above human nature. Thus, to those who recognize the Revealer of doctrines in the prophets and the apostles, we say that much glory also appears, which is seen in the second advent of the Word." [125]

In the same series of commentaries on Matthew's Gospel, Origen speaks of the "inward coming of Christ in glory to the soul," uniting the believer to Himself in a union so intense that the chosen one leaves behind the limitations of this mortal state and is raised to be one spirit with the Lord—an experience somewhat similar to the ecstasy of the Neoplatonist Plotinus.[126] In this experience the believer enters the kingdom of God, which the Alexandrian doctor variously interprets to be the indwelling of the Word, the implanting of the seeds of truth in the soul, or the apprehension of divine truth or spiritual reality.[127]

Having reinterpreted the doctrine of the second advent, Origen proceeded to speculate about the resurrection of the dead—an issue to which he devoted an entire treatise, of which only sparse fragments have been preserved.[128] Fortunately, he does expound on the matter elsewhere also. Although it is clear that Origen was fully committed to the spirituality and immortality of the soul and that he shared the Platonic aversion toward the flesh,[129] this did not preclude for him an equally strong commitment to the notion of a future resurrection. As he wrote: "Let no one . . . suspect that . . . we belong to those . . . who set aside the doctrine of the resurrection as it is taught in Scripture. . . . We preserve both the doctrine of the Church of Christ and the grandeur of the divine promise." [130] And he did, as he went about avoiding the crude literalism of those who spoke of the reanimation of the flesh, while preserving the Biblical idea of an actual resurrection body—for a time, anyway.

There will be a physical resurrection in the next world. Each soul will be reunited with its body—the same body that it bore on earth, yet adapted to a new existence in a new world.[131] Hence, though its form, or *eidos*, will be the same, since it represents the natural, outward expression of its abiding individuality, its essence, or material substrata, will be totally different, because it will be adapted to a new aeon, on the one hand, and to the varying degrees of the soul's purity or impurity, on the other hand.[132] And the resurrection body of the wicked will be different from that of the righteous, although it too will be incorruptible.[133] As mankind goes through the succession of world cycles, experiencing a gradual purgation from evil, the resurrected bodies will increase in subtlety until they completely disappear and all the redeemed are pure intelligences once again: "All corporeal creatures must exchange their material for subtle and spiritual bodies and . . . all substance must become one pure and inconceivably bright body, of which the human mind can at present form no conception." And " 'if all are to be made subject to God, all shall lay aside their bodies; and then all bodily existence shall be brought to nought. . . . All substance shall be refined into its most perfect form and rarified into aether which is a pure and uncompounded essence.' " [134]

As might be expected from the foregoing, Origen was one of the severest critics of millenarianism.[135] He castigated the follies of those literalist interpreters of the Bible who cherished and promoted dreams of dwelling in an earthly Jerusalem, where they would revel in sensual pleasures to their hearts' content. Such individuals "understand the divine Scriptures in a sort of Jewish sense, drawing from them nothing worthy of the divine promises." [136] However, those who read the Scriptures with the proper understanding look forward to the experience of eating "the bread of life, which may nourish the soul with the food of truth and wisdom, and enlighten the mind, and cause it to drink from the cup of divine wisdom. . . . By this food of wisdom, the understanding, being nourished to an entire and perfect condition like that in which man was made at the beginning, is restored to the image and likeness of God." [137]

While the righteous can anticipate the eternal enjoyment of divine wisdom, the damned will have to endure painful sufferings—but of a spiritual kind. Referring to Isaiah 50:11,[138] Origen comments: "Every sinner kindles for himself the flame of his own fire, and is not plunged into some fire which has been already kindled by another, or was in existence before himself. Of this fire the fuel and food are our sins." [139] In other words, the punishments of the wicked are "the pangs of guilty consciences when by God's power the memory of our trangressions is set before our eyes. . . . 'Thus it is the fire of conscience and the stings of remorse which torture the mind as it looks back on former self-indulgence.' " [140] These are the torments of hell to be endured by sinners eternally, though not necessarily endlessly.[141] For punishment has a healing and redemptive purpose, and it will come to an end when this has been accomplished.[142] No matter how obdurate or wicked the soul, slowly yet certainly a change for the better will come. It may take many aeons of suffering through several cycles of worlds before the healing is completed, but it will ultimately happen.

This is Origen at his Neoplatonic best, propounding the doctrine of *apokatastasis,* or universal restoration of all things to their original, purely spiritual, state, for "the end is always like the beginning." [143] This is the culmination and conclusion of the souls' evolutions through the vast cosmic cycles. Origen found his Biblical foundation for this eschatological universal restoration in 1 Corinthians 15:24-28,[144] which prophesies the eventual subjection of all enemies to Christ, and the delivery of the kingdom by Christ to the Father, who then will be "all in all." It was his conviction that the goodness of God through Christ would eventually recall all His creatures to one good end——even His enemies, including death and the devil himself.[145] God would not truly be "all in all" until "the end has been restored to the beginning, and the termination of things compared with their commencement. . . . And when death shall no longer anywhere exist, nor the sting of death, nor any evil at all, then verily God will be 'all in all.' " [146]

This universal restoration, or *apokatastasis,* may not last, however, but be itself a passing phase. Influenced as he was by Hellenistic thought, Origen reluctantly envisaged the possibility that the perfect souls while exercising their freedom may apostatize from good and turn once again to evil. Such a relapse would necessitate yet another creation, and the whole redemptive process would have to start again.[147] He much preferred to think, however, that since "love never fails," when the purified souls have truly learned to love God, the very love that is greater than anything else will prevent them from relapsing and rebelling.[148]

Regardless of one's judgment of Origen's eschatological speculations, they must be viewed as very significant because of his preeminent position as "the theologian" of the Eastern churches in the third century. The depth, breadth, and outreach of his enormous literary output helped to shape the thinking of many Christians for several generations.

Significant also is what his ideas represented. The urgent apostolic expectation of the parousia and the catastrophic consummation of the world, resulting in a new, eternal cosmic order, had now been replaced by a long and tortuous Spirit-guided march to perfection. In the protracted ideological contest between Christianity and syncretistic Gnosticism, it appeared that the latter had finally won a round. The Biblical gnostic from Alexandria had shown a way back to God through constantly expanded and deepened knowledge. He had also addressed the critical problem of the delay of the second advent by pointing out that there really had been no postponement at all. Christians had simply been looking for the wrong thing, because of their simplistic, literalistic interpretation of the apostolic kerygma. Instead of looking up to the heavens, they were urged to look inward for the Lord, who had already come and who kept coming again.

Also worthy of note is the inordinate attention that Origen gave to what may be called the "accessories" of the advent hope: matters pertaining to the origin and nature of the soul, the state of the dead, the composition of resurrected bodies, rewards and punishments, the conclusion of the plan of salvation, the fate of the devil, and the nature of eternal bliss. This is evidence of the fact that as the keen attention that was at first concentrated on the second advent continued to wane, the eschatological interests of Christians became much more diffused and speculative. What had once been kept in the shade by the splendor of the parousia now gained increased exposure as Christian thinkers began to rival the speculative extravagance of earlier Greek and Jewish writers. Origen provides a good example of this trend. However, while his radical reinterpretation of the advent hope may have tickled the fancy of the intelligentsia, it proved to be too radical, too speculative, and too extravagant for the majority of Christians. They were not about to jettison the inherited apostolic *regula fidei* with its clear and simple statement of hope in Christ's "second coming from the heavens in the glory of the Father to sum up all things and to raise up all flesh of all humanity, so that . . . He may make a just judgment among all men, sending into everlasting fire the spiritual powers of evil and the angels who trangressed and fell into rebellion, and the impious, . . . but upon the just . . . bestowing life and immortality and securing to them everlasting glory." [149]

The Revival of the Advent Hope in the Face of Sporadic Persecutions (A.D. 250-313)

In addition to what has just been said, the deterioration of relations between state and church during the third century resulted in a general social climate in the Christian congregations that was not particularly receptive to Origen's spiritualized notions about the course of history. The temper of the times called for a more affirmative statement of the Christian view about the future at hand. In A.D. 250, believers throughout the empire were violently persecuted by order of Emperor Decius. Origen himelf died (a few years later) from the tortures inflicted upon him. After abating for a short period, anti-Christian hostilities broke out into the open once again, in 257, during the reign of Valerian. Then, quite unexpectedly, in 260 Gallienus pronounced Christianity a *religio licita* ("legal religion"). For the next forty years the church was left to go its way, until the final and most bloody onslaught upon it was unleashed by Emperors Diocletian and Galerius, beginning in 303 and lasting for a decade, until the proclamation of the edict of toleration of 313, by Constantine[150] brought relief, at least in the West.

During this period of turmoil and suffering, the members of the Christian churches frequently expressed their longing for the return of their Lord and for deliverance from their sad and mad world. This is quite consistent with the general pattern that in the darker periods of history the eschatological hope shines the brightest.[151] One of the frequent responses to persecution and suffering is the belief that God wants and intends to deliver His children in their hour of distress. This is expressed not merely in timid, hopeful terms, but through confident affirmations of the certainty that God and good *will* shortly triumph. This is the heart of John's Apocalypse, penned during the dark days of Domitian's repression. And it was the heart of the apocalyptic messages proclaimed and written in the course of the third and early fourth centuries by such men as Jude,[152] Firmilian of Caesarea (in Cappadocia),[153] Nepos of Arsinoë,[154] Cyprian of Carthage,[155] Methodius of Olympus,[156] Commodianus,[157] Victorinus of Pettau,[158] and Lactantius.[159]

Very much attuned to the course of world events unfolding around them, these men interpreted all physical catastrophes and all political and social upheavals—including their persecution—as clear signs of the impending end of the world and of the second advent of Christ.[160] The antichrist of Bible prophecy was about to launch his last offensive against God's saints.[161] Following traditional thinking, he was expected to be a Roman, one of the Caesars. Victorinus of Pettau went as far as to revive the old belief of *Nero redivivus,* first found in the writings of the Roman historians Suetonius and Tacitus, and later borrowed and adapted by Christian authors. According to this concept, the first Roman persecutor of the Christians—the tyrant Nero—would someday reappear and resume his bloody extermination of the faithful.[162] The manifestation of antichrist would be terrifying, but, as Cyprian reminded his readers, "above him comes Christ also. The enemy goeth about and rageth, but immediately the Lord follows to avenge our sufferings and our wounds. The adversary is enraged and threatens, but there is One who can deliver us from his hands."[163] Believers need not be disheartened, for everything was going according to Christ's predictions, and "already His second coming draws near to us."[164]

There is a distinct tone of urgency here, missing for many years, that is reminiscent of the fervor found in the New Testament. In their distress, Christians fervently prayed for and, according to Cyprian, craved for[165] the promised deliverance. And they felt quite certain that God would not allow them to endure suffering for very long—seven years at the most, according to Vitorinus' exegesis of Revelation 11.[166] "The kingdom of God," wrote Cyprian, "is beginning to be at hand; the reward of life, and the rejoicing of eternal salvation, and the perpetual gladness and possession lately lost of paradise, are now coming, with the passing away of the world." [167]

In contrast to Origen's spiritualized notions about the second advent, the Christians of what might be termed the "Martyr Period" looked for a literal parousia of Christ in glory, to be witnessed by the whole world. " 'Behold,' " exclaimed Victorinus, " 'He shall come with clouds, and every eye shall see Him.' For He who at first came hidden in the manhood that He had undertaken shall after a little while come to judgment manifest in majesty and glory." [168] All the angels will be with Him, and, said Lactantius, "the heaven shall be opened in a tempest, and Christ shall descend with great power, and there shall go before Him a fiery brightness" that will destroy the wicked, while at the same time resurrecting the righteous.[169]

It would appear that Origen's speculations about the resurrection and the nature of the resurrection body were not widely shared by his immediate successors, who preferred to affirm the Biblical doctrine of a literal resurrection, defending it as before by means of appeals to Divine Omnipotence. Thus, Methodius asserts, against Origen, that "the body shall rise, with bones again joined and compacted with flesh," [170] just as Christ was raised in the same body that He bore on the cross,[171] as His encounter with doubting Thomas demonstrates. To be sure, resurrected bodies will have new qualities, such as immortality, impassibility, and glory—the same qualities that they possessed before the Fall—but they will be materially identical with our present earthly bodies.[172] Not all shared these views, however, as evidenced by Cyprian, who appears to have short-circuited the whole problem by neglecting the doctrine of the resurrection in favor of the notion that believers enter paradise and the heavenly kingdom at the time of their death. This is certainly the case of the martyrs, who close their eyes on the world "and at once . . . open them to look upon God and Christ," being "suddenly taken away from earth, to be placed in the heavenly kingdoms," joining the glorious company of the patriarchs, the prophets, the apostles, the saints, and dear ones.[173]

On the subject of Christ's millennial reign on earth, despite the strong influence of Origen and his disciples—especially Dionysius of Alexandria—who had eliminated the doctrine from their eschatology,[174] it still appears in the writings of Commodianus, Methodius, Victorinus, and Lactantius. Using very traditional language, they picture Christ reigning with the resurrected saints in the New Jerusalem, sharing a period of peace, prosperity, and pleasure. Some among the righteous are even marrying and begetting children during this time.[175] Methodius, however, objected to this "Jewish" exegesis of Revelation 20, which failed to perceive "the deep things of the Scriptures." He preferred to spiritualize the paradisiacal pleasures of the saints, pointing out that "the vine . . . refers to the Lord Himself, and the fig tree to the Holy Spirit, as the Lord 'maketh glad the hearts of men,' and the Spirit healeth them." [176]

The end of the seventh millennium will usher in the last judgment, the consignment of the devil and the wicked to their everlasting punishment, and the total re-creation of the earth for the benefit of the righteous. No redemptive punishment for the condemned and no universal salvation in some distant future are being contemplated here. In the words of Cyprian, there will not "be any source whence at any time they may have either respite or end to their torments. . . . The pain of punishment will then be without the fruit of penitence; weeping will be useless, and prayer ineffectual. Too late they will believe in eternal punishment who would not believe in eternal life." [177] The saints, by contrast, "shall be glorious together with Christ, blessed of God the Father, always rejoicing with perpetual pleasures in the sight of God, and ever giving thanks to God. For none can be other than always glad and grateful, who, having been once subject to death, has been made secure in the possession of immortality." [178]

Thus, the eschatological realism of the church's early days and the fervor of its hope in the *soon*, literal return of Christ reappeared for a brief period, during the trying decades of the late third and early fourth centuries. Amazingly, however, what the Christians were to witness was not the fulfillment of their hopes, but the totally unexpected "Christianization" of the empire under Constantine.

The Advent Hope in the "Christianized" Empire Down to Saint Augustine

With the conversion of Emperor Constantine to Christianity and the official recognition of the Christian religion by the state in 313, the eschatological hope of the church underwent yet another transformation. Given the violence of the preceding decade, the sudden and startling turn of events seemed truly miraculous; Constantine *had* to have been divinely raised to be the deliverer and protector of God's people. It was also painfully obvious that the prophetic interpretations and predictions about the future by some of the church's best minds had once again been less than trustworthy. The new times demanded, so it seemed, a complete reassessment of the course of salvation history. Now that the persecutions had ceased and favored status had been granted to Christianity, the Roman imperial government could hardly be identified with the antichrist! On the contrary, the state had now become the ally of the church of Christ. [179] And since it was determined to favor Christianity at every turn, ecclesiastical leaders stretched out their hands to receive all that they could get. State patronage increasingly usurped eschatological vindication as the new goal of the Christian bishops. Caesar and not Christ was what the majority were "looking for and hastening unto" (cf. 2 Peter 3:12). And no church that comes to such favorable terms with the state can honestly yearn for any kind of apocalyptic divine reversal or nurture for long the hope of a sudden, terminal divine intervention. As could be expected, ideas began to emerge to the effect that the "Christianized" empire was the promised kingdom of God on earth. The current dispensation was the time of its realization, and the establishment of the church on earth was the mode of its fulfillment. [180]

The best representative of this type of thinking was the bishop Eusebius of Caesarea (died c. 340), who lived through the whole transformation and whose theology underwent a radical reorientation during this period. He started out expounding with great clarity the future hope of "the second coming of Christ, which the prophecies predict will be glorious and bring in the Divine Kingdom." [181] This divine kingdom, ushered in by the parousia, would succeed the Roman Empire and would last forever. [182]

A few short years later, the same writer was showering Emperor Constantine with praises, hailing him as "perfect in wisdom, in justice, in courage, in piety, in devotion to God." [183]Aware that an abundance of every blessing was being poured on him by God, Eusebius came to see the Christian emperor as the new and greater Moses whose empire was "the imitation of the monarchical power in heaven," because Constantine had consciously modeled his government after that in heaven and because he governed mankind by the divine archetypal pattern, calling all men to higher knowledge.[184] Eusebius went as far as to suggest that Constantine's restoration of Jerusalem was a fulfillment of Revelation 21:2, "that second and new Jerusalem spoken of in the predictions of the prophets." [185]

It would appear that for the bishop of Caesarea, the divine kingdom had been established by Constantine through the providence of God. The new Christian empire was obviously constituted and organized for continuity. It had taken on the task of redeeming the pagan world for Christ, and as it set out to accomplish this mission, it was becoming increasingly clear that its Christian citizens were no longer living in the urgent expectation of the parousia. The brewing controversies over the Trinity, the preexistent nature of the Son, and the nature of Christ in the Incarnation are further evidences that the theological focus of attention had shifted a long way from eschatological matters.[186]

It would be a mistake, however, to suppose that the members of the churches in the fourth century had lost sight of the transcendent goal altogether. Indeed, they had not, and the vicissitudes of their earthly existence only served to reinforce their feelings that the contemporary world order had to be a mere prelude to an ultimate, other-worldly kingdom of God. Thus, the advent hope, stripped of its aura of immediacy, remained an important component of the inherited body of Christian doctrines, marking the terminus ad quem of the history of salvation.

The second coming was depicted in many treatises, sermons, and lectures, with little to suggest that it was taken otherwise than literally. The favorite way to present the doctrine was to contrast it with the first advent:

In the first advent, Christ came
> From the earth (referring to the Incarnation).
> In lowliness.
> In humble guise.
> Wrapped in swaddling clothes.
> In patience.
> To reveal the Father.
> To suffer.
> To endure the cross.
> Not to overthrow the Roman Empire.

In the second advent, Christ will come
> From heaven, escorted by tens of thousands of angels, drawn by streams of fire, with a luminous cross to impress those who crucified Him.
> In divine glory.
> In His own magnificence.
> Covered with light and receiving glory from the attending angels.
> As a conquering king.
> To bring the eternal crown.

To sit in judgment.

To render to all the fruit of His cross.

To end the world, including the Roman Empire.

In addition,

He shall roll up the heavens and darken the sun and the moon.

He will be seen by all.

The wicked will try to hide from His face, but joy will illumine the countenance of the righteous believers.

The elect will be gathered by angels and ride toward Christ on chariots of clouds.

None of the saints shall be forgotten—no matter how lowly.

All His enemies will be subdued.

His kingdom shall have no end.[187]

Christians could now give thanks for the first advent, in the past, but look forward to the second advent in the future. Moreover, they could know that the parousia was approaching by taking note of the many predictive signs enumerated by Christ in the Gospels. While it might not be imminent, Cyril of Jerusalem was convinced that "the end of the world is . . . drawing near."[188]

At the second coming the resurrection of the dead will occur. This remained an unquestioned article of the Christian faith. And while the majority of believers were content to accept the "fact" of it, some revived the speculations of Origen or contributed new explanations of their own. Thus, Cyril of Jerusalem suggested that the resurrection body will be made spiritual and eternal—"a marvelous thing, such as we cannot worthily speak of."[189] This means that the sinners will also "receive an eternal body, fitted to endure the penalties of sins, that [they] may burn eternally in fire, nor ever be consumed."[190] Hilary of Poitiers thought that God would reconstitute the bodies from the identical matter of which they were once composed, while altering their quality so as to fit them for their new condition.[191] This was also the view of Ambrose, who insisted that the body must be resurrected because it has shared in this life in the actions of the soul and therefore should come up with it to judgment. He envisaged two resurrections: At the first, the righteous will be raised, without needing to come before the judgment. Believers who have lapsed into sin will be raised, judged, and will have to endure the pains of a purgatorial fire until the second resurrection, when they will be redeemed. At that time also, the wicked will be brought forth to "the punishment of darkness."[192]

It is significant to note that the chiliastic ideas of the early patristic age had pretty well disappeared by this time. As Jerome bluntly put it: "The saints will never have an earthly kingdom, but a heavenly. Then let the story of the thousand years cease."[193] The general consensus was that the millennium had either begun with Constantine or, as the theologians Tyconius and Augustine were to suggest, the final millennium represented the total duration of the Christian church on this earth.

In the absence of the Biblical millennium, the final judgment tended to be placed at the time of the parousia. None would escape it. This was especially the view of the theologians in the Eastern empire.[194] Western Christians preferred to think that while all would appear before the judgment of Christ at the last day, only those whose lives have been a mixture of good and evil would in the strict sense be judged. The saints are already saved and need no judgment, and the wicked have been judged already.[195] Of those appearing before the divine assize, an exact accounting of every action, every thought, and every motive will be required. Most tended to view the experience in spiritualized terms, however. While not going all the way with Origen, they believed, in the words of Gregory of Nazianzus, that God will "set before us . . . our sins . . . till at last He leads us away self-convicted and self-condemned, no longer able to say that we are being unjustly treated." [196] In other words, at the judgment the real accusers will be our own conscience and our own sins.[197]

That the wicked would endure the torments of an eternal fire was also universally believed. It is interesting to note, however, that Origen's doctrine of redemptive punishment had gained favor with many theologians throughout the empire. The Easterners Didymus the Blind and Gregory of Nyssa went as far as to accept the Alexandrian's idea of *apokatastasis*—the final universal restoration of all creation and the complete victory of good over evil.[198] Westerners, while not promoting universalism, did envisage the possibility that the chastisement of Christian sinners would be only of limited duration, leading to their ultimate salvation.[199] This view seemed more consistent with their understanding of a loving God than the idea of the Creator existing in eternal estrangement from so many of His creatures for whom He already gave so much.

On the subject of the rewards of the righteous, the predominant emphasis was upon the "beatific vision"—the contemplation and knowledge of God. In the words of Cyril of Alexandria: "Without needing any figure, riddle, or parable, we shall contemplate, as it were with face uncovered, and with unencumbered mind, the beauty of the divine nature of our God and Father." [200] This will be to the redeemed the source of their greatest happiness.[201] The prospect of meeting and fellowshipping with the saints was also a popular notion—especially among the membership at large. Chrysostom wrote about meeting with Paul, "the wrestler of Christ," and Peter, the "leader of the choir of the saints." [202] Jerome looked forward to sharing the company of Mary, the mother of the Lord; Anna, the prophetess of the Gospel; and "many whom before I have not known." [203] Also to be looked forward to was the transformation of human nature into divine perfection, assuming the qualities of immortality, perfect knowledge, glory, honor, and power.[204]

Many of the concepts outlined above were admirably synthesized into a coherent system by that most important figure in the history of Christianity, Saint Augustine of Hippo. A gifted and well-read scholar, he was influenced in his eschatological speculations by the doctrines of those who had come before him, and in particular by the Donatist theologian Tyconius, a little-known figure of the late fourth century. Using the allegorical method of Bible interpretation, the Donatist theologian sought to give credence to the idea that the seventh millennium should be reckoned, not from the second advent of Christ, but from the beginning of the Christian Era.[205] This idea, in the hands of Augustine, was to administer the coup de grace to the remnants of chiliasm. Tyconius also provided him with a philosophical framework to interpret the course of human history, by positing that all creation is the battleground between two contending powers—the City of God against the City of the Devil.[206] And methodologically, he gave him a set of seven rules with which to interpret apocalyptic materials—rules that Augustine admitted using as "keys to open the secrets of Scripture."[207]

Thus equipped, the bishop of Hippo set about writing his famous treatise *The City of God*, in which he describes the history of God's chosen people in the world. Building on the ideas of Tyconius, he asserts that the millennial reign of Christ upon the earth had begun with the career of Jesus, who bound the strong man Satan (see Mark 3:27). Ever since that time the devil has been confined to the abyss, in order that he may not seduce the nations from which the church is gathered, and over whom he held sway before Jesus appeared. But the abyss, for Augustine, is not a chaotic pit in the regions beneath the earth, but "the countless multitude of the wicked, whose hearts are unfathomably deep in malignity against the Church of God."[208] Thus Satan's realm is not the Roman government, which at that point was still nominally Christian; rather, it is that group of scoffing unbelievers who continue their hostility toward the church. While the devil remains bound, the saints reign with Christ a thousand years, even as the author of Revelation affirms. It is the present church that is the kingdom of Christ and the kingdom of heaven, where the saints reign both while living and after their death. This militant spiritual regime is to grow more prosperous with the passing of time, according to Augustine, "until we come to that most peaceful kingdom in which we shall reign without an enemy, and it is of this first resurrection in the present life, that the Apocalypse speaks."[209]

Although the present world is not to grow worse as the end approaches, yet Augustine accepts the statement in Revelation 20:7, interpreting it to say that Satan is to be loosed from the abyss for a short time before the end of the thousand years. This loosing is interpreted to mean that the enemies of the church will be essentially active in their opposition for three and a half years, before the inauguration of the final judgment. During this brief time the antichrist may prevent some from embracing the Christian faith, and he may even cause a few to fall away, but such will be no loss to the church, since "these do not belong to the predestined number of the sons of God."[210] The true church will stand firm and pass gloriously through this period of tribulation, which will usher in the second advent of Christ—a belief that "the whole church of the true God holds and professes."[211] This final second advent is prefigured presently by the unseen coming of Christ that "continually occurs in His church, that is, in His members, in which He comes little by little, and piece by piece, since the whole church is His body."[212] Christ's coming to the members of His church now does not preclude, however, as it did in Origen, His glorious return from heaven, which will also signal the resurrection of the dead and the final judgment.[213]

There is every indication to suggest that Augustine believed in a literal, physical resurrection. He writes that the bodies of the saints will be perfect and entire, with all their organs; only that which is ugly will have been changed.[214] Both the saints and the wicked will be endowed with immortality—in the case of the latter so that their punishment may be everlasting.[215]

Following the resurrection, all humanity will be subjected to the judgment. No one will be spared. And as the books are opened, "every one shall recall to memory all his own works, whether good or evil, and shall mentally survey them with a marvellous rapidity, so that this knowledge will either accuse or excuse the conscience, and thus all and each shall be simultaneously judged."[216] The wicked will be consigned to eternal fire, the nature and location of which are unknown, "unless perhaps the divine Spirit reveal it to someone."[217] Then the world will be transmuted, but not completely destroyed, by a universal conflagration in which "the qualities of the corruptible elements which suited our corruptible bodies shall utterly perish, and our substance shall receive such qualities as shall, by a wonderful transmutation, harmonize with our immortal bodies, so that, as the world itself is renewed to some better thing, it is fitly accommodated to men, themselves renewed in their flesh to some better thing."[218] Thus will be established the New Jerusalem, the eternal dwelling of the saints, who with glorified eyes shall behold God, who "shall be the end of [their] desires, who shall be contemplated without ceasing, loved without cloy, praised without weariness," in an eternal Sabbath.[219] Such was the eschatological hope of Augustine, who was to influence Christian thinking for centuries to come.

Summary

This essay has sought to show the fate of the advent hope as the early Christian church emerged and spread into the Greco-Roman world, expressing its faith in modes of thought that successively were shaped by Jewish, Greek, and fnally Latin insights. The use of these modes was accompanied by a lessening of the eschatological expectation, owing to the fact of its delay and to changing social and political circumstances. Thus the imminently awaited advent of the late first and early second centuries gradually gave way to a "doctrine" of the advent—one of the essential components of the "history of salvation." This essential doctrine was in turn spiritualized away by those who insisted on promoting a type of "realized eschatology," more in character with the superior religious gnosis represented by Christianity (to Hellenistic minds).

Changing conditions brought a revival of the earlier expectancy, only to have it fulfilled in a totally unexpected manner: The kingdom of God supposedly was initiated by the advent of the Christian emperor Constantine. The victory of the Christian church came to be viewed as a close approximation of the coming of God's reign. Nevertheless, even the citizens of the City of God still felt themselves very much earthbound, and the hope of the parousia—now once again an "essential" Christian doctrine—remained very much alive in their thinking about the future, even as it cast a long beam of light on their present lives and conduct.

NOTES

[1] The dual significance of the Christian sacraments—representing what has already happened and pointing to what is yet to come—is well summarized in G.W.H. Lampe, "Early Patristic Eschatology," in W. Manson, et al., *Eschatotology: Four Papers Read to the Society for the Study of Theology* (Edinburgh, © 1952), pp. 22-24. See also on baptism: P. Lundberg, *La typologie baptismale dans l'ancienne église* (Uppsala, 1942); G.W.H. Lampe, *The Seal of the Spirit*, 2d ed. (London, 1967), pp. 97-148; J.N.D. Kelly, *Early Christian Doctrines*, rev. ed. (New York, 1978), pp. 193-195, 207-211. On the Eucharist, see Hans Lietzmann, *Messe und Herrenmahl*, 3d ed. (Berlin, 1955), pp. 249-263; E. Schweitzer, "Das Abendmahl eine Vergegenwaertigung des Todes Jesu oder ein eschatologisches Freudenmahl," *Theologische Zeitschrift* 2 (1946): 81-90.

[2] See 2 Clement 7:6. All references to the Apostolic Fathers are to the text of Karl Bihlmeyer, *Die Apostolische Väter*, 2d ed. (Tübingen, 1956). Cf. Justin Martyr *Dialogue With Trypho* 14; Cyril of Jerusalem *Catechetical Lectures* 20. 5, 6.

[3] Ignatius *To the Ephesians* 20.

[4] Rev. 19:9.

[5] Clement *To the Corinthians* 2:2, 3; Ignatius *To the Philadelphians*, introduction. Cf. Irenaeus *Against Heresies* 5. 8. 1.

[6] Barnabas 7:9, 10; 2 Clement 17:5.

[7] Clement of Rome, Ignatius, Hermas, Polycarp, Papias, and the authors of the epistles of Barnabas, 2 Clement, to Diognetus, and of the Didache.

[8] See Clement *Corinthians* 24:1; 50:3; Barnabas 5:7; 6:13; Ignatius *To the Romans* 4:3; *To the Smyrnaeans* 6:2; *To Polycarp* 3:2; 6:2; Hermas *Visions* 3. 8. 9; *Similitudes* 9. 12. 3. See also C. H. Dodd, *The Apostolic Preaching and Its Development* (New York, 1964), pp. 31-35.

[9] *To the Ephesians* 11:1.

[10] *To Polycarp* 3:2.

[11] Didache 16:1. The Didache was a handbook of instruction prepared for the use of the Christian communities in Syria, probably in the first decade of the second century. See also 2 Clement 12:1.

[12] Hermas *Visions* 3. 8. 9.

[13] Barnabas 21:3.

[14] Chapter 15.

[15] Didache 16:8. Cf. Barnabas 4:3; Hermas *Visions* 4. 2. 1-5.

[16] Ignatius *To the Trallians* 9:2.

[17] Clement *Corinthians* 23-26.

[18] See Ps. 3:5; 23:4; Job 19:26.

[19] According to the legend, the phoenix bird, after living five or six hundred years, either burnt itself to ashes or died in a nest of frankincense and myrrh. From the ashes or the decaying flesh it came back to life again with renewed youth. See Ovid *Metamorphoses* 15. 392-407 and Pliny *Natural History* 10. 2. See also J. Hubaux and M. Leroy, *Le Mythe du phénix dans les litteratures grecque et latine* (Liège, 1939), and R. van den Broek, *The Myth of the Phoenix According to Classical and Early Christian Traditions* (Leiden, 1972).

[20] Ignatius *To the Smyrnaeans* 3:1-3. See also Ignatius *To the Trallians* 9:2; 2 Clement 9:5; Clement *Corinthians* 26:3; Polycarp *To the Philippians* 7:1.

[21] 2 Clement 9:1.

[22] See Leon Morris, *The Biblical Doctrine of Judgment* (Grand Rapids, 1960); H. Ringgren, "Jüdische Apokalyptik," *Die Religion in Geschichte und Gegenwart*, 3d ed. (Tübingen, 1957), vol. 1, cols. 464-466; George F. Moore, *Judaism in the First Centuries of the Christian Era*, 3 vols. (Cambridge, Mass., 1927-1930), vol. 2, pp. 287-395; Samuel Sandmel, *Judaism and Christian Beginnings* (New York, 1978), pp. 83-89, 188-208, passim; Emil Schürer, *The History of the Jewish People in the Age of Jesus Christ*, new ed. (Edinburgh, 1979), vol. 2, pp. 544-547; T. W. Manson, *The Teaching of Jesus*, 2d ed. (London, 1963), pp. 261-284; G. R. Beasley-Murray, *Jesus and the Future* (London, 1954); Joachim Jeremias, *The Parables of Jesus*, rev. ed. (New York, 1963), pp. 221-227; Dodd, *Apostolic Preaching*; Ethelbert Stauffer, *New Testament Theology* (New York, 1955), pp. 220-222.

[23] Epistle to Diognetus 7:6. See also 2 Clement 1:1; Polycarp *To the Philippians* 2:1; Barnabas 7:2.

[24] 2 Clement 17:4.

[25] Hermas *Similitudes* 4. 1-4. See also Polycarp *To the Philippians* 7:1, 2; Clement *Corinthians* 28:1; 2 Clement 17:4-7.

[26] Barnabas 4:12.

[27] Ignatius *To the Ephesians* 16:2; Hermas *Similitudes* 9. 18. 2.

[28] Clement *Corinthians* 35:2.

[29] *Ibid.*, 50:3; 2 Clement 19:4; Hermas *Visions* 2. 2. 7; *Similitudes* 9. 27. 3.

[30] Irenaeus *Against Heresies* 5. 33. 3, 4.

[31] D. H. Kromminga, *The Millennium in the Church: Studies in the History of Christian Chiliasm* (Grand Rapids, 1945), p. 56. See also Leonhard Atzberger, *Geschichte des christlichen Eschatologie innerhalb der vornicänischen Zeit* (Freiburg, 1896), vol. 1, pp. 90-92.

[32] Chap. 16:3. Cf. 2 Peter 3:10, 12, 13.

[33] Hermas *Visions* 4. 3. 3; 1. 3. 4.

[34] While not radical to Jewish minds conditioned by a tradition of apocalyptic pronouncements, the Christian message went against everything that the classical world view stood for. See Pierre Duhem, *Le système du monde. Histoire des doctrines cosmologiques de Platon à Copernic* (Paris, 1924), vol. 1, chaps. 1, 2; Marc Lods, *Précis d'histoire de la théologie chrétienne du IIe au debut du IVe siècle* (Neuchâtel, 1966), pp. 117-120; Oscar Cullmann, *Christ and Time*, 3d rev. ed. (London, 1962), pp. 51-60.

[35] This was the basis for the pagan thinker Celsus' contention that "there will neither be more nor less good and evil among mortals." For "God does not need to amend his work afresh."—In Origen *Against Celsus* 4. 69. See also the criticism of the Christian view of the cataclysmic end of the world by the Skeptic philosopher Caecilius Natalis, in the *Octavius of Minucius Felix* 10: "Because they threaten conflagration to the whole world, and to the universe itself, with all its stars, are they meditating its destruction? As if either the eternal order constituted by the divine laws of nature would be disturbed, or the league of all the elements would be broken up, and the heavenly structure dissolved, and that fabric in which it is contained and bound together would be overthrown." Again, in chapter 11, he wrote: "It is a twofold madness to denounce destruction to the heaven and the stars, which we leave just as we find them."

[36] The point is well made by Aristotle in his *De Generatione et Corruptione* 2. 11: "What is 'of necessity' coincides with what is 'always,' since that which 'must be' cannot possibly 'not-be.' Hence a thing is eternal if its 'being' is necessary: and if it is eternal, its 'being' is necessary. And if, therefore, the 'coming-to-be' of a thing is necessary, its 'coming-to-be' is eternal; and if eternal, necessary. It follows that the 'coming-to-be' of anything, if it is absolutely necessary, must be cyclical—i.e. must return upon itself. . . . It is a circular movement, therefore, and in cyclical coming-to-be that the 'absolutely necessary' is to be found." On the notion of the circular motion in Greek philosophy, see J. Chevalier, *La notion du nécessaire chez Aristote et ches ses prédécesseurs, particulièrement chez Platon* (Paris, 1915), pp. 160-189; O. Hamelin, *Le système d'Aristote*, 2d ed. (Paris, 1831), pp. 335-338.

[37] "Eschatology in the Patristic Age: An Introduction," *Greek Orthodox Theological Review* 2 (1956): 32.

[38] Origen *Against Celsus* 4. 14; "It is the nature of a mortal, indeed, to undergo change and remoulding, but of an immortal to remain the same and unaltered. God, then, could not admit of such a change.

[39] *Octavius* 11. The Greeks, nurtured in the belief of the immortality of the soul, were shocked by the idea of the "resurrection of the dead" *(anastasis nekrōn)*—literally, a "standing up of corpses." See in this connection the following works: Erwin Rohde, *Psyche: The Cult of Souls and Belief in Immortality Among the Greeks*, 2 vols., reprint ed. (New York, 1968); Clifford H. Moore, *The Religious Thought of the Greeks*, 2d rev. ed. (Cambridge, Mass., 1925), pp. 144-182 passim; Krister Stendahl, ed., *Immortality and Resurrection* (New York, 1965); Henry Chadwick, "Origen, Celsus, and the Resurrection of the Body," *Harvard Theological Review* 41 (1948): 83-102; Charles N. Cochrane, *Christianity and*

Classical Culture (New York, 1957), pp. 114-176 passim.

[40] Origen *Against Celsus* 5. 14. See also 2. 55, 77; *Octavius* 11.

[41] Origen *Against Celsus* 4. 10.

[42] *Ibid.*, 5. 14.

[43] See Justin *Dialogue With Trypho* 80. See also Irenaeus *Against Heresies* 5. 31. 1; Origen *Commentarium in 1 Corinthians,* in *Journal of Theological Studies* 10 (1909): 46, 47; Gospel of Philip 73: 1-3 (James Robinson, ed., *The Nag Hammadi Library* [New York, 1978], p. 144); 57: 19, 20 *(NHL,* p. 135). An interesting exception to this generalization is the Gnostic *Treatise on Resurrection,* written in the latter part of the second century by an anonymous Valentinian teacher to his student Rheginos, in response to questions regarding death and the afterlife. It does refer to a "spiritual resurrection" immediately following death, involving the ascension of a spiritual body composed of invisible members covered with a "spiritual flesh," which is absorbed in the pleroma—the "all" of God. See the text in Michel Malinine, Henri-Charles Puech, et al., *De Resurrectione,* and the recent English translation in *NHL,* pp. 50-53. See also the detailed monograph by Malcolm L. Peel, *The Epistle to Rheginos* (Philadelphia, 1969). On Gnostic thought, dualism, and eschatology, see Ugo Bianchi, ed., *The Origins of Gnosticism/Le origini dello gnosticismo* (Leiden, 1967), especially pp. 62-68, 109-125, 221-223, 517; R. M. Wilson, *Gnosis and the New Testament* (Philadelphia, 1968), pp. 60-84, 103-111, 117-124; Hans Jonas, *The Gnostic Religion,* 2d ed. rev. (Boston, 1963); Elaine Pagels, *The Gnostic Gospels* (New York, 1979), pp. 3-27.

[44] Lampe, "Early Patristic Eschatology," p. 18.

[45] Martin Werner, in his work *Die Entstehung des christlichen Dogmas* (Bern, 1941), abridged English translation, *The Formation of Christian Dogma* (New York, 1957), argues that the delay of the parousia was the single most important factor in shaping the development of Christian doctrines during the second and third centuries. His work represents an expansion of a thesis first put forward by Albert Schweitzer in *The Quest of the Historical Jesus* (London, 1910), pp. 330-397. The thesis had originally been drafted by J. Weiss, in his work *Die Predigt Jesu vom Reiche Gottes,* 2d ed. (Göttingen, 1900). See also R.P.C. Hanson, *The Continuity of Christian Doctrine* (New York, 1981), pp. 34-50; J. Pelikan, *Historical Theology: Continuity and Change in Christian Doctrine* (Philadelphia, 1971), pp. 72-76; *idem, The Emergence of the Catholic Tradition, 100-600,* vol. 1 of *The Christian Tradition* (Chicago, 1971), pp. 123-132. For a sociological and psychological approach to the problem caused by the delay of the parousia in the early church, see John Gager, *Kingdom and Community: The Social World of Early Christianity* (Englewood Cliffs, N.J., 1975). This work is based on a major study by Leon Festinger, *A Theory of Cognitive Dissonance* (Evanston, Ill., 1957), and the more recent application of it in Leon Festinger et al., *When Prophecy Fails* (New York, 1964).

[46] Schweitzer's theory of "Enteschatologisierung" is developed in his *Quest of the Historical Jesus,* pp. 330-397. In his autobiographical work *Out of My Life and Thought,* rev. ed. (New York, 1949), pp. 32-59, he gives an account of how he arrived at this conclusion.

[47] Tertullian *Apology* 39. 2 (italics supplied); cf. 32. 1. On the word *Maranatha,* see Didache 10:6; on the various usages of the term, see G. Kittel, ed., *Theological Dictionary of the New Testament,* 10 vols. (Grand Rapids, 1964-1976), *s.v.* "Maranatha," by K. G. Kuhn.

[48] Verses 15, 9, 11, 12, R.S.V.

[49] 2 Clement 12:5, 6; see also verses 1-4. The logion used by Clement is also found in Clement of Alexandria, *Stromata* 3. 13. 92, 93. There are also allusions to it in the apocryphal Acts of Peter 38. Its origin is disputed among scholars. H. Leisegang, *Die Gnosis,* 4th ed. (Stuttgart, 1955), p. 19, and W. Schneemelcher, in Edgarr Hennecke, *New Testament Apocrypha* (Philadelphia, 1963), vol. 1, p. 169, attribute it to the Gnostic *Gospel of the Egyptians.* W. C. van Unnik rejects the idea, since the logion does not occur in the Nag Hammadi document bearing that title. See his *Newly Discovered Gnostic Writings and Early Christianity* (New York, 1959), pp. 123, 124. G. F. Moore, in *Judaism,* vol. 2, p. 191, and vol. 3, p. 190, has suggested that it might be Jewish in origin. For an overall discussion of the questions raised by this logion, see Oscar Cullmann, "Quand viendra le Royaume de Dieu?" *Revue d'histoire et de philosophie religieuses* 18 (1938): 183-185.

[50] See Mark 13:10 and Matt. 24:14.

[51] As evidenced by the author of the religious romance known as the Pseudo-Clementine Homilies (2. 15-17). On the origin of the Pseudo-Clementines, see H. Waitz, "Die Pseudo-klementinen und ihre Quellenschriften," *Zeitschrift für die neutestamentliche Wissenschaft* 28 (1929): 241-272. See also J. Lowe, "The First Christian Novel: A Review of the Pseudo-Clementines," *Canadian Journal of Religious Thought* 7 (1931): 292-301.

[52] Origen *Commentary on the Epistle to the Romans* 2. 4 (in O. Baeurfeind, ed., *Der Romerbrief des Origines* [Leipzig, 1923]).

[53] Enoch 47:4; 4 Ezra 4:36; 2 Baruch 23:4, 5; 30:2.

[54] 1 Clement 2:4; 58:2; 59:2. See also W. C. van Unnik, "Le nombre des elus dans la lere Epitre de Clément," *Revue d'histoire et de philosophie religieuses* 42 (1962): 237-246.

[55] Justin *Dialogue With Trypho* 39. See also chapters 35 and 44.

[56] *1 Apology* 45.

[57] *Ibid.,* 28. In regard to salvation, cf. chapters 3 and 6.

[58] *Didascalia,* F. X. Funk, ed. (Paderborn, 1905) 5. 15. 3; *Constitutions of the Holy Apostles* 8. 5. 6 and 22.3.

[59] For the rabbinic texts, see Hermann L. Strack and Paul Billerbeck, *Kommentar zum Neuen Testament aus Talmud und Midrash: Excurse zu einzelnen Stellen des Neuen Testaments* (Munich, 1956), vol. 2, pp. 992, 977-988; see also Moore, *Judaism,* vol. 2, pp. 350-371. For the Jewish background, see K. Hruby, "Die rabbinische Exegese messianischer Schriftstellen," *Judaica* 21 (1965): 100-122; *idem,* "Anzeichen für das Kommen der messianischen Zeit," *Judaica* 20 (1964): 73-90; J. Klausner, *The Messianic Idea in Israel* (New York, 1955), pp. 408-419; Schürer, *History,* vol. 2, pp. 514-525.

[60] Though the Messianic age had already started, the actual appearance of the Messiah was being delayed because of the transgression of His people. See Babylonian Talmud, Sanhedrin 97a. See also Moore, *Judaism,* vol. 2, pp. 352, 357. It was also widely believed that God had set a definite time for sending the Messiah that not even the unrepented sins of Israel could postpone. *Ibid.,* p. 351.

[61] Echoes of this explanation can also be found in the canonical 2 Peter 3:8.

[62] Barnabas 4:3. Cf. Enoch 89:61-64; 90:17.

[63] Barnabas 4:9.

[64] Chap. 15:4.

[65] Verse 5.

[66] See, for example, Justin *Dialogue With Trypho* 81:3; Irenaeus *Against Heresies* 5. 25. 1-3; 28. 1-3; Hippolytus of Rome *Commentary on Daniel* 4. 23, 24; *Treatise on Christ and Antichrist* 60-67; Lactantius *Divine Institutes* 7. 14-26; Victorinus of Pettau *On the Creation of the World*, passim; Commodianus *Instructions* 35; 43. See also A. Luneau, *L'histoire du salut chez les pères de l'Église: La doctrine des âges du monde* (Paris, 1964); Jean Daniélou, "La Typologie millénariste de la semaine dans le chiliasme primitif," *Vigiliae Christianae* 2 (1948): 1-16; Atzberger, *Christlichen Eschatologie*, vol. 1, pp. 566-573; 583-611; A.J.B. Higgins, "Jewish Messianic Belief in Justin Martyr's 'Dialogue With Tryphon,' " *Novum Testamentum* 9 (1967): 298-305.

[67] Lampe, "Early Patristic Eschatology," pp. 22-24, suggests that the apostolic doctrine and the sacraments were "the most powerful factors" in preventing early Christian eschatology from degenerating into individualistic mysticism or a quasi-Judaistic hope of reward for the faithful after death. See also Gregory Dix, *The Shape of the Liturgy* (London, 1945), pp. 127-130, 185, 186, 225-267.

[68] On the connection between persecutions and the renewal of the eschatological hope, see Lods, *Précis d'histoire*, pp. 132-134; *idem, Confesseurs et martyrs: successeurs des prophètes dans l'Église des trois premiers siècles* (Neuchâtel, 1958), pp. 44-54; W.H.C. Frend, *Martyrdom and Persecution in the Early Church* (New York, 1967), pp. 149-152, 219, 220, 274, 275, 410, 411; E. Stauffer, "Märtyrertheologie und Täuferbewegung," *Zeitschrift für Kirchengeschichte* 3 (1933): 545-609; H. von Campenhausen, *Die Idee des Martyriums in der alten Kirche* (Göttingen, 1936), pp. 68-82, passim.

[69] According to Festinger et al., *When Prophecy Fails*, p. 28, proselytism is one of the most common and effective ways of dealing with cognitive dissonance, the assumption being that "if more and more people can be persuaded that the system of belief is correct, then clearly it must, after all, be correct." See also Gager, *Kingdom and Community*, pp. 37-40.

[70] *Apology* 16. See also Melito's *Petition*, cited in Eusebius *Ecclesiastical History of the Church* 4. 26. 7; Tertullian *Apology* 32; 40; Arnobius of Sicca *Against the Heathen* 1. 6.

[71] Hippolytus *Discourse on the Holy Theophany* 8, 9.

[72] Lampe, "Early Patristic Eschatology," p. 20.

[73] See Aristides of Athens *Apology* 15; Justin *Dialogue With Trypho* 110, 116, 117; *1 Apology* 14; Tertullian *Prescription Against Heretics* 14; *On Repentance* 7; 2.

[74] Tertullian *Apology* 39; Hippolytus *Commentary on Daniel*, 4. 12. 2; 4. 5, 3, 4; Lactantius *Divine Institutes* 7. 25.

[75] Hippolytus *Daniel* 4. 4, referring to Rev. 17:10; Irenaeus *Against Heresies* 5. 28. 3.

[76] Hippolytus *Daniel* 4. 4-6.

[77] Tertullian *Against Marcion* 3. 13. See also Justin *Dialogue With Trypho* 110.

[78] Irenaeus *Against Heresies* 5. 25. 3, quoting Dan. 7:25. Irenaeus offers three possible interpretations of the number 666: It could mean Evanthas, Teitan, or Lateinos. While refusing to come to a definitive conclusion, he appears to favor the last one, because it is "the name of the last kingdom [of the four seen by Daniel]. For the Latins are they who at present bear rule."—*Ibid.* chap. 30. 3. See also chapters 28 and 29. Cf. Justin *Dialogue With Trypho* 32; 110; Hippolytus of Rome, who devoted an entire treatise on the subject *(Treatise on Christ and Antichrist)*; his *Daniel* 4. 7, 22, 39-43; 7. 7; 12. 1, 2, 7; Tertullian *On the Soul* 50; *On the Resurrection of the Flesh* 25; *Concerning Flight in Persecution* 12.

[79] Hippolytus *Daniel* 7. 17. Cf. Irenaeus *Against Heresies* 5. 35. 1; Justin *Dialogue With Trypho* 80; *1 Apology* 52.

[80] Justin *Dialogue With Trypho* 139. See also chapter 81; Irenaeus *Against Heresies* 5. 28. 3; 31. 1, 2; 32. 1, 2; 33. 3, 4; 35. 1, 2; Hippolytus *Daniel* 4. 55, 56; Tertullian *Against Marcion* 3. 24; 4. 31; 5. 15; *The Shows* 30. 1; *The Chaplet* 13.

[81] Irenaeus *Against Heresies* 5. 36. 1. See also chaps. 32; 36. 1-3; Justin *Dialogue With Trypho* 81; 139; Tertullian *Apology* 32; *On the Resurrection* 22; *Against Marcion* 3. 24; 25; Hippolytus *Against Plato, On the Cause of the Universe* 3.

[82] Justin *Dialogue With Trypho* 14; 40; 51. On Christ's literal return in glory and power, see chapters 14; 31; 32; 34; *1 Apology* 51; 52.

[83] Justin *Dialogue With Trypho* 6. He rejects quite specifically the Platonic view (see chapter 5), as did Irenaeus *Against Heresies* 2. 34. 4; Tatian *Address to the Greeks* 13; Theophilus *To Autolycus* 2. 24; 27; Arnobius of Sicca *Against the Heathen* 2. 14; 32; Lactantius *Divine Institutes* 7. 5; and others. See also the essay by Harry A. Wolfson, "Immortality and Resurrection in the Philosophy of the Church Fathers," in his *Religious Philosophy: A Group of Essays* (Cambridge, Mass., 1961), pp. 69-103; Claude Tresmontant, *La métaphysique du Christianisme et la naissance de la philosophie chrétienne* (Paris, 1961), pp. 577-583; Kelly, *Christian Doctrines*, pp. 466, 467; Adolf von Harnack, *History of Dogma*, reprint ed. (New York, 1961), vol. 2, pp. 169-229 passim; Atzberger, *Christlichen Eschatologie*, vol. 1, pp. 116-121, 221-223, 292-295; and the books by J. Pelikan, *The Shape of Death* (London, 1962); Heinrich Knapp, *Probleme altchristlicher Anthropologie* (Gütersloh, 1950); and Alfred Rush, *Death and Burial in Christian Antiquity* (Washington, D.C., 1941).

[84] Tatian *Address to the Greeks* 13.

[85] Irenaeus *Against Heresies* 5. 2. 2, 3; 20. 1.

[86] *Ibid.* 5. 14. 1-4.

[87] *Ibid.* 2. 29. 2.

[88] Justin *1 Apology* 19 and Tertullian *On the Resurrection* 57, both quoting Matt. 19:26. Cf. Luke 18:27. See also Hippolytus *Against Plato, On the Cause of the Universe* 2.

[89] Justin *Dialogue With Trypho* 80.

[90] Irenaeus *Against Heresies* 5. 34. 1, 2; 35. 1. See chapters 33-36, especially 35. 1.

[91] Kelly, *Christian Doctrines* p. 469.

[92] No unanimity of opinion existed among the Fathers on the subject of the final retribution. Some believed that the wicked would suffer "everlasting punishment" (Tertullian *On the Resurrection* 35); others believed that they were destined to "everlasting destruction"—meaning annihilation (Arnobius of Sicca, *Against the Heathen* 2. 14).

[93] Justin *Dialogue With Trypho* 124. See also his *1 Apology* 10; 52; Tatian *Address to the Greeks* 13.

[94] Irenaeus *Against Heresies* 5. 8. 1; 4. 20. 5, 6. See also J. Gross, *La divinisation du chrétien d'apres les Pères Grecs: Contribution a la doctrine de la grâce*, 2d ed. (Paris, 1946); and the articles by M. J. Congar, "La déification dans la tradition spirituelle de l'Orient," *La vie spirituelle* 43 (1935), supplément, pp. 91-107; A. J. Festugière, "Divinisation du chrétien," *La vie spirituelle* 47 (1939): 97-106; M. Lot-Borodine, "La doctrine de la 'deification' dans l'Eglise grecque jusqu'au XIe siècle," *Revue de l'histoire des religions* 105 (1932): 5-43; 106 (1932): 525-574; Atzberger, *Christlichen Eschatologie*, vol. 1, pp. 131-143; Michel Aubineau, "Incorruptibilité et divinisation selon St. Irénée," *Recherches de science religieuse* 44 (1956): 25-52.

[95] Tertullian *On the Soul* 55.

[96] Irenaeus *Against Heresies* 5. 31. 2. See also Hippolytus, fragment on Luke 23 *(ANF* 5:194). On this subject, see J.

Kroll, *Gott und Hölle: der Mythos vom Descensuskampfe* (Leipzig and Berlin, 1932), especially the first chapter; Atzberger, *Christlichen Eschatologie*, vol. 1, pp. 139, 140, 145, 245, 246, 276-281. It would appear that only the souls of the martyrs were spared the experience of descending into the underworld. It was believed that they ascended directly into the presence of God. See Tertullian *On the Soul* 55-58; Irenaeus *Against Heresies* 4. 33. 9. The idea goes back to the earliest days of Christianity, as evidenced by the writings of Ignatius *To the Ephesians* 12. 2; *To the Smyrnaeans* 4. 2; *To the Romans* 4. 1; 7. 2; *To Polycarp* 2. 3.

[97] Hippolytus *Against Plato* 1. See also Justin *Dialogue With Trypho* 5.

[98] Hippolytus *Against Plato* 1.

[99] *Ibid.*, 2.

[100] For the construction of such a personal eschatology, frequent appeals were made to the parable of the rich man and Lazarus (Matt. 16:19-31). See, for example, Irenaeus *Against Heresies* 2. 34. 1; Tertullian *On the Soul* 58.

[101] The movement has quite appropriately been called by one of its best exponents, Pierre de Labriolle, *La crise du Montanisme* (Paris, 1913). See also his *Les sources de l'histoire du Montanisme: Textes grecques, latins, syriaques* (Fribourg, 1913), and the more recent studies by Kurt Aland, "Bemerkungen zum Montanismus und zur frühchristlichen Eschatologie," in *Kirchengeschichtliche Entwürfe* (Gütersloh, 1960), pp. 105-148, and "Das Montanismus und die kleinasiatische Theologie," *Zeitschrift für die neutestamentliche Wissenschaft* 54 (1955): 109-116. Also helpful are H. Kraft, "Die altchristliche Prophetie und die Enstehung des Montanismus," *Theologische Zeitschrift* 11 (1955): 249-271; R. G. Smith, "Tertullian and Montanism," *Theology* 46 (1943): 127-139; Wilhelm Schepelern, *Der Montanismus une die phrygischen Kulte: Eine geschichtliche Untersuchung* (Tübingen, 1929).

[102] Nathanael Bonwetsch, *Geschichte des Montanismus* (Erlangen, 1881), p. 139, cited in Pelikan, *Emergence of Catholic Tradition*, p. 98.

[103] Jean Daniélou and Henri Marrou, *The First Six Hundred Years*, vol. 1 of *The Christian Centuries* (New York, 1964), p. 101. See also Kraft, "Altchristliche Prophetie," pp. 268-270; De Labriolle, *Crise du Montanisme*, pp. 30, 34, 35.

[104] Eusebius *Eccl. Hist.* 5. 14; 16.

[105] Epiphanius of Salamis *Panarion* 48. 2. 4. See also J. Pelikan, "Eschatology of Tertullian," *Church History* 21 (1952): 118, 119.

[106] Eusebius *Eccl. Hist.* 5. 16. 18.

[107] Epiphanius *Panarion* 49. 1. 3; 48. 14. 1; Eusebius *Eccl. Hist.* 5. 18. 2; Jerome, *Letter 41* (to Marcella), 3. 2.

[108] *Against Marcion* 3. 24.

[109] Eusebius *Eccl. Hist.* 5. 18. 2; Hippolytus *Daniel* 4. 18, 19. Celibacy as a mark of genuine Christianity conformed to popular ideas among the early Christians. See 1 Clement *Corinthians* 38:2; Ignatius *To Polycarp* 5: 2, 3; Athenagoras *A Plea for the Christians* 33; Tertullian *Apology* 9; *On Monogamy* 8; *To His Wife* 1. 3; *On Purity* 16; Origen *Romans* 9. 1; *Homily on Numbers* 6. See also Derrick Bailey, *Sexual Relation in Christian Thought* (New York, 1959), pp. 19-102.

[110] The concept of "guard duty" accounts for the military name *statio* that was applied to it. See Hermas *Parables* 5. 1; Tertullian *On Fasting* 10; *On Prayer* 19. "The Christian stood 'on guard' in order to give the Lord a worthy reception when He returned," writes Hans Lietzmann, in *The Founding of the Church Universal*, rev. trans. (Cleveland, 1953), p. 133. On the fasting practices of the Montanists, see Tertullian *On Fasting* 1; 2; 10; 17; Jerome, *Letter 41* (to Marcella), 3. Cf. Hippolytus *Refutation of All Heresies* 8. 12.

[111] See Tertullian *Concerning Flight in Persecution* 1; *On Repentance* 7; 9.

[112] De Labriolle, *Crise du Montanisme*, p. 146.

[113] Noteworthy is the absence in the earliest anti-Montanist polemics of any mention of cultic or doctrinal aberrations. In contrast with the Gnostics who rejected the Old Testament, the Montanists revered it. Where the Gnostics were Docetists, the Montanists affirmed the reality of Christ's body and the resurrection of the flesh. Against the Gnostic repudiation of the Christian eschatological hope, the Montanists proclaimed the imminent return of Christ. Unlike some Gnostics, the Montanists were rigorists. Montanism offered little that could be seized upon as contrary to the canon of Scripture and the apostolic tradition.

[114] Eusebius *Eccl. Hist.* 5. 16-18; Hippolytus *Refutation of All Heresies* 8. 12.

[115] Gager, *Kingdom and Community*, p. 45.

[116] Lietzmann, *Founding of the Church*, p. 298. This was also the view of Porphyry as quoted by Eusebius *Eccl. Hist.* 6. 19:5-8. On Origen's eclecticism and philosophical background, see Charles Bigg, *The Christian Platonists of Alexandria* (London, 1913), pp. 63-72, 151-191; Eugene de Faye, *Origene: sa vie, son oeuvre, sa pensée*, 3 vols. (Paris, 1923-1928), especially vol. 2, which details Origen's indebtedness to Hellenistic thought; Hal Koch, *Pronoia und Paideusis. Studien über Origenes und sein Verhältnis zum Platonismus* (Leipzig, 1932), especially pp. 163-304; Jean Daniélou, *Origène* (Paris, 1948), pp. 24-40, 85-108.

[117] See the article by Gustave Bardy, in *Dictionnaire de théologie catholique*, s.v. "Origène," vol. 11, cols. 1489-1565, which seeks to underscore the Biblical foundation of Origen's thought. See also the books by René Cadiou, *Introduction au système d'Origène* (Paris, 1932), pp. 29-58; and Daniélou, *Origène*, pp. 137-174.

[118] Origen *On First Principles* 2. 1. 3; 3. 6. 9.

[119] *Ibid.*, 1. 6. 2, 3; cf. 3. 5. 4, 5; *Against Celsus* 7. 32.

[120] *Idem.*, *On First Principles* 3. 5. 3. See also 2. 3. 1; Jerome, *Letter 124* (to Avitus), 5.

[121] Origen *On First Principles* 1. 6. 1, 2.

[122] *Ibid.*, 3. 6. 2, 3; Jerome, *Letter 124* (to Avitus), 5.

[123] Origen *Commentary on Matthew* 12:30. For a detailed exposition of Origen's views on the Second Advent, see Atzberger, *Christlichen Eschatologie*, vol. 2, pp. 427-431.

[124] In *Matthaem Commentariorum Series (Series of Commentaries on Matthew)* 32. See also chap. 70. The series is found in Migne, *Patrologia graeca*, vol. 13. Cf. Origen, *Commentary on Matthew* 12:30.

[125] *Series on Matthew* 50. (Italics supplied.) See also Atzberger, *Christlichen Eschatologie*, vol. 2, p. 429.

[126] *Series on Matthew* 50; 56; 70. Cf. *Commentary on Matthew* 12:30; *On First Principles* 3. 6. 9; see also Plotinus *Enneads* 3. 8. 6; 5. 3. 17; 5. 5. 7; 6. 7. 34; 6. 9. 4.

[127] *Commentary on Matthew* 10:14; 12:14, 36. See also *Homilies on Jeremiah* 14, 10; *Commentary on the Canticle of Canticles* 1; *Commentary on John* 19.

[128] Eusebius mentions two volumes (*Eccl. Hist.* 6. 24. 2), and Origen himself speaks of "treatises" (*On First Principles* 2. 10. 1). It seems that the two works were at one time combined into one treatise (see Jerome *Against John of Jerusalem* 25). The fragments are found in Methodius of Philippi *On the Resurrection;* Pamphilus *Apology for Origen* 7; and

Jerome *Against John of Jerusalem* 25, 26. On Origen's doctrine of the resurrection, see W. L. Knox, "Origen's Conception of the Resurrection of the Body," *Harvard Theological Review* 41 (1948): 83-102; Atzberger, *Christlichen Eschatologie*, vol. 2, pp. 431-449; Tresmontant, *Métaphysique du Christianisme*, pp. 613-618, 630-639.

[129] Atzberger, *Christlichen Eschatologie*, vol. 2, pp. 367-372.

[130] *Against Celsus* 5. 22.

[131] *On First Principles* 2. 10. 1.

[132] See *On First Principles* 2. 10. 1-8; 3. 6. 5, 6; *Against Celsus* 5. 23; 7. 32; 4. 56. Cf. Methodius *On the Resurrection* 2. 10-21; Epiphanius *Panarion* 64, 12.

[133] Origen, *On First Principles* 2. 10. 2, 3. Cf. book 3. 6. 4.

[134] Jerome, describing Origen's belief, in his letter to Avitus, No. 124, 11 and 5. See also Origen *Against Celsus* 7. 32.

[135] Atzberger, *Christlichen Eschatologie*, vol. 2, pp. 393-401; Kromminga, *Millennium*, pp. 104-107.

[136] *On First Principles* 2. 11. 2.

[137] *Ibid.*, 2. 11. 3.

[138] "Behold, all you who kindle a fire, who set brands alight. Walk by the light of your fire, and by the brands which you have kindled! This shall you have from my hand: you shall lie down in torment" (R.S.V.).

[139] *Ibid.*, 10. 4.

[140] Jerome, Letter 124 (to Avitus), 7. See also Origen, *On First Principles* 2. 10. 4; Atzberger, *Christlichen Eschatologie*, vol. 2, pp. 449, 450.

[141] See Origen's *Homilies on Exodus* 6. 13, where "from age to age" *(in saeculum et in saeculum)* is viewed as a long period of time, "but there is some end." And even if something longer is indicated, "an end is set." See also *Against Celsus* 6. 26.

[142] Daniélou, *Origène*, pp. 271-281, and Henry Chadwick, *Early Christian Thought and the Classical Tradition* (New York, 1966), p. 93.

[143] *On First Principles* 1. 6. 2. See also Atzberger, *Christlichen Eschatologie*, vol. 2, pp. 451-456; Johannes Quasten, *Anti-Nicene Literature After Irenaeus*, vol. 2 of *Patrology* (Westminster, Md., 1950-1961), pp. 87-90; *Reallexikon für Antique und Christentum*, s.v. "Apokatastasis," by C. Lenz, vol. 1, 510-516; and Tresmontant, *Métaphysique du Christianisme*, pp. 395-457.

[144] *On First Principles*, 1. 6. 2.

[145] *Ibid.*, 1. 6. 3; 5. 3; *Series On Matthew* 33. When Origen was taken to task on the question of the repentance and salvation of the devil, he protested that he had never held such a theory. See Rufinus of Aquileia, "The Book Concerning the Adulteration of the Works of Origen," in *Nicene and Post-Nicene Fathers*, 2d series, Vol. III, p. 423.

[146] Origen, *On First Principles* 3. 6. 3.

[147] *Ibid.*, 3. 5. 3. See also Quasten, *Patrology*, vol. 2, pp. 89, 90; Chadwick, *Christian Thought*, p. 94.

[148] *On Romans* 5, 10.

[149] Irenaeus *Against Heresies* 1. 10. 1. Cf. Tertullian *Prescription Against Heretics* 13.

[150] See the outstanding account of these developments in Lietzmann, *Founding of the Church*, pp. 166-172, and *From Constantine to Julian* (Cleveland, 1953), pp. 17-81. Also Frend, *Martyrdom and Persecution*, pp. 285-392.

[151] Lods, *Précis d'histoire*, pp. 132-134. Also the old work by Herbert Workman, *Persecution in the Early Church* (London, 1906), pp. 125-155; Michael Barkun, *Disaster and the Millennium* (New Haven, Conn., 1974), pp. 34-61; Lampe, "Early Patristic Eschatology," pp. 26, 27.

[152] According to Eusebius *(Eccl. Hist.* 6. 7), Jude wrote a treatise on Daniel's seventy weeks in which he announced the imminent arrival of the antichrist.

[153] See his letter to Cyprian (A.D. 256), in *Epistles of Cyprian* 74. 10, 11, where he reports the activities of a would-be prophetess in his province during the persecutions of Julius Maximinus, the Thracian.

[154] Eusebius *(Eccl. Hist.* 7. 24) reports (about the time of the Decian persecution) that Nepos wrote a millenarian treatise (apparently against Origen) that drew heavily on the Revelation of John, entitled *The Allegorists Refuted.*

[155] Cyprian, the Christian bishop of Carthage, was martyred in 258. His eschatological ideas are scattered throughout his many epistles and treatises, especially *On the Mortality*, *Exhortation to Martyrdom*, and *On the Lord's Prayer.*

[156] Methodius was one of Origen's most erudite opponents. He authored many works, most of which are no longer extant. His apocalyptic views are best expressed in his book *On the Resurrection* and his dialogue *Banquet of the Ten Virgins.*

[157] Historians still hold divergent opinions regarding the period when Commodianus wrote his treatises. We tend to side with those scholars who cite the years 250-258. See A. d'Alès, "Commodien et son temps," *Recherches de science religieuse* 2 (1911): 480-520; 599-619; O. Bardenhewer, *Geschichte der altkirchlichen Literatur*, 2d ed. (Freiburg im Breisgau, 1914), vol. 2, pp. 647-657; J. Gage, "Commodien et le mouvement millénariste du IIIe siècle," *Revue d'histoire et de philosophie religieuses* 41 (1961): 355-378. Of interest are Commodianus' *Instructions* and his *Apologetic Poem*, both of which draw heavily on various apocalyptic sources, including the Sibylline Oracles.

[158] Victorinus of Pettau, who was martyred about 304, has left us two works revealing strong millenarian and apocalyptic leanings: *Commentary on the Apocalypse* and a fragment from his treatise *On the Creation of the World.*

[159] Lactantius probably composed his *Divine Institutes* during the great Diocletianic persecution (c. 308). The seventh and last book of this strange work, entitled "On the Happy Life," focuses extensively on eschatology. His work *On the Death of the Persecutors* is of importance as a source for Diocletian's persecutions. See also Daniélou, "Typologie millénariste," pp. 14, 15.

[160] See Firmilian's Epistle to Cyprian, in *Epistles of Cyprian* 74. 10; Cyprian *Mortality* 2, 14-16; *Address to Demetrianus* 5, 23; Commodianus *Instructions* 43; Victorinus *Apocalypse* 6:5, 7-9, 12; Lactantius *Divine Institutes* 7. 16; *Epitome of the Divine Institutes* 71.

[161] Already at the beginning of the third century, a Christian author by the name of Jude, in a treatise on Daniel's seventy weeks, predicted, according to Eusebius, "that the much talked about advent of antichrist would take place at any moment—so completely had the persecution set in motion against us at that time overthrown many off their balance" (*Eccl. Hist.* 6. 7).

[162] Suetonius *Lives of the Caesars* 6. 57; Tacitus *Histories* 2. 8, 9; Victorinus *Apocalypse* 11:7. See also the Sibylline Oracles 2. 216-223; Commodianus *Apologetic Poem*, as cited by Adolf Harnack in *Chronologie der altchristlicher Literatur* (Leipzig, 1904), vol. 2, pp. 433-442.

[163] Cyprian, Epistle 55 (to the people of Thibaris), 7.
[164] *Idem*, Epistle 62 (to Caecilius), 18. See also the Epistle to the Clergy and Christians in Spain, No. 67, 7, and Epistle 57 (to Lucius of Rome), 2.
[165] *Idem, On the Lord's Prayer* 13.
[166] Victorinus *Apocalypse* 11:3. According to Lactantius *Divine Institutes* 7. 17, it would be only three and a half years.
[167] Cyprian *Mortality* 2.
[168] Victorinus *Apocalypse* 1:7.
[169] Lactantius *Epitome* 72. Cf. Cyprian *Three Books of Testimonies Against the Jews* 2. 30; Methodius *Banquet* 6. 4.
[170] Methodius *Banquet* 9. 2.
[171] *On the Resurrection* 3. 13.
[172] *Ibid.*, 7, 12. See also Commodianus *Instructions* 44.
[173] Cyprian *Exhortation to Martyrdom* 13; *Mortality* 26.
[174] See Dionysius' response to the chiliast Nepos of Arsinoë, in his *On the Promises*, in which he not only debunks the doctrine but calls into question the canonicity of John's Apocalypse. See Eusebius *Eccl. Hist.* 7. 24, 25.
[175] Commodianus *Instructions* 44; Lactantius *Divine Institutes* 7. 24; Victorinus *Apocalypse* 20:1-3, in the *Corpus Scriptorum Ecclesiasticorum Latinorum* (Vienna, 1916), vol. 49. Jerome's edition purposely omits the millenarian passages, including the reference to Papias.
[176] Methodius *Banquet* 10. 5; see also 9. 1, 4.
[177] Cyprian *To Demetrianus* 24.
[178] *Ibid.*, 25.
[179] On the Constantinian empire and the church, see the following excellent studies: N. H. Baynes, "Constantine the Great and the Christian Church," *Proceedings of the British Academy* 15 (1929): 341-442; H. Kraft, *Kaiser Konstantins religiöse Entwicklung* (Tübingen, 1955); K. Aland, "Die religiöse Haltung Kaiser Konstantins," *Texte und Untersuchungen* 53 (1957): 549-600; Hermann Doerries, *Constantine the Great* (New York, 1972); Jean Gaudemet, *L'Eglise dans l'Empire roman (IVe-Ve siècles)* (Paris, 1958); idem, "La législation religieuse de Constantin," *Revue de l'histoire de l'Eglise de France* 33 (1947): 25-61; A. Piganiol, *L'Empereur Constantin* (Paris, 1932); H. Karpp, "Konstantin des Grosse und die Kirche," *Theologische Rundschau*, N.F. 19 (1950): 1-21.
[180] Leroy E. Froom, *The Prophetic Faith of Our Fathers*, 4 vols. (Washington, D.C., 1946-1954), vol. 1, p. 373.
[181] Eusebius *Proof of the Gospel* 4. 16; see also 9. 17.
[182] *Ibid.*, fragment of book 15.
[183] *Idem, Oration in Praise of the Emperor Constantine* 5.
[184] *Ibid.*, 2-4; see also his *Life of Constantine* 1. 13; 24; 4. 75; S. L. Greenslade, *Church and State From Constantine to Theodosius* (London, 1954), pp. 10, 11. In addition, see the excellent monograph by Timothy D. Barnes, *Constantine and Eusebius* (Cambridge, Mass., 1981), especially pp. 224-271. Also the following: F. E. Kranz, "Kingdom and Polity in Eusebius of Caesarea," *Harvard Theological Review* 45 (1952): 47-66; Gustave Bardy, "La théologie d'Eusèbe de Césarée d'après l'*Histoire Ecclésiastique*," *Revue d'histoire ecclésiatique* 50 (1935): 5-20; R. Farina, *L'impero e l'imperatore criatiano in Eusebio di Cesarea: la prima teologica politica del Cristianesimo* (Zurich, 1966), especially pp. 120-154; N. H. Baynes, "Eusebius and the Christian Empire," in *Byzantine Studies and Other Essays* (London, 1955), pp. 168-172.
[185] Eusebius *Life of Constantine* 3. 33.
[186] Note in this connection the terse reference to the Second Coming in the Nicene Creed: ". . . and will come to judge the living and the dead." (J.N.D. Kelly, *Early Christian Creeds*, 2d ed. [New York, 1960], pp. 205-230).
[187] The contrasts are drawn from Athanasius *On the Incarnation of the Word* 56; Cyril of Jerusalem *Catechetical Lectures* 15; Ambrose *Homilies on the Psalms* 43. 7; Jerome *Commentary on Daniel* 2. 40; 7. 11, 13; Letter 121 (to Algasia), in Migne, *Patrologia latina*, 22: 1036; Chrysostom, *Homilies on 1 Thessalonians* 8; Theodoret *Commentary on the Visions of the Prophet Daniel* 2.
[188] Cyril of Jerusalem *Catechetical Lectures* 15. 12.
[189] *Ibid.*, 18. 18.
[190] *Ibid.*, 18. 19.
[191] Hilary of Poitiers *Homilies on the Psalms* 2. 41.
[192] Ambrose *On the Belief in the Resurrection* 52; *Homilies on the Psalms* 1. 54, 56.
[193] Jerome *Daniel* 7. 25.
[194] Cyril of Jerusalem *Catechetical Lectures* 15. 23, 24; Athanasius *On the Incarnation* 56.
[195] Ambrose *Homilies on the Psalms* 1. 54, 56; Ambrosiaster *Commentary on 1 Corinthians* 15. 15-53; Hilary of Poitiers *Homilies on the Psalms* 1. 15-18.
[196] Gregory of Nazianzen *Orations* 16. 8.
[197] See Cyril of Jerusalem *Catechetical Lectures* 15. 25. Cf. Basil the Great, *Homilies on the Psalms* 33. 4.
[198] They did not, however, accept Origen's idea of the possibility of another Fall. On Didymus, see Jerome's *Apology Against Rufinus* 1. 6; Gregory of Nyssa *The Great Catechism* 26.
[199] Ambrosiaster *On 1 Corinthians* 15. 33; Jerome Letter 118 (to Julian), 6, 7; Ambrose *Homilies on the Psalms* 1. 56.
[200] Cyril of Alexandria *Commentary on St. John* 16. 25. See also Cyril of Jerusalem *Catechetical Lectures* 18. 28, 29; Chrysostom *Homily on Romans* 32. 3; Basil the Great *Homilies on the Psalms* 33. 11; Ambrose *The Consolation* 29, 31, 37, 39.
[201] Cyril of Alexandria *St. John* 14. 4.
[202] Chrysostom *Homily on Romans* 32. 24.
[203] Jerome Letter 39 (to Paula), 7.
[204] Gregory of Nazianzen *Orations* 7. 23; Gregory of Nyssa, *On the Soul and the Resurrection* (NPNF/2 5:453); Chrysostom *Homily on Romans* 32. 3, 4; *On 1 Corinthians* 34.
[205] See Gennadius *Lives of Illustrious Men* (addition to Jerome's treatise) 18. See also Traugott Hahn, *Tyconius-Studien: Ein Beitrag zur Kirchen- und Dogmengeschichte des vierten Jahrhunderts* (Leipzig, 1900), pp. 87-91. Also useful for a general introduction to Tyconius is the account in P. Monceaux, *Histoire littéraire de l'Afrique chrétienne* (Paris, 1919), vol. 5, pp. 165-219.
[206] Hahn, *Tyconius*, pp. 42-62. See also R. A. Markus, *Saeculum: History and Society in the Theology of Saint Augustine* (London, 1970), pp. 116-119.
[207] Augustine *On Christian Doctrine* 3. 30. On the seven rules, see Francis C. Burkitt, ed., *The Book of Rules of*

Tychonius (Cambridge, 1894).

[208] Augustine *City of God* 20. 7. On Augustine's eschatological views, see Eugène Portalié, *A Guide to the Thought of Saint Augustine* (Chicago, 1960), pp. 289-303; A. Wachtel, *Beiträge zur Geschichtstheologie des Aurelius Augustinus* (Bonn, 1960), pp. 120-126; G. Folliet, "La typologie du sabbat chez Saint Augustin: son interpretation millénariste entre 388 et 400," *Revue des études augustiniennes* 2 (1956); T. E. Mommsen, "Saint Augustine and the Christian Idea of Progress," *Journal of the History of Ideas* 12 (1951):346-374.

[209] Augustine *City of God* 20. 9.

[210] *Ibid.*, 20. 8.

[211] *Ibid.*, 20. 1.

[212] *Ibid.*, 20. 5.

[213] *Ibid.*, 20. 1, 6, 30.

[214] *Ibid.*, 22. 19.

[215] *Idem, Enchiridion* 92.

[216] *Idem, City of God* 20. 14.

[217] *Ibid.*, 20. 16.

[218] *Ibid.*, 20. 14; *idem, Enchiridion* 92.

[219] *Idem, City of God* 22. 30.

CHAPTER 5

The Advent Hope
in the Middle Ages

Richard K. Emmerson

MEDIEVAL Christians, although troubled by the passage of time, confidently awaited the second advent of Christ. As the twelfth-century Cistercian father Guerric of Igny states, "I am absolutely sure that in the end he will appear and will prove not to have deceived me; so in spite of the delay he imposes I shall go on waiting for him confidently, because he certainly will come and will not be later than the most timely day." [1] The fervor of these words from Guerric's first sermon for the advent season may surprise some readers, for typically, Protestant Christians have been taught that the advent hope was lost during the Middle Ages. Nothing could be further from the truth.

Unfortunately, the period from Augustine to Luther is often misunderstood, perhaps because during the sixteenth century, Reformers, who at first attacked a corrupt Papacy, increasingly directed their opposition to Roman Catholic theology. These polemics, legitimately aimed at real administrative and spiritual abuses, sometimes misrepresented the key doctrines of medieval theology in order to show what the Reformers considered to be their un-Biblical bases, their excessive use of allegory, and their dependence on a corrupt tradition. As a result, Protestants, as heirs of the Reformation, tend to concentrate on the doctrines that divide them from the Roman Catholic tradition developing from the Middle Ages and often do not recognize the continuity of the Christian faith, the numerous beliefs that they share with medieval Christians, or the extent to which Reformation theology developed from a fluid medieval spirituality. Like the Reformers, medieval exegetes and theologians sought the truth through careful interpretation of scripture. It is therefore unfortunate that conservative Protestants sometimes fail to recognize the great theologians of the Latin church among the fathers of the faith.[2]

Christian belief during the Middle Ages was not static, for it developed through a thousand years to meet the needs of a Christianized Europe, reacting to various heresies and non-Christian threats, and shifting with the growing institutionalization of the church. Generally, historians divide medieval history into three lengthy periods: the Early Middle Ages (500-1000), the High Middle Ages (1000-1300), and the Late Middle Ages (1300-1500). The religious history of each of these periods has its particular concerns and reflects changes in the intellectual and political climate of the time. In general, the religious beliefs of the Early Middle Ages, highly influenced by the fathers and monastic spirituality, are best illustrated by scriptural glosses and homiletic and didactic works, whereas the representative doctrines of the High Middle Ages, a period that witnessed a growing historical awareness coupled with theological speculation, are reflected in universal histories, encyclopedias, scholastic summae, and in many visual and literary works of art. During the Late Middle Ages traditional teachings remained standard, but beginning with popular and learned dissatisfaction with hierarchical authority, and fueled by movements considered heretical by the church, new forms of spirituality and unorthodox belief flourished, as is evident in the numerous mystical and polemical tracts of the time.

Throughout the Middle Ages, however, there was a general body of catholic (universal) doctrines. Central to these was the belief that history had a beginning, middle, and end, based on the "three advents" of Christ: at the beginning as Creator, at the center of history as the God-incarnate Redeemer, and at the end as Judge. Thus medieval Christians expected the return of Christ at the end of time, specifically to resurrect the dead, to judge mankind, and to inaugurate a new world. This doctrine, clearly stated in the New Testament and taught by the early Christian church, is included in all early Christian and medieval creeds.[3]

The medieval Christian expectation of Christ's second advent was firmly established by Augustine (354-430), the complex and sometimes controversial bishop of Hippo who has been called "the single most influential thinker in the Western intellectual tradition." [4] Augustine, whose work tends to synthesize many strands of early Christian thought, is often described as antiapocalyptic and as almost single-handedly sounding the death knell of chiliasm.[5] Although he explains in his magisterial *City of God* that at first he believed in a millenium to follow the bodily resurrection of the dead at the end of the world, he came to reject the doctrine primarily because he felt that it led to an excessively materialistic conception of the millennium: "But in fact those people assert that those who have risen again will spend their rest in the most unrestrained material feasts, in which there will be so much to eat and drink that not only will those supplies keep within no bounds of moderation but will also exceed the limits even of incredibility. But this can only be believed by materialists." [6] In contrast, Augustine argued that the millennium ought to be understood as beginning with the establishment of the church by Christ, whom he understood as binding Satan. As Revelation 20:7 makes clear, at the end of time the dragon will be loosed, signifying the horrors of the last days before Christ's second coming. However, "in the meantime, while the Devil is bound for a thousand years, the saints reign with Christ, also for a thousand years; which are without doubt to be taken in the same sense, and as denoting the same period, that is, the period beginning with Christ's first coming." [7]

This view that "the church even now is the kingdom of Christ and the kingdom of heaven" is neither without Biblical bases, nor is it original with Augustine. As

Jaroslav Pelikan notes, early Christian liturgical practice reflects a double understanding of Christ's coming: "The coming of Christ was 'already' and 'not yet': He had come already in the Incarnation, and on the basis of the Incarnation would come in the Eucharist; He had come already in the Eucharist, and would come at the last in the new cup that He would drink with them in His Father's kingdom." [8] It is true that Augustine's understanding of the millennium could reduce the sense of urgency concerning the times and moderate an earlier emphasis on the imminence of Christ's second coming, especially when merged with the Tyconian understanding of the church as the body of Christ and the later medieval insistence on the real presence of Christ in the mass.[9] However, to designate Augustine as antiapocalyptic is misleading if we understand such to mean that to Augustine the Christian expectation of the end and the second advent of Christ was not of central importance. Augustine was concerned not only with the second advent but also with such last-day expectations as the release of Gog and Magog, the coming of Antichrist, the resurrection of the dead, and the destruction of the world, although he did not wish to be dogmatic concerning the exact nature and ordering of these events.[10]

Augustine spoke primarily against those whose apocalyptic concern with the future he considered excessive, whose theories he understood to be not only a waste of time but also dangerous. He opposed attempts to second guess the Lord, to recklessly manipulate scripture to specify the course of the future, and to impudently set dates concerning the events of the end and the return of Christ. He resisted the temptation of identifying contemporary calamities with the signs of the end, and called on those who sought to enumerate precisely the persecutions the Christian church would suffer before the final persecution of Antichrist and the end of the world "to renounce the audacious presumption of making any pronouncement on the question." He also reminded those wishing to determine when Christ would return that in Acts 1:6, 7 Christ refused to reveal such even to the apostles: "It is vain, therefore, that we try to reckon and put a limit to the number of years that remain for this world, since we hear from the mouth of the Truth that it is not for us to know this. And yet some have asserted that four hundred, five hundred, or as much as one thousand years may be completed between the Lord's ascension and His final coming. But to show how each of them supports his opinion would take too long; and in any case it is unnecessary, for they make use of human conjectures, and quote no decisive evidence from the authority of canonical Scripture. In fact, to all those who make such calculations on this subject, comes the command, 'Relax your fingers, and give them a rest.' And it comes from him who says, 'It is not for you to know the times, which the Father has reserved for His own control.' " [11]

In general Augustine not only expects the second advent but indeed bases his entire theology of the two cities, and, as we shall see later, his concept of history, on that expectation. In the *City of God* he devotes book 20 to a discussion of the last judgment—including an extensive examination of Biblical prophecies—book 21 to the punishment of evil and the reward of the righteous, and book 22 to the resurrection of the body and to the bliss of heaven. These are the events that finally establish who is and who is not truly a citizen of the city of God and they all assume Christ's second advent, an expectation held, according to Augustine, by all Christians: "Now it is a belief held by the whole church of the true God, in private confession and also in public profession, that Christ is to come from heaven to judge both the living and the dead, and this is what we call the last day, the day of divine judgment.[12]

Thus, during the twilight of the ancient world, Augustine established what would become the received medieval understanding of the advent hope: Christ's return in glory at the end of time to judge and save is certain, although not necessarily imminent and certainly unpredictable. The Christian church represents the beginning of the kingdom of God, a spiritualized millennial kingdom, but the earthly church is temporal, to be brought to its conclusion by the son of God who will inaugurate the eternal kingdom, the inheritance of the righteous. This world is not the Christian's home, and life in this world is only a pilgrimage directed to claiming that inheritance: "In this world we are given an earnest of that inheritance, and we shall at the appointed time come into the inheritance of which this is a pledge; but at present we go on our way in hope, and we make progress from day to day as we 'put to death the evil actions of the body by the power of the Spirit.' " [13]

The Augustinian perspective on the advent hope remained relatively constant throughout the Early and High Middle Ages. The belief in the ultimate return of Christ, in fact, was the cornerstone on which other key Christian doctrines were built. Medieval theologians thus often cite this eschatological doctrine to support their theologies of history, salvation, and the nature of Christ. The second advent and last judgment bring Christian history to its destined conclusion; they "guarantee," as Jaroslav Pelikan notes, "the objectivity of salvation"; and they establish Christ as the "Lord of History." [14]

Theologians continued to teach that Christians were living in the last age and that the second coming would not be put off for long, although refusing to date the parousia or even claim that the end was imminent. For example, in a letter to King Ethelbert (June, 601), Gregory the Great, although citing the political and natural upheavals of the Early Middle Ages as signs of the times, retreats from identifying them with the signs of the end. Certainly "the end of the present world is already near," he affirms, but the horrors of the end "are not to come in our own days, but they will all follow upon our times." As encouragement he adds: "If you are aware of some of them happening in your land, do not be disturbed, for these signs of the end of the world are sent ahead so that we may have a concern for our souls." [15] Thus Pope Gregory I sets forth the middle position so typical of medieval theology. It is not wise to identify the expected signs of the end with contemporary events, for one cannot be sure when Christ will return, but it is certain that He will return in the not-too-distant future, and, for the sake of our souls, Christians should always remember the end of time and doomsday. As Guerric of Igny notes, although the Lord "does command that He should be awaited with patience, in another place He promises that He will be coming quickly. On the one hand He is giving some idea of the great persistence needed, on the other He is strengthening the fainthearted, terrifying the improvident, and rousing up the lazy." [16]

In fact, only a very few medieval theologians thoroughly spiritualized eschatology, and by and large their teachings were rejected by the Christian tradition, or even condemned as heretical. Interestingly, even spiritualized cosmologies did not do away with the concept of "the end of time." For example, John Scotus Eriugena (c. 810-c. 877), highly influenced by Greek mysticism, interpreted the parable of the wise and foolish virgins in an eschatological sense, noting that the delay of the bridegroom (Matt. 25:5) represents "The interval of time between the first and the second coming of the Lord, or from the beginning of the world to its end." [17] Eriugena's hellenizing theology, though, considered the return of Christ and His judgment to be spiritual, not literal, to take place within the Christian's enlightened conscience. Following Origen, he also understood the resurrection as preceding universal salvation, and rejected the concept of eternal damnation. Partly because of its teachings concerning the end of the world, a Parisian council in 1210 condemned the *Periphyseon* as an influence on heretics and ordered the book burned.[18]

The eschatology of most medieval theologians, however, was more orthodox and did not suffer the fate of the *Periphyseon*. In fact, the physical and bodily return of Christ is stressed repeatedly not only in theological argument but also in more popularized works. According to the *Memoriale Credencium*, a late Middle English compilation of various moral works intended to instruct laymen in the basics of Christian theology, Christ ascended to heaven "with flesh and blood, body and soul," and "shall come at the day of doom in man's form glorified." [19] This is the "hope of all peoples," the expectation that unifies the "body of Christ on earth," and relates the Christian church to its Old Testament predecessor. As Guerric of Igny states: "Just as the church awaited in the holy ones of old the first coming, so in us she is expecting the second. Just as she steadfastly hoped in the first for the price of her redemption, so she hopes in the second for the reward of her earnings." Thus, although concerned with the apparent delay of Christ's return, Guerric continually emphasized the promise of the second advent to be held in faith and to be anticipated with hope. "In this the soul does not have just a bare hope; it overflows with hope, hope mounting upon hope as trial comes upon trial, delay upon delay." [20]

Guerric of Igny, as well as other medieval writers, makes clear that the advent hope should transform Christians and lead the church to reject this world's false rewards: "This looking forward in hope raises her above earthly concerns; her eyes are fixed with joyous longing upon those of heaven. There are some, impatient to find happiness in the affairs of this present life, who neglect the Lord's advice and make every effort to snatch the prizes this world offers. But blessed is the man whose whole hope rests in the Lord's name and who takes no notice of spurious and empty foolishness." [21] The time of the delay is thus a time of trial and temptation, but it is also a time of mercy when sinful man can repent and prepare to meet Christ. "So, if you are wise, give an eye to yourself and see how you are using this delay. If you are a sinner do not be heedless but take the opportunity to repent. If you are holy the time is given you to progress in holiness, not to slip away from the faith." [22]

Such concern, of course, follows naturally from the medieval Christian belief that the second advent inaugurates a literal courtlike judgment resulting in the eternal punishment of evil as well as eternal bliss of the saved. In a sermon delivered in Rome, Leo the Great (c. 400-461) summarized this expectation: "For the Lord will come in His glorious majesty, as He Himself foretold, and there will be with Him an innumerable host of angel legions radiant in their splendor. Before the throne of His power will all the nations of the world be gathered; and all the men that in all ages and on all the face of the earth have been born, shall stand in the Judge's sight. Then shall be separated the just from the unjust, the guiltless from the guilty; and when the sons of piety, their works of mercy reviewed, have received the kingdom prepared for them, the unjust shall be upbraided for their utter barrenness, and those on the left having naught in common with those on the right, shall by the condemnation of the Almighty Judge be cast into the fire prepared for the torture of the devil and his angels, with him to share the punishment, whose will they choose to do." [23]

The theological concern with eschatology is evident as well in medieval commentaries on the Bible. During the Early Middle Ages exegetes, sharing Augustine's concern with the excesses of predicting the end of time and his understanding of the church as the millennium on earth, preferred to describe the nature and significance of Christ's return rather than its timing. At the end of time, Christ will appear in majesty to judge all mankind, to damn the wicked, and to save the righteous. The second coming will be the final confrontation in the war between good and evil waged within church history and will bring to an end the *psychomachia,* the moral conflict fought within the souls of individual Christians. Moral arguments rather than historical conjecture are emphasized. Thus, interpretations of Revelation generally reject both chiliasm and any attempts to mathematically determine the last days. Important early commentators such as Bede(c. 672-735), Beatus of Liebana (d. c. 800), Alcuin (d. 804), and Haimo of Auxerre (c. 843) believed that Revelation contained *nihil historicus,* nothing historical. They approached the symbols and images of Revelation as prophetic clues to the spiritual world, prophecy being understood as dealing with that which, to quote Thomas Aquinas, is not "knowable by men except from divine revelation." [24]

Prophecy is not limited to prediction of the future, but includes all spiritual things, whether past, present, or future. The final book of the Bible was understood both as surveying the future and providing moral exhortation based on a sense of evil at work in the present, its symbolism representing the cosmic battle between good and evil as evident in the life of the church now and to be witnessed in the final battle of the future. Many early commentaries thus provide a double interpretation of particular symbols, in terms of both the present and the future. Ambrosius Autpertus (died c. 781), for instance, understands the triumphant vision of Revelation 11:15-18 as representing "the two advents of the Lord . . . the first and the second, the humble and the exalted, the secret and the manifest." Similarly, Berengaudus understands the fall of Babylon (Rev. 18:2) as signifying on the one hand the contemporary victory of the church by means of gospel preaching, and on the other hand the destruction of evil in the last days.[25]

Because of the significance of Revelation as Scripture's concluding book and as a Christian prophecy of the future, exegetes devoted much time to examining the symbols and images of John's vision, attempting to explain its message for the contemporary church, but always recognizing that their interpretations were speculative. Through proper study and the awareness of exegetical rules—specifically those outlined by the Donatist writer Tyconius—the Christian exegete could arrive at a level of certitude concerning the spiritual. Nevertheless, much remains hidden; there is much conjecture. In *On Christian Doctrine,* Augustine chastised Tyconius for claiming that with his rules "whatever is closed will be opened, and whatever is obscure will be illuminated." With his usual common sense, Augustine charts a middle course, arguing that some or even much "that is closed will be opened," but unfortunately much remains uncertain.[26] Nevertheless, the symbols and images of Revelation, when subjected to the rules of Tyconius, could help explain the spiritual battle between the two cities. The Biblical text is not approached as a continuous narrative but as a series of recapitulative sections, usually patterns of seven. Following the seventh rule of Tyconius, concerning "the devil and his body," exegetes populated their commentaries with generalized and timeless figures that continually reappear: the virtues and vices, the true and false churches, Satan and Christ, demons and angels, the faithful and—especially in the eschatological passages—Antichrist. This last representative of evil appears throughout these commentaries, taking on a life of his own.[27]

One of the best examples of the importance of Antichrist in the Early Middle Ages is the little treatise by the tenth-century monk, Adso of Montier-en-Der, the *Libellus de Antichristo*. A work of great influence in the High Middle Ages, the *Libellus* analyzes the "prophecies" concerning Antichrist, both Biblical and sibylline. Adso created a full prophetic "life" of the final representative of evil, understood by medieval theologians to be a human parody of Christ with devilish connections who would appear in the last days both to deceive and to persecute the church. Adso, although writing during a time often considered by historians to be charged with apocalyptic expectation, was careful to avoid a sense of impending doom. After the destruction of Antichrist, he points out, comes a time of penance for those earlier deceived by Antichrist; furthermore, "no one knows how much time there may be after they shall have completed this penance until the Lord comes to judgment; but it remains in the providence of God who will judge the world in that hour in which for all eternity He predetermined it was to be judged." [28]

Although the earlier interest in the generalized conflict between the forces of good and evil and such eschatological figures as Antichrist continued in the High Middle Ages, this later period was also much more historically minded. Along with allegorical and moral concerns, theologians and exegetes became more interested in "the human universe of sacred history." [29] Beginning in the twelfth century, the increased interest in historical order particularly influenced interpretations of the book of Revelation, as is evident in the commentaries of Rupert of Deutz (d. 1129), Richard of Saint Victor (d. 1173), and Joachim of Fiore (c. 1135-1202).[30] In contrast to the nonhistorical understanding of Revelation primarily in moral terms evident in the Early Middle Ages, commentaries now see the last book of the Bible as an outline of church history. According to the earlier Augustinian vision of salvation history, exegetes and historians could trace stages of history from Creation to the Incarnation, but since the establishment of the Christian church represents the culmination of salvation history (following, as Augustine argued, the chaining of the dragon and the institution of the millennium), historical development ceases. The twelfth-century commentators, however, elaborated the Augustinian structure by further subdividing the present age of the church into historical periods. Commenting on the opening of the seven seals (Rev. 6:1-8:5) as a prophetic *Geistesgeschichte*, for example, Anselm of Havelburg (d. 1158) traced various persecutions and heresies afflicting the Christian church within history up to the appearance of Antichrist at the end of the world.[31]

The reading of the Apocalypse as *historia* was most fully developed in the commentary of Alexander Minorita of Bremen, a work that influenced such important later exegetes as Hugh of Saint-Cher (c. 1190-1263) and Nicholas of Lyra (1270-1340) and through them Reformation commentaries.[32] Writing circa 1242, Alexander understood the last book of the Bible to be a prophecy largely fulfilled, a narrative established in time and unchanging, an outline of Christian history from its first-century origins to the establishment of the fraternal orders in the thirteenth century. From the perspective of the thirteenth century and with the aid of chronicles and universal histories, the exegete could establish the truth and explicate the apocalyptic symbols and images with factual certitude. Recapitulation is abandoned and the narrative sequence of the text emphasized. The images and events of Revelation are not isolated but a temporal series. The Franciscan commentator identified the symbols with specific emperors, kings, generals, and ecclesiastics, the events of Scripture with particular battles, persecutions, and heresies. The undifferentiated figures of the cosmic battle between good and evil are now replaced by historical characters such as Nero, Titus, Domitian, Trajan, Pelagius, Justinian, Saint Benedict, Charlemagne, and Mohammed. Moving chronologically through time, the images of Revelation lead ultimately to the final vision, the return of Christ in majesty.

Reflecting the growing interest in post-Biblical history, the High Middle Ages also witnessed the compilation of numerous chronicles and universal histories. Generally beginning with Creation and tracing both Biblical and secular (especially Roman) history to the institution of Christianity and the establishment of the various medieval kingdoms and city-states, these works often concluded with the last things and the expected second advent. Once again, the influence of Augustine cannot be overemphasized. The *City of God*, with its concern to trace the history of the two cities from Cain and Abel through secular and salvation history to the end of time, provided a model for universal histories. Furthermore, Augustine's structuring of history according to the "three advents" of Christ—in Creation, in the Incarnation, and at Doomsday—meant that historians needed not only to concentrate on origins and past events but also to keep an eye on the conclusion of history. Particularly influential was Augustine's concept of the six ages of world history based on Creation week, the first five days of the week symbolizing five ages from Creation to the Incarnation, the sixth day the age of the church to be followed by a sabbath age, interpreted variously as the rest of the saved after death or as heavenly rest.[33] This pattern is especially passed on to the Middle Ages by Isidore of Seville (c. 560-636), whose *Etymologiae* details the six ages, and later by Bede (c. 673-735), who traces the six ages in his *De Temporum Ratione*.

The importance of the last things in medieval history is evident in the works of two significant and influential historians, Otto of Freising and Vincent of Beauvais. Otto, an early twelfth-century bishop and uncle of Frederick Barbarossa, traces history from Adam to the year 1146 in the first seven books of his *Chronica sive Historia de Duabus Civitatibus*. In the eighth book he then treats the eschatological future, including the persecution of Antichrist, the signs of doomsday, and the second coming. Following Augustine, Otto interprets the millennium as the present, the thousand years representing "the fullness of the time," after which Satan will be loosed from his hellish imprisonment.[34] It is perhaps symptomatic of many modern investigations and attitudes toward medieval historiography that the editors of Otto's *Chronica* for the prestigious series *Monumenta Germaniae Historiae* argued whether or not the eighth book, since it deals with eschatology, ought to be included in their edition. But this attempt to distinguish between history and eschatology clearly reflects modern bias and is not medieval. Fortunately, the eighth book was included in the edition. Its eschatological concerns are an essential component of the Christian philosophy of history and thus an essential part of Otto's outline of both religious and secular history. It is "an integral part of the whole composition." [35]

Similarly, the historian and encyclopedist, Vincent of Beauvais, concluded his *Speculum Historiale* (written c. 1250) with a discussion of future history—the events of the last days. Following its account of the Christian crusades against the Saracens, the *Speculum* considers the great iniquity of the times, Biblical and popular prophecies concerning the last days, the life of Antichrist, the signs of doomsday, and the last judgment.[36]

That eschatology continued to play a major role in Christian history at the end of the Middle Ages is evident in Hartmann Schedel's *Liber Chronicarum*, published in Nuremberg in 1493. Like other universal histories in the Augustinian tradition, the so-called Nuremberg Chronicle divides history according to the six ages. Antichrist is expected to conclude the sixth age, thus ushering in the eschatological future, the last things, and judgment day. Schedel, however, allowed for a short intervening time between the present and the last days. At the conclusion of his discussion of the first six ages, which he brought down to the year 1492, he left six blank pages before beginning the discussion of the eschatological future.[37] The reader is expected to chronicle the last events of world history for himself. These events and their exact timing remain uncertain, but it is clear that Schedel did not expect them to fill many pages of history. He was certain, however, that the unknown would be followed by the prophetically known, the events of the future introduced by Antichrist's appearance. Thus from the fifth-century Orosius to the fifteenth-century Schedel, medieval historians, like most medieval theologians and exegetes, were concerned with eschatology, especially the second coming of Christ and the last judgment. The last things represented the goal of history and provided their works with coherence and meaning. Historians thus emphasized eschatology and the advent hope, placing these events in the near, although not imminent, future.

The Christian understanding of history was not limited, of course, to commentaries on Revelation or to universal chronicles. It also influenced Christian worship and was celebrated in the liturgy. Their apocalyptic outlook meant that—in contrast to the Greeks, who describe history as cyclical (a movement from and a return to a "golden age")—Christians understood history as linear. Moving from Creation to doomsday, history does not repeat itself, a point Augustine vehemently makes. Referring to the Greek cyclical view, he states, "Heaven forbid, I repeat, that we should believe this. For 'Christ died once for all for our sins'; and 'in rising from the dead he is never to die again.' " [38] Nevertheless, in its commemoration of salvation history, the liturgical calendar does move, like the seasons themselves, in a circular pattern, although medievals would probably prefer to describe this pattern as a spiral.[39] Since it is based on the life of Christ, it appears to repeat itself in the two advents, both celebrated in the advent season. Yet, as a fifteenth-century Middle English collection of sermons makes clear, "Holy Church makes mention of the coming of Christ in two ways. The first was to buy man out of bondage and thralldom of the devil to bring him to bliss. The other coming shall be at the day of doom when God shall reward and judge every man and woman as they have deserved." [40]

Readings for the advent season included not only prophecies of the nativity of Christ, but also of the end of the world and the second advent. The Gospel for the first week in advent (Luke 21:27) refers to the coming of the Son of man. Readings also included the most popular Biblical source for the medieval Antichrist tradition, 2 Thessalonians 2:1-13. In the early development of the liturgy, furthermore, what Josef Jungmann calls "a sort of pre-Advent" emphasizing the second coming of Christ ended the liturgical year just as advent began the liturgical year. "In this pre-Advent period, the idea of the final coming of our Lord, of the parousia, is predominant, as it is in Advent itself. By remembering this second and glorious Advent, we prepare ourselves to celebrate the remembrance of the first advent." [41]

The fact that advent season was intended not only to celebrate the nativity of Christ but also to prepare the Christian for the second coming and the final judgment meant that it was both a joyous and a solemn season. The *Legenda Aurea,* an extremely popular hagiographic compilation by Jacobus de Voragine (c. 1228-1298), explains: "Thus the Advent fast is both a joyous fast, and a fast of penance. It is a joyous fast because it recalls the advent of the Lord in the flesh; and it is a fast of penance in anticipation of the advent of the last judgment." [42] This mixture of joyous love for the Christ child with fear of the Judge is particularly evident in advent sermons as well as in the particular chants and rituals of the season. John Mirk's *Festial,* a popular collection of sermons, not only exemplifies the standard medieval teaching concerning the liturgy, but also suggests how Christians may have felt concerning the second advent. "But this first coming of Christ Jesus into the world brought joy and bliss . . . to all Christian creatures. Wherefore Holy Church uses songs of melody and gladness, as 'Alleluia.' But the second coming of Christ Jesus shall be so cruel and with such vengeance that no tongue can tell. Wherefore in token of this dreadful coming of Christ to the judgment, Holy Church lays down this Advent time the songs of melody, as 'Te Deum,' 'Gloria in excelsis,' and 'Ite, missa est' and such others. Also in this holy time solemnizations of matrimony and weddings are ceased and left, for after the day of judgment there shall never be weddings more." [43]

The liturgical celebration of the second advent of Christ thus emphasized the awesomeness of Christ's return in majesty and the fear of the final judgment of all sinners. Few realize, for example, that the famous sequence by Thomas of Celano (c. 1200-c. 1255), the *Dies Irae* ("Day of Wrath"), was originally written for the Sunday before advent.[44] This "supreme expression of hope and fear in the face of the judgment," however, was not alone in reminding Christians of doomsday. Throughout the Middle Ages both liturgical and vernacular lyrics forcefully described the terrors of the end, as is evident in the ninth-century Latin poem "Quique cupitis audire," as well as in the responsory of the mass for the dead.[45]

This emphasis on the justice of Christ's judgment and the pains to be suffered by the damned was reinforced by the notion that the world as the locale of sin was to be held in contempt by the Christian, that he should not tarry in sin on his pilgrimage of life. During the Early Middle Ages, when Christian Europe was faced with repeated attacks from both barbarian and Islamic peoples, life was extremely difficult and the rejection of this world followed naturally from hardship. Furthermore, the *contemptus mundi* outlook was institutionalized by monastic asceticism, which, in teaching the importance of the inner life and the rejection of the world, also emphasized the fear of judgment and punishment. Thus the highly influential *Rule of Saint Benedict,* in addition to prescribing as instruments of good works the Ten Commandments, the love of Christ, the love of enemy, and the desire of eternal life, also teaches the monks "to know for certain that God sees all everywhere," "to see death before one daily," "to fear judgment day," and "to fear Hell." [46] One effect of such an outlook is that some Christians came to look upon the second coming of Christ not so much as a blessed hope but as a time of fear, the final installment in a life of misery. Perhaps the best known example of such an outlook on the end of time is expressed in the *De Miseriis Humane Conditionis* of Pope Innocent III (1160-1216), with its detailed description of judgment day and enumeration of the various punishments of hell.[47]

As an aid to the imagination in crystallizing the reality of doomsday, popular works also described the judgment at length. Developing the language of secular courts and trials, the *Legenda Aurea* details the number of accusers and witnesses to be present, the categories of mankind to be judged, and the nature of the sentence to be passed. Christ the judge "will be inexorably severe," and must be distinguished from earthly judges easily influenced: "He will not be influenced by fear, since He is all-powerful, nor by bribes, since He is abundance itself, nor by hate, since He is benevolence itself, nor by love, since He is justice itself, nor by error, since He is wisdom itself. Against His wisdom neither the pleading of advocates nor the sophisms of philosophers nor the discourses of orators nor the tricks of hypocrites will prevail." [48] Such arguments, of course, were intended to convince the average Christian that the judgment was to be real and would have no appeal. Sharing the same purpose, medieval sermons especially emphasized the finality of the last things. As seems typical of preachers at all times, sermons during the Middle Ages made great use of the horrors of the end and threats of judgment to prod Christians to repent their sins and lead lives devoted to good.

The literary and visual arts, furthermore, supported these homiletic appeals. Twelfth-century Latin plays represented the parable of the wise and foolish virgins and the deceitful appearance of Antichrist, whereas the great cycles of vernacular mystery plays developed during the fifteenth century always concluded their dramatizations of salvation history with the last judgment. These popular plays usually staged Christ the judge, several angels and devils, and balanced groups of saved and damned representing the various estates of medieval society. Often speaking directly to the audience, these characters either praise the mercy of God or mourn their evil lives and the fact that it is now too late to repent. For example, the Chester *Doomsday* presents a sinful pope who complains:

"Alas, alas, alas, alas!
Now am I worse than ever I was.
My body again the soul has

That long has been in hell.
Together they be—now is no grace—
Defiled before thy face,
And after my death here in this place
In pain ever to dwell." [49]

Similarly, the mosaics decorating the apses of early Christian and Byzantine basilicas and the magnificent mural frescoes and carved stone tympana of Romanesque and Gothic cathedrals presented medieval Christians with specific realizations of Christ's majestic return, the resurrection of the dead, the weighing of the souls witnessed anxiously by angels and demons, and the respective rewards of the saved and the damned. Often, as in the famous tympanum of Saint Lazare, *Autun,* designed by Gislebertus, the horrors of hell receive particular emphasis.[50]

But it would be misleading to imply that medieval Christians only looked to the end in fear. The judgment plays, for example, always describe at some length the joys of the saved, and even popular secular works, such as Chaucer's *Canterbury Tales,* conclude with the promise of "the endelees blissee of hevene." By portraying Christ at the second coming marked with the wounds of the cross, moreover, many manuscript illustrations make clear that He will return as Saviour as well as a judge. Similarly, not all preachers taught that Christians need fear an awful doomsday. Here once again Augustine opposed the excessive use of apocalyptic expectation to make an impression. Although he could on occasion urge the people of Hippo, "Do not be slow to turn to the Lord, nor delay from day to day, for His wrath shall come when you know not," commenting that "God knows how I tremble on my bishop's throne when I hear that warning," generally he opposed those who wished to scare Christians into a life of righteousness. In response to the Pelagian emphasis on the terrors of the last judgment, Augustine perceptively noted that "a man who is afraid of sinning because of hellfire, is afraid, not of sinning, but of burning." [51]

Particularly in the High Middle Ages, with its greater emphasis on a suffering Christ who through the cross became Saviour, the judgment—although real enough—was also perceived as evidence of the grace of Christ and His love for us. As the great Franciscan minister-general Bonaventura (c. 1221-1274) urged, "If you are concerned with judgment, it is to Christ that the power of judgment pertains; and we should gladly choose to have Him as a judge, for He loves us. We should say to Him: 'Lord, You must judge us; but make it so that Your blood atones for us.' " [52] Similarly, in his sixth sermon on the Song of Songs, Bernard of Clairvaux (1090-1153) argued that the fear of judgment must be balanced by the hope of salvation, for "a man who thinks only of the judgment will fall into the pit of despair." Bernard spoke from his own experience: "And if, as happened at times, I should grow forgetful of His mercy, and with a stricken conscience become too deeply involved in the thought of the judgment, sooner or later I was cast down in unbelievable fear and shameful misery, enveloped in a frightful gloom out of which I cried in dismay: 'Who has yet felt the full force of Your fury, or learnt to fear the violence of Your rage'?" The conclusion of Bernard's sermon is one of the most eloquent medieval statements of the advent hope: "Mercy and judgment will be the theme of my songs in the house of my pilgrimage, until one day when mercy triumphs over judgment, my wretchedness will cease to smart, and my heart, silent no longer, will sing to You. It will be the end of sorrow." [53]

To this point this essay has outlined the continuity of the Augustinian vision of the last days and the second advent from the Early to the High Middle Ages. In the Late Middle Ages this tradition continued to be standard in the work of orthodox writers. After the twelfth century, however, an increasing number of works discussed the expectation of the last things, and many of these departed from the more conservative orthodox teachings of the fathers and doctors. These departures, influenced by a greater sense of the urgency of the times and the corruption of the church, include a new emphasis upon the imminence of the end; the expropriation of apocalypticism by radical religious, political, and social movements; and the revival of chiliasm.

As noted earlier, Augustine opposed attempts to date the exact timing of the second advent. Following Augustine, most medieval theologians, although teaching that Christians were now living in the last age (the millennium of the church), similarly opposed self-proclaimed prophets who predicted the imminent end of the world. No doubt reflecting a typical reaction of ecclesiastics to contemporary apocalyptic predictions, Boniface VIII (pontificate, 1294-1303) is reported to have asked, "Why do these fools expect the end of the world?" [54] Theological works in general avoided identifying the evils of the time with the exact signs of the end. Sermon literature was the one exception, however. Preachers particularly liked to dwell on the signs of the end of time as visual proofs that indeed the end was near and thus immediate repentance was necessary. For example, Abbo of Fleury (c. 945-1004), writing around 995, notes that as a young man he heard a sermon preached in Paris predicting the appearance of Antichrist and the last judgment around the year 1000.[55] Perhaps the most interesting examples, however, are the Old English sermons of Wulfstan (d. 1023), who served as archbishop of York and Worcester. Eschatological themes pervade his work, which set out to convince the Anglo-Saxons that contemporary sufferings, including the Danish attacks, were the results of their sins. Although refusing to forecast a specific date for the end, Wulfstan did argue that it was imminent.[56]

During the later Middle Ages, however, this concern with the imminent end was not restricted to homiletic works. Troubled by the continuing disputes between church and empire, savage wars, economic dislocation, and the protean appearance of numerous heterodox and heretical movements, concerned theologians and reformers from the twelfth through the fifteenth century often pointed to contemporary events as signaling the end of time. In his *Fourth Watch of the Night,* the German polemicist Gerhoh von Reichersberg (1093-1169) attacked political opponents of the church and described the second coming as "approaching or already soon imminent." Similarly, the Spanish Dominican Vincent Ferrer (c. 1350-1419) in his report written for Pope Benedict XIII concluded that "the time of the Antichrist and of the end of the world will be soon and quite soon and very shortly." [57]

Not all late medieval writers, however, were satisfied with such relatively safe and general statements concerning the imminent end of the world. Ignoring scripture and the orthodox medieval tradition, self-appointed prophets set specific dates for the appearance of Antichrist and the inauguration of the last things. Arguing that "it would be ridiculous for the church to spread the gospel about the end and consummation of the world daily and not to attend to the approach of the event," Arnold of Villanova (c. 1240-1311) confidently predicted that "the time of the persecution of the Antichrist will fall within the fourteenth century from the birth of Christ, about the seventy-eighth year of that century." [58] Such concerns were echoed in more popular works as well. For example, in a sermon preached in London in 1388, "Redde Rationem Villicationes Tue," Thomas Wimbledon, referring to specific evils of the time, explained that a certain doctor had predicted the appearance of antichrist around 1400. Wimbledon included this detail to convince his audience that, just as the life of every man passes through sickness and old age and finally comes to an end, so the world, sickened by the great evils of the time and suffering the pangs of old age (pestilences and earthquakes), must also come to an end.[59]

During the fourteenth century natural calamities and the obvious corruption of the church particularly fueled apocalyptic expectations. The Black Death, which killed about a third (about 25 million) of Europe's population, was understood as a sign of the imminent destruction of the world. As Barbara Tuchman comments: "A scourge so sweeping and unsparing without any visible cause could only be seen as divine punishment upon mankind for its sins. It might even be God's terminal disappointment in His creature. Matteo Villani compared the plague to the Flood in ultimate purpose and believed he was recording 'the extermination of mankind.' " [60]

The political machinations and overwhelming wealth of the papal court, its transference from Rome to Avignon (which contemporary reformers called the Babylonian captivity), and ultimately the Great Schism were also considered to be signs of the end.[61] As a result many in the later Middle Ages, from conservative ecclesiastics to serious reformers and revolutionary fanatics, identified their opponents (both religious and political) as Antichrists. Apocalypticism, rather than providing Christians with a unifying hope, reflected the political and religious polemics tearing Christendom asunder. The Oxford scholastic John Wycliffe (c. 1329-1384) particularly reflects this polemical use of apocalypticism. His writings, which do not develop in detail traditional expectations of the second advent, repeatedly condemn many aspects of orthodox belief and church structure as belonging to Antichrist.[62]

The dislocations of the later Middle Ages also influenced artists and poets. Although their works generally remain orthodox, they do reflect the heightened apocalyptic expectations of the time. Especially after the mid-thirteenth century, illustrations of the book of Revelation particularly became popular with both lay and religious patrons. The images of John's prophetic vision became the subject of frescoes and wall hangings and were painted in numerous Bibles and religious encyclopedias, in the margins of the sumptuous books of hours, and in independent apocalyptic books.[63] Eschatological themes, such as the triumph of death and the last judgment, also dominated late medieval art, becoming both more common and more intense after the plague. Commenting on Francesco Traini's last judgment fresco in Pisa, for instance, Millard Meiss recognizes a new attitude in the representation of Christ. In contrast to high Gothic judgments, which remind the viewer of Christ's mercy, Traini portrayed Christ addressing "the damned alone, turning on them with an angry mien, his arm upraised in a powerful gesture of denunciation." [64] Literary works similarly reflected the religious and social strains of the Late Middle Ages. The greatest poet of medieval Catholicism, Dante (1265-1321), ruthlessly condemned papal wealth and corruption, relegating two simoniac popes (Nicholas III and Boniface VIII) to hell, for example, in the nineteenth canto of the *Inferno.* By drawing on the iconography of the medieval Antichrist tradition, developing apocalyptic symbols such as the whore of Babylon, and alluding to the last judgment, "Dante achieves true prophetic stature in his denunciation of papal corruption." [65] Also condemning church corruption, the Middle English poem *Piers Plowman* concludes with a vision of the last days, including Antichrist's assault on the true Christian church.[66] It should be noted that both the *Divine Comedy* and *Piers Plowman* condemn particular ecclesiastical problems, not the doctrine or structure of the church nor the institution of the papacy.

This use of apocalyptic imagery to condemn the evils of the time and to urge reform reflects the pessimistic expression of the advent hope. A more optimistic expression, however, is evident in the revival of chiliasm in the later Middle Ages. Of course, expectations of an age of peace and Godlike rule had been kept alive in the Middle Ages in Jewish apocalypticism, especially in connection with what Gershom Scholem calls "acute Messianism." [67] Throughout the Middle Ages, Jewish teachers and commentators, studying Old Testament prophecy and even astronomical phenomena, predicted the appearance of the Messiah and the establishment of a Messianic kingdom. "The hope of the Messiah did not," as Abba Hillel Silver notes, "at any time disappear in Israel." [68] The *Book of Elijah*, for example, expected the end shortly after the Arab conquest of Persia in 641, whereas the *Revelations of Simeon ben Yohai* expected the Messiah to come around 750. Other Jewish speculations, often based on the 2300-day prophecy of Daniel 8:14, expected the appearance of the Messiah in 968, 1210, 1300, 1306, 1324, 1334, 1340, and 1403, whereas the famous commentator, Rashi (1040-1105), expected the Messiah for the year 1352 or 1478.[69]

Even the great philosopher Maimonides (1135-1204), who like Augustine often opposed attempts to calculate the end, related a tradition passed on through his family that pointed to the year 1216 as the time when prophecy would be restored in Israel, a sign of the Messiah's imminent appearance. To Maimonides, belief in the Messiah is an essential article of faith: "King Messiah will arise in the future and will restore the kingship of David to its ancient condition, to its rule as it was at first. And he will rebuild the Temple and gather the exiled of Israel. And in his days all the laws will return as they were in the past." [70]

Particularly of interest in medieval Jewish Messianism is its doubling of the Messiah into two figures, Messiah ben Joseph and Messiah ben David. Messiah ben Joseph will be killed by the powerful leader of all evil on earth, Armilus (who in many details closely resembles Antichrist), whereas Messiah ben David, expected to defeat Gog and Magog as well as Armilus, will prepare the way for the end of time.[71] Thus the medieval Jewish expectation of the last things included both a suffering and a triumphant Messiah. It also included belief in a resurrection of the dead, a last judgment, and a New Jerusalem. But these are not accomplished by the Messiah, but the Lord God. The Jewish aggadic tradition considers the Messiah as a human agent of God, as the last of the great kings of the world. One apocalyptic midrash states: "Ten kings ruled from one end of the world to the other. The first king is the Holy One, blessed be He, who rules in heaven and earth." Other kings include Nimrod, Joseph, Solomon, Ahab, Nebuchadnezzar, Cyrus, and Alexander the Great. At the end of history will come the ninth king, the Messiah "who will rule from one end of the world to the other, as it is said, *And the stone that smote the image became a great mountain, and filled the whole earth* (Dan. 2:35). The tenth king: Kingship will return to its owner: He who was the first king, He is the last king." [72]

As Raphael Patai comments, "the era of Messianic rule was conceived as a rule of God over the whole world" when all nations would accept the Lord as ruler. "In this great triumph of the Lord over idolatrous mankind, the Messiah—the human agent whose heroic valor brought it about—becomes almost superfluous. Once the kingdom of heaven over the earth is established, his active role has come to an end, and nothing more is left for him than to sit on David's throne in Jerusalem and be the visible but passive representative of God in the world of man." [73] This expectation of a human savior, along with the notion of a double Messiah, to suffer and to conquer, to be not only defeated by an Antichristlike figure but also to overwhelm Gog and Magog, resembles in many respects the millennial Christian expectation developing in the Early Middle Ages of a future last world emperor. He would be a political leader, a new Roman (or French or German) emperor who would destroy the opponents of Christianity (especially Gog and Magog). Expected to establish his universal rule in Jerusalem and institute a time of peace and righteousness, he would ultimately resign his crown and rulership before the appearance of Antichrist.[74]

After the twelfth century, millenarian hopes were given a more explicitly spiritual and a new philosophical basis by the work of Joachim of Fiore (c. 1135-c. 1202), a Cistercian mystic who established in his own lifetime a reputation as a prophetic interpreter of history and the future. His trinitarian interpretation of salvation history was both subtle and complex and remains the subject of much dispute. To simplify, however, Joachim believed that just as the New Testament age of the Son followed the Old Testament age of the Father, so the present age would pass into a new *status* after the defeat of Antichrist. Taking place within history, this age would be characterized by a reformed church under the direction of spiritual orders. As Bernard McGinn states, Joachim's "scheme was in one sense a revival of early Christian millenarianism; but it was also much more, a distinctive form of utopianism that sought not only to give ultimate historical validation to the institutions to which Joachim was most devoted, especially monasticism, but which also represented an original viewpoint on the theme of *reformatio* conceived of as a new divine irruption into history rather than as a return to the past." [75]

It is not clear that Joachim conceived this new age as the millennium. He described it as a time of "justice on earth and an abundance of peace," when the Jews would be converted and the dragon imprisoned "in the remaining nations which are at the ends of the earth." [76] Yet he remained orthodox in refusing to predict its exact timing and duration, and there is some evidence that he thought of the age as a relatively short period before the final battle with Gog and Magog and the advent of Christ.[77] Unfortunately, as Morton Bloomfield has recently observed, in the later Middle Ages "Joachim's name became a byword for every fanatic and apocalyptic." [78] Joachim's followers at first conceived of the new age in largely spiritual terms, to begin in the year 1260. With the passage of time, however, Joachim's restrained conclusions based on careful exegesis were replaced by a more fervent millenarianism. Expectations of a future age of peace and righteousness to take place within history before the second advent of Christ became politicized, polemical weapons in the continuing conflict between papacy and empire. They were also taken over by a wide range of late medieval radical groups, from the Spiritual Franciscans, who condemned papal corruption, on the one hand, to various revolutionary and communistic movements attempting to usher in the millennium before the second coming of Christ.[79]

Thus the Late Middle Ages witnessed some of the more radical excesses of millenarianism, the very developments that Augustine had sought to forestall in his opposition to chiliasm and popular apocalypticism. Nevertheless, our modern fascination with this late medieval radicalism, its opposition to the papacy, and its "pre-Reformation" prophetic zeal should not blind us to the fact that even in the Late Middle Ages the advent hope was an essential element of orthodox Christian belief, generally Augustinian in emphasis and usually rejecting millenarianism and deterministic predictions concerning the end of time. Medieval Christians continued to believe that they were living in the last age and that man's pilgrimage in a sinful world would soon end. The hope of Christ's return as judge and Saviour remained constant throughout the Middle Ages.

NOTES

[1] Guerric of Igny, *Liturgical Sermons I,* Cistercian Fathers Series 8 (Shannon; 1971), p. 3.

[2] For example, in his wide-ranging study, *The Prophetic Faith of Our Fathers: The Historical Development of Prophetic Interpretation* (Washington, D.C., 1950), LeRoy Edwin Froom refers to "the prophetic faith of the fathers of the early Christian church, the fathers of the Reformation church, and of the colonial American church, as well as those of more modern times" (Vol. I, p. 16). The fathers of the medieval church are conspicuously absent here, and when Froom does discuss their work it is often in a negative light. In general Froom's compilation of sources is helpful, but his commentary on the medieval theologians and his conclusions should be read with caution. A very helpful recent work emphasizing the continuity of medieval and reformation thought is Stephen Ozment's *The Age of Reform, 1250-1550: An Intellectual and Religious History of Late Medieval and Reformation Europe* (New Haven, 1980).

[3] See Henry Bettenson, ed., *Documents of the Christian Church,* 2d ed. (London, 1963), pp. 23-36.

[4] Ozment, *The Age of Reform,* p. 2. See also Peter Brown, *Augustine of Hippo* (Berkeley, 1967).

[5] According to Bernard McGinn, Augustine "was the most incisive opponent of the apocalyptic interpretation of history in the patristic period," and "the fountainhead of all antiapocalyptic eschatology in the Middle Ages." See *Visions of the End: Apocalyptic Traditions in the Middle Ages,* Records of Civilization: Sources and Studies 96 (New York, 1979), p. 26. This excellent collection of medieval apocalyptic materials henceforth will be cited as McGinn, *VE.*

[6] Augustine *City of God* 20. 7, trans. David Knowles (Baltimore, 1972). All references to the *City of God* are to this translation.

[7] *Ibid.,* 20. 9.

[8] J. Pelikan, *The Emergence of the Catholic Tradition (100-600),* vol. 1 of *The Christian Tradition: A History of the Development of Doctrine* (Chicago, 1971), p. 126. See also Augustine *City of God* 20. 9.

[9] See G. C. Berkouwer, *The Return of Christ,* trans. and ed. James Van Oosterom, and Marlin J. Van Elderen (Grand Rapids, 1972), pp. 141-146.

[10] See Augustine *City of God* 20. 11-12. 13. 19. 23. 30; Richard Kenneth Emmerson, *Antichrist in the Middle Ages: A Study of Medieval Apocalypticism, Art, and Literature* (Seattle, 1981), pp. 65, 66. Henceforth cited as Emmerson, *AMA.*

[11] Augustine *City of God* 18. 53. See also 52.

[12] *Ibid.,* 20. 1.

[13] *Ibid.,* 21. 15.

[14] Pelikan, *The Growth of Medieval Theology (600-1300),* vol. 3 of *The Christian Tradition* (Chicago, 1978), p. 156. Froom, *Prophetic Faith of Our Fathers,* states that "it is not to be supposed that the doctrine of the Second Advent itself was abandoned or spiritualized away after Augustine's time."—Vol. I, p. 490.

[15] McGinn, *VE,* p. 64.

[16] Guerric of Igny, *Liturgical Sermons,* p. 6.

[17] John Scotus *Periphyseon* 5. 38, ed. and trans. Myra L. Uhlfelder (Indianapolis, 1976). According to Richard C. Dales, Eriugena argued that the world was both eternal and made by God. It "is eternal through participation in its eternal cause, the Word of God"; however, its "corporeal multiplicity" is temporal, beginning with the fall of man and concluding "with the reunion of man (and with him the physical universe) with God." See "Discussions of the Eternity of the World During the First Half of the Twelfth Century," *Speculum* 57 (1982): 496.

[18] John Scotus *Periphyseon* 5. 37. On Eriugena, see Pelikan, *Growth of Medieval Theology,* pp/ 95-105.

[19] J.H.L. Kengen ed., *Memoriale Credencium: A Late Middle English Manual of Theology for Lay People* (diss., University of Nijmegen, 1979), p. 203. I have modernized the original Middle English.

[20] Guerric of Igny, *Liturgical Sermons,* pp. 2, 3.

[21] *Ibid.,* p. 2.

[22] *Ibid.,* p. 3.

[23] Leo the Great, Sermon IX, in Charles Lett Feltoe, trans., *A Select Library of Nicene and Post-Nicene Fathers of the Christian Church,* 2d. ser. 1894; rpt. (Grand Rapids, 1979), pp. 118, 119.

[24] Thomas Aquinas *Summa Theologiae* 2a2ae. 171. 3, in Roland Potter, ed. trans., *Summa Theologiae* (New York,

1970), vol. 45, p. 17. To Thomas, prophecy deals not only with future events but also with "all that is needed for the instruction of the believing people of God." See Potter, ed., *Summa Theologiae*, p. 19. On the interpretation of Revelation in the Middle Ages, see Wilhelm Kamlah, *Apokalypse und Geschichtstheologie: Die mittelalterliche Auslegung der Apokalypse vor Joachim vor Fiore*, Historische Studien 285 (Berlin, 1935). For a brief survey of the early medieval commentaries, see Barbara Nolan, *The Gothic Visionary Perspective* (Princeton, 1977), pp. 5-9. Nolan's work properly emphasizes the importance of the Apocalypse in medieval culture, although her "prophetic" readings of medieval literature are uneven. See my review in *Modern Philology* 77 (1980): 409-411.

[25] Ambrosius Autpertus *Expositionis in Apocalypsin Libri X*, ed. R. Weber, Corpus Christianorum Continuatio Mediaevalis (Tournrai, 1975), p. 437. I have translated the original Latin. Berengaudus, *Expositio Super Septem Visiones Libra Apocalypsis*, ed. Jacques Paul Migne, *Patrologia Latina*, vol. 17, p. 916. The identity of Berengaudus is uncertain; his works are included with those of Ambrose.

[26] Augustine *On Christian Doctrine* 3. 30. 43, trans. D. W. Robertson, Jr., Library of Liberal Arts (Indianapolis, 1958).

[27] For the medieval identification of apocalyptic images with Antichrist, see Emmerson, *AMA*, pp. 34-49. For a recent discussion of the Tyconian concept of recapitulation, see Yves Christe, "Traditions litteraires et iconographiques dans l'interpretation des images apocalyptiques," in *L'Apocalypse de Jean: Traditions Exegetiques et Iconographiques, IIIe-XIIIe Siecles*, Etudes et Documents 11, Section d'Histoire de la Faculte des Lettres de l'Universite de Geneve (Geneva, 1979), pp. 109-134.

[28] Adso *Libellus de Antichristo*, trans. Bernard McGinn, *Apocalyptic Spirituality* (New York, 1979), p. 96. On the work's significance, see Emmerson, "Antichrist as Anti-Saint: The Significance of Abbot Adso's *Libellus de Antichristo*," *American Benedictine Review* 30 (1979): 175-190. The time expected to follow the destruction of Antichrist becomes especially important in later medieval discussions of the last things. See Robert E. Lerner's excellent essay, "Refreshment of the Saints: The Time After Antichrist as a Station for Earthly Progress in Medieval Thought," *Traditio* 32 (1976): 97-144.

[29] See M. D. Chenu's excellent essay, "Theology and the New Awareness of History," in Jerome Taylor and Lester K. Little, ed. and trans. *Nature, Man, and Society in the Twelfth Century: Essays on New Theological Perspectives in the Latin West* (Chicago, 1968), pp.162-201.

[30] Rupert of Deutz, *Commentariorum in Ioannis Apocalypsin* (Nuremberg, 1526); Richard of St. Victor, *In Apocalypsim Ioannis*, ed. Jacques Paul Migne, *Patrologia latina*, 196:683-888; and Joachim of Fiore, *Expositio in Apocalypsim Ioannis* (Venice, 1527; rpt. Frankfurt, 1964).

[31] See Emmerson, *AMA*, p. 19; and Kamlah, *Apokalypse und Geschichtstheologie*, pp. 64-70.

[32] Alexander Minorita, *Expositio in Apocalypsim*, ed. Alois Wachtel, Monumenta Germaniae Historica, Quellen zur Geistesgeschichte des Mittelalters 1 (Weimar, 1955). For Hugh of St. Cher, see his *Postillae in Universa Biblia*, printed in various fifteenth- and sixteenth-century editions; for Nicholas of Lyra, see his *Postillae*, which often accompanies the interlinear commentaries of the *Glossa Ordinaria*, available in numerous early editions, including *Biblia Sacra Cum Glossis* (Venice, 1588).

[33] On the concept of world ages, see Emmerson, *AMA*, pp. 12-18.

[34] Otto of Freising, *The Two Cities, Records of Civilization*, trans. Charles C. Mierow (New York, 1928), p. 456.

[35] Felix Fellner, "The 'Two Cities' of Otto of Freising and its Influence on the Catholic Philosophy of History," *Catholic Historical Review* 20 (1934-1935): 169.

[36] Vincent of Beauvais, *Speculum Historiale* (Strassburg, 1473), book 32, vol. 4, pp. 106-110.

[37] Hartmann Schedel, *Liber Chronicarum* (Nuremberg, 1493). The blank folios are cclviii-cclxi. Antichrist is introduced by a powerful woodcut on folio cclxii.

[38] Augustine *City of God*, 12. 13.

[39] A circular pattern limited to this sinful world is vicious, whereas a spiral, while apparently imitating the motion of the circle, can move from this to the next world. Thus Augustine condemns the ungodly to "walk in a circle" (*ibid.*) and Dante describes the damned in the *Inferno* as eternally imprisoned in the circles of hell. Interestingly, *Purgatorio* is structured as a spiral and *Paradiso* as a series of circles, no longer vicious since heaven is not stained by sin.

[40] Susan Powell, ed., *The Advent and Nativity Sermons From a Fifteenth-Century Revision of John Mirk's Festial*, Middle English Texts 13 (Heidelberg, 1981), p. 65. I have modernized the original Middle English in all quotations from this edition.

[41] Josef Jungmann, *The Early Liturgy to the Time of Gregory the Great*, trans. Francis A. Brunner, Liturgical Studies (Notre Dame, Ind., 1959), p. 276.

[42] Jacobus de Voragine, *Legenda Aurea*, trans. Granger Ryan and Helmust Ripperger (1941; rpt. New York, 1969), pp. 2, 3.

[43] Powell, *Advent and Nativity Sermons*, pp. 65, 66.

[44] Peter G. Cobb, "The Calendar: The History of the Christian Year," in Cheslyn Jones et al., ed., *The Study of Liturgy* (New York, 1978), p. 416.

[45] See F.J.E. Raby, *A History of Christian-Latin Poetry From the Beginnings to the Close of the Middle Ages*, 2d ed. (Oxford, 1953), pp. 443-452. On the "Quique cupitis audire" see Emmerson, *AMA*, p. 162.

[46] Anthony C. Meisel and M. L. del Mastro trans., *The Rule of Saint Benedict*, Image Books (Garden City, N.Y., 1975), pp. 52, 53.

[47] Margaret Mary Dietz, trans., *On the Misery of the Human Condition*, Library of Liberal Arts 3 (Indianapolis, 1969), books 8-17, pp. 74-85.

[48] De Voragine, *Legenda Aurea*, p. 5.

[49] R. M. Lumiansky and David Mills, ed., *The Chester Mystery Cycle*, Early English Text Society, Supplementary Series 3 (London, 1974), p. 444, ll. 173-180. I have modernized the original Middle English. On Antichrist and the last judgment in medieval drama see Emmerson, *AMA*, pp. 163-187 and the essays in *Homo, Memento Finis: The Just Judgment in Medieval Art and Drama* (Kalamazoo: Medieval Institute Publications, 1985).

[50] For a recent study, see Don Denny, "The Last Judgment Tympanum at Autun: Its Sources and Meaning," *Speculum* 57 (1982): 532-547.

[51] Brown, *Augustine of Hippo*, pp. 250, 372.

[52] Bonaventura *Collationes in Hexaemeron* 18. 10, in Jose de Vinck, trans., *The Works of Bonaventure*, vol. 5 (Paterson, N.J., 1970), p. 272.

[53] Bernard of Clairvaux *On the Song of Songs* 1, in Kilian Walsh, trans., Cistercian Fathers Series 4 (Kalamazoo, 1976), p. 37.

[54] "Cur fatui expectant finem mundi?" in Heinrich Finke, *Aus den Tagen Bonifaz VIII: Funde und Forschungen,* Vorreformationsgeschichtliche Forschungen 2 (Munster, 1902), p. 222.

[55] See the extracts from Abbo's *Apologeticus,* in McGinn, *VE,* pp. 89, 90.

[56] On eschatological themes in Old English sermons, see Milton McC. Gatch, *Preaching and Theology in Anglo-Saxon England: Aelfric and Wulfstan* (Toronto, 1977); see also Emmerson, *AMA,* pp. 150-155. Latin theological works translated into the vernacular were often given a greater sense of urgency. See, for example, Emmerson, "From *Epistola* to *Sermo:* The Old English Version of Adso's *Libellus de Antichristo,*" *Journal of English and Germanic Philology,* 82 (1983): 1-10.

[57] For Gerhoh, see McGinn, *VE,* p. 106; for Vincent, see p. 257.

[58] For Arnold, see McGinn, *VE,* pp. 223, 224.

[59] See Ione Kemp Knight, ed., *Wimbledon's Sermon,* Duquesne Studies, Philological Series 9 (Pittsburgh, 1967). On predictions of Antichrist and the end, see Emmerson, *AMA,* pp. 54-56.

[60] *A Distant Mirror: The Calamitous Fourteenth Century* (New York, 1978), p. 103. On the plague see also Otto Friedrich, *The End of the World: A History* (New York, 1982), pp. 111-142.

[61] See Marjorie Reeves, *The Influence of Prophecy in the Later Middle Ages: A Study of Joachimism* (Oxford, 1969), pp. 416-428.

[62] On the polemical use of the Antichrist tradition, see Emmerson, *AMA,* pp. 66-73.

[63] On medieval apocalyptic illustrations, see Richard Kenneth Emmerson and Suzanne Lewis, "Census an Bibliography of Medieval Manuscripts Containing Apocalypse Illustrations, c. 800-1500," *Traditio* 40 (1984), 41 (1985), and 42 (1986).

[64] Millard Meiss, *Painting in Florence and Siena After the Black Death: The Arts, Religion, and Society in the Mid-Fourteenth Century* (Princeton, 1951), p. 76.

[65] Richard Kenneth Emmerson and Ronald B. Herzman, "Antichrist, Simon Magus, and Dante's *Inferno* XIX," *Traditio* 36 (1980): 398.

[66] Emmerson, *AMA,* pp. 193-203.

[67] Gershom Scholem, "Toward an Understanding of the Messianic Idea in Judaism," *The Messianic Idea in Judaism and Other Essays on Jewish Spirituality* (New York, 1971), pp. 1-36.

[68] Abba Hillel Silver, *A History of Messianic Speculation in Israel From the First Through the Seventeenth Centuries* (Boston, 1959), p. 36.

[69] Raphael Patai, *The Messiah Texts* (New York, 1979), pp. 55, 56; see also Silver, *Messianic Speculation,* pp. 42-45, 54, 55.

[70] Quoted in Patai, *Messiah Texts,* pp. 323, 324. Maimonides' opposition to calculations of the end is best stated in his *Yad haHazaga:* "Neither should one calculate the end. The sages said, 'May the spirit of those who calculate the end be blown away.' But let him wait and believe in the matter generally, as we have explained."—Patai, *Messiah Texts,* p. 326. See also Silver, *Messianic Speculation,* pp. 66, 74, 75.

[71] Patai, *Messiah Texts,* pp. xxxiii, xxxiv. See also Scholem, "Messianic Idea in Judaism," p. 18.

[72] *Ibid.,* p. 194.

[73] *Ibid.,* p. 190.

[74] See Emmerson, *AMA,* p. 89. McGinn, *VE,* pp. 43-50, translates the early sources of the legend. For expectations of the last world emperor in the later Middle Ages and Renaissance, see Reeves, *The Influence of Prophecy in the Later Middle Ages,* pp. 295-392.

[75] McGinn, *VE,* p. 129. See also Bernard McGinn, *The Calabrian Abbot: Joachim of Fiore in the History of Western Thought* (New York, 1985).

[76] Joachim, *Liber Figurarum,* in McGinn, *VE,* p. 138.

[77] See E. R. Daniel's introduction to his edition of Joachim's *De Ultimis Tribulationibus* in Ann Williams, ed., *Prophecy and Millenarianism: Essays in Honour of Marjorie Reeves* (Harlow, 1980), pp. 165-171. In *AMA* I state that Joachim's third *status* is "a modification of the traditional millennium" and that Joachim "postpones the *eschaton* by placing Antichrist's defeat long before the end of the world." Robert Lerner, in his review of *AMA,* disagrees. He argues that "Joachim never explicitly postponed the *eschaton* by any concrete measure of time and almost certainly assumed that the third *status* between Antichrist and the end would be of very short duration. It may well be that Joachim's exegetical innovations helped clear new paths for millennialism after old ones had been blocked off, but it will not do to state without qualification that "Joachim's third *status* is a millennial age." See *Speculum* 57 (1982): 603; and "Joachim of Fiore's Breakthrough to Chiliasm," *Christianesimo nella Storia* 6 (1985): 489-512.

[78] Bloomfield, "Recent Scholarship on Joachim of Fiore and His Influence," in Williams, *Prophecy and Millenarianism,* p. 38.

[79] The standard study of radical millenarianism in the Middle Ages is Norman Cohn's *The Pursuit of the Millennium: Revolutionay Millenarians and Mystical Anarchists of the Middle Ages,* rev. ed. (New York, 1970). See also the essays by Cohn, Howard Kaminsky, and Donald Weinstein in Sylvia L. Thrupp, ed., *Millennial Dreams in Action: Studies in Revolutionary Religious Movements* (New York, 1970).

CHAPTER 6

The Christian Hope in the
Reformation of the Sixteenth Century

V. Norskov Olsen

THE Reformation of the sixteenth century took place, theologically and religiously, in the charged atmosphere of the latter days. The Protestant Reformers acknowledged in the events of the time—whether religious, political, or social in nature—the signs of the imminence of the second advent of Christ. In an intense eschatological consciousness they saw in the historical process of the time the convulsion signifying the great day of judgment, the end of the world, and the beginning of the consummation of all things. It is more and more realized how widely eschatological preconception pervaded European intellectual and religious life in the sixteenth century, and how much people considered their own age an apocalyptic era.

Luther and Calvin, the two foremost Protestant Reformers, emphasized that the believers should look forward to and prepare for the second advent of Christ. They were convinced that a culmination of worldly history was not only real but imminent. They renewed the attitude of the early Christians regarding the last day.

Accordingly, Luther states: "I hold that the last day is not far away." The Christian is longing for that day. Luther prays: "Help us, dear Lord, and hasten the day of Thy second coming, so that we may be delivered from this evil world, the devil's kingdom, and redeemed from the terrible suffering we endure, inwardly from our conscience and outwardly from the wicked . . ., that we may obtain bodies freed from all physical and spiritual distress and fashioned like Thine own glorified body, dear Lord Jesus Christ." Commenting on the text 'Looking for that blessed hope, and the glorious appearing of the great God and our Saviour Jesus Christ" (Titus 2:13), Luther admonished his listeners with these words: "Our life ought to be one of such modesty in relation to ourselves, to our neighbour, and to God that we can confidently expect the appearing of our Lord." Next he asked this question: "Is this not the most comfort?"[1] The answer is implied.

115

Calvin says that we should "desire the advent of the Lord not in wish only, but with earnest sighs, as the most propitious of all events. He will come as a Redeemer to deliver us from an immense abyss of evil and misery, and lead us to the blessed inheritance of his life and glory." [2] Realizing that many did not have this desire, he admonished: "Woe to our stupidity, therefore, which exercises such power over us, that we never think seriously about the coming of Christ, to which we ought to give our whole attention." [3] On account of the significance of this event, "Satan aims directly at the throat of the church, when he destroys faith in the coming of Christ." [4]

The believer's faith in the second advent of Christ would be a spur to holier living; likewise, the hope of the advent would sustain the Christian in the sorrows and burdens of life and bring peace and joy into his existence. Calvin tells us that if "heaven is our country, what can the earth be but a place of exile" [5] where we are preparing for the glory of the heavenly kingdom. "For the Lord hath ordained, that those who are ultimately to be crowned in heaven must maintain a previous warfare on earth, that they may not triumph before they have overcome the difficulties of war, and obtained the victory. Another reason is that we here begin to experience in various ways a foretaste of the divine benignity, in order that our hope and desire may be whetted for its full manifestation." [6]

Luther was fond of table discussions on all aspects of doctrine and life. These table talks have been preserved for posterity to read and evaluate. On such an occasion in 1532 the last day was the theme of discussion. Luther's answer to a question was "I hope I may live until the last day." The statement, of course, needed clarification, and Luther gave it: "The last day is just before the door. My calendar has run out; I know of no more in my Scriptures." Luther identified himself with Noah confronting an unbelieving world. In 1541 he noted that there were 126 years between the death of Adam and the birth of Noah, and that the same number of years had transpired since the death of Huss. [7]

Calvin did not, like Luther, emphasize a more or less exact time for the advent, nor did he fall for the temptation, so common in the century, to calculate apocalyptic time periods. He solved the problem of the imminent advent in these words: "The solution is easy, for it is at hand with regard to God, with whom 'one day is as a thousand years' (2 Peter 3:8). In the meantime, the Lord would have us be constantly waiting for him in such a way as not to limit him to a certain time. 'Watch,' says he, 'for ye know neither the day nor the hour' (Matt. 24:42)." [8] His real concern was "that believers may be prepared at all times." "Now Christ designed that the day of his coming should be hid from us, that, being in suspense, we might be as it were upon watch." [9] Since the final age had already begun with the first advent of Christ, "we must remember this principle that from the time when Christ once appeared, there is nothing left for the faithful, but with suspended minds ever to look forward to his second coming." [10] In his comments on the resurrection chapter of 1 Corinthians 15 he reminds his readers that the second advent should "be looked for by the saints every hour." [11]

Christ's sermons regarding the signs of His coming and the end of the world, as recorded in the Gospels, in Matthew 24, Mark 13, and Luke 17 and 21, formed the basis for the Reformers' discussion of the same topic. Says Luther: "I do not wish to force anyone to believe as I do; neither will I permit anyone to deny me the right to believe that the last day is near at hand. These words and signs of Christ (Luke

21:25-36) compel me to believe that such is the case." [12]

The words of Christ "And this gospel of the kingdom shall be preached in all the world for a witness unto all nations; and then shall the end come" (Matt. 24:14) were fulfilled in the Protestant Reformation with its renewal of the gospel, and this fulfillment had but one meaning: the imminent approach of the end. [13] Writes Luther: "I believe that the last day is not far off, for the gospel is now making its last effort." He compares the preached gospel to a light that brings forth a great burst of illumination just prior to its extinction, or to a sick man who just before he dies appears as if restored, and then in an instant is gone. [14] While no age had seen so many signs on earth and in the sky, nothing witnessed so much to the nearness of the end as the brightness of the evangelical light. Since the days of the apostles there had not been such a light. With the return to the study of the Bible in its original languages, the gospel was preached nearly as purely as in the time of the apostles. It was at least purer than at the time of Augustine and Jerome. [15]

The preaching of the gospel included a proclamation of warning regarding the final judgment, for Christ was appointed by the Father to judge the world. The true ministers of Christ are called "the criers or apparitors of the highest judge." [16] Although the preaching of the gospel was a sign of the end, Luther and Calvin did not believe in the conversion of mankind at large. On the contrary, the majority would not accept the warning message. Accordingly Calvin states: "There is no reason, therefore, why any person should expect the conversion of the world." [17] This state of indifference was another sign of the last days, fulfilling the prediction of Christ "As the days of Noe were, so shall also the coming of the Son of man be" (Matt. 24:37). "So now Christ declares that the last age of the world will be in a state of stupid indifference, so that men will think of nothing but the present life, and will extend their cases to a long period, pursuing their ordinary course of life, as if the world were always to remain in the same condition." [18]

The final phase prior to the second advent is noticeable not only by a renewal of the gospel but also by the appearance of Antichrist; it is marked by the final struggle between the true church and the false, or apostate, church, culminating in the second advent of Christ. From the vantage point of this struggle, Luther and the other Reformers looked back upon history and perceived the fall of the church and the development of Antichrist, which had its seat within the church in the form of the papacy.

During the stormy year of 1520 Luther wrote a treatise, *On the Babylonian Captivity of the Church,* that deals with the seven sacraments and marks his final break with the Church of Rome. Here we find the following statement:
"The papacy is of a truth the kingdom of Babylon, yea, very Antichrist! For who is 'the man of sin' and 'the son of perdition' but he that with his doctrines and his law increased sins and the perdition of souls in the church, while he sitteth in the church as if he were God? All this the papal tyranny has fulfilled, and more than fulfilled, these many centuries; it has extinguished faith, obscured the sacraments, and oppressed the gospel; but its own laws, which are not only impious and sacrilegious, but even barbarous and foolish, it has enjoined and multiplied world without end." [19]

In the eschatological scene of Luther the threats of the Turks assumed a prominent place. He associated the Turks with the papacy and the battle of Armageddon. The pope, being Antichrist, sat in the temple of God, while the

Turks, being the beast of Revelation, persecuted Christ from outside the church. Thus the papacy and the Turks were respectively the internal and external enemy of the church and became the apocalyptic people of Gog and Magog. When Luther heard of a reported treaty between the turks and the papacy, he expressed the opinion that the world would not long exist. The Turks were God's punishment against the social injustices and the religious indifference of the German people. What the Jews and the city of Jerusalem had once suffered, the German nation would now experience, for after the light of the gospel had shone, there would come contempt, followed by the last judgment. The church of Christ remained as a poor little band, while the church of Antichrist comprised the greater number. The abomination would remain to the judgment day; the church of Christ should therefore guard itself from deterioration until the return of Christ.[20]

Luther often referred to the saying of Christ that the last days would be like those of Noah before the Flood. There was no doubt in his mind that the present age was comparable with Noah's. The contempt of the world for the Word of God and the incredible decay in every aspect of life, which had come as a natural consequence of the indifference to the gospel, seemed obvious. That which previously had happened before the Flood, before the destruction of Sodom and Gomorrah, before the Babylonian captivity, and before the destruction of Jerusalem, now was taking place in Germany. The conflict between the unbelieving world and the followers of Christ could only be resolved by the second advent of Christ.[21]

Luther therefore emphasized that while the signs of the last days "are numerous and great," yet "very few will understand and see them as signs." Therefore, "the last day comes so unexpectedly that the world, though it could see and hear the signs of the last day, does not believe but rather lives in great security and laughs it off with the words 'Oh, you dear fool, are you afraid that the heavens are caving in and that we are living in the last day?'" On the other hand, Luther described the true followers of Christ as those who will be looking on these signs as genuine even though they do not know the day or the hour.[22]

The achievements of the Renaissance and humanism prior to the Reformation were considerable. The liberal arts flourished, including the study of Hebrew, Greek, Latin, and classical literature. The enthusiasm for learning was enhanced by new inventions such as Gutenberg's typecasting mold. During Luther's time or later, Copernicus, Tycho Brahe, and Johannes Kepler gave man a new view of the universe. Columbus, Vasco da Gama, and Magellan opened a new vista of the world in which man lived.

Luther asserted: "The history of the centuries that have passed since the birth of Christ nowhere reveals conditions like those of the present." It is revealed in much building and planting, eating and drinking. Clothing seems to have reached its limit in expensiveness, commerce encircles the globe, and all kinds of art have been produced. Men are looking "into the mysteries of things, [so] that today a boy of twenty knows more than twenty doctors formerly knew." Reference was also made to inventions such as firearms and other implements of war. The increased knowledge of languages, which had made the restoration of the gospel possible, was a special sign that the world had its opportune moment. Accordingly Luther acknowledged his debt to humanistic studies, Writing to the humanist Eobanus

Hessus, he told that the revival of languages stood to the Reformation as John the Baptist to Christ. To Luther all this indicated that he lived in the latter days. Likewise, the social and political conditions of the time indicated the same. True enough, there had always been distress and perplexity among the nations, but never so intense as in Luther's own time.[23]

The strange phenomena in nature—the darkening of the sun and moon, the falling of the stars, earthquakes, et cetera—predicted by Christ as signs of the end were also discussed by the Reformers.[24] These signs were considered as having been fulfilled in eclipses, fallen meteors, earthquakes, floods, et cetera, that had taken place in their own time.

The first advent of Christ was largely unknown save to the Jews, but His second coming will be public and universal. He will come in physical form and all will see Him (Rev 1:7), and the heavenly host will accompany Him. It is a day of joy for those who look for Him.[25]

Calvin expressed his firm conviction regarding the second advent of Christ: "For he will descend from heaven in visible form, in like manner as he was seen to ascend, and appear to all, with the ineffable majesty of his kingdom, the splendour of immortality, the boundless power of divinity, and an attending company of angels. Hence we are told to wait for the Redeemer against that day on which he will separate the sheep from the goats, and the elect from the reprobate, and when not one individual either of the living or the dead shall escape his judgment. From the extremities of the universe shall be heard the clang of the trumpet summoning all to his tribunal; both those whom that day shall find alive, and those whom death shall previously have removed from the society of the living." [26]

In a sermon on Matthew 25:31-46, where Christ discussed the last judgment, Luther gives a vivid picture of Christ's second coming: "He will return on the last day with great power, and glorious majesty, and with him the full army of angels. He will sit on the clouds and all will see him. None can hide or flee; rather he must appear. It will be a beautiful judgment and an unspeakably glorious majesty with all the angels present and he in their midst." [27]

Luther's hope in the second advent of Christ was maintained among his pupils and friends. Nikolaus Herman expresses it in this way:

> "For your coming, Lord, we're waiting all,
> and listening for the trumpet's call.
> Lord Jesus, come—do not delay.
> And help your church—we are afraid." [28]

In His great prophetic talk Christ had warned against time-setting for His second coming, and had also warned that false Christs would arise. Over and over again during the Christian Era, Messianic movements arose within Judaism, fixing dates for the coming of the Messiah or led by someone claiming to be the Anointed One.[29] Messianic speculations that were especially prominent among sixteenth-century Jews continued on into the seventeenth century.

Messianism generally thrives on suffering. At the close of the fifteenth century Jews were expelled from Spain, Portugal, and many German provinces. In the sixteenth century they were the object of fierce persecution in Italy. Messianic interest was also prompted by the political and religious situation, as for example the increased power of the Turks in Europe, the decline of the papacy, and the rift in Christendom. Abba Hillel Silver mentions three pseudomessiahs who appeared in the first half of the sixteenth century and ten major Messianic calculators setting various dates for the coming of the Messiah also in the same century.[30]

The eschatological thoughts of the sixteenth century were formulated within the framework of millennialism. The Reformers of the classical Protestant movements adhered to an Augustinian millennial view in a modified form: Their era, the last period of history, would culminate in the literal second advent of Christ, the resurrection of the dead, the destruction of the present world, and the creation of a new earth. Extreme Radical Reformers (Thomas Münzer being a typical example), just as those of Puritan England in the seventeenth century, held the premillenial chiliastic concept that Christ would reign upon the earth, through the spiritual kingdom of His saints, for a thousand years. This glorious reign of Christ would precede the everlasting kingdom. Accordingly, the fifth kingdom of Daniel was still to be fulfilled in a golden age, and it was not, as in the Augustinian view, brought to consummation in the Christian church.

Opposition to the latter view drove the Radicals to break with the *corpus Christianum* since the time of Constantine. In their millennial views they considered themselves in perfect harmony with the Apostolic and Ante-Nicene Fathers. Seeing themselves as God's chosen instrument to herald the new millennial age, the Radicals saw their task not as a reformation, but as a restitution of what they believed to be apostolic Christianity. In their different eschatological concepts, the magisterial and Radical Reformers both recognized that there was a gulf between them that neither was able to bridge. The Radicals' relationship to the state and the magisterial church, as well as their soteriological outlook, were shaped by their eschatology.

The two basic concepts of the millennium, with variations, reflect different views of eschatology during the period under study. Protestant time-setting for the advent is likewise rooted here. English expositors illustrate the latter.

The Venerable Bede (673?-735), the father of English historiography, firmly established the Augustinian philosophy of history.[31] Likewise, Thomas Aquinas (1225?-1274), the "Angelic Doctor" of the Latin Church, perpetuated the Augustinian historiography as the orthodox version. At the same time he also asserted that the "thousand two hundred sixty days mentioned in the Apocalypse . . . denote all the time during which the church endures, and not any definite number of years."[32] This is undoubtedly a criticism of Joachim of Floris' periodization of church history.

In his book *The Last Age of the Church (1356)*, John Wycliffe (1329?-1384) expressed his belief that the present age was the last.[33] Two Lollard treatises of the fourteenth century, *The Praier and Complaynte of the Ploweman Unto Christe*[34] and the *Lanterne of Light*,[35] spoke about the struggle with the papacy, which to them was Antichrist, stressing that this struggle would culminate in the second advent of Christ and the final judgment.

William Tyndale (1492?-1536), with whom English Protestant historiography began, believed that history was moving toward the second advent of Christ, a literal resurrection, and the eternal kingdom. With Luther, he believed that the origin of the papal apostasy began about A.D. 600, around the time of Boniface III and Emperor Phocas. Tyndale gradually developed the theme of the great controversy between Christ and Satan in the three works *The Parable of the Wicked Mammon, The Obedience of a Christian Man,* and *The Practice of Prelates* until, with the help of Biblical apocalyptic imagery, the papacy was clearly identified as Antichrist. In Tyndale's particular reinterpretation of English history, several aspects appear significant. In medieval England from the archbishops of Canterbury Anselm and Becket to the cardinal Thomas Wolsey had been part of an international conspiracy led by Antichrist disguised as the pope, seeking to make the English kings their submissive servants. During this period the original Christianity that had been planted in England early in the Christian Era was gradually corrupted. In spite of the force of Antichrist, God had repeatedly sent "prophets" to rebuke and warn the peoples as well as to lead them back to the Scriptures as the true foundation of truth. The lesson to be drawn from the war between the elect and the apostate church was that God's elect could expect pitiless persecution before the true gospel could finally prevail. Here in embryo is the Protestantizing of English history.

It is within the framework of Tyndale's view of English church history that men such as Robert Barnes, Nicholas Ridley, Hugh Latimer, John Philpot, John Bradford, John Hooper, and Thomas Cranmer preached, wrote, and even suffered martyrdom.

John Bale (1495-1563) in his major work, *The Image of Both Churches,* expounds historically the struggle between the true church and the false church, culminating in the second coming of Christ.[36] His familiarity with expositors of the Apocalypse is obvious from his tabulations of interpreters from Justin Martyr and Irenaeus to Luther and Calvin.[37]

The major steps in the changes of the interpretation of the millennium and related apocalyptic time periods and images, with resulting changes in eschatology, are traceable in the works of John Bale, John Foxe, John Napier, and Thomas Brightman.

John Foxe (1516-1587) is best known for his signal work *Acts and Monuments,* commonly called *The Book of Martyrs,* but he also authored a Latin exposition of the first seventeen chapters of the Apocalypse.[38] He towers above all the Englishmen who contributed to shaping English history into a Protestant mold.[39]

The Magisterial Reformers sought to establish the validity of the Protestant Reformation in the light of a Protestant view of church history. Having modified the Augustinian millennial view with the eschatology of Christ and Paul, they saw the Protestant revival of the gospel, as opposed to Antichrist's teachings, as a sign of the end. Not only the Reformers' actual relationship to the state but also their view of history entitled them to be called Magisterial Reformers. Constantine and later emperors who supported the church were, from their viewpoint, with good reason called Christian emperors.

Rome had become Antichrist by usurping the power of Christian emperors, but the Reformation sought to restore godly princes to their former Christian responsibility and authority, which should be used in a positive way to advance the evangelical church. That a godly ruler should become a second Josiah or Constantine was a necessary part of the struggle against Antichrist. For example, Luther and others considered Frederick the Wise to be the eschatological emperor,[40] and Wittenberg itself was elected to be God's chosen city as Jerusalem had been in former days. But any national self-consciousness that emerged as a result of the religious leadership of the godly prince was framed within the eschatological view of the end, and included neither the chiliastic concepts of the early church nor the millennial view of the Radical Reformers and the Puritans of the civil war years.

John Foxe's work *Acts and Monuments* was written in the atmosphere of the last days, and Foxe, with the Reformers in general, posited a one-directional movement of history toward the second advent of Christ. John Sleidan writes that the believers should "not be discouraged, but should waite for deliuerance by the comming of Christ, who will come shortly after these afflictions." [41] Interpreting Revelation 14:14: "And I looked, and behold a white cloud, and upon the cloud one sat like unto the Son of man, having . . . in his hand a sharp sickle," Bale comments: "This sickle received he of his everlasting Father, such time as he gave over unto him his universal judgments. By the order of this vision should the preachers seem in the last age of the church much to admonish the people of the latter day, with the coming of Christ again to judge both the quick and the dead, as is in their creed or belief." Bale also writes that "the time is at hand to reap: for we are those upon whom the ends of the world are come." [42]

As Magisterial Reformers, Bale and Foxe placed great importance upon the ruling monarch and expressed great hopes for their country and the Reformation; however, the advent was always looming on the horizon. John Jewel, who had undoubtedly heard the hundred sermons that Bullinger preached on the Apocalypse, [43] expresses the apocalyptic views of the latter in his exposition upon the two Epistles of Paul to the Thessalonians. [44] Jewel advocates the apocalyptic idea that the Messiah can be expected to come "out of the blue." Believers should stand "in readiness, and watch, and pray, that we may be caught up into the clouds to meet our Redeemer." He says, "You shall be caught up into the clouds to meet the Lord," and he emphasizes, "We which shall see all these things shall also be caught up ourselves." [45]

John Bradford's attitude toward England is reminiscent of John Aylmer's, as quoted by William Haller, [46] in Bradford's statement that "no people heretofore hath had or now hath such cause and so great occasion . . . to be thankful, as we have." [47] But in a meditation, "On the Coming of Christ to Judgment," and a treatise, "Meditation on the Kingdom of Christ," he refers to the "Messiah out of the blue" idea. [48]

Thomas Becon calls the Church of England "a glorious church" and compares it to "a pleasant and goodly vineyard" planted by God "in the realm of England." Furthermore, God is "dressing and trimming it after the best manner." [49] Becon also refers to such apocalyptic literature as the book of Daniel, the Revelation, and 2 Thessalonians. [50] Concerning the advent of Christ, he writes that "we are not certain of the day and hour; yet we may plainly perceive that it is not far off." [51]

Edwin Sandys in one of his sermons speaks about "the mercies of God toward the church of England," and mentions, among the blessings, that God "hath given us Moses our sovereign, a prudent and gentle magistrate, who seeketh not revenge, but beareth with the muttering of the people." [52] He also offers a beautiful prayer for the queen, comparing God's help to England with the deliverance of the people out of Egypt. [53] However, in another sermon Sandys emphasizes that "all things do shew that the end of all things is at hand." [54]

These statements from Bradford, Becon, and Sandys combine a concept of a national church, or Christian commonwealth, with the idea of the Messiah soon to come in the clouds of heaven. John Foxe did the same. Incidentally, he complained that one of the faults of the papists was that they did not desire "the Lord to come in the clouds." [55]

Foxe followed the common medieval concept when he counted the binding of Satan and the beginning of the thousand-year period from the birth of Christ. However, the later and more typical view of Foxe was that the period spanned the time from Constantine to Wycliffe, or to be exact, from A.D. 324 to A.D. 1324. In making this change, Foxe formulated a church history periodization that was original with him. Foxe arrived at this new view while studying the persecution of the early church in light of the book of Revelation, especially the numbers in chapters 11, 12, and 13.[56] In these chapters several time periods of the church are mentioned in connection with the persecution. The periods are listed as 1260 days; three and a half days; a time, times, and half a time; and forty-two months. According to Foxe, these numbers all refer to the same time period; yet the problem he faced was that "all this by computation coming but to three years and a half, came nothing near the long continuance of these persecutions, which lasted three hundred years." [57]

In Foxe's study of this vexing problem, a voice said within him, "Thou fool, count these months by sabbaths, as the weeks of Daniel are counted as sabbaths." [58] Thus, multiplying the forty-two months by seven, he was given 294 days. Then, reckoning each day for a year, he arrived at 294 years, which should comprise the length of the persecution in the early church. Foxe counted this period from A.D. 30 to A.D. 324. By this calculation, Foxe established some specific points: (1) the importance of Constantine as a Christian emperor; (2) the cessation of the ten persecutions of the early church at the time of Constantine; (3) a thousand-year period from Constantine to Wycliffe (A.D. 324-A.D.1324); (4) the loosing of Satan about A.D.1324 by the decay of the papacy, developed during the previous centuries; (5) a new three-hundred-year period of ten persecutions dating from the time when Wycliffe began to preach the gospel; and (6) a time calculation that fixed the coming of the Lord at the end of the second 294-year period. The actual date he gives is 1586, but, he says, "the Lord knows whether the period will be shortened for the elect's sake." [59] In another connection he writes that this period "appears to leave only eight years." [60] Foxe's study of the various symbols of the book of Revelation also convinced him that the Lord could be expected in his own time.

In his closing remarks about the seventh trumpet, Foxe brings the nearness of the second advent into renewed focus when he writes: "This seventh trumpet certainly is not far off, when by a marvellous inversion of things and times the past shall grow old and all things new, a new heaven and a new earth shall be constituted." [61] Like the seventh trumpet, the seventh vial[62] describes last events and points out the time of "the supreme day of judgment, which will bring an end to all things and all times." [63]

Whatever message Foxe conveys in his interpretations of the various images of the Revelation, his explanations are always written in the charged atmosphere of the last days. The same is the case in the *Acts and Monuments,* in which Foxe compares worldly soldiers with the soldiers of Christ. Referring to the latter, he states: "To be shorte, they declare to the worlde what true fortitude is, and a way to conquer, which standeth not in the power of man, but in the hope of the resurrection, to come, and is now, I trust, at hand." [64] In the opening paragraph of his letter "To the True and Faithful Congregation of Christes Vniuersall Church," Foxe wishes "aboundance of all peace and tranquilities, with the speedy commying of Christ the Spouse, to make an ende of all mortall miserie." [65] The picture of the two witnesses of Revelation 11 illustrates the resurgence of the gospel, signifying to Foxe the imminent approach of the end. [66]

John Foxe was followed by John Napier (1550-1617), a distinguished Scottish mathematician and devoted adherent of the Protestant cause who likewise began the thousand-year period with the cessation of persecution at the time of Constantine. [67] However, there were some basic differences in their views of church history. For Foxe the thousand years meant a period of no major persecution against the church. He considered the condition of the visible church excellent in the beginning of the period, and tolerable for several centuries following, but toward the end of the period anti-Christian forces became evident. For Napier, on the other hand, the thousand years covered from its very beginning a time of apostasy in the visible church, and the binding of Satan meant that he was held back from stirring up universal wars. Accordingly, the loosing of Satan was fulfilled in the wars begun by Osman I about A.D. 1300. [68]

Like Foxe, Napier finds a very close connection between the 1260 days of chapter 12 of the book of Revelation and the thousand years of chapter 20, [69] but here also the application reveals Napier's different concept of the visible church since the time of Constantine. In his exposition of the book of Revelation, Napier lays down thirty-six basic propositions. The first states that "in propheticall dates of daies, weekes, moneths, yeares, euerie common propheticall day is taken for a yeare." [70] Accordingly, the 1260 days stand for 1260 literal years. In the calculations of Napier these 1260 years began about A.D. 300 [71] and covered the reign of Antichrist.

Napier writes "that betwixt the yeare of Christ 300, and 316, hath the Antichristian and Papisticall reign begun, reigning vniuersalle and without any debatable contradiction 1260 yeares; and so (as is said) about the yeare of God 1560 began their first publike decay, and the open repining against their kingdom to their confusion, ever more and more." [72] During these years "the whole outward visible church lay whollie as dead, and corrupted with Papisticall errours, and began not to bee raised vp nor quickened by the work of life, till after the yeare of God, a thousande three hundred." [73] During these years only the invisible church was the true church. [74]

Thus Napier reacted against Foxe and the Magisterial Reformers' concept of the golden era of the Constantinian church. However, he was still within a modified Augustinian view of the millennium, believing that the era in which he lived was the last. He fixed a number of dates by manipulating apocalyptic numbers. The 1260 years ended in 1576, and other apocalyptic periods expired respectively in 1541, 1590, 1639, 1688, and the last in 1786. On account of the belief that God would shorten the time for the sake of the elect, he expected the final judgment to take place sometime between 1688 and 1700. [75]

At the close of the Elizabethan reign the premillennial idea was advocated. Accordingly, it should be noticed that Napier believed, with the Reformers, in the second advent of Christ, bringing the last judgment, the resurrection, the second and everlasting death, followed by eternity.[76] The description of the New Jerusalem in Revelation 21 refers to the eternal heavenly kingdom; thus he speaks against the sect of "Chiliasts or Millenaries, who thought our reign with Christ to be on earth, and temporal."[77] It should be noticed that Napier's exposition on the Revelation "occupies a prominent place in Scottish ecclesiastical history, for it is the earliest Scottish work on the interpretation of the scriptures."[78]

Napier's concept of the church was further emphasized by Thomas Brightman (1562-1607), a Puritan scholar and one of the founders of English Presbyterianism. Like Foxe and Napier, he explained the thousand years as the span of time from Constantine to Wycliffe.[79] That Satan was bound during this period meant that there was "brought in such a manner of government, as left the open enemies no power to dominere and tyrannize in and over the church, as they had been accustomed to do in former times."[80] However, Brightman also emphasized that Antichrist reigned during the thousand years,[81] since this period and the 1260 years began at the same time.[82] Thus Brightman and Napier were one in their application of the 1260 years but differed from Foxe.

In evaluating the role played by Constantine in the history of the church, as viewed by Foxe, Napier, and Brightman, we must distinguish two points: the importance of Constantine at a certain given time in history and then the status of the church from the time of Constantine. Foxe praises both Constantine and the visible church for some centuries after Constantine. Napier and Brightman do the former in no less glowing terms than Foxe, but not the latter.

In spite of this specific role predicted and fulfilled in Constantine, according to Brightman, Antichrist, "vvish Beast is the Pope of Rome vvho sprunge vp at once vvith Constantine, vvas made great by the Nicene Counceel,"[83] and for a thousand years "from Constantine the church abidinge in most secret lurkinge places, vvas together with Christ, but did not great metter famous and remarkeable by the vvorld. Those 1000 yeares being ended, Wicklefe preacheth the gospel in the world."[84] Napier and Brightman seem to say that Constantine, in granting peace to the church, fulfilled the role given him by God, yet the visible church became the seat of Antichrist. Therefore, although Queen Elizabeth had played a God-given part in the Reformation, her established church could still become the seat of Antichrist.

So far Brightman agrees with Napier, but he moves a major step further from Foxe by making a double application of the thousand-year period. He writes: "And they shall reigne vvith him a thousand yeares. These thousand yeares begin, where the former ended, that is in the yeare 1300; whereby continuance of the truth is promised for a thousand yeares, from the restoring thereof (of which we haue spoken) in these our nations of Europe of which also this first resurrection belongeth."[85]

Understood spiritually, a second "first resurrection" would take place and, in comparison with the first at the time of Constantine, it would be greater, for Christ would reign "most gloriously uupon earth, by ministery of his seruants, so as he shall aduance his church vnto the highest honour that can be, euen aboue all empire that is."[86] The Holy City and the new earth of Revelation (chapters 21 and 22) are symbols describing the new millennial church, which the Jews will join; thus, Jerusalem "shall be sealed vpon earth."[87]

We have seen an evolution in the writings of Bale, Foxe, Napier, and

Brightman regarding the millennium. Bale and at first Foxe held the Augustinian concept, but Foxe modified it by placing the beginning with Constantine and giving the period an exact numerical value. Napier adhered to the Foxian interpretation, including the importance of Constantine, but he saw in Bishop Sylvester the embryo of Antichrist (being a member of the Kirk of Scotland and one of the Edinburgh commissioners to the general assembly in 1588, and in 1593 appointed one of the committee members to ensure the safety of the Kirk, Napier favored the Presbyterian form of church government), and therefore fixed the beginning of the 1260 years at the same time as the beginning of the millennium. However, he adhered to the Augustinian idea of the last age.

Brightman, being one of the fathers of English Presbyterianism, held Napier's view of the 1000- and 1260-year periods; thus both men reacted against Foxe's view of the Constantinian church. From a reference to the Whitgift-Cartwright controversy (episcopacy versus presbytery) it is evident that Brightman stood on the side of the latter.[88] When Foxe praised Constantine and Elizabeth, it was as a Magisterial Reformer, but when Brightman did the same, it was within the framework of what became seventeenth-century apocalyptic expectations of the millennium as a new age on earth. Thus there was a great gulf between Foxe and Brightman, and not the former but the latter was the ancestor of the apocalyptic hopes of the 1640s.

Joseph Mead, or Mede (1586-1638), broke fully away from the Augustinian-Foxian tradition and is the link between Brightman and the premillenialism of the seventeenth century. His work *Clavis Apocalyptica* was first published in 1627 and reprinted in 1632. He thus belongs to the seventeenth century.

Reference has been made to the Radical Reformers, and some specific features of their eschatology should be noticed. Past historians spoke only about the Reformation initiated by the Protestant Reformers, and opposition to it by the Roman Catholics in the Counter-Reformation. Now a third and equally important movement is recognized: the Radical Reformation. We refer to their leaders as Radical Reformers.

Michael Servetus, who on account of his anti-Trinitarian views was arrested and put to death by the city council of Geneva in 1553 under the direction of Calvin and with the approval of most other Reformers, exemplifies, in the application of the 1260-day period of Revelation 12, a shift that reflects the Radicals' view of the fall of the church.[89]

Servetus' main theological work is his *Christianismi Restitutio,* in which he claims to be a restorer of Christianity, no doubt in opposition to Calvin's *Institutes of the Christian Religion.* Like Joachim of Floris, he considered the 1260 days to be actual years, but covering a period in which the true church of God's elect was found, not in, but outside the *corpus Christianum.* The period began with Constantine and the Council of Nicaea. It was believed that the doctrines of the Trinity and infant baptism were endorsed at that time and that church and state were molded into one entity, resulting in the establishment of the papacy under Pope Sylvester. The age of Antichrist was thus calculated from 325 to 1585, making that year the eschatological moment; consequently, it could only be expected that the Radicals would consider the Protestant magisterial churches within the anti-Christian domain.

In this connection it should be noticed that there seems to be a relationship between the Radicals' apocalyptic periodization and Arian tendencies. The underlying philosophy was that because the fall of the church took place at the time of Constantine, the Trinitarian doctrine endorsed by the apostate church must be heretical. Their apocalyptic view of the fall of the church thus had its share in shaping an anti-Trinitarian theology. In England the distinctive feature of the Radical Reformation "was the close interrelationship of Libertinism, anti-Trinitarianism, Anabaptism of the Melchiorite strain, and Spiritualism." [90] Foxe's records of the public hearings of the Anabaptists and his own pleading with them reveal that they did not seem able to present or substantiate an orthodox view of the incarnation and the nature of Christ. This phenomenon has often appeared within extreme apocalyptic movements; the present-day sect of Jehovah's Witnesses is a typical example.

Since the termination of the 1260 years was near, so was the end of Antichrist's reign. Joachim's concept of a third age of the Holy Spirit at the end of 1260 years was never forgotten. According to George H. Williams, for Radical leaders such as David Joris, Anthony Pocquet, and William Postel, the third age had begun with their respective conversions and rebirths.[91] Further, already in the middle of the second century Montanus had reacted against the formalism of the church by proclaiming himself an instrument of the Holy Spirit for the inauguration of its new dispensation. The Radicals were also able to refer to Tertullian as one who had joined the Montanists. Accordingly, an apocalyptic expectation of the Holy Spirit was anticipated in connection with the final phase of the great controversy between Christ and Satan—or the elect and Antichrist—and the ushering in of the new millennial age.

An early exponent of chiliasm was Thomas Münzer, who came into confrontation with Luther and Melanchthon. As a Lutheran preacher at Zwickau in 1520, he called for extreme religious and social reforms. Here he linked up with the so-called Zwickau prophets, who believed in the millennium and direct personal revelation through visions and dreams. Next we find him in Bohemia, where his Prague Manifesto of 1521 advocated a chiliasm that justified violence by the elect. He returned to Germany but was expelled from the various places where he settled. He joined the Peasants' Revolt but was captured and executed in 1525.

The classic example of chiliasm was the endeavor to make the city of Münster into the New Jerusalem of the Apocalpyse. As a background for this story we must begin with Melchior Hofmann, (1496?-?1544). In the 1520s he was a Lutheran lay preacher in Livonia (Latvia and Estonia), Sweden, and Denmark. During these years he developed eschatological ideas and preached the approaching end of the world. In 1529 he arrived in Strassburg, where in 1530 he joined the Anabaptists. Because of his views on baptism and eschatology he had to flee the city, and for three years worked successfully as an apostle for Anabaptism in Friesland and Holland. He returned to Strassburg, which he expected to be the New Jerusalem, but was arrested and imprisoned for life. His followers became known as Melchiorites.

The Melchiorite leader John Matthijs, ministering in Amsterdam, ordained a group of apostles, among them John of Leiden. The latter visited Münster in 1533 and found that Bernhard Rothmann, a Lutheran pastor of the large church of St. Lambert, publicly expressed doubt about infant baptism. The following year he was baptized by one of the apostles ordained by John Matthijs. Within a week he and his assistants baptized 1,400 citizens of Münster.[92]

Melchiorites made their way from all parts of Holland and Zeeland to Münster in what was considered to be a mass movement.[93] Among the pilgrims were John Matthijs and John of Leiden. The latter took over the leadership of the city and was proclaimed king. They asserted that God had rejected Strassburg and had chosen Münster as the New Jerusalem. The mastery of the city lasted only a little more than a year. The hope of realizing an apocalyptic utopia ended when the army captured the city on June 25, 1535.

There is a definite parallel between extreme ante-Nicene chiliasm and the Post-Nicene Fathers' reaction against it and the apocalypticism of Thomas Münzer, the Zwickau prophets, the Melchiorites, and the events of Münster and the Protestant Reformers' opposition to them. Both Luther and Calvin refuted the error of chiliasm. The Augsburg Confession, A.D. 1530, condemns those "who scatter Jewish opinions, that, before the resurrection of the dead, the godly shall occupy the kingdom of the world, the wicked being everywhere suppressed; the saints alone, the pious, shall have a worldly kingdom, and shall exterminate all the godless."[94]

The opposition of the Protestant Reformers to the results of extreme chiliasm is understandable. However, in view of the fact that most of the Radicals denied infant baptism, past church historians have unfortunately characterized the entire Anabaptist movement as revolutionary, so doing the grossest injustice to the movement as a whole. As already noted, this picture has been changed. While Anabaptists of the sixteenth century have been placed within the Radical Reformation as such, it is now evident that when we speak about eschatology among them, we must distinguish between those who held extreme chiliastic views and sought to realize them by force, as we have observed, and those who held to a peaceful eschatology.[95]

Menno Simons (1496-1561), a reformed parish priest in Friesland who became an Anabaptist, did much to consolidate and heal the Anabaptist movement after the catastrophe of Münster. We are fortunate in having his complete writings.[96] He wrote a pamphlet, *The Blasphemy of John of Leiden*, 1535, in which he states:

"And so it may be plainly understood that not by Christians is the Babylonian harlot to be destroyed; also that Christians should not exterminate. A Theudas may rise up and cause a disturbance, but he shall not succeed. There may rise up a Judas of Galilee and make a commotion, but he shall perish and all his followers shall perish and be scattered. Therefore let every person beware and observe the Scriptures carefully, and he shall see that the Lord Himself will destroy at His coming and punish all His enemies who would not submit to Him. . . . This scripture clearly testifies that the Lord Christ must first come again before all His enemies are punished. And how Christ will come again He Himself testifies, saying, For the Son of man shall come in the glory of his Father with his angels; and then he shall reward every man according to his works. Again, For as the lightning cometh out of the east, and shineth even unto the west; so shall also the coming of the Son of man be. . . . And then shall appear the sign of the Son of man in heaven: and then shall all the tribes of the earth mourn, and they shall see the Son of man coming in the clouds of heaven with power and great glory. The two angels also testified how Christ would come again, saying, Ye men of Galilee, why stand ye gazing up into heaven? this same Jesus, which is taken up from you into heaven, shall so come in like manner as ye have seen him go into heaven."[97]

In a treatise, *The Foundation of Christian Doctrine*, 1539, he refers to John of Leiden in these words: "And if anyone declares himself king in the kingdom and dominion of Christ, as John of Leiden did at Münster, he with Adonijah shall not go unpunished, for the true Solomon, Christ Jesus Himself, must possess the kingdom and sit eternally upon the throne of David."[98]

While a small group expressed hope that Christ would come to Münster in 1538, or another that Münster again would be conquered by the Anabaptists by 1540, chiliasm among the Anabaptists had disappeared by 1540. We have noticed that Menno Simon rejected chiliasm, and the Mennonite confessions of faith published in the sixteenth and seventeenth centuries make no reference to chiliasm. Leaders of the Swiss, Dutch, and German Anabaptist churches wrote voluminously, but, as John C. Wenger asserts, "none of these leaders exhibits chiliastic views." He further contends that "all the major leaders held to views which would now be called amillennial (nonmillennial)."[99]

As the sixteenth century moved on, Protestant theology, in the words of Robert Friedmann, "abandoned the idea of a second coming of Christ: concentrating exclusively on the personal certitude of salvation *(Heils-gewissheit)*. There was simply no room left for a meaningful eschatology within the late Lutheran and post-Lutheran theology. The only place where such ideas were kept alive and had a legitimate function was the left way of the Reformation, or, as we all now call it, the Radical Reformation; Anabaptism and related movements."[100]

In this branch of the Reformation the advent hope shined brightly. To be ready and to be vigilant for the second coming of Christ became the eschatological framework within which great missionary zeal and endeavors were manifested.

NOTES

[1] *D. Martin Luthers Werke. Kritische Gesamtausgabe* (Weimar, 1883-   ). Hereafter referred to as *WA. WA* 10/1, 2:93; 41:317; 25:52.

[2] John Calvin, *Institutes of the Christian Religion* (Grand Rapids, 1957), book II, p. 30; book III, IX, 5.

[3] *Idem, Commentaries on the Epistles to Timothy, Titus, and Philemon* (Edinburgh, 1956), p. 263 (comments on 2 Tim. 4:8).

[4] *Idem, Commentaries on the Catholic Epistles* (Edinburgh, 1855), p. 415 (comments on 2 Peter 3:4).

[5] *Idem, Institutes*, book III, IX, 4.

[6] *Ibid.*, book III, IX, 3.

[7] *D. Martin Luthers Werke. Tischreden* (Weimar, 1912-1921). Hereafter referred to as *WATR. WATR* 2:1291, 1297; *WA* 53:40.

[8] John Calvin, *Commentaries on the Epistles of Paul the Apostle to the Philippians, Colossians, and Thessalonians* (Edinburgh, 1851), p. 324 (comments on 2 Thess. 2:2).

[9] *Ibid.*, pp. 283, 285 (comments on 1 Thess. 4:15; 5:1).

[10] *Idem, Catholic Epistles*, p. 128 (comments on 1 Peter 4:8).

[11] *Idem, Commentary on the Epistles of Paul the Apostle to the Corinthians* (Edinburgh, 1849), Vol. II, p. 60 (comments on 1 Cor. 15:52).

[12] *WA* 10/1, 2:95.

[13] *Ibid.*, 93-98.

[14] *WATR* 5:54-88.

[15] *WA* 11:380; 17/1:389; 15:39.

[16] Calvin, *Philippians, Colossians, and Thessalonians*, p. 286 (comments on 1 Thess. 2:3); *Commentary Upon the Acts of the Apostles* (Edinburgh, 1859), Vol. II, p. 151 (comments on Acts 18:31).

[17] *Idem, Commentary on a Harmony of the Evangelists, Matthew, Mark, and Luke* (Edinburgh, 1846), Vol. III, p. 147 (comments on Matt. 24:30).

[18] *Ibid.*, p. 157 (comments on Matt. 24:37).

[19] Martin Luther, *Three Treatises* (Philadelphia, 1943), p. 186.

[20] *WA* 42:634, 635; *WATR* 10:553; *WA* 44:346; 51:623, 624; *WATR 5:5512; WA* 45:47; 51:553.

[21] *WA* 42:320, 321, 288; 25:357, 358; *WATR* 10:309, 442, 443.

[22] *WA* 10/1, 2:93-95.

[23] *Ibid.*, 95; 15:36-42; *WATR* 3:50.

[24] Calvin, *Commentary on a Harmony of the Evangelists*, Vol. III, p. 146; *WA* 10/1, 2:107.

[25] *WA* 10/1, 2:109.

[26] Calvin, *Institutes*, book II, XVI, 17.

[27] *WA* 45:325.

[28] Quoted in Paul Althaus, *The Theology of Martin Luther* (Philadelphia, 1966), p. 422.

[29] Abba Hillel Silver, *A History of Messianic Spekulations in Israel, From the First Through the Seventeenth Centuries* (Boston, 1959).

[30] *Ibid.*, pp. 110-150.

[31] The Venerable Bede, *Baedae Opera Historica*, trans. J. E. King (London and New York, 1930); *The Explanation of the Apocalypse by Venerable Bede*, trans. Edward Marshall (Oxford and London, 1978).

[32] Thomas Aquinas, *Summa Theologia* (part 3, "Supplement," p. 77, arts. 1, 2), trans. Fathers of the English Dominican Province (London, 1932), pp. 142-144.

[33] Even if Wycliffe was not the author, as Lechler thinks (see Gotthard Lechler, *John Wycliffe and His English Precursors* [London, 1844], p. 63), the tract no doubt reflects his views.

[34] *The Praier and Complaynte of the Ploweman Unto Christe* (Antwerp, 1531).

[35] *Lanterne of Light* ed. Lilian M. Swinburn (London, 1917).

[36] John Bale, *The Image of Both Churches*, in *Select Works of John Bale* (Cambridge, 1849).

[37] *Ibid.*, pp. 255-258.

[38] John Foxe, *Eicasmi seu Meditations in Sacrem Apocalypsin* (London, 1587). (Hereafter referred to as *Apoc.*)

[39] For a study of John Foxe, see V. Norskov Olsen, *John Foxe and the Elizabethan Church* (Berkeley, Calif.; Los Angeles; London, 1973).

[40] *WA* 8:475, 476.

[41] John Sleidan, *A Briefe Chronicle of the Foure Principall Empyres*, trans. Stephan Wythes (London, 1563), sig. 104v.

[42] Bale, *The Image of Both Churches,* pp. 463, 464.

[43] The sermons of Bullinger were translated into English; see Henry Bullinger, *A Hundred Sermons Upon the Apocalips of Jesu Christe* (n.p., 1561). In his sermons Bullinger expresses himself in terms similar to that of Jewel and other expositors. See, for example, pp. 24 and 699.

[44] John Jewel, *Works,* (Cambridge, 1847), Vol. II, pp. 813-946.

[45] *Ibid.*, pp. 873, 871, 870.

[46] William Haller, "John Foxe and the Puritan Revolution," in *The Seventeenth Century: Studies in the History of English Thought and Literature from Bacon to Pope*, ed. Richard F. Jones (Stanford, 1951), p. 209.

[47] John Bradford, *Sermons* (Cambridge, 1848), p. 13.

[48] *Ibid.*, pp. 185-187; Bradford, *Letters* (Cambridge, 1853), pp. 359-362.

[49] Thomas Becon, *Prayers* (Cambridge, 1844), pp. 11, 206.

[50] *Ibid.*, pp. 405, 505, 511, 517, 519; Becon, *Catechism* (Cambridge, 1844), pp. 152, 409.

[51] Becon, *Prayers,* p. 624; see also p. 286.

[52] Edwin Sandys, *Sermons* (Cambridge, 1842), pp. 217, 218.

[53] *Ibid.*, pp. 415, 349.

[54] *Ibid.*, p. 364; see pp. 364-369, 387, 388.

[55] John Foxe, *A Sermon of Christ Crucified* (London, 1831), p. 93.

[56] *Idem, The Ecclesiasticall History* (London, 1570), Vol. I, p. 139.

[57] *Ibid.*, p. 290.

[58] *Idem, The Acts and Monuments*, ed. Josiah Pratt (London, 1853-1870), Vol. I, p. 290.

[59] *Apoc.*, p. 147.

[60] *Ibid.*, p. 123.

[61] *Ibid.*, p. 195.

[62] Rev. 16:17-21.

[63] *Apoc.*, p. 387.

[64] John Foxe, "A Declaration Concerning the Utilitie and Profite of Thys History," preface in John Foxe, *Acts and Monuments* (London, 1563).

[65] *Idem,* "To the True and Faithfull Confregation of Christes Vniuersall Church," preface in John Foxe, *The Ecclesiasticall History* (London, 1570).

[66] *Apoc.*, pp. 149-177.

[67] John Napier, *A Plaine Discovery of the Whole Revelation of Saint John* (Edinburgh, 1593), p. 62.

[68] *Ibid.*, pp. 62-74, 232-235.

[69] *Ibid.*, pp. 237, 238.

[70] *Ibid.*, p. 1.

[71] *Ibid.*, p. 64.

[72] *Ibid.*, p. 68.

[73] *Ibid.*, p. 234.

[74] *Ibid.*, pp. 161, 162.

[75] *Ibid.*, pp. 9, 12, 15, 16, 21, 22, 179.

[76] *Ibid.*, pp. 236-240.

[77] *Ibid.*, p. 240.

[78] Joseph Frederick Scott, "John Napier," *Encyclopaedia Britannica* (Chicago, 1964), vol. 16, p. 77.

[79] Thomas Brightman, *A Revelation of the Revelation* (Amsterdam, 1615), p. 840.

[80] *Ibid.*,

[81] *Ibid.*, p. 841.

[82] *Ibid.*, p. 840.

[83] *Ibid.*, sig. B$_2$v.

[84] *Ibid.*, sig. B$_3$r.

[85] *Ibid.*, p. 851.

[86] *Ibid.*, p. 842.

[87] *Ibid.*, p. 878.

[88] *Ibid.*, p. 139.

[89] Philip Schaff, *History of the Christian Church* (Grand Rapids, 1953-1959), Vol. VIII, pp. 732-757.

[90] George Hunston Williams, *The Radical Reformation* (London, 1962), p. 778.

[91] *Ibid.*, p. 848.

[92] *Ibid.*, pp. 368, 369.
[93] Cornelius Krahn, *Dutch Anabaptism: Origin, Spread, Life, and Thought,* 1450-1600 (The Hague, 1968), p. 147.
[94] *WA* 41:121; Calvin, *Institutes,* book III, XXV, 5; "The Augsburg Confession," A.D. 1530, Part I, Art. VII, printed in *The Creeds of Christendom* (New York, 1919), Vol. III, p. 18.
[95] See Robert Friedmann, *The Theology of Anabaptism* (Scottdale, Pa., 1973), pp. 101-115.
[96] *The Complete Writings of Menno Simons* (Scottdale, Pa., 1959).
[97] *Ibid.*, p. 47.
[98] *Ibid.*, p. 199.
[99] John C. Wenger, "Chiliasm," *Mennonite Encyclopedia* (Scottdale, Pa., 1955), Vol. I, p. 557.
[100] Friedmann, *Theology of Anabaptism,* p. 102.

CHAPTER 7

Eschatological Hope

in Puritan England

Bryan W. Ball

THE passing of the English crown from the Tudors to the Stuarts was to prove a significant milestone in the development of Protestant thought. With the accession of James I, in 1603, the Puritan movement, which had taken root in the later years of Elizabeth's reign, progressively came to shape the views of many believers, and this notwithstanding the king's early threat to 'harry' Puritans out of the land and the later restrictions imposed by the repressive Archbishop Laud. William Haller remarks that from this time Puritan preachers "increased in number and influence faster than before, finding a growing audience ever more willing to listen."[1] As the years passed and the Bible became more and more the basis of Puritan preaching and writing, clergy and laity alike became increasingly aware of an eschatological emphasis in Scripture. The hope of Christ's second coming, together with its associated doctrines, appears as one of the important outcomes of Puritanism's rediscovery of the essential Biblical message. Probably at no other time in English history has the doctrine of the second advent been so widely proclaimed or so readily accepted as in the heyday of Puritanism.*

It is the broad sweep of eschatological hope in the seventeenth century that emerges as a major conclusion to the study of Puritan literature. From an ecclesiastical standpoint, the doctrine of Christ's second coming was proclaimed by Anglican and Nonconforming Puritans alike. John Durant, the Independent Puritan who preached in Canterbury Cathedral, could say in 1653 that among Protestants of every loyalty, "prelatical, presbyterian, independent, or anabaptist," advocates could be found even of the extremer millenarian eschatology that had appeared by that time. Certainly in the preceding half century or so, many of

---

* The terms "Puritan" and "Puritanism" are used in this chapter for those English believers in the seventeenth century both within and beyond the Anglican fold, whose chief concern was for purity of doctrine and life, rather than for those within the Church of England whose main desire was for its structural reform, cf. E.F. Kevan, *The Grace of Law* (London, 1964), pp. 17-19.

the most influential clergy in the British Isles had associated themselves with the more moderate advent hope. To those Anglicans of an earlier generation who had preached the doctrine of Christ's coming—Hugh Latimer, Edwin Sandys, John Bradford, and John Rogers, among others—could be added the names of James Ussher, archbishop of Armagh; Patrick Forbes, bishop of Aberdeen; Joseph Hall, bishop of Norwich; and John Donne, dean of St. Paul's.

Beyond the ranks of such prominent Anglicans, the second advent literature was rapidly augmented by works from leading Puritan theologians. The Presbyterians Thomas Brightman, Thomas Hall, and James Durham would have differed ecclesiastically from Independents such as Thomas Goodwin, Nathaniel Homes, William Strong, and John Owen, who preferred the Congregational way. Matters of church government aside, however, the hope of Christ's coming became a prominent and common factor in their theology, each contributing significantly to the advent literature that was read and reread in England during the seventeenth century. Other great Puritan divines would have agreed that the recovery of truth and its impartation to the individual believer was of far greater consequence than the arid debate over church government, and names such as Thomas Taylor, Richard Sibbes, and Richard Baxter cannot be excluded from the list of prominent Puritans who espoused and proclaimed the advent hope.

Socially, the doctrine of Christ's coming was evident on an even broader plane. Innumerable commentaries, expositions. pamphlets, and sermons from clergy of every rank were complemented by works of various laymen from a wide cross section of public and private life. From James I to James Ussher, from the mathematician John Napier and the statesman William Alexander, earl of Stirling, to the seventeenth century poets John Donne, George Wither, and John Milton, the advent hope found a lucid and compelling expression. Aspects of second advent doctrine investigated by Sir Henry Finch, the lawyer; Samuel Hartlib, the economist; and the schoolmasters Thomas Hayne, William Burton, and James Toppe, were reexamined and restated not only by theologians but by other laymen—by Leonard Busher, for example, the early advocate of religious toleration, and by Robert Purnell, the devout Baptist elder from Bristol. The readiness with which the church as a whole took to itself the hope of Christ's coming is one reason for the warmth of spiritual life so characteristic of the Puritan era.

Geographically, the national spread of second advent hope was considerable. Certain areas of the country, in view of their associations with early Protestantism and the Puritan movement, could be expected to have been more susceptible to the challenge of a new Biblical emphasis. East Anglia and the Southeast accordingly provided a number of second advent preachers and prophetic expositors. Joseph Mede studied and lectured at Cambridge; William Bridge had been appointed town preacher at Great Yarmouth; and Joseph Hall, nominally at least, was still bishop of Norwich when he wrote *The Revelation Unrevealed*.

In the West, Richard Bernard, the Anglican rector of Batcombe in Somerset; the Presbyterian John Seagar from Devon; and Robert Purnell of Bristol, all espoused the advent hope and contributed to its literature. Wales provided the fiery Vavasour Powell and the mystical Morgan Llywd, and Ireland the renowned James Ussher. Among the names that could be cited from Midland counties are Thomas Hall from Warwickshire, who wrote at least two books concerned with the last events; Robert Bolton from Northamptonshire, author of *The Four Last Things;* and Richard Baxter from Kidderminster in Worcestershire, whose *Saints' Everlasting Rest* is one of the classics of Puritan devotion.

Scotland provided an impressive list of theologians committed to a reemphasis of New Testament eschatological hope. James Durham, William Guild, and David Dickson were university professors at Glasgow, Aberdeen, and Glasgow and Edinburgh respectively, whose writings all betray a deep interest in the events of the last days.

It is clear that many of the most eloquent advocates of the second advent in the seventeenth century were prominent theologians loyal to the norms of accepted doctrinal orthodoxy. Baxter is thoroughly representative when he says:* "This is most clear, that to this end will Christ come again to receive His people to Himself, that where He is, there they may be also . . . The Bridegroom's departure was not upon divorce. He did not leave us with a purpose to return no more; He hath left pledges enough to assure us. We have His Word, His many promises, His sacraments which show forth His death till He come, and His Spirit to direct, sanctify, and comfort till He return. . . . He that would come to suffer will surely come to triumph. And He that would come to purchase will surely come to possess." [2]

The Doctrine of the Second Advent

The certainty with which the church in Puritan England anticipated the *eschaton* is matched only by the clarity with which it understood related issues of second advent doctrine. Samuel Smith, one of the many Puritan divines ejected at the Restoration,[†] had, in 1618, written *The Great Assize, or, Day of Jubilee,* a popular work that had been through no less than thirty-nine editions by the turn of the century and must have been read by many thousands throughout the land. "He shall come as a king," Smith declared, "full of majesty and glory, guarded and attended upon with many thousands of heavenly soldiers, even all His holy angels." [3]

There was little deviation in the seventeenth century from this view that Christ's coming would be literal, personal, and glorious, "in the flesh," to quote John Seagar, another Puritan preacher. Seagar's *Discovery of the World to Come,* an important contribution to the second advent literature at a time when extremer views were beginning to gather momentum, examined virtually every aspect of the advent hope, emphasizing that the bodily and visible return of Christ at the end of the age was to be distinguished from any spiritual "comings" to the individual believer through the immediacy of the Holy Spirit. [4]

This point was taken up again by Christopher Love, a Presbyterian preacher who also wrote at great length on the advent hope as set forth in Scripture. Love pointed out that the concept of a spiritualized second advent was a third century deviation introduced by Origen, and that it should not be regarded as Biblical. On

---

*Spelling and punctuation in quotations from seventeenth-century authors have been modernized throughout.

†The restoration of the monarchy, in 1660, was rapidly followed by government legislation that effectually proscribed Puritanism in England and curtailed the continuing development of the Puritan evangelical impulse. It is variously estimated that between 1,700 and 2,000 clergymen, "the cream of English evangelical preachers," were removed from their livings on August 17, 1662, by the Act of Uniformity.

this point Love explains: "It was the great mistake of Origen, though he holds for the coming of Christ again, that he pleads for the coming of Christ in spirit. Therefore the text where it is said, 'You shall see the Son of man coming in the clouds of heaven,' Origen understands by the clouds, to be the saints, because it is mentioned in Scripture, that the believers are a cloud of witnesses. Now this is to pervert the whole letter of the Bible, and turn all the Scripture into an allegory and metaphorical sense. . . . I only mention this to confute those that follow the conceit of Origen, merely to make Christ's coming to be but a spiritual coming, a coming in the hearts of saints." [5]

In harmony with many Biblical exegetes of the time, Love recognized that the Bible appeared to refer to the coming, or appearing, of Christ in several ways. In *Heaven's Glory, Hell's Terror,* Love drew attention to three apparent comings of Christ mentioned in Scripture, the first in the flesh at the Incarnation, the second "spiritual" coming through the gospel, and the third, a final appearance to judgment at the last day. Love stressed that it was this final coming to judgment that was referred to in both Colossians 3:4 and John 14:3, the texts on which his *Heaven's Glory* and *Penitent Pardoned* were respectively based. Hence, "by Christ's appearing here, is meant that glorious manifestation of Jesus Christ upon earth at the time when He shall come at the last day," [6] and "the same Jesus that you saw ascend, shall descend, so that it cannot be Christ in His spirit, but in His person." [7]

Apart from the certainty with which Christ's second coming was anticipated, there is possibly no point of wider agreement among Puritan theologians than on what Love here describes as "a glorious manifestation." Ussher's description of Christ's coming at the end "environed with a flame of fire, attended with all the host of the elect angels," [8] is matched by Robert Bolton's "coming in the clouds of heaven with power and great glory." [9] John Owen's exposition of the Epistle to the Hebrews, written in 1680, speaks of an "illustrious appearance filling the whole world with the beams of it," [10] a late echo of Thomas Taylor's earlier description of the advent as it appeared in his commentary on Titus, published in Cambridge in 1619, "in such glory as neither the tongue can utter, nor the mind of man conceive." [11]

Baxter adds, "methinks I see Him coming in the clouds, with the attendants of His angels in majesty, and in glory." [12] There are few exponents of the second advent doctrine in the seventeenth century who transmit a note of hope more than does Baxter: "If there be such cutting down of boughs and spreading of garments, and crying hosanna, to One that comes into Jerusalem riding on an ass; what will there be when He comes with His angels in His glory? If they that heard Him preach the gospel of the kingdom, have their hearts turned within them, that they return and say, 'Never man spake like this man: then sure they that behold His majesty and His kingdom, will say 'There was never glory like this glory.' " [13]

In attempting to explain the exact nature of the second advent, Puritan theologians often compared Christ's second coming at the end of time with His first coming at the Incarnation. "When our Saviour Jesus Christ lived on earth, He came in misery, very base and lowly," said Samuel Smith, "but now, He shall come as a king, full of majesty and glory." [14]

Christopher Love, again, is unambiguous in describing the manner of the advent: "When Christ first appeared, He appeared in the form of a servant; at His second appearing He shall appear in majesty as a king. In His first appearing He appeared in contempt in a manger, in His second He shall shine in glory in the clouds. In His first appearing He had only beasts to be His companions; in His second appearing He shall have saints and angels to be His attendants." [15]

Such concise theological statements concerning the manner in which Christ would come had been prefigured in Sir William Alexander's epic poem of some fourteen hundred stanzas, "Dooms-day; or the Great Day of the Lord's Judgment" (1614):

> Who can abide the Glory of that sight,
> Which kills the living, and the dead doth raise,
> With squadrons compass'd, angels flaming bright.
> Whom thousands serve, Ten thousand thousands praise?
> My soul entranced is ravished with that light,
> Which in a moment shall the world amaze. [16]

If the poetry was not all it might have been, the theology was above reproach, and men widely concurred in expecting a glorious, visible advent and a personal and literal appearance of Christ at the end of the age.

But when would the advent occur? In attempting to provide an answer to this tantalizing question, Puritan theologians and preachers were aware that they were wrestling with a problem that went back to the earliest days of the Christian church. Thomas Hall is representative of his own age in reechoing the New Testament note of imminence when he says, "The days we live in are the last days. Our times are the last times . . . this is the last hour . . . and upon us the ends of the world are come." [17]

The Puritans of the seventeenth century were essentially children of the Reformation, and within the context of Reformation theology, itself contained within the framework of the New Testament, there was but one answer that could be given. Christ would come soon. The end of the present order was imminent. As Hall again points out: "If the apostle thought the day of the Lord was at hand sixteen hundred years ago, we may well conclude that it is near now." [18]

The Puritan preachers did not seek to disassociate themselves with the New Testament emphasis on the imminence of the advent, or from the reiteration of that emphasis that succeeding generations had noted. Henry Symons takes a middle road between restrained anticipation and unrestrained speculation: "It will not be long before this Judge comes, though I dare not say with Alsted in his Chronol: that 1657 should be the year, because the numeral letters are found in *Mundi Conflagratio;* nor yet with Napier that 1688 shall be the year, for those are *Arcana coeli:* yet I may say with Bucanon, if sixteen hundred and sixty years ago were *ultimum tempus,* then this is *ultimum temporis.* I may say with Tertullian, this is *clausulum seculi:* with Austin, Christ is *in proximo:* with Cyprian, he is *supra caput;* yea, I may say of some here as was said of Simeon, they shall not depart this life before they shall see the Lord's Christ. . . . He is on the wing, He comes post, He will be here before most are aware." [19] The appeal to the Fathers gave added respectability to the doctrine of Christ's coming, setting it again within the context of New Testament and immediate post-New Testament theology.

This conviction that Christ's coming was at hand became widespread in England in the seventeenth century, but, as Henry Symons and many others

136

plainly demonstrate, it was a conviction that could be held without becoming involved in capricious date-setting or the subjective interpretation of prophecy. When these men and their contemporaries studied the Bible they discovered a recurring eschatological emphasis. They saw that Christ Himself had spoken at length of the last days and the consummation of world history, and that the early church had gone forth on its world mission seemingly sustained in the hope of an early fulfillment of Christ's promises.

As the Puritan apologist strove to recapture the spirit as well as the letter of New Testament eschatology, he inevitably identified with the hopes of the early church. Thus to Richard Baxter, the eventful day is "approaching," "not far off," "comes apace," and Thomas Adams, whose prodigious exposition of 2 Peter went to more than sixteen hundred folio pages, explained, "the time from Christ's ascension to the world's end, is called *Dies extrema*, the last day, because it immediately (without any general alteration) goes before it. The end in the apostles time was not far off, now it must be very near: if that were *ultima dies*, this is *ultima hora:* or if that were *ultima hora*, the last hour, this is *ultimum horae*, the last minute." [20]

Hall is one of many in the seventeenth century who see the entire post-New Testament age in an eschatological sense. The last days began with the apostles and it behooves good Christians to live always in the expectation of a final fulfillment. In professing the hope of an imminent advent, the preachers of Puritanism clearly felt an affinity with the first apostles of Christ, and Baxter speaks for many when he exclaims "How near is that most blessed joyful day? It comes apace, even He that comes will come, and will not tarry." [21]

The Basis of Eschatological Hope

The root of eschatological hope in the seventeenth century was the unqualified acceptance of Scripture as the sole source of faith and doctrine. The Puritan apologist wishing to substantiate a point of doctrine turned instinctively to the Bible. James Ussher argued, "The books of Holy Scripture are so sufficient for the knowledge of Christian religion, that they do most plentifully contain all doctrine necessary to salvation." [22] Richard Baxter's *Saints' Everlasting Rest* similarly proclaimed, "The Scripture promising that rest to us, is the perfect infallible word and law of God." [23] Christopher Love exhorts his readers to "be sure you make the Word of God to be the standard by which you try and prove all doctrines that you hear, and if there be anything preached (although it should be by an angel from heaven) that is not according to the Word of God, believe it not." [24]

To the true Puritan the Bible was authoritative, not only in its record of the past and in its guidance for the present life and doctrine of the believer, but equally so in its delineation of future consummation for the church. John White, who figured prominently in the formation of the Massachusetts Company, and who was also a member of the Westminster Assembly, ably argued the intrinsic relationship in Scripture between past, present, and future:

"Whatsoever things were written aforehand were written for our learning . . .; the laws for our direction; the prophecies for observation of their accomplishment in answerable events; the promises for our comfort and consolation; the examples of evil for caution, of good for imitation; and lastly the events, ordered by the wisdom and providence of God, for precedents and patterns, representing our state and condition, either what it is at present, and why so, or what we are to expect it may be hereafter."[25]

The validity of past and present is thus in their ultimate fulfillment in the future. Emerging from this bibliocentric eschatological hope comes a recognition of the intrinsic rightness and historicity of belief in Christ's second coming in Puritan theology. In the *Penitent Pardoned*, Christopher Love sets forth the doctrine of the second advent as an intregal element in the historic Christian faith. On John 14:3 Love comments, "This text contains in it the most material and fundamental points of all the doctrine of Christianity," notably "the great doctrine of Christ's second coming."[26]

John Owen, eminent Puritan theologian, similarly argued, "Christ's appearance the second time, His return from heaven to complete the salvation of the church, is the great fundamental principle of our faith and hope."[27]

Richard Sibbes (1577-1635), an earlier exponent of the second advent whose works were published posthumously between 1635 and 1650, had suggested that since the coming of Christ was fundamental to Christian doctrine, it should be desired by the church: "Such is the disposition of the church that, before Christ was come, good people were known by the desire of His coming. And therefore it was the description of holy men that they waited for the consolation of Israel. O Lord, come quickly, come in the flesh. But now the first coming is past they desire as much His second coming, and therefore they are described in the Epistle of St. Paul to be such as love and long for the appearing of Christ."[28]

Such expectancy was, moreover, a characteristic of the true church, the espoused bride of the heavenly Bridegroom. Sibbes also notes, "As in civil marriage there is a contract, so here, in the spiritual; and seeing there is a contract, there is also an assent to the second coming of Christ; the contracted spouse must needs say 'Amen' to the marriage day."[29] The second advent hope in Puritan theology was related to the revealed purpose of God for His people. William Jenkyn logically enquired, "If the other predictions in Scripture, particularly those concerning the first coming of Christ, have truly come to pass, why should we doubt of the truth of Christ's second appearance?"[30] Jenkyn's question, rhetorical though it was, had already been answered by Richard Baxter: "As Christ failed not to come in the fulness of time, even when Daniel and others had foretold His coming, so in the fulness and fitness of time will His second coming be."[31]

The foregoing statements suggest that a relationship was recognized in Puritan eschatology between the Incarnation and Christ's coming at the end. This relationship, in fact, saw the second advent as a necessary and inevitable theological sequel to the first advent. "The first and second coming of Christ are of so near connection," Richard Sibbes argued, "that oftentimes they are comprised together, as the regeneration of our souls and the regeneration of our bodies, the adoption of our souls and the adoption of our bodies, the redemption of our souls and the redemption of our bodies."[32] Christ must come again to complete the work of salvation that He had begun at His first coming to earth. Indeed, many would argue that that work could not be complete or efficacious until Christ had returned.

The concept that a theological link existed between Christ's two advents and that it related ultimately to the redemptive purposes of God in Christ, was nowhere put more forcibly than by John Durant in his introduction to *The Salvation of the Saints by the Appearances of Christ* (1653). Durant explained that it was his conviction that many Christians were content to go no further in appreciating the redemptive work of Christ than in obtaining an understanding of what had been accomplished on the cross. In Durant's view this was unfortunate, since the final and total salvation of man depended also on the work that Christ accomplished after His death and resurrection. While it was not to be disputed that the sacrifice of Christ as an atonement lay at the heart of God's redemptive plan, yet it did not constitute the whole of Christ's work. Although it was the *medium impetrationis,* it was not the *medium applicationis.* Salvation had been *purchased* but not *completed.* Beyond the cross "there remained a great deal more to be done . . . to apply it unto us." [33] Thus the divine redemptive purpose had been greatly furthered through Christ's priestly ministry in heaven, and would culminate at His second coming.

To Durant, as to many other theologians in the seventeenth century, a believer's salvation was now in hope, at a distance, as the rightful, though suspended, inheritance of an heir under age. While accomplished and assured, it was not yet a tangible reality, although Durant was careful to point out that it was "as safe as if you had it." [34] The robe had been provided, as had the crown, and at His coming the Lord would deliver both. "Christ keeps the crown till the day of His appearance and kingdom, and in that day He will give it to you." [35] Sibbes had said that at His second coming Christ "shall perfect our salvation"; Love, that "you shall then be saved to the uttermost"; and John Owen, with a little more finesse, added, "The end of His appearance is *eis sōtērion,* the salvation of them that look for Him." [36]

Whether it was to effect or complete a believer's salvation, or to make it a reality, or to receive the saint to himself, it was clear to believers in Puritan England that the final chapter in the saga of human redemption could not be written until Christ had returned as He had promised at the end of days.

The Soteriological Significance of the Second Advent

William Haller has drawn attention to the theological sequence by which a believer in the seventeenth century eventually attained to salvation. "Election — →vocation ——→justification ——→sanctification ——→glorification was more than an abstract formula. It became the pattern of the most profound experience of men through many generation." [37] In the understanding of most Puritans, glorification at Christ's coming would set the seal upon his experience in this present life and effectively prepare him for the life to come. Milton drew an argument for the necessity of the second advent from the doctrine of "perfect glorification." In his *Treatise on Christian Doctrine* Milton contrasts the "imperfect glorification to which believers attain in this life" with the "perfect glorification which is effected in eternity." Of the latter he states, "Its fulfilment and consummation will commence from the period of Christ's second coming to judgment, and the resurrection of the dead." [38] To Milton, a believer's glorification is an essential factor in the redemptive purpose of the gospel. It is a process that begins in this life but that is not fully realized until the second advent.

Other Puritan theologians shared similar views on the doctrine of glorification. To Christopher Love, glorification was essentially the future, eternal state of the believer "that we shall enjoy with Christ, when the world is ended," and that would become a reality when Christ "shall appear to judge the world."[39] Thomas Brooks, writing in *The Glorious Day of the Saints Appearance,* states succinctly, "When He shall appear the second time . . . He shall appear glorious, and so shall all His saints."[40] To Milton, Love, and Brooks alike, the believer's glorification is bound up with the ultimate purpose of the gospel and is contingent upon the second advent.

The men of the seventeenth century saw another aspect to the completion of Christ's redemptive work. Not only was it essential that Christ should finish that work for the sake of man, it was equally essential as far as He was concerned Himself. He had begun a work and it was unthinkable that He should leave it unfinished. Having undertaken the restoration of man to the fullness of fellowship with God, and having, through the atoning act on the cross, achieved reconciliation between God and man, it was incumbent on Him now to bring everything to a just and satisfactory conclusion. This He would do and could do only at His second coming.

Richard Sibbes had been persuaded by this argument, suggesting that the second advent would bring to perfection not only the church and the individual believer, but even Christ Himself. "Christ is in some sort imperfect till the latter day, till His second coming," Sibbes stated, explaining: "The mystical body of Christ is His fulness. Christ is our fulness, and we are His fulness; now Christ's fulness is made up, when all the members of His mystical body are gathered and united together; the head and the members make but one natural body . . . Christ in this sense is not fully glorious therefore till that time."[41] The emphasis is almost that of a divine obligation, self-imposed by the very nature of deity, to bring all to a glorious completion. Sibbes wrote on another occasion that Christ must come the second time "to make an end of what He hath begun."[42]

A further turn to this argument came from the logic of what may be described as the continuity of Christ's work for man. As Haller's soteriological formula suggests, the believer in the seventeenth century came to realize that Christ's involvement with mankind was to be seen not merely as one act at a given time in history, but rather as a continuous and contemporaneous fact. Christopher Love thus saw the second advent not as an isolated event at the end of time but as part of an unceasing process that moved toward the ultimate complete and harmonious restoration of fellowship between man and God. This process, having begun at the cross, had continued ever since, and included, in succession, Christ's ascension to heaven, His priestly ministry in heaven, His second advent, the resurrection of the dead, and "the great doctrine of that everlasting communion that the saints shall have with Christ in heaven."[43]

The writings of both Christopher Love and John Durant suggest that if Christ's ascension and priestly ministry could be shown as necessary parts of this continuous work, then it would naturally follow that the second advent, with its outcomes of restoration and restored fellowship, would be seen in a similar light. Therefore Love, before he discusses the second advent, emphasizes the importance in the total work of Christ of His mediatorial ministry in heaven. He "is entered into the very heavens, that He might appear before God for us."[44]

140

Love goes on to argue that the intercessory ministry of Christ in heaven is to be regarded as even more essential than His personal presence on earth. Only as Christ fulfills the office of high priest in heaven can He adequately make intercession for all men. This He could not do by being bodily present on earth, "therefore we have great advantage by Christ's going into heaven." [45]

John Durant drew an analogy from the sanctuary service of Old Testament Israel. In the sanctuary ritual it was not sufficient, Durant argued, for the sacrifice merely to be offered. It was also necessary for the blood of the sacrifice to be taken into the tabernacle itself. The significance of the sacrificial system was incomplete until the blood had been thus ministered. Durant then continues: "When Christ died, the sacrifice was slain, the blood was shed, there was no more sacrifice to succeed, all was finished in that respect; but yet all was not done till the blood of Christ was carried into the holy places, which was not till Christ went to heaven, to appear as our high priest." [46]

Having thus established the necessity of Christ's high priestly ministry, both Love and Durant then proceed to discuss the doctrine of the second advent in its logical sequence as the consummation of Christ's work for man. Christ had voluntarily undertaken man's salvation in response to human need, and the moral constraint to complete this work was indisputable.

Another dimension was given to the doctrine of Christ's second coming by Richard Baxter. "Fellow Christians, what a day will that be, when we who have been kept prisoners by sin, by sinners, by the grave, shall be fetched out by the Lord Himself." [47] Baxter suggests here a hope that is related to a definitive event in time. It is "by the grave," as well as by sin, that men have been bound and prevented from enjoying the fullness of fellowship with God for which they were created. Thus only as the grave is conquered and its captive released can the believer enter into eternal life in the widest sense.

The limitations of mortality must be overcome, and when Baxter speaks of an everlasting rest for the saints he speaks of more than the liberation of the soul from the body at death. To be sure, in Baxter's view, the saint's rest begins at death when the soul is liberated from the body, but this is only a partial rest. The fullness of the saint's rest is not achieved until after the resurrection when soul and body are united again, and Baxter looks forward confidently to the day when "perfect soul and body together" come into the presence of God. [48] This essential reunification of body and soul will take place at "that most blessed joyful day," that is, at the second coming of Christ. In this assurance Baxter can trustingly commit his whole being to the grave: "O hasten that great resurrection day! When thy command shall go forth, and none shall disobey; when the sea and earth shall yield up their hostages, and all that slept in the graves shall awake, and the dead in Christ shall first arise; . . . therefore dare I lay down my carcass in the dust, entrusting it, not to a grave, but to Thee: and therefore my flesh shall rest in hope, till Thou raise it to the possession of the everlasting rest." [49] Through the redemptive act on the cross, "Christ bought the whole man, so shall the whole partake of the everlasting benefits of the purchase." [50] In short, the fullness and blessedness of eternal life can only be realized through the resurrection of the body.

This again is Christopher Love's message when he argues that the "main end of Christ's coming again" is the resurrection of the body. [51] It is what John Durant means when he declares, "Salvation is only yours, at the last day." [52] The whole doctrine of the resurrection of the body is thus very much a question of a believer's personal salvation. "You are already redeemed in your souls," says Durant, "but your bodies are not yet redeemed . . . in that day you shall have not only soul-salvation, but body-salvation." [53] The consensus of opinion in Puritan England was that Christian hope lay less in the survival of the soul after death, as universal as that doctrine undoubtedly was, than in the new creation of the whole being. When David Dickson spoke of "the full accomplishment of the salvation of the believers," he spoke in terms of Christ's coming and the resurrection of the body. [54] He who had in the first place fashioned man from the dust of the ground and pronounced him perfect, would yet bring forth from the grave a multitude of men with bodies not subject to "diseases and distempers, infirmities and deformities, maimedness and monstrous shapes." [55] Here again is the element of glorification, the hope of personal and perfect salvation. In professing that hope, the saints in seventeenth-century England were not ashamed.

The Effect of Prophetic Interpretation

A renewed interest in the interpretation of apocalyptic prophecy came as the English Reformation developed. Of the books of Daniel and Revelation, the learned Joseph Mede observed, "I conceive Daniel to be Apocalypsis contracta, and the Apocalypse Daniel explicate, in that both treat about the same subject." [56] This relationship between Daniel and the Revelation was never in doubt among Puritan expositors, and as the seventeenth century progressed the study of prophecy came to be a factor of far-reaching consequence. A modern historian, William Lamont, has noted the influence of sixteenth-century theologians on later apocalyptic interpreters, particularly on Thomas Brightman, who, to quote Lamont, "acknowledged his debt to 'our John Foxe' for his pioneer labours in the field of apocalyptic interpretation." [57] In the event, however, Foxe's contribution to the interpretation of prophecy in England did not prove as influential as that of his disciple, for it is not until the sixteenth century had passed that the study of Daniel and the Revelation reached its most significant point.

With Brightman, we come to one of a group of men in the early years of Puritanism whose attempts to popularize the books of Daniel and Revelation were destined to have a more far-reaching influence on the interpretation of prophecy in England than any of them could possibly have imagined. Together with John Napier, the Scottish mathematician and inventor of logarithms; Arthur Dent, the Puritan rector of South Shoebury in Essex; and Joseph Mede, the Cambridge scholar whom the *Dictionary of National Biography* describes as "a man of encyclopedic information," Brightman gave to the study of prophecy a relevance in keeping with the eschatological tone of the age. Prophetic interpretation owed the respectability that it certainly enjoyed throughout the seventeenth century to these four early expositors.

Napier's work, *A Plain Discovery of the Whole Revelation of St. John*, appeared first in 1593 and was reprinted in 1594, 1611, 1641, and 1645, as well as being published twice in Dutch and four times in French between 1600 and 1607. Froom notes the later comment of Adam Clarke on the widespread influence of Napier's work: "So very plausible were the reasonings and calculations of Lord Napier, that there was scarcely a Protestant in Europe, who read his work, that was not of the same opinion." [58]

Arthur Dent's *The Ruin of Rome,* an exposition of the Revelation that is omitted from Froom's *Prophetic Faith of Our Fathers,* enjoyed an even greater popularity than Napier's work, going through at least eleven printings between 1603 and 1662. Brightman's interest in prophetic interpretation included both the books of Daniel and the Song of Solomon as well as the book of Revelation, although the latter was undoubtedly the most popular of his works, issued first in Latin in 1609 and 1612, and in English in 1611, 1615, 1616, and 1644.

The learned Joseph Mede was unquestionably the most prolific and influential writer of this early group. Mede's *Clavis Apocalyptica,* the first and most significant of his works on prophecy, was issued three times in Latin and three times in English between 1627 and 1650. Mede's other eschatological works, along with his correspondence on latter-day events with many prominent men of the time, were reprinted, together with the *Clavis Apocalyptica* or *Key to the Revelation,* in his works, which appeared in 1648, 1663, 1664, 1672, and 1677.

Napier had recognized that the inclusion of the books of Daniel and Revelation in the canon of Scripture had an immediate implication. "To what effect were the prophecies of Daniel and of the Revelation given to the church . . . if God had appointed the same to be never known or understood?" [59] he asked. Arthur Dent had gone further, laying the responsibility of explaining the book of Revelation squarely on the shoulders of the ministry: "I hold that every minister of the gospel standeth bound as much as in him lieth, to preach the doctrine of the Apocalypse to his particular charge and congregation." [60]

The premise that the books of Daniel and Revelation were an essential part of the sacred canon, was as fundamental to the Baptist pastor as it was to the Anglican scholar. William Hicks, in the midst of the foment created by the Fifth Monarchy extremists, wrote a commentary on the book of Revelation expressly intended "for the keeping the saints feet straight, in not stumbling by a false interpreting and applying of this book of prophecies." [61] Hick's *Revelation Revealed,* although intended as a corrective to "wild applications" of prophetic symbolism, nevertheless maintained that "the things represented in this book are no more mysteries and hidden things, but as clear and accomplished acts unto us." [62] *The Revelation Revealed* was one of the last in a long line of works between 1590 and 1660 that endeavored to set the interpretation of prophecy fairly within the context of accepted doctrinal orthodoxy.

As the Puritan preachers endeavored to understand the meaning of apocalyptic prophecy, an overwhelming majority came to the conclusion that the only valid approach to the books of Daniel and Revelation was that which would later be known as historicism. Both the early and later Puritan expositors are virtually unanimous that Daniel and the Revelation should be understood in the framework of the historicist construction. Brightman, in commenting on Revelation 1:1, explained "the matters should be begun by and by, and should flow from thence with a perpetual course without interruption, although the final consummation should be afterward for many ages." [63]

David Pareus, a continental expositor whose commentary on the book of Revelation was widely read in England, stated that the time covered by its prophecies was "from the giving of the Revelation, even unto the end of the world."[64] The preface to William Guild's exposition of Revelation stated quite clearly that the scope of its prophecies was from "John's days to Christ's second coming."[65] It was thus within the context of this historicist approach, which viewed both the prophecies of Daniel and the Revelation as a panorama of successively unfolding events spanning twenty centuries or more of church history, that the Puritan preachers endeavored to understand the purposes of God as outlined in prophecy.

The practical application of the historicist hermeneutic to the books of Daniel and Revelation, in conjunction with the rediscovery of the advent hope throughout Scripture, resulted in a new emphasis on the kingdom of God soon to come. Joseph Mede believed simply that the kingdom, which he identified with the church, would go through two stages, the church/kingdom "militant," which had been established at Christ's first coming, and the church/kingdom "triumphant," which would be inaugurated at the second coming.[66]

Thomas Goodwin's view of the kingdom was based on an interpretation of Daniel's vision of the stone that referred to the establishment of Christ's kingdom on earth through the successful preaching of the gospel in the time of the fourth world empire.* The eschatological phase of this kingdom, "the world to come," would be realized by an ultimate transformation of the present world order.[67]

Nathaniel Holmes also saw the kingdom in two phases. Taking his position from Daniel's prophecy, Holmes argued that the kingdom of the stone represented the first stage, from the founding of the church until the end of the world, while the kingdom of the mountain depicted the divine kingdom as it would exist after the final overthrow of the powers of evil.[68]

There is a common element in these arguments that sees all history moving toward the ultimate realization of the kingdom of God. When they speak of the kingdom in an eschatological sense, they speak of the reasoned culmination to an agelong development. The divine kingdom is destined to supersede all earthly kingdoms simply because God is God. Daniel had said of God, "He removeth kings, and setteth up kings," and the course of earthly empires is always subordinated to the ultimate conquest of all by an eternal and divine kingdom.

Hope in the establishment of this kingdom brought a new problem, for the Puritan theologian committed to the historicist interpretation of prophecy was obliged to include in his scheme of events the millennium of Revelation 20. As the serious study of prophecy became more respectable, the question of the millennium became increasingly problematic when expositors recognized the difficulties associated with the thousand years of Satan's bondage and the saints' reign. The chief concerns eventually came to be those of relating the second advent to the millennial period and the end of the world, of ascertaining the nature of the millennium, and of placing all in a sequence that did not contradict the total revelation of Scripture.

In the seventeenth century the arguments on some of these points were, to say the least, intense, but, given the perspective of history, it is possible to bring some order out of confusion and to see that the millenarian views that developed in Puritan England fell largely into one of three categories, broadly analogous to the later classifications of amillennialism, premillennialism, and postmillennialism.

---

*The four world empires prefigured in Daniel 2 and 7 were, in Puritan exposition, almost exclusively Babylon, Medo-Persia, Greece, and Rome.

Strictly speaking, the amillennialists cannot be described as millenarians, since they held to the view that the thousand-year period belonged to the past and had no further place in any scheme of future events. The premillennialist stressed that the millennium was to be inaugurated by the literal and personal second coming of Christ. The postmillennialist also anticipated a future millennium, but emphasized, generally, that a literal second advent would not take place until the end of the millennium.

The view that placed the thousand years of Revelation 20 in the past was a continuation of early Reformation theology, and beyond that could be attributed to Augustine, who had equated the millennium with the entire era between Christ's two comings. The seventeenth century began with a reiteration of the Augustinian concept, although in a form modified by the passing of sixteen hundred years. Early seventeenth-century expositors almost exclusively saw the millennium as a literal period of time, the chief characteristics of which were the binding of Satan and the reign of the church. The neo-Augustinian concept of the millennium continued to attract many expositors, even through the years when a more extreme millenarianism was becoming popular. In 1656 William Guild argued for a fulfilled millennium, and the following year Thomas Hall stated, "All the orthodox do unanimously agree and conclude, that those thousand years are already past and gone." [69]

The obvious difficulty with attempting to place the millennium in the past was that no period as long as a thousand years could be found in history during which the devil had been effectively bound and during which the church had enjoyed an era of undisturbed peace and spiritual advancement. Nathaniel Holmes could agree with Bishop Prideaux of Worcester that the time of Satan's binding concurred with that of the Saints' reign, but disagreed with the bishop's argument that the time was now past. "The saints have not yet reigned; no, not in the picked thousand years of the doctor's; but errors, persecutions, wars, etc., pressing down the churches, as ye have heard, have that time abounded." [70]

If the thousand years were to follow the reign of antichrist, and if antichrist was to rule for 1260 years, and if the supremacy of antichrist was to be marked by errors, blasphemy, idolatry, and persecution, it could only be concluded that the millennium should be placed in the future. Such arguments spoke with force both to the academic mind schooled in the disciplines of logic and theology and to the more humble believer versed only in the teachings of Scripture. The premillennialism of which Holmes was a later advocate had begun to appear in England during the last 1620s, and from that time many believers in England began to entertain a premillennial advent hope.

Most of those in the seventeenth century who are now labeled millenarians were in fact premillennialists, looking for the personal, glorious, and imminent coming of Christ and the subsequent establishment of His kingdom. The premillennialists themselves were divided, disproportionately, between a larger conservative wing who believed in a spiritual reign of Christ through His saints, and a more radical element who expected that He would reign in person on earth for the duration of the thousand years. Apart from this divergence, the two wings of premillennialism were broadly agreed on the major events associated with the thousand years of Revelation: a literal, personal advent; two literal resurrections, preceding and following the millennium; a postmillennial judgment; and the ultimate resignation of authority to the Father forever. Within this broad framework of millennial expectation there were always exceptions, but the overwhelming popularity of what has just been described as conservative premillennialism is a characteristic of eschatological hope in Puritan England, and is the unique contribution of the seventeenth century to the interpretation of the millennium in succeeding ages.[71]

The Effect of the Advent Hope

The Puritan eschatological emphasis taught men that hope was an essential element in the Christian faith. As devout and erudite scholars diligently studied Scripture they learned of a hope set before them, of a hope laid up in heaven, of a hope that the body would be resurrected at the last day. They read that the Christian believer was begotten unto a lively hope, that he was the heir of the hope of eternal life, that he was to look for the blessed hope, the glorious appearing of Christ. It all spoke of a future consummation in time, and in professing such a hope the saints in seventeenth-century England were not ashamed.

It was precisely this hope that encouraged the believer along the path to sanctification and ultimate glorification. The goal to be reached by traveling this path was godliness, the evidence of fitness for eternity to be spent in the presence of a holy God and holy angels. "If a man hope for this coming of Christ, he will purify himself for it, even as He is pure. He will not appear in his foul clothes, but . . . will fit himself as the bride for the coming of the bridegroom."[72] Even as the earthly bride did not spend the time of her betrothal dreaming of bliss to come, but in acquiring apparel suitable for the wedding and in the exacting task of preparation for a new life, even so the church and the individual believer alike were to spend the remaining time in preparation for Christ's coming and eternity to follow. As Alexander Nisbet declared, belief in Christ's second coming "is a special means to make Christians thrive in grace and holiness."[73]

Richard Sibbes emphasized that the converse was also true. If the hope of Christ's coming is not seen to work efficaciously in the present life of the believer, "it is but a false conceit and lying fancy."[74] Sibbes also notes the positive effect of Christian hope: "If we say this truly, come Lord Jesus, undoubtedly it will have an influence into our lives. It will stir up all graces in the soul; as faith, to lay hold upon it; hope, to expect it; love to embrace; patience, to endure anything for it; heavenly mindedness, to fit and prepare for it."[75] True Christians, therefore, "always live in expectation of the Lord Jesus in the clouds" with oil in their lamps and "prepared for His coming."[76]

All this recaptures both the letter and the spirit of New Testament eschatological hope. Thomas Goodwin is one of many seventeenth-century writers who recognized that the church in the New Testament lived constantly in the expectation of an early fulfillment of Christ's promise to return. The early church "had that day in their eye," and "walked in view of it"; consequently, they were "set forth as a pattern" to succeeding generations in the church.[77] Thus, in Goodwin's view, the whole gamut of eschatological doctrine—belief in Christ's coming, the interpretation of apocalyptic prophecy, the computation of Biblical chronology, an understanding of the age, the future of the Papacy, the millennium, and the kingdom—was, in the last analysis, to be measured by one criterion. "The only use of knowing them," declared Goodwin is "to prepare for them. . . . The day and year of the accomplishment of the great matters are hid from us, so that each day and year we may be found ready, whenever they shall come."[78] It was the eschatological emphasis in the New Testament and in the outlook of the early church that constrained Durant's exhortation "It is your work and wisdom, to cleanse yourselves from all filth, and to perfect holiness in a filial fear of God."[79] The conservative bishop Joseph Hall recognized the inevitable consequence of true eschatological hope when he said that a true Christian is always ready for the coming of the Lord.[80]

While the Puritan believer looked forward to a definitive point in time for the ultimate realization of his hopes, he also understood that the future emerged from the present. Eschatological hope was not posited solely on an isolated event at the end of time but rather in the culmination of a divine, agelong process. For the world, this process had been in operation from the beginning of history; for the individual, it had begun with the outworking of divine grace at conversion. There was no future, no hope, for the man who lived only for the present. The true hope associated with the last events led both church and individual saint toward a future final event along the path of present and total commitment.

Christopher Love preached ten sermons on the coming of Christ and the glory of the future life as mentioned in Colossians 3:4. The sermons were all based on the three propositions, that Christ is the life of the believer now, that Christ will appear in glory at the end of time, and that when He does appear the saints will appear in glory with Him. As noted already, Love argued that there are three appearings, or comings, of Christ set forth in Scripture: first His appearing in the flesh, when He lived a holy life on earth; second, His appearing in and through the lives of the believers by the gospel; and finally, His appearing in glory at the last day. Love's argument is that the saints will appear with Christ in glory at the end only as His holy life is manifest in them now.[81]

Richard Sibbes also understands this relationship between the believer's present life and the future, and uses the analogy of the marriage of the bride with the heavenly Bridegroom at the end of time. Before this marriage can be finally ratified, there is to be a threefold union of Christ with His church: a union of nature, a union of grace, and a union of glory. To Sibbes, the union of nature came through the incarnation, when Christ took upon Himself human nature. The union of grace comes through the effective outworking of the gospel in human experience, when man partakes of the divine nature. The union of glory will be at the end when the church, duly prepared and perfected, will be in heaven, in the presence of Christ.[82] The marriage cannot be consummated until this union of glory, but that union itself is not possible without either those of nature or grace. The future, either of church or of individual believer, cannot be isolated from the present. It is part of it, the culmination in time of a process in history and in life.

The reality of this hope in the personal experience of the individual believer finds expression in many ways in the writings of Puritan Adventists. Richard Sibbes, for instance, sees it as an effective antidote to sin: "The soul is never in such a tune, as when the thoughts of those glorious times have raised the affections to the highest pitch . . . so long as it is so affected, it cannot sin . . . so long then, as we keep our hearts in a blessed frame of faith, and in a love of the appearing of Christ, they are impregnable."[83]

To Thomas Goodwin, hope is a barrier against the machinations of Satan.

"The devil, the shorter his time is, the more he rages and . . . seeing these are the last days . . . the more should we endeavor to do God service." [84] To Thomas Brooks, it is a challenge to prepare the whole man for eternity. "Those that have hopes to reign with Christ in glory, that have set their hearts on that pure and blissful state . . . they will purify both their insides, and their outsides, both body and soul." [85] The total effect of hope on the life of the believer is wide indeed. It is an incentive to duty and obedience.[86] It is the spring of brotherly love.[87] It is a stimulus to work and to pray for others.[88] It is the root of happiness and contentment in the present life.[89] There is, in short, no aspect of Christian life and doctrine that is not quickened and ennobled by the influence of a positive eschatological hope.

This theology of hope is an effective agent that breaks down the barrier between present and future by bringing the future into the present in a form that is accessible to every aspiring believer. In the language of the time, it is eloquently summarized by Thomas Brooks in the introduction to his *Heaven on Earth:* "Holiness is the very marrow and quintessence of all religion. Holiness is God stamped and printed upon the soul; it is Christ formed in the heart; it is our light, our life, our beauty, our glory, our joy, our crown, our heaven, our all. The holy soul is happy in life, and blessed in death, and shall be transcendently glorious in the morning of the resurrection, when Christ shall say, 'Lo, here am I, and My holy ones, who are My joy; lo, here am I, and My holy ones, who are My crown; and therefore, upon the heads of these holy ones, will I set an immortal crown.' Even so, Amen, Lord Jesus." [90] It is difficult to avoid the conclusion that the advent hope was an indispensable factor, perhaps even the chief factor, in the vitality and spirituality that characterized both church and individual believer in the seventeenth century.

We turn again to Richard Sibbes to note the immediate significance of the relationship between eschatological hope in the life of the believer and in the life of the church. The fundamental unity of the believer with Christ and the consequential unity of believer with believer within the church were both seen in direct relationship to a positive belief in the coming of Christ. Sibbes had repeatedly argued, "The contracted spouse must needs say 'Amen' to the marriage day." "It is the disposition of a gracious heart, to desire the glorious coming of Christ Jesus." "The more we have of Christ in us, the more shall we desire His coming to us." [91] The conclusion to such an emphasis must be understood: "Let us labor to have all the corners of the heart filled up with the spirit of Christ: our understandings, with knowledge; our affections, with love and delight; and our wills, with obedience. The Scripture calls it being filled with all the fullness of God. Now, the more we enter into the kingdom of heaven, by growth in grace here, the fitter shall we be for it, and the more shall we desire it." [92] To Sibbes as to multitudes beside him, fellowship with Christ in glory was measurably dependent on fellowship with Christ in grace. The relationship was unalterable but not unattainable, and belief in the second advent effectually contributed to the believer's present spiritual condition.

Yet the end of Christian unity was more than a personal relationship between Christ and the individual believer that would culminate at a point in the future. The entire church was to draw a blessing from the second advent hope, a blessing related to the unity of believer with believer, and it was at this precise point that

Sibbes found cause for concern. In the preface to his *Glorious Feast of the Gospel* he regrets that many have apparently lost this necessary relationship: "Alas, Christians have lost much of their communion with Christ and His saints." [93] The very experience upon which the future glory of both church and believer rested was being eroded, and the reason was clear: "They have woefully disputed away, and dispirited the life of religion and the power of godliness into dry and sapless controversies about government of church and state." [94] Matters of secondary consequence have come to claim the attention of many, and Sibbes' point of concern is apparent. Let the message of the church take precedence over its machinery. Let believers recapture a unity with Christ and with each other through a rediscovery of essentials. From this premise, Sibbes went on to set forth the doctrine of the second advent as an intregal part of the total message of the New Testament.

Other influential preachers in the seventeenth century voiced similar sentiments. Edmund Calamy and Stephen Marshall, both moderate and esteemed, deplored the divisions that had appeared in church and kingdom. Marshall described the multiplicity of sects into which the church had been divided as an "epidemical disease . . . pleasing to Satan." [95] The divisions within the church were clearly an obstacle to the realization of the divine purpose, and while some undoubtedly expected the desired unity to be realized through acts of Parliament and the establishment of a state church, there were many whose discernment was more far-reaching. William Strong's eschatological hope of "perfect and sweet communion one with another" is contingent upon the communion of each individual believer with God, in Christ.[96] The cure for division, according to the moderator of the Westminster Assembly, lay in a universal acceptance and an individual application of the essentials of the Christian faith. The last word thus belongs to Jeremiah Whitaker: "The way to cure the bleeding distempers of Christendom is for all men to endeavor to get inward persuasions answerable to their outward professions, for as these main principles are more or less believed, so is the heart and life of men better or worse ordered. When the soul is once fully persuaded that Christ is God, that He is the true Messiah, that there is another life besides this, that the Lord Christ is ready to come to judgment, and His reward is with Him, then the soul begins to seek and beg an interest in Christ, to flee from wrath to come, to assure the hopes of heaven, whilst we are on earth. And this hope, when once truly attained, carries the soul far above the comforts of life, and beyond the fears of death." [97]

There is more here than mere concern with ecclesiastical politics or church government, more than the unrealistic ambitions of a radical millenarian minority. Hope, the future, Christ's coming, eternal life; these, in the context of a complete Christocentric gospel and in the experience of each believer, are the basis of a valid ecumenism, the assurance of an ultimate triumph. Many in the seventeenth century died in that hope, and counted it a privilege to do so. They had not received the promises, but with the eye of faith had seen them afar off. The church in Puritan England was stronger for the advent hope it cherished and for its effect on the lives of those who embraced it.

NOTES

[1] William Haller, *The Rise of Puritanism* (New York, 1957), p. 50.
[2] Richard Baxter, *The Saints' Everlasting Rest* (London, 1650), p. 50.
[3] Samuel Smith, *The Great Assize, or, Day of Jubilee* (London, 1628), p. 21.
[4] John Seagar, *A Discovery of the World to Come According to the Scriptures* (London, 1650), pp. 76, 94, 95.
[5] Christopher Love, *The Penitent Pardoned* (London, 1657), p. 175.
[6] Christopher Love, *Heaven's Glory, Hell's Terror* (London, 1653), p. 32.
[7] Love, *The Penitent Pardoned*, p. 176.
[8] James Ussher, *A Body of Divinity* (London, 1645), p. 477.
[9] Robert Bolton, *Mr. Bolton's Last and Learned Work of the Four Last Things, Death, Judgement, Hell, and Heaven* (London, 1632), p. 87.
[10] John Owen, *A Continuation of the Exposition of the Epistle of Paul the Apostle to the Hebrews* (London, 1680), p. 470.
[11] Thomas Taylor, *A Commentary Upon the Epistle of Saint Paul Written to Titus* (Cambridge, 1619), p. 480.
[12] Baxter, *The Saints' Everlasting Rest*, p. 791.
[13] *Ibid.*, p. 776.
[14] Smith, *The Great Assize*, p. 21.
[15] Love, *Heaven's Glory*, p. 38.
[16] William Alexander, "Dooms-day; or the Great Day of the Lord's Judgment," in *Recreations With the Muses* (London, 1637), p. 48.
[17] Thomas Hall, *A Practical and Polemical Commentary of Exposition Upon the Third and Fourth Chapters of the Latter Epistle of Saint Paul to Timothy* (London, 1658), p. 7.
[18] *Ibid.*
[19] Henry Symons, *The Lord Jesus His Commission* (London, 1657), pp. 35, 36.
[20] Thomas Adams, *A commentary or Exposition Upon the Divine Second Epistle General, Written by the Blessed Apostle St. Peter* (London, 1633), p. 1130.
[21] Baxter, *The Saints' Everlasting Rest*, p. 254.
[22] Ussher, *A Body of Divinity*, p. 18.
[23] Baxter, *The Saints' Everlasting Rest*, title page.
[24] Christopher Love, *A Christian's Duty and Safety in Evil Times* (London, 1653), p. 82.
[25] John White, *The Troubles of Jerusalem's Restoration* (London, 1646), p. 1.
[26] Love, *The Penitent Pardoned*, p. 115.
[27] Owen, *Exposition of . . . Hebrews*, p. 471.
[28] Richard Sibbes, *The Bride's Longing for Her Bridegroom's Second Coming* (London, 1638), pp. 55,56.
[29] *Ibid.*, p. 15.
[30] William Jenkyn, *An Exposition of the Epistle of Jude* (London, 1652), Part I, p. 537.
[31] Baxter, *The Saints' Everlasting Rest*, p. 92.
[32] Sibbes, *The Bride's Longing*, p. 72.
[33] John Durant, *The Salvation of the Saints* (London, 1653), Epistle to the Reader, sig. A₇r.
[34] *Ibid.*, p. 221.
[35] *Ibid.*
[36] Richard Sibbes, *An Exposition of the Third Chapter of the Epistle of St. Paul to the Philippians* (London, 1639), p. 225; Love, *Heaven's Glory*, p. 51; Owen, *Exposition of . . . Hebrews*, p. 470.
[37] Haller, *The Rise of Puritanism*, p. 93.
[38] John Milton, "A Treatise on Christian Doctrine," in *The Works of John Milton* (New York, 1931), Vol. XVI, p. 337. The *De Doctrina Christiana*, a two-volume dogmatic theology written originally in Latin, drew the following comment from A. H. Strong: "Though unfortunately it has never yet gained wide recognition in the theological world, this 'Treatise of Christian Doctrine' is so original and so able a discussion of fundamental truth that it merits careful attention."—*The Great Poets and Their Theology* (Philadelphia, 1897), p. 257. The validity of this comment may be due in part to the fact that the *De Doctrina Christiana* was not published until 1825, after it had lain unrecognized in the State Paper office for 150 years, discarded as "dangerous rubbish."
[39] Love, *Heaven's Glory*, pp. 4, 6.
[40] Thomas Brooks, *The Glorious Day of the Saints' Appearance* (London, 1648), p. 6.
[41] Sibbes, *The Bride's Longing*, pp. 50, 51.
[42] Richard Sibbes, "The Churches' Echo," p. 107, in *Beams of Divine Light* (London, 1639).
[43] Love, *The Penitent Pardoned*, p. 115.
[44] *Ibid.*, p. 122.
[45] *Ibid.*
[46] Durant, *The Salvation of the Saints*, pp. 48, 49.
[47] Baxter, *The Saints' Everlasting Rest*, p. 47.
[48] *Ibid.*, p. 836.
[49] *Ibid.*, pp. 837, 838.
[50] *Ibid.*, p. 29.
[51] Love, *The Penitent Pardoned*, p. 197.
[52] Durant, *The Salvation of the Saints*, ep. ded., sig. A₄v.
[53] *Ibid.*, pp. 224, 225.
[54] David Dickson, *A Short Explanation of the Epistle of Paul to the Hebrews* (Aberdeen, 1635), p. 193. Advocates of the less popular doctrine of conditional immortality in seventeenth-century England are noted by L. E. Froom, *The conditionalist Faith of our Fathers* (Washington, 1965), Volume II, and N. T. Burns, *Christian Mortalism From Tyndale to Milton* (Cambridge, Mass., 1972). This latter work is important for its clarification of the three schools of mortalist thought that developed during the English Reformation. The earlier Annihilationists held that the soul died eternally with the body and that there would be neither resurrection of soul or body at the end, thus falling beyond any strict classification of conditionalists. The Thnetophsychists maintained that the soul had no existence as an entity apart from the body, and that it therefore "died" when the body died, to await resurrection, with the body, at the last day. The Psychopannychists declared the soul to be a separate, immortal, entity that did not, however, enjoy existence

in isolation from the body, and that slept in unconsciousness after death until the resurrection. Burns rightly points out that the soul-sleep of Thnetopsychism is figurative (*Christian Mortalism*, p. 18), and the resurrection of body and soul is therefore, more correctly, re-creation of the whole man. More extended analysis of the doctrine of conditional immortality in seventeenth-century England by the present author may be found in *The English Connection* (Cambridge, 1981), chapter 9.

[55] Bolton, *The Four Last Things*, p. 129.

[56] Joseph Mede, 'Epistles,' in *The Works of . . . Joseph Mede* (London, 1672), p. 787.

[57] William Lamont, *Marginal Prynne, 1600-1669* (London, 1963), p. 59.

[58] Adam Clarke, *The Holy Bible . . . With a Commentary and Critical Notes* (New York, 1850), vol. i, p. 21, in LeRoy Froom, *The Prophetic Faith of Our Fathers* (Washington, D.C., 1948), vol. 2, p. 457.

[59] John Napier, *A Plaine Discovery of the Whole Revelation of Saint John* (Edinburgh, 1593), p. 18.

[60] Arthur Dent, *The Ruine of Rome: or an Expostion Upon the Whole Revelation* (London, 1603), Epistle to the Reader, sig. aalv.

[61] William Hicks, ΑΠΟΚΑΛτΨΙΖ ΑΠΟΚΑΛτΨΕπΣ or, *The Revelation Revealed* (London, 1659), Epistle to the Reader, sig. blv.

[62] *Ibid.*, preface, sig. Clv.

[63] Thomas Brightman, *A Revelation of the Revelation* (London, 1615), p. 3.

[64] David Pareus, *A Commentary Upon the Divine Revelation of the Apostle and Evangelist John* (Amsterdam, 1644, tr. E. Arhold), p. 16.

[65] William Guild, *The Sealed Book Opened* (London, 1656), preface.

[66] Mede, 'Diatribae', in *Works*, p. 104.

[67] Thomas Goodwin, *The Works of Thomas Goodwin* (London, 1681), Vol. I, Part I, p. 454.

[68] Nathaniel Holmes, ΑΠΟΚΑΛτΨΙΣ ΑΝΑΣΤΑΣΕπΣ: *The Resurrection Revealed* (London, 1653), p. 237.

[69] Guild, *The Sealed Book Opened*, p. 304; Thomas Hall, *Chiliastomastix Redivivus* (London, 1657), p. 66.

[70] Holmes, *The Resurrection Revealed*, p. 456.

[71] For a more extended investigation of English seventeenth-century millenarianism see B. W. Ball, *A Great Expectation: Eschatological Thought in English Protestantism to 1660* (Leiden, 1975), chapter 5, "Last Events and the Millennial Rule of Jesus."

[72] Sibbes, *The Bride's Longing*, pp. 73, 74.

[73] Alexander Nisbet, *A Brief Exposition of the First and Second Epistles General of St. Peter* (London, 1658), p. 330.

[74] Sibbes, *The Bride's Longing*, pp. 73, 74.

[75] *Ibid.*, p. 79.

[76] Ussher, *A Body of Divinity*, p. 451.

[77] Goodwin, *Works*, Vol. V, Part II, p. 25.

[78] *Ibid.*, Vol. II, Part I, p. 190.

[79] Durant, *The Salvation of the Saints*, ep. ded., sig. A₅r.

[80] Joseph Hall, *The Revelation Unrevealed* (London, 1650), p. 233.

[81] Love, *Heaven's Glory*, pp. 4, 5.

[82] Sibbes, *Beams of Divine Light*, p. 102.

[83] Sibbes, *The Bride's Longing*, pp. 105, 106.

[84] Goodwin, *Works*, Vol. I, Part III, p. 133.

[85] Thomas Brooks, *Heaven on Earth* (London, 1654), p. 540.

[86] Love, *Heaven's Glory*, p. 47.

[87] Holmes, *The Resurrection Revealed*, p. 542.

[88] Sibbes, *An Exposition of . . . Philippians*, p. 230.

[89] Taylor, *Commentary on Titus*, p. 492.

[90] Brooks, *Heaven on Earth*, pp. 606, 607.

[91] Sibbes, *The Bride's Longing*, pp. 15, 48, 84.

[92] *Ibid.*, pp. 84, 85.

[93] Richard Sibbes, *The Glorious Feast of the Gospel* (London, 1650), preface.

[94] *Ibid.*

[95] Stephen Marshall, *A Sermon . . . The Unity of the Saints with Christ* (London, 1653), pp. 21, 37.

[96] William Strong, *The Trust and Account of a Steward* (London, 1647), p. 29.

[97] Jeremiah Whitaker, *The Christian's Hope Triumphing* (London, 1645), ep. ded.

CHAPTER 8

The Great Second Advent

Awakening to 1844

Godfrey T. Anderson

T HE year 1831 was not an ordinary year, even in a period of great ferment in American society. Andrew Jackson was in the midst of his first term as President. His coming to the White House marked the climax of a seemingly inexorable trend in the direction of democracy and the common man, a trend that had been developing over a period of years.

In the year 1831 in England, Michael Faraday discovered the principle of electromagnetic induction, upon which rests our modern world of dynamos and motors. The *world* was never to be the same again.

In the year 1831 in Virginia, Nat Turner led out in the South's most terrifying slave insurrection; while in New England, William Lloyd Garrison was launching his uncompromising and incendiary attack on the South's "peculiar institution," slavery. These events signalized the increasingly bitter North-South debate that culminated three decades later in the bloody fratricidal conflict known as the American Civil War, or the War Between the States. *America* was never to be the same again.

In the year 1831 in Rochester, New York, Charles Grandison Finney conducted a successful revival that in dramatic fashion united personal religion with a reform crusade that had definite social implications.[1]

It was in this same year that an honest New York farmer, after a period of intensive study of the Bible, began to preach publicly the imminence of the literal, visible coming of Christ to this planet about the year 1843. And the *religious world* was never to be quite the same again.

New England and New York, where Millerism had its greatest early successes, were in the throes of change greater even than usual for the burgeoning and bumptious Republic. Reform was rampant and spared nothing in its sweep. "It was a day of universal reform—a day when almost every man you met might draw a plan for a new society or a new government from his pocket; a day of infinite hope and infinite discontent. Every institution was called before the bar of reason, and of sentiment, too: the church, the state, the law, the army, the family, property—and required to justify itself. Nothing was immune, nothing was sacred, nothing was taken for granted, nothing but the right of inquiry."[2]

It is very probable that "in the history of the world the doctrine of reform never had such scope" as during this period. "The Advent movement in America, led by William Miller, is synchronized with the period of New England's great social revolution."[3]

The religious picture in the area most affected by Miller's message was complex and somewhat contradictory. One Baptist minister explained that his congregation consisted of "some nominal Baptists, Presbyterians, Congregationalists; . . . several Universalists; and . . . a number of nothingarians, and profane vulgarists."[4]

Along with a seeming trend toward a type of ecumenism there existed a tendency in the direction of a narrow sectarianism. "All Protestant churches united in condemning Catholics. All evangelical sects united, too, against Universalists and Unitarians. Methodists, Baptists, and Presbyterians could share their hatred of Christians. Baptists and Presbyterians cooperated in damning Methodists and Free Will Baptists. Presbyterians all too often proved disagreeably intolerant of Baptists. To cap the climax, both Baptists and Presbyterians, particularly the latter, maintained a constant and bitter strife between the enthusiasts and the conservatives in their own ranks."[5]

While Miller was in a sense the first one to proclaim "the Advent near" in a manner that roused the interest and curiosity of large numbers, he was by no means the first to embrace this concept. Beginning with the apostolic church and following something of a cyclical pattern since that time, the belief in the imminence of Christ's return had been espoused by a variety of individuals and groups. In the apostolic age "it was universally believed that the end of the world and the kingdom of heaven was at hand."[6] Periods of prosperity and moral laxity in the church were followed by times when dissenting groups appeared, many of them advocating millenarian views.[7]

Times of stress and social and political upheaval have tended to give birth to apocalyptic beliefs and to predictions of the end of time. This was true of the Reformation, the Peasants' Revolt, and the English, French, and American revolutions. There were those who expected Christ to come in the years 500, 1000, 1365, at the time of the Hussite Wars, and on many other occasions, especially when the times seemed out of joint.[8]

Belief in the imminent return of Christ to this earth was threatened near the end of the eighteenth century by theories of an English commentator, Dr. Daniel Whitby. He had taught that the world would be converted before the second advent and that a thousand years of peace and righteousness would precede Christ's coming. This view has been described as a "spiritualizing system" that tended to obscure the literal advent of Christ. By the early nineteenth century this position had been adopted by a majority of evangelical divines, and thus the preaching of a literal second advent was largely neglected by the ministry. Among those who in the eighteenth century sought to restore the premillennial view were Isaac Newton and John and Charles Wesley.[9]

"With this apostasy from the primitive faith . . . , and the wide prevalence of skepticism in the land, the church was in a state of peril; at this time of need came the great Advent Awakening in this country, the call back to the apostolic faith and to the voice of prophecy." [10]

William Miller, by whose name the Advent Awakening was to become known, was born in Pittsfield, Massachusetts, in 1782. He spent almost his entire life in and around Low Hampton, New York, on the border of Vermont. The oldest of sixteen children, Miller was instructed by his godly parents to honor and revere God and His revelation as contained in the Bible. Miller's early years were characterized by a love of books and learning, but circumstances prevented his securing an advanced formal education.

When he was 21 Miller married and established his home and farm at Poultney, Vermont. What he felt were inconsistencies in the lives of some professed Christians and in the Bible led him to embrace deism, which was still popular for a time following the American Revolution. Miller accepted deistic views after studying carefully and at some length the works of Voltaire, Hume, Volney, Paine, Ethan Allen, and others. This phase of his life extended for a dozen years, until 1816. [11]

Following his marriage Miller demonstrated his leadership and public service concerns by serving as constable, justice of the peace, and sheriff. During the War of 1812, in which Miller served as a captain of infantry and saw action in the battle of Plattsburgh, he began to move back toward the religion of his earlier years. Some indications of his beginning to doubt his doubts are reflected in letters that he wrote to his wife and others during this period.

Following the end of the War of 1812 and until 1823 Miller studied the Bible intensively, without commentaries, reaching a series of conclusions that became the message of his later public ministry. His studies brought him to these convictions: 1. Christ would return to this earth, personally and visibly, and the earth would be destroyed by fire. The advent would occur about 1843. 2. The righteous dead would be raised at Christ's coming and would be given immortality and reign with Him eternally upon a restored earth. 3. The millennium would begin with the second advent of Christ and end with the final destruction of the wicked. [12]

Speaking of his method of Bible study in this period, Miller explained: "I determined to lay aside all my prepossessions, to thoroughly compare scripture with scripture, and to pursue its study in a regular and methodical manner. I commenced with Genesis, and read verse by verse, proceeding no faster than the meaning of the several passages should be so unfolded as to leave me free from embarrassment respecting any mysticisms or contradictions. Whenever I found anything obscure, my practice was to compare it with all collateral passages; and, by the help of Cruden, I examined all the texts of Scripture in which were found any of the prominent words contained in any obscure portion. Then, by letting every word have its proper bearing on the subject of the text, if my view of it harmonized with every collateral passage in the Bible, it ceased to be a difficulty. In this way I pursued the study of the Bible, in my first perusal of it, for about two years and was fully satisfied that it is its own interpreter." [13]

Fourteen rules of Bible interpretation were asseverated by Miller. These included his basic belief that the Bible could be understood by diligent application and study and that nothing revealed would be hid from those who seek in faith to know; that Scripture must be its own expositor; that parables and visions and figures are used by God in the Bible to give its message; and that figures always have a figurative meaning and are used in prophecy to represent future times and events. His final rule was "You must have *faith*." [14]

About the time that Miller completed his intensive study of the Bible, he drew up a statement of his faith, which extended to twenty articles. Those dealing with Christ's coming stated:

> I believe Jesus Christ will come again in his glory and person to our earth, where he will accomplish his divine purposes in the saving of his people, destroying the wicked from the earth, and taking away the sin of the world.

> I believe that the second coming of Jesus Christ is near, even at the door, even within twenty-one years—on or before 1843.*

> I believe that before Christ comes in his glory, all sectarian principles will be shaken, and the votaries of the several sects scattered to the four winds; and that none will be able to stand but those who are built on the word of God. [15]

In the fateful year 1831 William Miller was prepared to begin public preaching, although he did so hesitatingly and reluctantly at first. One present-day historian, not particularly sympathetic to the Millerite movement, has evaluated the advent preacher in these words: "William Miller was temperamentally conservative: an ingenious logician with a resourceful mind; not an inspired prophet but a solid, sober, sincere student, driven only by the irresistible conclusions of patient research; and withal, an utterly literal-minded soul." [16]

A more recent interpretation of Miller's particular appeal in his day stresses his acceptability by the social and economic groups that to a large extent made up his following: "What Miller added to the traditional fire-and-brimstone mixture was the ingredient of mathematical computation as an 'infallible' method of unravelling mysterious prophecies. This appealed strongly to Yankee ingenuity, and challenged the competitive spirit of thousands of amateur Bible interpreters. In addition, he laid great stress upon the imminent casting down of the mighty, the wealthy, and the educated from their exalted seats, and the raising up of the weak and humble and faithful to replace them. More than that, in an age of competing utopias, when reformers were sprouting everywhere and promising everything . . . Miller outbid them all." [17]

Recent studies of Millerism have tended to stress the influence of such economic factors as the Panic of 1837 upon the state of mind that welcomed Miller's message. The effects of the 1837 depression continued well into the 1840s and contributed to the complex setting in which Miller's teachings were given consideration. [18]

While most of those who embraced Millerism were of limited education, there

---

*Miller's selection of this date for Christ's coming was based on his interpretation of the prophecy of Daniel 8:44. The "sanctuary" was this world, and its cleansing would be accomplished by Christ's return. Miller interpreted the 2,300 days as 2,300 literal years. Considering the vision of Daniel 9 as an enlargement on Daniel 8:44, Miller saw the beginning of the time period as 457 B.C., when Artaxerxes issued an enabling decree for the Jews to restore Jerusalem. The 2,300 years would terminate, Miller calculated, in A.D. 1843.

were important exceptions to the general characterization of Miller's followers as being the unlearned. An example is Professor N. N. Whiting, a Greek and Hebrew scholar who translated the New Testament from the Greek.[19] Others included Henry Dana Ward (M.A., Harvard); J. P. Weethee (M.A., Ohio State), a meteorologist for the State of Pennsylvania; and Elon Galusha, a leader among the Baptists and the son of a governor of Vermont. There were also a few who proclaimed the second advent who were graduates or former students of Yale, Bowdoin, Andover, or Oberlin.[20]

Charles Fitch sought supporters at Oberlin College but received only a mixed reception. Charles Grandison Finney and Asa Mahan, president of Oberlin, received Fitch kindly but not his message.

Students of Millerism have sought to establish the social views held by Miller at various periods of his career. After early bitter denunciation of the abolition movement, he later (by 1839) supported it. In the mid-thirties he had referred to abolitionists as fire-skulled, fanatical, and suicidal.[21] He opposed war at a time when neither abolition nor war was popular in the country. Also, Miller was an arch Mason and a Democrat.

Miller was nearly 50 years of age when he gave his first sermon at Dresden, near his home, on August 14, 1831. He had been invited to speak to the members of the Baptist church. During the previous nine years since he had worked out his religious views, he had discussed them with individuals but shied away from public preaching of his beliefs. Increasingly he felt the call to warn the world of the end of all things earthly. In the end "it was largely the public address of William Miller that launched the Second Advent Movement in America, and for fifteen years guided it on its way." [22]

The launching of Miller's public ministry came at a time when interest in the second coming in England in particular had reached a high point. The Albury Parish Park conference in England from 1826 to 1830 dealt with aspects of the second coming. In the eight years following the first Albury conference, six prophetic journals were launched in the British Isles, and in the same period some fifty volumes of prophetic interpretations were published in Great Britain. "Within fifteen years after the first conference at Albury, three hundred ministers of the Church of England . . . were proclaiming the speedy end." [23]

In America in the early nineteenth century there was less interest and activity regarding the second coming than in Europe. Still, a number of prominent ministers were speaking on the subject. Some were speculating on the meaning of the 2300-day prophecy. More than one hundred books on the second advent were published before 1840 in America.[24]

A series of sixteen articles by Miller appeared in the Baptist Vermont *Telegraph* in 1832. These were submitted anonymously, but when Miller's initials were added he was identified by readers as the author of the series. His first pamphlet appeared the following year under the title "Evidences From Scripture and History of the Second Coming of Christ About the Year 1843." Later in 1833 he was licensed to preach by the Baptist church of which he was a member. About this time eight or nine ministers were preaching his views.

As Miller extended his preaching tours he went about on a self-supporting basis. The only money he received to support his preaching up to 1836 was one dollar given him while on a tour that took him into Canada. At this time Miller published in book form his lectures dealing with the evidences of the second coming. These later expanded, went through five editions, and helped to acquaint a large number with the man and his message. Miller noted that he had given eight hundred lectures from October, 1834, to June 9, 1838. In an address in January, 1844, he stated that he had preached about 4,500 lectures to at least 500,000 people in twelve years.[25]

A new phase in the work of Miller came in 1839 when he met for the first time Joshua V. Himes, minister of the Chardon Street Chapel of Boston. Although Himes was impressed with Miller's message and potential, he did not agree with him in every detail. He expressed himself in these words: "As it respects the general views of Mr. Miller, we consider them in the main to be in accordance with the word of God. We do not, however, adopt the peculiarities of any man. We call no man master. Yet we frankly avow that there is much in his theory that we approve and embrace as gospel truth. . . . The advent is near. It is *possible* that we may be mistaken in the chronology. It may vary a few years, but we are persuaded that the end cannot be far distant." [26]

About this time other influential spiritual leaders also gave their support to Miller, among them Charles Fitch (Congregational), Josiah Litch (Methodist), and Joseph Bates (Christian Connection). Previously Elder J. Fuller (Baptist) and Elder Truman Hendryx (Baptist) had embraced Miller's teachings.

Of those associated with William Miller, Joshua Vaughan Himes was without question the leading figure in widening the influence of Miller's teachings. He was the organizer of the movement and its publicist without peer. One critic referred to him as Miller's "shield and fortress, helmet and buckler." [27]

Himes arranged for invitations for Miller to preach in the large centers of population of the Northeast. Himes was the publishing genius of the movement. From his base at the Chardon Street Chapel, known for its support of many reform movements, notably antislavery sentiments of the Garrison variety, Himes took hold of Millerism and made it for a time almost a household word in the Northeastern United States.

The presses under Himes's direction sent forth a steady stream of pamphlets, tracts, books, charts, broadsides, handbills, and even songbooks. Soon after meeting with Miller, Himes in 1840 launched *The Signs of the Times and the Expositor of Prophecy* (changed in 1844 to *The Christian Herald*), which soon had an estimated fifty thousand readers.[28] Two years later, in support of a Miller lecture series in New York City, Himes established *The Midnight Cry,* printing ten thousand copies daily for several weeks and later making of it a weekly. These were followed by publications in Philadelphia; Cleveland; Washington, D.C.; Baltimore; and Canada. In 1844 Hines published three quarterly issues of a paper for the ladies, called *Advent Message to the Daughters of Zion*.[29]

Miller's estimate of Himes's contribution to the advent movement can be judged by the testimony that he gave of his friend: "I cannot here withhold my testimony to the efficiency and integrity of my brother Himes. He has stood by me at all times, perilled his reputation, and, by the position in which he has been placed, has been more instrumental in the spread of these views than any other ten men who have embarked in the cause. His course, both in laboring as a lecturer and in the manner that he had managed his publications, meets my full approval." [30]

The success of Millerism, which came with the masterly promotion of Joshua Himes, also generated outright opposition. Now for the first time churches were being closed to Miller's preaching. The press and some ministers began to speak out in opposition. One clergyman in Lynn, Massachusetts, said it was "as great a sin for church members to go to these Miller lectures as to the theatre." [31]

Two pamphlets appeared in 1840; one, by an anonymous Roman Catholic, was entitled "Millerism Overthrown, or a False Prophet Confounded." Its tone can be seen in this passage: "His manner of dealing with his subject is reprehensible. He not only strains the meaning of the text, gives forced and unnatural constructions, but also abounds in probable falsehoods, and evinces a vindictive and intolerant spirit, better becoming an imp of Satan than a follower of Jesus Christ our Lord." [32] The writer accused Miller of an anti-Catholic bias, and he confessed to misgivings "that William Miller is anti-Christ."

Another work appeared that was even more damaging to Miller's program. The author was a Baptist minister of Providence, Rhode Island, Dr. John Dowling. His attack was entitled "An Exposition of the Prophecy Supposed by William Miller to Predict the Second Coming of Christ in 1843." Dowling also wrote the text of a seven-point refutation of Miller's interpretation, in an article that appeared in an extra edition of Horace Greeley's New York *Tribune*, March 2, 1843. Joshua Himes gave his evaluation of the effectiveness of Dowling's writings: "I do not hesitate to say . . . that Mr. D's Review of Miller has done more harm to the spiritual interests of the world, and closed more eyes against the light by putting an end to inquiry on their part, than all that has appeared besides, whether by Christians, Universalists, or infidels." [33]

Another critic saw both good and evil in Miller's preaching. It had done good, he said, in getting people to study their Bibles, but evil in building their hopes in the second coming at a specific time. If the event did not take place, he felt, "a greater evil must be the result." [34]

Thus as Miller's work gained momentum, a body of opposition literature developed, only to be met by counterrebuttals from Miller and his supporters, especially from Josiah Litch, who, next to Himes, was probably Miller's most effective Lieutenant.

From another quarter, the *Signs* reported that a Millerite student of Dartmouth College had been denied aid by the American Education Society because of his views, characterized, along with women's rights and nonresistance, as one of the "radicalisms of the day." [35]

Meanwhile Miller continued his itineraries and expanded the geographic area of his ministry. He estimated that during the twelve-month period ending October 1, 1840, he had traveled 4,560 miles, given 627 lectures, and had brought about the conversion of five thousand people. [36]

Early in 1840, while Miller was preaching in Portland, Maine, Ellen Harmon and her family heard him and embraced his views. Two and a half years later James White heard Miller and Himes preach. White had previously accepted the views set forth. Both these young people, James White and Ellen Harmon (White), became influential later in founding and nurturing the Seventh-day Adventist Church.

With the increase in the number preaching the coming of Christ, a need was felt for a general meeting or conference to help coordinate the views of those preaching the message and bring about a needed unity of effort. Among the sixteen signers of the call for this first "general conference," to be held at Chardon Street Chapel in Boston in October, 1840, was Joseph Bates, who was also to become a leading figure in the founding of the Seventh-day Adventist Church. The object of the meeting on the second coming was definitely not to create a new organization of believers or to attack the opposers of Millerism. Rather, it was "to discuss the whole subject faithfully and fairly. . . . By so doing we may accomplish much in the rapid, general, and powerful spread of 'the everlasting gospel of the kingdom' at hand, that the way of the Lord may be speedily prepared, whatever may be the precise period of His coming." [37]

Specific subjects for discussion were (1) The second advent, (2) chronology of prophecy, (3) the restoration of Israel, (4) history and doctrine of the millenium, (5) the kingdom of heaven, (6) the judgment. [38]

The deliberate attempt to interest and include those of various denominations is apparent from their address: "We are agreed and harmonize with the published creed of the Episcopal, Dutch Reformed, Presbyterian, and Methodist churches, together with the Cambridge Platform of the Congregational Church, and the Lutheran and Roman Catholic churches, in maintaining that Christ's second and only coming now will be 'to judge the world at the last day.' " [39]

The conference, attended by more than a score of ministers and many laymen to a total of two hundred in all, lasted for two days and accomplished a unifying purpose, closing with a communion service of the Lord's Supper. In his opening address the chairman, Henry Dana Ward, emphasized that the message they were engaged in proclaiming was not something new, but had a very long history in the church. [40] Illness prevented the attendance of Miller, but the discourses that he was to give, one on prophetic chronology and the other on the judgment, were read by Himes.

Ten thousand copies of the 175-page report of the meetings were distributed far and wide, going to theological schools and to ministers and interested laymen at home and abroad. In a "circular" address adopted by the conference, the position of the group was set forth, and the premillenial views were reaffirmed. The conference provided for the holding of additional general conferences; sixteen such meetings were held in the following four years, as were numerous local conferences. Thus was the work vastly unified and strengthened in spite of differences of views on some details among Adventist believers in the year 1840.

Regarding the spirit of the general conference, the *Signs* reported: "With views unmatured and uncompared, on the general subject, there was not, from first to last, a single contradiction, nor argument arrayed against argument, nor the least appearance of controversy, or contention on any point discussed; while there was the greatest harmony, apparent Christian union and good feeling, with deep and solemn interest manifested throughout the meetings, both for worship and business, so that in case of every vote or resolution moved and seconded, it passed unanimously." [41]

The series of general conferences held in various centers, including Low Hampton, Miller's hometown, served to coordinate the ideas and to formulate the plans for the advancement of the advent movement. The most far-reaching in results was the conference held in Boston in May, 1842. "It was one of the most important gatherings ever held in the history of the advent movement." [42] Joseph

Bates was chairman, and Joshua V. Himes, his friend dating back to New Bedford days, served as secretary. At this meeting some of the positions of the group were more sharply defined, and the doctrines of a temporal millenium and the restoration of the Jews to Palestine were rejected. Approval was voted at this meeting for lithographing three hundred prophetic charts that had been developed by Apollos Hale and Charles Fitch.

Another significant step was taken at this session when the idea of holding camp meetings was adopted, an idea borrowed from the Methodists. In June, 1842, the first Millerite camp meeting in America was held at Hatley, Quebec; in the three years from 1842 to 1844 more than a hundred camp meetings were held in the geographic area of the Millerites' chief activity, with additional ones being held in England in the year 1844. An estimated half million persons attended these meetings during this three-year period.[43]

At this Boston conference also, thirteen resolutions were adopted reaffirming the position of the believers on the imminence of Christ's return. One of these indicated their general agreement on the culmination of all things earthly in the year 1843.

During 1842, second advent associations were launched for "the purpose of strengthening and comforting each other with these truths, and in every practical way to disseminate knowledge in the subject and, . . . to promote the glory of God."[44]

At an earlier general conference it had been agreed to establish a second advent library in every town and village. A sizable amount of Adventist literature ranging in size from small tracts to books was now coming from the presses. Reading and study halls were started, commencing with one in Boston at Himes's headquarters. The second advent library, including charts and broadsides and hymnals, contributed greatly to the spreading of the Millerite message near and far.

In November, 1842, *The Midnight Cry* announced that it considered it a religious duty to pay its printers and paper makers daily so that Christ would not come and find the publishers "keeping back the hire of the laborers."[45]

The methods of distributing advent writings included placing papers on ships headed for distant ports, and Adventists supplied lighthouses along the coast with the printed tidings of Christ's imminent return. In addition to supplying theological centers in America, such as Andover and Newton, with reports of the first Adventist general conference, copies were sent to missions in India, Burma, Siam, Persia, Jerusalem, and the Sandwich Islands.[46]

Himes, the promoter whose fertile mind developed a host of ideas, was responsible for the idea of a "monitory wafer." This was a seal to use in fastening letters, each seal containing an appropriate Scripture verse or thought dealing with the theme of the second coming.[47] Additional postage charges limited its use.

Thus did a variety of plans supplement the work of the preachers—Miller himself and a growing number of assistants—in the task. In 1842 a big tent was utilized for holding Millerite meetings. This tent also was used in connection with camp meetings and was the largest in the country at the time. The big tent was a curiosity and received much publicity as it was moved from place to place with remarkable dispatch. Its seating capacity in time reached about six thousand persons. As various churches closed their doors to Millerite preachers and as

160

permanent halls large enough to accommodate such crowds were unavailable, the tent became an extremely valuable adjunct to the Adventist crusade.

The major exception to the use of the big tent for Millerite meetings was in Boston (and in time in other large cities), where a large Millerite tabernacle was erected, and dedicated early in May, 1843. Thirty-five hundred persons attended the dedicatory services. The building drew much attention in Boston, particularly with reports that for the most part attempted to discredit the Millerites for betraying their beliefs by introducing the element of permanence in the building of such a structure.[48]

It would be misleading to suggest that there was complete agreement on all elements of William Miller's teachings among his coworkers and followers. A number, even of the leaders, avoided the setting of a special time for Christ to return to this earth. Such prominent Millerites as Henry Dana Ward, N. N. Whiting, and Henry Jones were among those who opposed setting a definite date. Miller himself did not accept a fixed date until just two weeks before October 22, 1844. In spite of the differences in viewpoints, the various conferences and programs, promoted mainly by Himes, tended to unify the believers and stiffen their resolve as the crucial time for the second coming approached.

As the fatidic year 1843 opened, Miller was confident that the culmination of everything earthly was about to occur. He addressed a message to his followers on January 1, 1843: "This year—O blessed year!—the captive will be released, the prison doors will be opened, death will have no more dominion over us, and life, eternal life, be our everlasting reward."[49]

In a synopsis of his views, Miller set forth sixteen detailed items, each beginning with "I believe." He closed the series with words that come as near any as he uttered, until early October, 1844, to setting a specific date for Christ's coming: "I am fully convinced that sometime between March 21, 1843, and March 21, 1844, according to the Jewish mode of computation of time, Christ will come, and bring all his saints with him; and that then he will reward every man as his works shall be."[50]

A number of natural phenomena in 1843 gave credence to the prediction of the Millerites that the end was near at hand. In late February an unheralded comet blazed across the sky and was visible each evening for more than a month. This was the most brilliant comet of the entire century. The Millerites treated this display with restraint. They did, however, interpret reports of severe storms, earth-quakes, and such indications as the increase of knowledge and the dishonoring of treaties by the nations as specific signs of the end of the world.

Because of the unusual natural phenomena of the times, and for other reasons, the year 1843 found revivals reaching new heights in the evangelical churches. Miller was incapacitated because of illness from March until about September, 1843. (Miller wrote, "My health is on the gain. . . . I have now *only* twenty-two boils, from the bigness of a grape to a walnut, on my shoulder, side, back, and arms."[51] Miller's colleague L. D. Fleming recommended as a remedy " '*one pound* of shot . . . [boiled] in a quart of sweet milk down to one *pint*,' taken in small quantities several times daily."[52]) Yet the warning went forward during the year and on into the early part of 1844. The newly dedicated Millerite tabernacle in Boston as well as the big tent and other meeting places were crowded to the limit with eager listeners.

Even the South, which had resisted Millerite speakers, began to warm to the advent message in the summer of 1843. A Millerite preacher was given a favorable hearing in Norfolk, Virginia, and in the nation's capital. Others met with success in the Carolinas and Delaware. In the North, special efforts were put forth to bring the advent message to negroes, especially in such centers as Boston and Philadelphia.

By the summer of 1843 the *Signs* was accepting only three-month subscriptions because, it was explained, time would not continue long. Advent preachers were crisscrossing the New England area, New York, and beyond. Calls for literature were coming in from all over the South and from England.

Robert Winter, an Englishman, had set up a press in London in 1843 and claimed to have printed fifteen thousand copies of Millerite literature. During the summer a British edition of *The Midnight Cry* appeared in England, and an estimated two to three thousand became believers during the peak of the movement, between 1842 and 1845. Their "great disappointment" occurred, however, about a year after that in America, on October 10, 1845.

"There was, however, a far less marked tendency in Britain than in America to concentrate upon a specific date. The movement (if such it may be called) was therefore . . . more diverse, and consequently less easy to trace. It was a delta with many often shallow channels, some broad, some narrow, but all eventually running into the sand, whether of non-Adventist extremism . . . or simply sheer disillusionment.[53]

In addition Adventist tracts were being printed in French and German, and Adventist book agencies were operating in large cities in America, extending from Boston and Montreal to St. Louis and Louisville. One who participated in the movement recalled later that the year 1843 was a memorable epoch and that the air seemed full of the sound "Behold, he cometh with clouds"[54]

The widespread interest in and acceptance by many of the advent message at this time is not difficult to understand. In addition to the milieu of the times was the fact that the Millerite message was a basically orthodox teaching: "The Advent movement's most distinctive feature was in fact its extreme closeness to orthodoxy. Any church might profit from hearing the message, whether or not it chose to follow the letter of the doctrine. For all expected some grand event soon, either the Advent or the millenium, and all should prepare. Every Protestant sect in the region [western New York], excepting possibly the Episcopal and the Presbyterian, achieved a new height of revival fervor and conversions in 1843."[55]

Yet in spite of all this, the Millerites in 1843 had to face not only widespread apathy and indifference but out-and-out opposition as well. Many of the "learned divines" of the mainline churches and seminaries, whom Miller castigated consistently, took issue with many of his views. Some of them presented papers and lectures pointing out what in their view were the errors of Miller and his followers.

Of the newspapers that joined the attack on Millerism, a Methodist paper the *Olive Branch,* published in Boston, was perhaps the most vituperative in its attacks. Ironically, the infidel Boston *Investigator* reflected the most "Christian" charity toward Millerism.[56]

In addition to being ridiculed and taunted in certain quarters, the Millerites were actually persecuted. This is understandable in a time when religious intolerance was on the rise, as evidenced by the anti-Catholic riots occurring at this very time. In one place a highly respected businessman known by his associates to be a sincere and devout Christian was attacked "because of his faith in the Second Advent, hung in effigy, lampooned in the public press, and hissed in the streets. . . . Also on more than one occasion mobs compelled Advent preachers to flee or suffer insults and eggings because of the nature of the message they were preaching." [57]

Increasingly, especially after some Adventist leaders identified the churches as Babylon and cried, " 'Come out of her, my people,' " did opposition mount and bitterness develop to an extreme degree. In the summer of 1843 the Millerites began ordaining their own ministers. [58]

The application of the term *Babylon* to both Catholic and Protestant churches was strongly opposed by Miller and other responsible leaders. Charles Fitch was a proponent of the idea, which was pursued by many and received more support after the Millerites were expelled from many of the churches. Some churches closed their doors to Adventist preachers. As early as 1839 a Congregational church had been closed to Miller in Westford, Massachusetts, and in 1842 a Methodist minister who had embraced Millerism was barred from preaching in the Methodist church in Oxford, Connecticut. [59]

A resolution voted by the Methodist Episcopal conference of 1843 in Bath, Maine, stated "that the pecularities of that theory relative to the second coming of Christ and the end of the world, denominated Millerism, together with all its modifications, are contrary to the standards of our church, and we are constrained to regard them as among the erroneous and strange doctrines which we are pledged to banish and drive away." [60]

Another one of their resolutions stated "that though we appreciate the motives of those among us who have been engaged in disseminating these peculiarities, we can but regard their course in this respect, as irreconcilably inconsistent with their ecclesiastical obligations, and as having an immediate and more particularly an ultimte, disastrous tendency." [61]

In his public preaching Miller invariably impressed his hearers with his sincerity. His gestures were easy and expressive, and he used a topical or logical arrangement of his points, with usually three main divisions of his subject. He used a fluent, conversational style of address, with sufficient range to hold the attention of his audience. In his presentations he eschewed vocal pyrotechnics and he did not rant. While he evinced power in his preaching, he "was not a great orator, or a great logician, or a great preacher in the commonly accepted meaning of these terms." [62]

While Miller's discourses for the most part were mild and moderate, he was capable on occasion of being emphatic as well as dramatic in his presentations. Speaking on the text "We shall reign on the earth," he declared: "But you, O impenitent man or woman! where will you be then? When heaven shall resound with the mighty song, and distant realms shall echo back the sound, where, tell me, where will you be then? *In hell!* O think! *In hell!*—a dreadful word! Once more think! *In hell!* lifting up your eyes, being in torment. Stop, sinner; think! *In hell!* where shall be weeping, wailing, and gnashing of teeth. Stop, sinner, stop; consider on your latter end. *In hell!*" [63]

From time to time Miller would drop comments that expanded his expressed view that he preferred a single humble prayer to all the Hebrew, Greek, and Latin in the world. "The divinity taught in our schools is always founded on some sectarian creed. It may do to take a blank mind and impress it with this kind, but it will always end in bigotry. A free mind will never be satisfied with the views of others. Were I a teacher of youth in divinity, I would first learn their capacity, and mind. And if these were good I would make them study the Bible for themselves, and send them out free to do the world good. But if they had no mind, I would stamp them with another's mind, write bigot on their forehead, and send them out as slaves." [64]

In the course of time the persistent attacks of his critics led him to turn on them with a degree of vehemence. "I am sick of this continual harping upon words. Our learned critics are worse on the waters of truth than a school of sharks on the fishing banks of the north, and they have made more infidels in our world than all the heathen mythology in existence. What word in revelation has not been turned, twisted, racked, wrested, distorted, demolished, and annihilated by these voracious harpies in human shape, until the public have become so bewildered they know not what to believe?" [65]

Miller was uncompromising in his strong feelings against Universalists, a very effective group but largely neglected by historians. A Universalist, O. A. Skinner, circulated a tract entitled "Miller's Theory Utterly Exploded." When challenged to a debate by a Universalist, Miller said, "I will not contend with them. . . . Michael would not contend with the devil." [66] A contemporary characterized the Universalists as irreligious, profane, Sabbathbreakers, drunkards, and haters of evangelical religion. [67]

With the passing of March 21, 1844 (and April 18, 1844, which some accepted on the basis of the Karaite Jewish reckoning), the end of the Jewish year during which Miller believed the end of the world would come, he reiterated his faith in the imminence of the great day. Writing to Himes, he said: "I am still looking for the dear Saviour, the Son of God from heaven, and for the fulfillment of the promise made to our fathers and confirmed under them. . . . The time as I have calculated it is now filled up; and I expect every moment to see the Saviour descend from heaven. I have now nothing to look for but this glorious hope." [68]

But to a substantial number of Miller's followers, the passing of the spring of 1844 without the appearance of Christ led to "a marked decline in enthusiasm."

Just before the expiration of the time that had been suggested for Christ's return, Miller and Himes conducted meetings in the nation's capital with great success. Of these Miller said: "They throng us constantly for papers, books, and tracts, which Brother Himes is scattering gratuitously by thousands, containing information on this subject. They send in from this vicinity and from 'old Virginia' for papers and lecturers; but the one hundredth part of their requests can never be complied with. Never have I been listened to with so deep a feeling, and with such intense interest, for hours." [69]

During these lectures a cannon exploded on the U.S.S. *Princeton* on the Potomac River, killing the Secretary of State, the Secretary of the Navy, and several others. President Tyler was on board this ship but escaped injury. Millerites and others read into this calamity the voice of God warning them, and after this incident a number of Congressmen as well as other prominent leaders came out to hear the lectures. *The Midnight Cry* commented: "The dread catastrophe on board . . . the *Princeton* called all to a most serious consideration of preparation to meet God. The event has aided us essentially in our work. It is hoped that it wll be instrumental in preparing many for the sounding of the 'last trump.' "[70]

With the passing of April, 1844, without the fulfillment of their hopes, the first major disappointment came to the advent believers. Reactions varied with individuals, but there were still many who now identified this period as "the tarrying time." They found assurance in this prophecy of Habakkuk: "For the vision is yet for an appointed time, but at the end it shall speak, and not lie: though it tarry, wait for it; because it will surely come, it will not tarry."

The year 1844 was unusual in many ways. It was a hectic Presidential campaign year in politics. The hustings resounded with screaming speeches and torchlight parades and the tub-thumping political songs of the contesting partisans of Clay, the Whig, and Polk, the Democrat. Political issues along with many others were clamoring for public attention, in addition to the warning that Christ could be expected to come before the year closed.

It was in the spring of 1844 that the telegraph sent its first jubilant message from Washington to Baltimore: "What hath God wrought!" Two days later it returned the more mundane tidings from Baltimore, where the Democratic convention was in session: "Polk nominated for the Presidency." It was in this same year that Karl Marx met Friedrich Engels in Paris; out of their friendship and collaboration came before long the *Communist Manifesto,* the basic scriptures of international communism. During this year Joseph Smith, leader of the Mormons, and his brother Hyrum were murdered by a mob at Carthage, Illinois. The passions engendered by the Nativist Movement were heating up, and there were serious and tragic anti-Catholic riots in Philadelphia.

In the summer of 1844, when the Millerites were at a loss to understand where their predictions had gone astray, a new interpretation was presented to them at a camp meeting held in Exeter, New Hampshire, August 12-17. Many Advent believers had gathered, hoping for and expecting new light. On the third day of the meetings, while Joseph Bates was speaking and trying without success to be convincing by repeating some of the clichés that had been used for several years, a woman in the audience interrupted him and said that "the Lord has servants here who have meat in due season for His household." The woman was a sister of Elder Samuel S. Snow, who had just arrived by horseback. Bates graciously invited Snow to the rostrum to present his message. The essence of the "new light" that Snow presented was that the correct date for the return of Christ was October 22, 1844. He continued his presentation the following day and was very convincing. Those in attendance, including Bates, left the meetings testifying that the granite hills of New Hampshire cried out now with the message "Behold, the bridegroom cometh; go ye out to meet him."

William Miller and Joshua Himes were preaching in the Midwest at the time and did not immediately accept this date. Later this was the only precise date that Miller ever endorsed as the one specific day on which Christ would appear.

The great tent that had been purchased in 1842 was again brought out, and the lecturers and laypeople who believed in the revised time schedule began to give this new warning to the people. In Cincinnati the great tent was crowded with listeners every night. At Louisville the crowds were immense, and the excitement ran high. Many knelt on the ground in contrition and prayer. At Albany, New York, there was an impressive revival.

It was about this time, and in spite of many protestations against sectarianism, that Miller and Himes joined with Fitch, Litch, Marsh, and others in advocation that the Millerites get out of the churches. This was a movement that had started about the middle of 1843. The opposition to the second advent movement, which had been gaining momentum, accelerated rapidly when the spring of 1844 had passed and the prophecies of Miller had been "proved false."[71] "By the summer of 1844 Millerism stood sharp and clear on the religious horizon as a well-defined and more or less separate movement, with ministers, Advent associations, and meetinghouses."[72]

No exact figures exist as to the number who accepted Miller's teachings. Estimates range up to a million, but careful and conservative estimates suggest that somewhat in excess of fifty thousand out of a population of about 20 million in the twenty-six states that made up the United States at that time could be identified as Millerites. Miller himself said on this point, "In nearly a thousand places, Advent congregations have been raised up, numbering, as nearly as I can estimate, some fifty thousand believers."[73] The relative strength of the movement in certain large urban areas is suggested by the following estimates: Philadelphia, 3,000; Cincinnati, 1,000; St. Louis, 250; Akron, 150; Rochester, 600; Oswego, 90."[74] Many other thousands played it safe by giving lip service to the teaching. Miller estimated that about two hundred ministers accepted his views in the United States and Canada and that about five hundred were giving Millerite lectures at one time.[75]

The majority of converts to Millerism had come from the Methodist, Baptist, and Christian churches. Relatively few came from the Unitarians, Presbyterians, and Episcopalians. For its size, the Christian Church furnished the largest proportion of converts to Millerism. Everett Dick in a doctoral dissertation projected figures on the church affiliation of 174 Millerite lecturers. These indicated that 44 percent were Methodist, 27 percent were Baptist, 9 percent were Congregationalist, 8 percent were Christian, and 7 percent were Presbyterian.[76]

Economically the Millerites were made up largely of farmers, shopkeepers, and laborers. The "intellectuals" by and large ignored the movement or spoke out against the harm that they felt time-setting would inevitably do to religion in general. William Ellery Channing, just before his death in 1842, presented an interpretation totally different from the very literal one that was being applied to Bible prophecy by the Millerites.

Stories have been told of great fanaticism throughout the country, of people who went insane under the strain, and of those who put on white ascension robes or behaved in irrational ways. No evidence has ever been produced to substantiate the stories of insanity and ascension robes. However, there were fanatical views promulgated. One who passed through the 1844 experience wrote at a later date: "About this time, fanaticism began to appear. . . . There were some who manifested a blind and bigoted zeal, denouncing all who would not sanction their course. Their fanatical ideas and exercises met with no sympathy from the great body of Adventists. . . . William Miller had no sympathy with those influences that led to fanaticism."[77]

James White, looking back at this period, said: "It was when they were left without definite time, during the summer of 1844, that extravagant views of being led by the Spirit prevailed, and to some extent brought in fanaticism, division, and wildfire, with their blighting results. . . . I here enter my solemn protest against making one grand Second Advent chowder of all that in any way has been connected with the great Advent movement, of truth and error, of wisdom from heaven, and the spirit and work of fanaticism, and then presenting it to the people as being all the work of Satan, or all the work of God." [78]

Those who truly and devoutly believed in the validity of October 22 made every preparation to meet Christ at that time. Some farmers who had planted crops in the spring demonstrated their faith by refusing to harvest them. Some storeowners set a day upon which to give away all their stock to any who wished to come and receive it. The two main advent papers, *The Advent Herald* and *The Midnight Cry,* put out their last editions. *The Midnight Cry* phrased its editorial in these words of Paul: "Finally, brethren, farewell, . . . be of good comfort, be of one mind, live in peace; and the God of love and peace shall be with you." *The Advent Herald* of October 16, 1844, carried a message from Himes: "As the date of the present number of the *Herald* is our last day of publication before the tenth day of the seventh month, we shall make no provision for issuing a paper for the week following. . . . We feel called upon to suspend our labors and await the result."

Not all the people throughout the country were seriously concerned with the predicted end of the world. One contemporary business leader, Philip Hone, who kept a diary during this period, in his entries of October 9, 14, and 29, 1844, made no mention of the waiting Adventists. Instead he observed, "The approaching Presidential election engrosses all interest and occupies the minds of all our citizens." Memoirs of the aged John Quincy Adams indicate that he was giving thought on October 22 to a minor point in a Whig political speech that he had made, rather than to the Millerite expectations. The New Hampshire *Patriot and State Gazette* on October 22 devoted its front pages to a meeting of the Merrimack County Agricultural Society, to plans to revise the state constitution, and to several antislavery items, but not a word regarding the expectations of the Millerites.

Most newspapers of the day manifested only a moderate interest in the activities of the Adventists as the fateful day approached. In September, 1844, the New Hampshire *Patriot and State Gazette* commented in a tone that was rather typical of other newspapers that commented at all: "Father Miller, nothing daunted by the nondestruction of the earth on the 23rd of March, is still holding forth on 'the end.' . . . He insists that the end is near, though he wisely concludes that he cannot name the day."

As the day approached, the devout watchers set about to right all wrongs and to make final confessions of their misdeeds. Stolen money was returned, and restitution was made for acts of dishonesty. Sums of money were received by government officials from people who wished to clear their consciences before the end of time.

On the climactic day, October 22, the Protestant Episcopal Church, without so much as a nod to the waiting Adventists, closed its annual convocation in Philadelphia, concerned with such items as a mission station in Turkey and a bishopric in China, but not with the second advent of Christ. On Sunday, October 20, in the Central Presbyterian church in Philadelphia, the Reverend Mr. Rood based his sermon on Christ's words "Of that day and hour knoweth no man, no, not the angels of heaven, but my Father only." The minister then solemnly concluded that every failure of a time prediction of the end of the world produced more scoffers and infidels and did more harm than good to religion.

During the days just before October 22, the scores of Millerite preachers returned to their homes to wait. The great tent was furled, and the presses ceased to print the advent literature. "The time immediately preceding the 22d of October was one of great calmness of mind and of pleasurable expectation on the part of those who regarded that point of time with interest. There was a nearness of approach to God, and a sweetness of communion with him, to which those who experienced it will ever recur with pleasure." [79]

The Adventists greeted what they believed to be earth's last sunrise with quiet confidence and joy. They prepared to gather together during the day in their meetinghouses, or lacking such, in homes of the members, that they might welcome the solemn event as bands of believers together. Accounts of their going to churchyards to wait by the graves of their loved ones, or to hilltops to be nearer heaven, were largely fabricated by those who wished to ridicule them. The records indicate that they actually met in their churches or in the homes of their fellow Adventists.

The body of advent believers saw midnight come and pass. They waited for the hours to creep along until morning, and their disappointment then became a certainty. Hiram Edson, one of the leaders of the Millerites, wrote of this hour: "Our fondest hopes and expectations were blasted, and such a spirit of weeping came over us as I never experienced before. It seemed that the loss of all earthly friends could have been no comparison. We wept, and wept, till the day dawn." [80]

October 22 found William Miller in his home in Low Hampton, New York, where he had gone to rest upon the completion of the work of proclaiming Christ's imminent return. Here Himes came to spend the day with his old friend and fellow laborer. The day no doubt brought to them a deeper disappointment than to any of the others, for they had been so intimately bound up in all phases of the movement.

Miller, confused and disappointed with the passing of October 22, was not ready, however, to disavow his faith. He wrote: "One thing I do know, I have preached nothing but what I believed; and God has been with me; his power has been manifested in the work, and much good has been effected." [81]

The spring following the Disappointment, Miller wrote from Low Hampton, accepting an importunate correspondent's invitation to speak at Albany: "I beg of you not to expect anything great from old Father Miller; he is old and broken, forgetful, and I think has lost all his energy. I have supposed my work was done; but your continual importunity has compelled me to yield." [82]

Miller remained at his farm after the Disappointment. He continued to study, but in three years suffered from impaired eyesight. He died in December, 1849. His published testimony written during those last years of his life affirmed his belief in the authenticity of his experience and his continuing belief that the second coming of Christ was near at hand.

Himes lived to be an old man. He affiliated himself with first-day Adventists until 1875, but spent the latter part of his life as a rector of the Episcopal Chuch in the Dakotas. To the end of his life, however, he defended the Millerite movement from those who would ridicule or belittle it.

Captain Joseph Bates, of Fairhaven, Massachusetts, who gave all of his considerable means, earned as a seaman, to the Millerite cause and who gave of himself without stint as a Millerite preacher, was deeply perplexed when the Disappointment came. Years later he told a friend that the following morning when he went out on the street on his way to purchase provisions, he wished the earth would swallow him up when children and others ridiculed him for his failure to go up as he had said he would on October 22.

From the peak of anticipation the Millerites were cast into the deepest gloom. There were serious problems for those who had given up all their possessions. Their businesses abandoned, their crops ungathered, they were confused, and many were in want. An organization was set up to care for the needs of such. In some places judges appointed probate officers to care for the neglected crops and property. In embarrassment the disappointed band now had to admit to the world that they had been mistaken in their hope, and take up the threads of life as best they could.

Many renewed their former memberships in the Methodist, Baptist, and other Protestant churches. One group joined the Shakers, who had a theory on the second coming of Christ. Some became atheists. A number who did not join other religious organizations continued to study independently and formed groups with divergent views on a variety of doctrinal subjects. Because debates on religious matters often tend to become very heated, the divisions grew.

Six months after the Disappointment a number of Adventists, including Miller, Himes, and many others of the leaders, but not including Bates, James White, and others who eventually became leaders of the Seventh-day Adventist group, met in Albany, New York, to chart a course for the future. They approved the following resolution: *"Resolved . . . that we have no fellowship with any of the new tests as conditions of salvation. . . . That we have no fellowship with Jewish fables and commandments of men, that turn from the truth, or for any of the distinctive characteristics of modern Judaism. And that the act of promiscuous feet-washing and the salutation kiss, as practiced by some professing Adventists as religious ceremonies, sitting on the floor as an act of voluntary humility, shaving the heads to humble oneself and acting like children in understanding, is not only unscriptural, but subversive—if persevered in—of purity and morality."* [83] The conference also stressed the continuing opportunity for salvation, thus rejecting the "shut door" concept.

The Albany conference was instrumental in holding together for the next few years those who had remained Adventists after the Disappointment. This was the final endeavor to organize the movement as a united body, includng all who had been part of the Millerite movement.

The process of splintering among Adventists continued for ten or fifteen years after the Disappointment. At least six groups of Adventists emerged as separate divisions during this period. These groups were Evangelical Adventists, Advent Christian Church, Sabbatarian Adventists, Church of God (Adventist), The Life and Advent Union, the Churches of God in Christ Jesus. Miller indicated his regret at the divisions that were developing among the Adventist body and stated that in one week he had received fifteen different Adventist papers in which, he said, there was little in common but the name.[84]

169

On April 7, 1845, Miller wrote to Himes: "This is a peculiar time. The greatest variety of fanciful interpretations of Scripture are now being presented by new luminaries, reflecting their rays of light and heat in every direction. Some of these are wandering stars, and some emit only twilight. I am sick of this everlasting changing; but, my dear brother, we must learn to have patience." [85]

Himes became the target of vicious accusations following the Disappointment: "Himes was represented as a dishonest man who had speculated on the fears of the community, a disturber of the peace, a rogue who had duped unsuspecting persons, then obtained large sums of money from them under false pretenses. He was accused of soliciting money for public purposes and appropriating it to private uses. Reports were circulated that he had absconded to Canada, Texas, and England. It was said he was liable to arrest under warrants already issued, or that he had already been arrested and was residing in jail. One report said that he had committed suicide. . . .

In his defense Himes opened himself for a complete investigation at the hands of any proper or interested person. He asked all those who had business dealings with him to make their records public. He opened his office books to a public investigation. Finally, he asked that anyone who felt he had been defrauded by him should make it known." [86]

In the course of time the Sabbatarian Adventist group had embraced the seventh-day Sabbath and the unconscious state of man in death (as well as the "shut door" position, which was shortly abandoned). Now, more than one and a third centuries after the great Disappointment, this church of some 4.5 million members, 85 percent of whom reside outside North America, is proclaiming the gospel of Christ, including the imminence of the second advent, in 185 countries and in about 600 languages and dialects of earth.

October 22, 1844, was a day to be remembered by the Adventists for its promise and for its heartbreak. Just after the Disappointment, William Miller wrote to Himes: "I have fixed my mind upon another time, and here I mean to stand until God gives me more light. And that is *Today*, TODAY, and TODAY, until He comes, and I see Him for whom my soul yearns." [87]

The extent to which a firm belief in the literal personal return of Jesus Christ to this earth on October 22, 1844, took hold of and shaped the lives of many sincere people was hard for their contemporaries to grasp, and it is hard also for descendants of the disappointed to understand sympathetically. But we can sense some of the amazement of contemporaries in the words that appeared in the Kennebec (Maine) *Journal* on November 15, 1844, with which the writer concluded his account of the day the Bridegroom tarried: "All of this in the middle of the nineteenth century, and in enlightened New England."

Little did contemporaries realize that the hope that flamed so brightly in 1844 would still be shining in the hearts of millions more than a century later. Faith in the certainty and imminence of Christ's return has persisted in a very real way down to our day. A meeting held in Lausanne, Switzerland, as recently as the summer of 1974 was attended by 2,400 Protestant evangelical leaders from 150 countries. In the course of its deliberations this congress expressed its faith in the second coming of Christ in these words: "We believe that Jesus Christ will return personally and visibly, in power and glory, to consummate His salvation and His judgment."

The great Advent Awakening, coming at its appointed time, alerted that generation to the concept of the return of Christ to Planet Earth. Today, several generations later, the effects of that earlier awakening are seen in a church growing more conscious of the urgency of its mission to warn the world of the literal, visible, and imminent coming of Christ, the King.

NOTES

[1] Whitney R. Cross, *The Burned-over District: The Social and Intellectual History of Enthusiastic Religion in Western New York, 1800-1850* (New York, 1965), p. 168.

[2] Henry S. Commager, *The Era of Reform, 1830-1860* (Princeton, N.J., 1960), p. 7.

[3] Reuben E. E. Harkness, "Social Origins of the Millerite Movement" (unpublished Ph.D. dissertation, University of Chicago, 1927), p. 105.

[4] Cross, *The Burned-over District*, p. 41.

[5] *Ibid.*, p. 43.

[6] G. Peck, "The Coming of Christ," *Methodist Quarterly Review* 24 (July, 1842): 352.

[7] Elmer T. Clark, *The Small Sects in America*, rev. ed. (New York, 1949), p. 32.

[8] *Ibid.*

[9] Dwight S. Banks, "The Rise and Growth of the Advent Christian Denomination From the Point of View of Its Doctrinal Development" (unpublished M.S.T. thesis, Gordon College of Theology, 1939), pp. 16, 17.

[10] Albert C. Johnson, *Advent Christian History: A Concise Narrative of the Origin and Progress, Doctrine and Work of This Body of Believers* (Boston, 1918), pp. 86, 87.

[11] *A Brief History of William Miller, the Great Pioneer in Adventual Faith*, 4th ed. (Boston, 1915), p. 35.

[12] Everett N. Dick, "The Adventist Crisis of 1843-1844" (unpublished Ph.D. dissertation, University of Wisconsin, 1930), pp. 12, 13; L. E. Froom, *The Prophetic Faith of Our Fathers*, 4 vols. (Washington, D.C. (1946-1954), Vol. IV, p. 463.

[13] *A Brief History of William Miller*, pp. 75, 76.

[14] Sylvester Bliss, *Memoirs of William Miller, Generally Known as a Lecturer on the Prophecies, and the Second Coming of Christ* (Boston, 1853), pp. 70, 71.

[15] James White, *Sketches of the Christian Life and Public Labors of William Miller* (Battle Creek, Mich., 1875), pp. 62, 63.

[16] Cross, *The Burned-over District*, p. 291.

[17] H. A. Larrabee, "The Trumpeter of Doomsday," *American Heritage*, April, 1964, p. 100.

[18] Billy Rojas, "The origins of Millennial Speculation During the 1840s: The Background and Development of the Millerite Movement" (unpublished master's degree thesis, Roosevelt University, 1966).

[19] David Tallmadge Arthur, "Joshua V. Himes and the Cause of Adventism, 1838-1845" (unpublished master's degree thesis, University of Chicago, 1961), p. 100.

[20] Dick, "The Adventist Crisis of 1843-1844," p. 266.

[21] In letter to Truman Hendryx, quoted in Cross, *The Burned-over District*, pp. 318, 319. For a distinction between the Millerites in general and post-1844 Sabbatarian Adventists on abolitionism, see Jonathan M. Butler, "Adventism and the American Experience," in Edwin Scott Gaustad, ed., *The Rise of Adventism* (New York, 1974), p. 146.

[22] Charles E. Weniger, "A Critical Analysis and Appraisal of the Public Address of William Miller, Early American Advent Lecturer" (unpublished Ph.D. dissertation, University of Southern California, 1948), p. 382.

[23] In Johnson, *Advent Christian History*, p. 540.

[24] Weniger, "A Critical Analysis," p. 40.

[25] Dick, "The Adventist Crisis of 1843-1844," p. 23.

[26] *Signs of the Times*, Feb. 1, 1841.

[27] *Ibid.*, Aug. 1, 1840.

[28] Banks, "Rise and Growth of Advent Christian Denomination," p. 48.

[29] Arthur, "Joshua V. Himes," pp. 132, 133.

[30] In *A Brief History of William Miller*, p. 154.

[31] *Signs of the Times*, April 15, 1840.

[32] A Cosmopolite, "Miller Overthrown, or the False Prophet Confounded" (Boston, 1840), p. 7.

[33] In Josiah Litch, "Refutation of Dowling's Reply to Miller on the Second Coming of Christ in 1843," The Second Advent Library, No. 11 (March 12, 1843).

[34] From a J.W.D. Hall lecture, Taunton, Mass., 1843 (Huntington Library, Rare Book Room, No. 190279).

[35] *Signs of the Times*, Aug. 1, 1840.

[36] Letter, to Hendryx, quoted in Weniger, "A Critical Analysis," p. 97.

[37] "Proceedings of the General Conference," *The First Report of the General Conference of Christians Expecting the Advent of the Lord Jesus Christ* (Boston, 1842), p. 1.

[38] *Signs of the Times*, Sept. 15, 1840.

[39] "Proceedings," *First Report of the General Conference*, p. 16.

[40] "Proceedings of Second Advent Conference," Second Advent Tracts, No. 1.

[41] *Signs of the Times*, Nov. 15, 1840.

[42] Dick, "The Adventist Crisis of 1843-1844," p. 45.

[43] Froom, *Prophetic Faith of Our Fathers*, Vol. IV, p. 651.

[44] In Froom, *Prophetic Faith*, Vol. IV, p. 762.

[45] *Midnight Cry*, Nov. 18, 1842.

[46] *Signs of the Times*, Feb. 15, 1841.

[47] Dick, "The Adventist Crisis of 1843-1844," p. 100.

[48] Francis D. Nichol, *The Midnight Cry* (Washington, D.C., 1944), pp. 138, 137.

[49] In *A Brief History of William Miller*, p. 180.

[50] "Synopsis of Miller's Views" (Boston, 1843).

[51] Letter, Miller to Himes, *Signs of the Times*, May 3, 1843.

[52] Cross, *The Burned-over District*, p. 80.

[53] D. S. Porter, "The Seventh-day Adventist Church in Britain" (unpublished manuscript).

[54] Luther Boutelle, *Sketch of the Life and Religious Experience of Elder Luther Boutelle* (Boston, 1891), p. 59.

[55] Cross, *The Burned-over District*, pp. 297, 298.

[56] Arthur, "Joshua V. Himes," pp. 90, 91.

[57] Banks, "Rise and Growth of the Advent Christian Denomination," pp. 57, 58.

[58] Rojas, "Origins of Millennial Speculation," p. 172.

[59] *A Brief History of William Miller*, p. 151; Banks, "Rise and Growth of the Advent Christian Denomination," p. 52.

[60] In Isaac C. Wellcome, *History of the Second Advent Message and Mission, Doctrine and People* (Yarmouth, Maine, 1874), p. 293.

[61] *Ibid.*

[62] Weniger, "A Critical Analysis," p. 381.

[63] In White, *William Miller*, pp. 229, 230.

[64] *Signs of the Times*, May 15, 1840.

[65] In White, *William Miller*, p. 218.

[66] *Ibid.*, p. 269.

[67] M. E. Marty, *The Infidel: Free Thought in American Religion* (Cleveland, 1961), pp. 218, 219.

[68] In *Advent Herald*, April 10, 1844.

[69] In Bliss, *Memoirs of William Miller*, p. 253.

[70] *Midnight Cry*, March 14, 1844.

[71] Banks, "Rise and Growth of the Advent Christian Denomination," pp. 55, 56.

[72] *SDA Encyclopedia*, rev. ed., Commentary Reference Series (Washington, D.C., 1976), vol. 10, p. 894.

[73] In White, *William Miller*, p. 361.

[74] Dick, "The Adventist Crisis of 1843-1844," p. 269.

[75] Johnson, *Advent Christian History*, p. 89.

[76] Dick, "The Adventist Crisis of 1843-1844," p. 267.

[77] Ellen G. White, *The Great Controversy Between Christ and Satan* (Mountain View, Calif., 1950), pp. 395, 396.

[78] James White and Ellen G. White, *Life Sketches* (Battle Creek, Mich., 1888), pp. 94-97.

[79] Sylvester Bliss, quoted in Wellcome, *History of the Second Advent Message*, p. 365.

[80] In Nichol, *The Midnight Cry*, pp. 247, 248.

[81] In Bliss, *Memoirs of William Miller*, p. 280.

[82] Letter, William Miller to T. Wrightson, Albany, N.Y., March 25, 1845. Original letter is in the Historical Society of Pennsylvania Library, Philadelphia.

[83] From *Proceedings of the Mutual Conference of Adventists* (New York, 1845), p. 16.

[84] Banks, "Rise and Growth of the Advent Christian Denomination," p. 59.

[85] In White, *William Miller*, p. 339.

[86] Arthur, "Joshua V. Himes," pp. 150, 151.

[87] In *The Midnight Cry*, Dec. 5, 1844.

CHAPTER 9

The Second Advent in Seventh-day Adventist History and Theology

Norval F. Pease

THE most definitive statement of Seventh-day Adventist doctrine is found in the *Church Manual.* In the summary of fundamental beliefs are the following statements referring either directly or indirectly to the second advent:

The nature of the advent: "The second coming of Christ is the hope of the church, the climax of the gospel, and the goal of the plan of redemption, when Jesus will come literally, personally, and visibly, with all His holy angels. Many signs of the times testify that His coming is at hand." [1]

The time of the advent: "the almost complete fulfillment of all the various lines of prophecy indicates that 'he is near, even at the doors.' " [2]

The effect of the advent on people: "The righteous dead will be raised to life at Christ's second advent. Together with the righteous living, they will be caught up to meet the Lord in the air, and will go with Him to heaven, there to spend the one thousand years known as the millennium. . . . The wicked who are living at the time of Christ's second advent will be slain by the brightness of His coming. These, with the wicked dead of all ages, will await the second resurrection, at the close of the one thousand years." [3]

The end of the controversy between good and evil: "At the end of the one thousand years, the following events will take place. *(a)* Christ and the righteous will descend from heaven, with the Holy City, the New Jerusalem; *(b)* the wicked dead will be resurrected for final judgment *(c)* the wicked will receive the final wages of sin when fire comes down from God out of heaven to consume them; and *(d)* this fire, which destroys the works of sin, will purify the earth. . . . The earth, cleansed by fire and renewed by the power of God, will become the eternal home of the redeemed." [4]

This, in condensed form, is the Seventh-day Adventist interpretation of the Biblical doctrine of the second advent.

A study of Seventh-day Adventist literature indicates that there has been no basic change in the concept of the second advent. For example, the editor of the

Review and Herald published the following summary of this doctrine as he understood it in 1925:[5]

Sign Prophecies of the Lord's Return

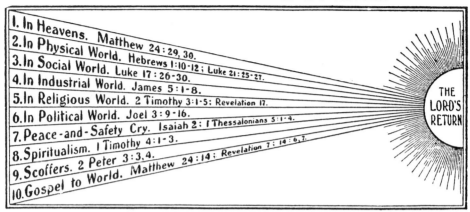

1. In Heavens. Matthew 24:29, 30.
2. In Physical World. Hebrews 1:10-12; Luke 21:25-27.
3. In Social World. Luke 17:26-30.
4. In Industrial World. James 5:1-8.
5. In Religious World. 2 Timothy 3:1-5: Revelation 17.
6. In Political World. Joel 3:9-16.
7. Peace-and-Safety Cry. Isaiah 2: 1 Thessalonians 5:1-4.
8. Spiritualism. 1 Timothy 4:1-3.
9. Scoffers. 2 Peter 3:3,4.
10. Gospel to World. Matthew 24:14; Revelation 7; 14:6,7.

THE LORD'S RETURN

Time Prophecies of the Lord's Return

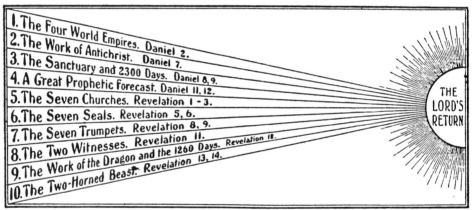

1. The Four World Empires. Daniel 2.
2. The Work of Antichrist. Daniel 7.
3. The Sanctuary and 2300 Days. Daniel 8, 9.
4. A Great Prophetic Forecast. Daniel 11, 12.
5. The Seven Churches. Revelation 1-3.
6. The Seven Seals. Revelation 5, 6.
7. The Seven Trumpets. Revelation 8, 9.
8. The Two Witnesses. Revelation 11.
9. The Work of the Dragon and the 1260 Days. Revelation 12.
10. The Two-Horned Beast. Revelation 13, 14.

THE LORD'S RETURN

Going back another thirty-six years, the *Seventh-day Adventist Yearbook* of 1889 dealt with the second advent as follows: "Seventh-day Adventists believe: . . .

"That the doctrine of the world's conversion and a temporal millennium is a fable of these last days, calculated to lull men into a state of carnal security, and cause them to be overtaken by the great day of the Lord as by a thief in the night (1 Thess. 5:3); that the second coming of Christ is to precede, not follow, the millennium; for until the Lord appears, the papal power, with all its abominations, is to continue (2 Thess. 2:8), the wheat and tares grow together (Matt. 13:29, 30, 39), and evil men and seducers wax worse and worse, as the Word of God declares (2 Tim. 3:1, 13)." [6]

"That the mistake of Adventists in 1844 pertained to the nature of the event then to transpire, not to the time; that no prophetic period is given to reach to the second advent, but the longest one, the two thousand and three hundred days of

Daniel 8:14, terminated in 1844, and brought us to an event called the cleansing of the sanctuary." [7]

"That God, in accordance with His uniform dealings with the race, sends forth a proclamation of the approach of the second advent of Christ; and that this work is symbolized by the three messages of Revelation 14." [8]

"That out of this prison-house of the grave, mankind are to be brought by a bodily resurrection; the righteous having part in the first resurrection, which takes place at the second coming of Christ." [9]

"That at the last trump, the living righteous are to be changed in a moment, in the twinkling of an eye, and with the risen righteous are to be caught up to meet the Lord in the air, so forever to be with the Lord (1 Thess. 4:16, 17; 1 Cor. 15:51, 52)." [10]

Going back to the beginning of Seventh-day Adventist history, James White stressed the doctrine of the second advent in terms that are still very familiar to Adventists: "He will *appear* the second time. . . .

"The second advent of Christ will be personal and visible. . . . Jesus, as He was addressing His disciples upon the subject of His second advent, pointed forward to the generation who would witness the signs of that event in the sun, moon, and stars, and said: 'They shall see the Son of man coming in the clouds of heaven with power and great glory' " (Matt. 24:30). . . .

"When the Lord shall be revealed from heaven in flaming fire, sinners then living will be destroyed, and the earth will be desolated. . . .

'When Christ appears the second time, the righteous dead will be raised, and the living righteous will be changed to immortality. . . .

"The church will then be no more separated from her adorable Redeemer; but with all the endowments of immortality, will 'ever be with the Lord.' " [11]

The foregoing samples of Seventh-day Adventist belief regarding the second advent extend over a period of a century and a quarter. If everything written and preached by Seventh-day Adventists regarding the second advent were to be analyzed and organized, a central core of doctrinal propositions might be stated somewhat as follows:

1. The second advent will be the climax of the plan of redemption.

2. The second advent is a prominent Biblical doctrine.

3. Bible prophecy indicates the "time of the end," but does not reveal the "day nor the hour" of the second advent.

4. The Bible foretells a series of signs in the physical, social, industrial, and religious worlds that indicate the imminence of the second advent.

5. The second advent will involve the resurrection of the dead who have been certified for eternal life in the pre-advent judgment.

6. The second advent will involve the destruction of those who have rejected the offer of salvation.

7. The second advent will be literal and visible.

8. The second advent will precede the millennium.

9. Preparation for the second advent involves a full acceptance of Christ as Saviour and Lord.

10. The church is directed to proclaim the message of the second advent to the world.

This list of propositions may not be complete. The order is not necessarily significant, and the wording is subject to revision. The basic ideas, however, are essential to Adventist theology.

Variety in Interpretation

The existence of a relatively constant theological position in regard to the second advent does not mean that the theme has had no variations. These variations have resulted from the basic fact of the passing of time, from changing conditions in the world and the church, and from continued reflection and evaluation on the part of the church's preachers, teachers, writers, and laymen. Selections in chronological order from church literature will illustrate the existence and the nature of variety in interpretation.

A writer in the *Review and Herald* of December 9, 1852, had the following to say about the beginning date of the "generation" of Matthew 24:34: " 'This generation' is clearly defined by our Lord. None other can reasonably apply, but the 'very generation' that are *eye-witnesses* to the fulfillment of 'all these things,' that is, the signs of the end of the world, and second coming of Christ, commencing with the darkening of the sun and the moon in 1780." [12]

Six years later the same contributor repeated his insistence on this point in a letter to the *Review*. The editor, Uriah Smith, disagreed: "We are . . . inclined to the opinion that the generation of which the Saviour declares that it shall not pass away, embraces all those in a situation to understand the proclamation of the First Angel, and who were taught to look upon the signs in the sun, moon, and stars *as* precursors of the great and notable day of the Lord." [13]

In 1871 James White, *Review* editor, wrote even more specifically: "It is our opinion that the Lord designed to teach that the people who should live at the time of the fulfillment of the last sign (the falling of the stars in 1833), and should hear the proclamation of the coming of Christ, based partly upon the fulfilled signs, should witness the scenes connected with His coming." [14]

In 1891 Uriah Smith was again editor of the *Review*, and his comment reflected the passing of time: "The generation living in 1844, when the great Advent proclamation was set before the world in such power, was the first generation that had these things presented to them in this manner. Many of them are still living, and will not have passed off the stage of action, before the angels are sent to gather the elect into the everlasting kingdom." [15]

The continued passing of time caused a contributor to the *Review* to make the following comment in 1905: "It is evident without argument that the end of this generation is now almost reached. 'This generation' to which the words of Christ referred is now represented only by hoary heads and feeble frames. They have reached the place in life's journey where death gathers his harvest from their number rapidly. A few more years at most must terminate the natural span of life for the few who yet remain. There remains only a brief part of the brief period which constitutes 'this generation.' " [16]

It is interesting to note in passing that in 1901 the scriptural statement "There shall be delay no longer" was adopted as a denominational slogan. The fact that this slogan was taken seriously is attested to by a reference to it made in 1905 in a *Review* editorial. [17]

As late as 1925 the phraseology that had become so popular over a period of seventy-five years appeared in a *Review* article: "History records in detail the fulfillment of our Lord's great prophecy regarding these signs and world conditions, and we are now unmistakably standing on the border of the eternal world, in the very closing days of the last generation." [18]

More than a half century has passed since the writing of this statement. The present generation has been faced with the absolute necessity of finding a viable explanation for the delay. This could have involved spiritualizing the second advent into some sort of "realized eschatology." It could have involved a complete rejection of the idea of imminence. But the belief in the second advent was too precious to the Adventist heart for these directions to be taken. A moving expression of the Adventist predicament and the Adventist faith is found in a 1968 statement by William A. Fagal, who was director of the Faith for Today telecast. This statement is included in this chapter because it is so representative of the virility of the advent hope, even in today's generation:

"For almost half a century now I have attended the Adventist Church and been exposed to its teachings. But important though this has been, the main religious influence on my life has not been church services but my parents' consistent, dedicated lives. . . .

"One thing they believed with all their hearts: Soon Jesus, keeping a centuries-old divine promise, will return to earth. And they taught me to believe this also. As I grew older and listened to sermons at church, camp meetings, . . . and occasional evangelistic services, I developed for myself the firm conviction that someday soon our Lord will return. I even felt concerned that He might come before I had a chance to complete my education and enter His service as a minister.

"But you see, it was evident back there—40 years ago—that the signs were taking place that Jesus had given in His Word to signal the approach of His advent. He must indeed come *soon*.

"Now I have been in the ministry more than 25 years, and my son looks forward to a place of service in God's cause. How do I feel now? With the passing of time have I concluded that "my Lord delayeth his coming" (Matt. 24:48)? Have I given up my faith and gone out to live a life full of worldly satisfactions but empty of that which really counts? No, I could not do that, because I believe more than ever that He is coming back to earth, and *soon*." [19]

Some may ask, How can a faith like that be maintained in view of the passing of the years? What theological rationale can enable the Adventist to continue his belief in the imminence of the Lord's return, despite the delay?

One answer to this question has been a growing emphasis in Seventh-day Adventist ranks on the hermeneutical principle of *conditional prophecy*. Probably the most complete treatment of this concept is found in L. E. Froom's *Movement of Destiny*, published in 1971. Froom phrases the issue thus: *"Just what is it that has delayed the promised return of our Lord? Can we know precisely why and wherein? And who and what are responsible? Has this been revealed, so that we are not left to bumbling guesswork? Or—have we been mistaken or misled in our basic expectation of the imminence of the Advent?"* [20]

Froom finds his answers to these questions in the writings of Ellen G. White. He recalls that in 1883 Ellen White was challenged to defend her 1851 statement that "time can last but a very little longer." [21] Her response, as Froom points out, was as follows: "The angels of God in their messages to men represent time as very short.

Thus it has always been presented to me. It is true that time has continued longer than we expected in the early days of this message. Our Saviour did not appear as soon as we hoped. But has the word of the Lord failed? Never! It should be remembered that the promises and threatenings of God are alike conditional." [22]

"It is the unbelief, the worldliness, unconsecration, and strife among the Lord's professed people that have kept us in this world of sin and sorrow so many years." [23]

This answer to the question of the delayed advent raises other questions: How about the sovereignty of God, whose purposes "know no haste and no delay"? [24] Can man's unfaithfulness postpone the advent indefinitely? Froom answers: "There are two sides to this crucial problem—God's side and ours. The times and the controls are in His hands. But the retardation or the speed-up largely rests with us—up to a point. They comprise our responsibility. It is chiefly a matter of our response and His enabling. God alone can bring the consummation to pass. He is sovereign. It is imperative that we understand these two sides, and rightly relate ourselves thereto." [25]

"There is in God's purpose and provision a moment, a time, a point, a climax—known only to Himself—beyond which our Lord will not tarry. His purposes and commitment will definitely and positively be carried out. A requisite proportion of His people *will* at last respond." [26]

Froom quotes another relevant Ellen G. White statement, made in 1868: "God's unwillingness to have His people perish has been the reason for so long delay." [27] He comments: "God is obviously more interested in the saving of precious souls, and in their being ready to meet the Lord, than in the precipitate fulfillment of His warnings." [28]

Froom traces the statements of Ellen White in regard to the delayed advent throughout her entire ministry. She always believed the advent to be imminent, though in 1901 she did say, "We may have to remain here in this world because of insubordination many more years." [29] The delaying factors were pointed out as the unreadiness of the church and the unfinished work of the gospel. But Ellen White stated clearly that "there is a limit beyond which the judgments of Jehovah can no longer be delayed." [30]

Froom's theology of the delayed advent is summarized in the following paragraphs: "God has made an irrevocable commitment—that sin and defiance shall not go beyond the line He has drawn, the point He has fixed, the time He has set. His predetermined *definitive outline* of the *redemptive provisions* will be fulfilled according to His convenanted commitment. There will and can be no failure here. The honor and integrity of God and His government—and of His declared Word—are at stake. The leeway ended, the extension concluded, then comes the destined finality, the avowed consumation—as surely as God is in His heaven.

"There is no unfaithfulness, no inconsistency or unawareness, no vacillation or uncertainty, no weakness or failure, on the part of God. Instead, there is infinite wisdom and understanding, mercy and justice, yearning love and inflexible righteousness. He has not abdicated His throne, nor relinquished His sovereign rulership.

"God is still at the controls of the universe. He is soon to bring His chosen ship Zion into the port of eternity. Despite any seeming appearances to the contrary, His is infinite, indefeasible, all-wise timing—as mankind will find. We would not have wished this deferment to have been otherwise, in the light of all the circumstances and contingencies—when viewed in the retrospective light of eternity. God knows best, and does what is best. He never errs. We can trust His wisdom and omnipotence."[31]

Herbert E. Douglass is one of the most recent proponents of the "conditional prophecy" theme. In an address given at a series of Bible conferences in 1974, Douglass developed his rationale for the delayed advent. He states his objective as follows: "We should renew our eschatological sense of urgency through the exposition of an adequate theology for the delay in the fulfillment of the Second Advent and thus to motivate to an accelerated completion of the task."[32]

The background of Adventist eschatology he summarizes as follows: "For over a century they [Seventh-day Adventists] have preached that Jesus could have returned within the lifetime of any generation living since 1844—long before there was a population explosion, ecological imbalances, nuclear weapons, an energy crisis, Adolf Hitler, World War II, or the modern nation of Israel. Adventist reasons for expecting the return of Jesus anytime within the last century have rested on sound principles of interpreting the Bible and not on sensational headlines in the morning newspapers.[33]

The principle of conditional prophecy Douglass introduces in the following statement, which he has underlined in his presentation: *"Only by employing a consistent hermeneutic, . . . that includes the Biblical principle of conditional prophecy, have Adventists been able to interpret Biblical promises and prophecies and yet avoid the mistakes and non sequiturs of other sincere Bible students."*[34]

He proceeds to defend the conditional principle and to establish boundaries for its application: "The principle of conditionality is not a hermeneutical gimmick contrived by Seventh-day Adventists to explain the delay in the Advent. Besides being a Biblical concept, this principle beautifully reflects the character of God. It tells us much about His way of dealing with men. He forces no one to do things His way; He waits for His people to 'catch on.' He is very patient and longsuffering; but eventually *what He promises does materialize*. What He says *will* be done *gets* done. However He often must wait until what He has purposed is indeed accomplished by men and women who have freedom of choice—for that is what the cosmic controversy is all about."[35]

Some would feel that Douglass overemphasizes the behavior of the church as a factor in determining the time of the advent and underemphasizes the ultimate sovereignty of God. It is true that Douglass does not stress the authority of God as much as does Froom; yet the above quotation indicates that he does not ignore it entirely.

Douglass stresses what he terms the "harvest principle"—namely, that "Jesus will return only when the harvest is ripe."[36] He argues that "the harvest principle in no way limits God's sovereignty."[37] His emphasis is on the development of a church that will be ready to meet its Lord. His position raises questions about the meaning of Christian perfection that are outside the boundaries of this study (Douglass's contribution was published in 1979 under the title *The End* [Pacific Press]).

Jack W. Provonsha, professor of religion and Christian ethics at Loma Linda University, has made a contemporary contribution to the theology of the second advent. Perhaps the keynote statement in his chapter "The God Who Comes to

Man," is: "Until Christians have learned what the second coming of Christ *means*, the event as something *that happens* may continue to be delayed."[38] Provonsha's quest for "meaning" leads him to declare: "The Second Coming is about the One who *comes* in history at a point of time as Jesus promised, but also One who ever comes. And make no mistake about it. That event in history is as certain as Jesus is trustworthy. That great event of the future points to an eternal truth about God's nature. It is God's nature to come to man."[39]

After developing further some of the "meanings" he sees in the doctrine of the second advent, Provonsha observes: "Unfortunately, out of concern for the time of the event, Adventists have often largely neglected these and other meanings which have so little to do with time. What they wanted to know is not What does it mean? but How? and When will it happen? The former of these they probably wouldn't understand, anyway, and the latter it was not for them to know, except relatively."[40]

Provonsha does not neglect the importance of signs. He says: "Signs of the times are, of course, useful as expressions of and reinforcement of this essential attitude of expectancy. While we are referring to signs, it might be well to observe that for the first time in history one of the major preconditions suggested by the Bible for the Second Coming now exists—*the whole world*. Never before has it been possible for issues to be really universal in their scope. There are no longer any truly isolated pockets of humanity. It is now technically possible for virtually every man, woman, and child on earth to experience any event or issue simultaneously. Communications technology has placed every man in everybody else's backyard. Nothing important happens anywhere but what can be known almost instantly everywhere. And this is what is most different about our day."[41]

Provonsha makes a unique contribution by discussing two reasons why modern man has difficulty in accepting the Biblical teaching of the second advent: (1) the seemingly interminable delay; and (2) the problem of harmonizing the phenomena of the second advent with modern scientific concepts. In answer to the first question the author states, "The Scriptures portray Him [God] as being both patient and compassionate. . . . He is in no hurry! . . . It is rather we who are impatient."[42] In answer to the second question, he declares, "The Scriptures speak of categories and qualities that must of necessity transcend the limits of time and space as we know them. . . . A skepticism that derives from human limitations may bear little relationship to what is ultimately real."[43]

There are places in the chapter where the reader has to read carefully to identify what the author means by "symbol," "objective reality," and "meaning." But he comes through clearly in his insistence on the reality of the second advent and the necessity of a deeper understanding of its significance.

God Meets Man, by Sakae Kubo, was published in 1978. Kubo was formerly a professor of New Testament at Andrews University and subsequently president of Newbold College, England. His book is divided into two sections, "The Meaning of the Sabbath" and "The Meaning of the Second Advent."

The section on the second advent is also divided into two sections, "The Advent and the Present Life" and "The Advent and Future Events." In the chapters under these headings are numerous paragraphs that give insights into the deeper significance of the second advent. The following selected quotations reflect some of the major concerns of the author:

"When we consider that the earth can support only 6 to 8 billion inhabitants, time is short for the human race before great catastrophies overtake us. Because of the population explosion and the insatiable needs of such increasing numbers, an insoluble dilemma presents itself. Men must decide either to choke to death from the pollutants they pour into the atmosphere or curtail their needs, be less comfortable, and eat less. If nuclear war does not wipe us out, we will eliminate ourselves by overpopulation and pollution. Such prospects lead only to despair." [44]

"The doctrine of last things is as important as that of first things. In Christian circles a crucial conflict took place over the understanding of the latter in the nineteenth century in the form of evolution versus Creation. At the same time the battle decided how one would interpret last things. If one considered Creation as unscientific and incongruous with science, it follows naturally that he would regard the return of Christ in the same way. Consequently, not as much open conflict rages over the doctrine of last things.

"Eschatology became a neglected area in Christian theology. For modern man it did not make sense. But with the neglect there arose a sense of futility. With no climax and objective to history, what sense did it make to live, to love others, to do good, to sacrifice, to discipline oneself? It is like sowing while knowing there would be no harvest, or practicing for a game that you know you would never play." [45]

"The resurrection, judgment, heaven, and hell constitute eschatology, but the central matter is the parousia, the appearance of our Lord and Saviour Jesus Christ. The ideas of the resurrection, judgment, heaven, and hell are not uniquely Christian. Other religions have some type of end-time events that seek to bring justice in an ultimate way. It is the parousia of Jesus Christ which is distinctive, the same Jesus Christ who is our Creator, who was incarnated, who lived among us, who was crucified, who was raised from the dead, and who ascended on high." [46]

"Redemption remains incomplete without the parousia; the righteous dead stay in their graves, and the righteous living stumble about in their sinful bodies in the midst of a sinful world, doomed to death." [47]

"The cross, the resurrection, and the ascension of Jesus make the coming of Christ an absolute certainty." [48]

"God is sovereign, and when His time comes, so will the day of the Lord. Besides, all that we do God has taken into consideration in His determination of the date, but the final decision is God's, not men's. It is well to keep this in mind so that we do not blasphemously think we can somehow by our own merely human efforts bring Christ down." [49]

"The man with an eschatological vision feels convinced of the validity of love, justice, right, and truth, which compels him to live all the more responsibly." [50]

"Thus God brings to fruition His desire for man. Sin and death have temporarily delayed its fulfillment, but ultimately God will accomplish His plan. The glorious appearing of Christ is a necessity if life is to have any meaning at all. Only with His coming will judgment and reward and final fruition take place. Then will all creatures say, " 'To him who sits upon the throne and to the Lamb be blessing and honor and glory and might for ever and ever!' " (Rev. 5:13, R.S.V.)." [51]

The quotations have been recorded without comment. They speak for themselves as examples of mature theological observations on the doctrine of the second advent.

A more recent contribution to the dialogue regarding conditional prophecy is a paper by William G. Johnsson, editor of the *Adventist Review,* entitled "Conditionality in Biblical Prophecy, With Particular Reference to Apocalyptic."

Dr. Johnsson's conclusions are as follows:

"1. Conditionality is a valid principle of Biblical interpretation. It arises from a due regard for the concern with human freedom that undergirds the Biblical accounts of God's dealings with the human race.

"2. Conditionality, however, may not be used indiscriminately in prophetic interpretation. Just as human freedom stands in tension with divine sovereignty in the Scriptures, so conditionality must give way to the fixed predictions of God in many prophetic passages. All Biblical predictions are not conditional.

"3. The prophecies made to Israel in a covenant setting are conditional. They are applications of the law of the covenant rather than predictive prophecies per se. They are the usual occurrence of conditional predictions in the Bible.

"4. Since conditionality is found most frequently in the covenant setting, the term 'conditional prophecy' itself is misleading.

"5. In prophecies of the first and second advents, conditionality is not a major factor. These predictions are predicated on the divine intervention in history as God asserts His sovereignty to effect His will in working out the plan of salvation.

"6. Apocalyptic predictions are usually unconditional. Only where the covenant setting with Israel predominates is conditionality present; and then it indeed is present. Elsewhere the divine sovereignty and foreknowledge portray history on a grand scale.

"7. It is therefore vital that any Biblical prophecy be carefully studied in interpretation. We by no means rule out conditionality; we merely suggest that we may not without due consideration employ conditionality as the key to interpretation. We must first study carefully the original context, noting the type of literature. (Is it general prophecy or apocalyptic? Does it fall within the covenant promises and threatenings?) Finally, we should see what application, if any, another inspired writer makes of the prophecy." [52]

Dr. Johnsson's insights provide a corrective to the tendency to believe that man can thwart the fulfillment of God's purposes.

The theme of variety in interpretation could be extended ad infinitum. Much could be written on the particular signs of the advent as they have been stressed at different times. In the earliest days much was said about the Dark Day and the falling of the stars, and some mention was even made of the aurora borealis. World conditions have always claimed their share of attention, with each new crisis being singled out as a harbinger of the advent. Every war has been the subject of serious concern. Natural disasters have been catalogued as they occurred. Strife between capital and labor could always be documented by fresh evidence. From the 1850s through the 1920s the "Eastern question" was a source of much speculation. The fate of the Turk was heralded as the trigger for earth's final conflict. "Many shall run to and fro, and knowledge shall be increased" (Dan. 12:4) was interpreted as applying to improvements in modes of transportation and new and greater scientific discoveries. Decline in moral standards was not difficult to document. While there was superficial variety in the preaching of the signs, a unified basic theme has remained surprisingly constant.

This unity can be observed by a perusal of the many "message" books and pamphlets that have been published by the Seventh-day Adventist Church as part of its evangelistic thrust. An analysis of these publications is beyond the limits of this chapter. A. O. Tait's *Heralds of the Morning* has been selected as a sample of this type of literature. It was published about "midstream" in Seventh-day Adventist history, appearing in five editions dated 1899, 1905, 1906, 1912, and 1915. An analysis of the 1915 edition reveals twenty-two chapters covering very thoroughly the Seventh-day Adventist teaching on the second advent. Both the prophecies and the signs are developed in detail. Tait, however, places less emphasis than some other authors on the signs in the heavens and the Eastern question.

Toward the close of his book Tait reveals his theological stance in regard to the second advent in the following statement: "The One who has inspired all the foregoing promises is no less a personage than He who created the universe. He possesses in Himself all the power that holds in place the vast world on which we live, guiding it in harmony with the countless number of vaster worlds which He is also sustaining and directing in space. In considering a statement or a promise, it is also proper to consider the power and ability of the one who makes it. Surely the One who has made this wealth of promises that Jesus the Lord will come again has ample power to sustain Him in making good His word. We may be sure that very part of it will be definitely and accurately fulfilled." [53]

Some arguments for the imminence of the second advent become less convincing with the passing time—for example, the Lisbon earthquake, the Dark Day, and the falling of the stars. These signs may be characterized as indications of the beginning of "the time of the end."

Other arguments become more compelling with the passing of time. One of these is the concept that the only alternative to the second advent is the self-destruction of the human race, as stressed by Kubo. This idea was proposed more than fifty years ago by Alonzo L. Baker, then an editor of *The Signs of the Times*. Baker wrote: "If the world should continue for long without some superhuman intervention, it would become one vast hospital, one great insane asylum, a charnel house whose walls are the four corners of the earth." [54]

Many frightening developments have taken place since Baker's book was written. The harnessing of nuclear energy has resulted in destructive weapons that threaten the survival of civilization on this planet. Pollution endangers human life by poisoning water and air, without which man cannot live. The population of the world threatens to grow larger than the world's known resources can support.

Modern believers in the second advent see in the declining quality of life on this planet a convincing sign that this is the end time described in the Bible. The rationale of their argument is that God will not permit the human race to self-destruct. The promised consummation of the plan of redemption must be sufficiently imminent to win the race with impending global disaster.

Theodore Carcich, formerly vice president of the General Conference of Seventh-day Adventists, declares: "For the first time in modern history men, religious or not, are envisaging the actual ending of man's adventure on earth." He quotes Toynbee's well-known statement: "If we have a nuclear war, too few people will be left alive to maintain civilization. If we do not, too many people will make life on this planet intolerable." [55] In a later article in the same series Carcich concludes: "The goal of history is the second coming of Christ and that the age-old warfare between good and evil will not drag on indefinitely and inconclusively."[56]

Robert H. Parr, then editor of the Australian *Signs of the Times* called attention to the problems of pollution and overpopulation, and reached the following conclusion: "These reasons are sufficient for me to believe that unless there is divine intervention man will either destroy the earth with his weapons of warfare or his pollutants, or he will starve himself because he cannot produce sufficient to feed the human family. Whether one of these horrors erupts first, or whether they all arrive together, this earth faces an insoluble crisis.

"I believe in the imminence of divine intervention. God has intervened in human affairs before—in Noah's day, for example. And such an intervention is the only thing that enables me to contemplate the future with equanimity. That, too, puts fervor into my prayer, 'Even so, come, Lord Jesus.' "[57]

Among other Seventh-day Adventist writers who have echoed these sentiments are H.M.S. Richards,[58] Earl E. Cleveland,[59] Horace E. Walsh,[60] and, more recently, Roy Allan Anderson.[61]

Current pessimism regarding the future of the world gives this argument an unprecedented cogency.

To the Adventist, whether in 1850 or later, "the doctrine of the second advent is the very keynote of the Sacred Scriptures."[62] Emphases might differ, vocabularies might change, but the basic theological principle remains constant. The long delay has necessitated some reflection on the Seventh-day Adventist position, but this reflection has resulted in clarification, not retrenchment.

The durability of this Seventh-day Adventist eschatology is attested to by a survey done in 1967 by C. Mervyn Maxwell, professor of church history at Andrews University, entitled "Trends in Second Coming Emphases and Interpretation Among Seventh-day Adventists." This research was reported to the Biblical Research Committee of the General Conference of Seventh-day Adventists. In his conclusions Maxwell stated: "This study has also attested a strong basic homogeneity among the kinds of people who responded. When the 1052 respondees were separated into 28 separate occupational, educational, and age groups, their responses on most issues were found to be remarkably similar. This observation, it may be stated, lends credence to the study as a valid sample of the type of people surveyed. All groups overwhelmingly acknowledged the second coming as a literal, personal, glorious appearance of Christ in the clouds. All groups overwhelmingly professed use of the phrase 'if time lasts' when announcing at least some of their plans. All groups accepted many if not all the same signs—and all agreed that 'mortal degradation' is the most impressive sign of all."[63]

Ellen G. White and the Second Advent

The second advent was one of Ellen White's most prominent themes. In her first vision she saw Jesus come, she saw the resurrection, and she was part of the group that was caught up to meet the Lord in the air.[64] According to her son, W. C. White, during her final illness she said, "Do not worry. I go only a little before the others."[65]

But to Ellen White, the second advent was more than a sentimental dream. She saw it as an integral part of the gospel: "The gospel message proclaimed by Christ's disciples was the announcement of His first advent to the world. It bore to men the good tidings of salvation through faith in Him. It pointed forward to His second coming in glory to redeem His people, and it set before men the hope, through faith and obedience, of sharing the inheritance of the saints in light. This message is given to men today, and at this time there is coupled with it the announcement of Christ's second coming as at hand. The signs which He Himself gave of His coming have been fulfilled, and by the teaching of God's Word we may know that the Lord is at the door.

"John in the Revelation foretells the proclamation of the gospel message just before Christ's second coming. He beholds an angel flying 'in the midst of heaven, having the everlasting gospel to preach unto them that dwell on the earth, and to every nation, and kindred, and tongue, and people, saying with a loud voice, Fear God, and give glory to him; for the hour of his judgment is come' (Rev. 14:6, 7).

"In the prophecy this warning of the judgment, with its connected messages, is followed by the coming of the Son of man in the clouds of heaven. The proclamation of the judgment is an announcement of Christ's second coming as at hand. And this proclamation is called the everlasting gospel. Thus the preaching of Christ's second coming, the announcement of its nearness, is shown to be an essential part of the gospel message." [66]

Ellen White's doctrine of the second advent is well summarized in chapter 17 of *The Great Controversy*, entitled "Heralds of the Morning." The author reviews the Biblical evidence of the second advent. Her list follows the classical Seventh-day Adventist pattern, except for the absence of any mention of the "Eastern question." She quotes from the Protestant Reformers to support her statement that "the coming of the Lord has been in all ages the hope of His true followers." [67] She reviews the well-known signs of the advent, beginning with the Lisbon earthquake of 1755. She explains the prophetic messages of Revelation 14, applying these messages to the nineteenth-century advent movement. She compares the failure of mankind to be ready for the first advent with the indifference of the world toward the second advent. This chapter is, in a sense, an introduction to the chapters that follow, tracing the advent movement from William Miller to the final events.

At this point Ellen White reveals the uniqueness of her testimony concerning the second advent. She alone could have written the chapter in *The Great Controversy* entitled "God's People Delivered," because she writes not only as an interpreter of Scripture, not only as a theologican, but as one who had witnessed a preview of the events. This chapter is a prime example of her claim, "Through the illumination of the Holy Spirit, the scenes of the long-continued conflict between good and evil have been opened to the writer of these pages." [68]

The eyewitness nature of the material is illustrated in the following quotations:

"The firmament appears to open and shut. The glory from the throne of God seems flashing through. The mountains shake like a reed in the wind, and ragged rocks are scattered on every side. There is a roar as of a coming tempest. The sea is lashed into fury. There is heard the shriek of the hurricane, like the voice of demons upon a mission of destruction. The whole earth heaves and swells like the waves of the sea. Its surface is breaking up. Its very foundations seem to be giving way. Mountain chains are sinking. Inhabited islands disappear. The seaports that have become like Sodom for wickedness, are swallowed up by the angry waters." [69]

"Soon there appears in the east a small black cloud, about half the size of a man's hand. It is the cloud which surrounds the Saviour, and which seems in the distance to be shrouded in darkness. . . . The firmament seems filled with radiant forms—'ten thousand times ten thousand, and thousands of thousands.' No human pen can portray the scene; no mortal mind is adequate to conceive its splendor." [70]

How the Holy Spirit revealed to the author the scenes of the second advent, we cannot and need not know. Also we need not assume that the picture she paints is complete in every detail. As a television serial gives a few glimpses of the next installment, so believers in the second advent are given a glimpse of that which is to come.

Previously in this chapter, the theme of conditional prophecy has been discussed. A summary of the teaching of Ellen White regarding the second advent would not be complete without reference to a doctoral dissertation by Ralph E. Neall, professor of religion at Union College, Lincoln, Nebraska. This dissertation, completed in 1982, is entitled, *The Nearness and the Delay of the Parousia in the Writings of Ellen G. White.* [71] In the abstract of his research, Neall states:

"While White consistently wrote of the nearness of the end throughout her ministry, she added the concept of contingency and delay in 1883, in reply to a critic's charge that she was a false prophet because Christ had not come. She said He had been delayed by the past and present sins of His people. Delay then became a new motive behind the same exhortations seen in the nearness stream of her thought.

"The tension between nearness and delay cannot be completely harmonized in Ellen White's writings, except perhaps by suggesting that the time of the end is fixed from God's viewpoint but delayed from man's." [72]

Neall summarizes the tension between "nearness" and "delay" in Seventh-day Adventist concepts of the second advent as follows:

"Alongside the belief that Christ is coming soon, there has developed in the church a belief that His coming has been delayed by the failure of church members to live holy lives and preach the message to the world. Taylor Grant Bunch, administrator and college Bible teacher, preached a widely distributed series of vesper sermons in 1937 which suggested that modern Seventh-day Adventists were repeating the experiences of the ancient Israelites who wandered in the wilderness for forty years because of their unbelief and disobedience. In the 1930s this interest was renewed by a spate of articles in popular Adventist magazines. In 1974 C. Mervyn Maxwell, chairman of the Department of Church History at the Seventh-day Adventist Theological Seminary at Andrews University, and Herbert E. Douglass, book editor for Pacific Press, wrote that Christ will come when the image of Christ is perfectly reflected in His children or, as Douglass put it, when the harvest is ripe. In this they were following the lead of M. L. Andreasen, administrator, teacher, and college president, who maintained that before He can come, the Lord needs a generation of holy people to demonstrate that the plan of salvation has been effective. . . . In other words, Christ's coming was seen as contingent on the state of the church and would materialize just as soon as the church 'swings into line' in cooperation with Christ, to use the words of Leroy Edwin Froom, seminary professor and for many years head of the Ministerial Association of the General Conference.

"On the other hand, works by Adventist scholars have appeared which deemphasize or ignore the element of contingency and delay in the coming of Christ. They say that the important thing is not the time when Christ will come, but the obligation to live in a constant state of readiness." [73]

The theme of readiness for the second advent raises the question of perfectionism. Neall quotes Ellen White as follows:

"No one is perfect. If one were perfect, he would be prepared for heaven. As long as we are not perfect, we have a work to do to get ready to be perfect. We have a mighty Saviour." [74]

Commenting on this quotation, Neall says:

"Ellen White consistently held up spotlessness as the goal for last-day saints and insisted that it could be reached but never claimed to have reached it herself. In this she was like Wesley, who preached the possibility of complete sanctification, but never claimed to have reached it himself. It is significant that in the statement above, after admitting that she was not perfect, White said, 'We have a mighty Saviour,' and 'I have that faith that takes hold of the promises of God.' It appears, therefore, that White's view of being ready to meet Christ at the parousia was to hold up perfection as the goal and justification as the assurance. The church ought to be and is called to be perfect yet it cannot claim it. Perfection is found only in Christ." [75]

Neall points out that Ellen White challenges the church not only to be *prepared* for the second advent, but also to *proclaim* the eschaton:

"White's thought that the Lord is *waiting* for the church to finish proclaiming three angels' messages must be seen in union with her parallel thought that the church must proclaim the message *because* the Lord is coming soon." [76]

Neall summarizes his concerns as follows:

"We see a profound paradox in White's eschatology. Nearness and delay stand in tension with each other. How can White speak of an appointed time for the return of Christ and yet say it is delayed by the failures of the church? How can she write of the first advent that 'God's purposes know no haste nor delay,' but of the second that 'the promises and threatenings of God are alike conditional'?

"The poles of the paradox can have wide-ranging effects in Christian faith and life. If the time of Christ's coming is in God's hand, the activities of man have no effect on it; if it depends on the deeds of men, it is not in God's hand. The first alternative can lead to passivity. Why should men be concerned if their activities have no effect on God's plans? But the second can lead to despair. If the generation of the apostles were not holy enough to meet the standard (for Christ did not come in their time), then what hope is there that any later generation will meet it?

"White's thought retains both poles. Is there any way of reconciling them? White suggested that the time of the end is certain from God's viewpoint but delayed from men's. While man has delayed the time, God still knows when the final date will be, just as He must have known the time when Israel would cross the Jordan and begin their conquest of Canaan. In 1883 White spoke of delay, but in 1888 she wrote that the seeming tarrying time was not in reality. Under this construction God retains His sovereignty in foreknowledge, but it is not completely satisfactory because the biblical view of God's sovereignty extends beyond mere foreknowledge. It does not really reconcile these two poles of divine sovereignty and human responsibility.

"In this final synthesis, we confess that we feel uncomfortable with the whole enterprise of harmonizing. If White herself did not really reconcile the two, why should we? Her writings were based on biblical, that is, Hebrew, modes of thought. It may be that our desire for logical harmony is more akin to Athens than to Jerusalem. In asking for logical harmony from White, we may be asking an illegitimate question. Like the Hebrew prophets, she was an evangelist, not a theologian." [77]

Synthesis

While this chapter is not intended to be apologetic, the author is taking the liberty of presenting a synthesis of the historic Seventh-day Adventist teachings regarding the second advent. It is hoped that this summary will stimulate further investigation and reflection.

1. The second advent is an act of God, a vital part of God's plan of salvation, and an important step in His solution of the sin problem.

2. The second advent is related to conditions in this world. Just as Christ came the first time when "the deception of sin had reached its height," [78] so He will come the second time before man succeeds in destroying himself by his pollution, his overpopulation, his bombs, or his sin. Through prophecy God revealed the "time of the end" in relative terms, with world conditions as one means of identifying the end-time.

3. The second advent is related to conditions in the church. God is holding the door of mercy open as long as His divine providence sees best. He is using every available means to persuade His church to be what He wants it to be and to do what He wants it to do.

4. There will come a time when God will decide that His plan for salvation demands that the world of wickedness be terminated and the door of mercy closed. *When nothing good can result from further delay, Jesus will come.* But the final issues are in the hands of God. It is true that prophecy is conditional. Man may *delay* the outworking of God's plans, but he cannot cancel it. The timing of His decision will reflect His love and His justice.

5. The second advent is more than a doctrine; it is the basis of a message. "This gospel of the kingdom shall be preached in all the world for a witness unto all nations; and then shall the end come" (Matt. 24:14). This is what Seventh-day Adventism is all about. The "gospel of the kingdom," "the everlasting gospel" (Rev. 14:6) is incomplete without the second advent. The message of the second advent is a part of the gospel, but it is not the whole gospel. The doctrine of the second advent would be meaningless apart from the incarnation, the life, the death, the resurrection, and the present ministry of our Lord. But the second advent is especially relevant now because it is the next major item on God's agenda, so far as this world is concerned.

The affirmation of a contemporary Seventh-day Adventist theologian aptly summarizes the doctrine of the second advent as currently understood by the Adventist Church:

"Salvation covers more than forgiveness, justification, and sanctification in this life. Salvation is more than the acceptance of those who believe in Him here. Complete salvation includes Christ's second advent. The plan of redemption cannot be finished without this. Complete redemption comes only by a new order from above." [79]

NOTES

[1] *Seventh-day Adventist Church Manual* (Washington, D.C., 1981), p. 289.
[2] *Ibid.*, p. 290.
[3] *Ibid.*, pp. 44, 45.
[4] *Ibid.*, p. 45.
[5] F. M. Wilcox, "Be Strong and of Good Courage," *Review and Herald*, Dec. 17, 1925.
[6] *Seventh-day Adventist Yearbook*, 1889, p. 148.
[7] *Ibid.*
[8] *Ibid.*, p. 150.
[9] *Ibid.*, p. 151.
[10] *Ibid.*
[11] James White, *Bible Adventism* (facsimile, Nashville, Tenn., 1972), pp. 42-44.
[12] Otis Nichols, "The Signs of the End of the World," *Review and Herald*, Dec. 9, 1852.
[13] Uriah Smith, *Review and Herald*, Nov. 18. 1958.
[14] James White, "Our Faith and Hope," *Review and Herald*, Jan. 10, 1871.
[15] Uriah Smith, "This Generation," *Review and Herald*, Nov. 17, 1891.
[16] L. A. Smith, "The End of 'This Generation,' " *Review and Herald*, Nov. 2, 1905.
[17] W. W. Prescott, "No More Delay," *Review and Herald*, Dec. 21, 1905.
[18] George W. Wells, "The Manner of His Coming and Signs Which Show His Coming Near," *Review and Herald*, June 25, 1925.
[19] William A. Fagal, "Lift Up Your Heads," *Review and Herald*, Aug. 1, 1968.
[20] LeRoy Edwin Froom, *Movement of Destiny* (Washington, D.C., 1971), p. 561.
[21] Ellen G. White, *Early Writings* (Battle Creek, Mich., 1900), p. 58.
[22] *Idem, Selected Messages* (Washington, D.C., 1958), book 1, p. 67.
[23] *Ibid.*, p. 69.
[24] *Idem, The Desire of Ages* (Mountain View, Calif., 1898), p. 32.
[25] Froom, *Movement of Destiny*, p. 566.
[26] *Ibid.*, p. 568.
[27] Ellen G. White, *Testimonies to the Church* (Mountain View, Calif., 1928), vol. 2, p. 194.
[28] Froom, *Movement of Destiny*, p. 578.
[29] Ellen G. White *Evangelism*, (Washington, D.C., 1946), p. 696.
[30] *Idem, Prophets and Kings* (Mountain View, Calif., 1917), p. 417.
[31] Froom, *Movement of Destiny*, p. 602.
[32] herbert E. Douglass, "The Unique Contribution of Adventist Eschatology," *North American Bible Conference—1974*, p. 1.
[33] *Ibid.*, p. 2.
[34] *Ibid.*, p. 10.
[35] *Ibid.*, p. 11.
[36] *Ibid.*, p. 15.
[37] *Ibid.*
[38] Jack W. Provonsha, *God Is With Us* (Washington, D.C., 1968), pp. 146, 147.
[39] *Ibid.*, p. 143.
[40] *Ibid.*, p. 145.
[41] *Ibid.*, p. 146.
[42] *Ibid.*, pp. 140, 141.
[43] *Ibid.*, pp. 141, 142.
[44] Sakae Kubo, *God Meets Man* (Nashville, Tenn., 1978), p. 76.
[45] *Ibid.*, p. 78.
[46] *Ibid.*, p. 81.
[47] *Ibid.*, p. 89.
[48] *Ibid.*, p. 99.
[49] *Ibid.*, p. 101.
[50] *Ibid.*, p. 111.
[51] *Ibid.*, p. 156.
[52] William G. Johnsson, "Conditionality in Biblical Perspective, With Particular Reference to Apocalyptic" (unpublished manuscript, quoted with the permission of the author), pp. 29, 30.
[53] Asa Oscar Tait, *Heralds of the Morning* (Washington, D.C., 1915), p. 360.
[54] Alonzo L. Baker, *The Hope of the World* (Mountain View, Calif., 1925), p. 82.
[55] Theodore Carcich, "The Relevance of Christ's Return," *Review and Herald*, July 20, 1972.
[56] *Ibid.*, Aug. 3, 1972.
[57] Robert H. Parr, "I Believe in the Imminent, Literal Coming of Christ," *Review and Herald*, April 13, 1972.
[58] H.M.S. Richards, "Loyalty to the Blessed Hope," *Review and Herald*, Sept. 29, 1966.
[59] Earl E. Cleveland, "The Day Is at Hand," *Review and Herald*, June 26, 1966.
[60] Horace E. Walsh, "The Necessity of Christ's Second Advent," *Review and Herald*, July 28, 1960; "Saturation Point," *Review and Herald*, July 22, 1965.
[61] Roy Allan Anderson, *Abandon Earth: Last Call* (Mountain View, Calif., 1982).
[62] Ellen G. White, *The Great Controversy* (Mountain View, Calif., 1931), p. 299.
[63] C. Mervyn Maxwell, "Trends in Second-Coming Emphasis and Interpretation Among Seventh-day Adventists

(unpublished report, 1971), p. 26.
[64] White, *Early Writings*, pp. 14-16.
[65] W. C. White, Letter to Editor, *Review and Herald*, June 17, 1915.
[66] Ellen G. White, *Christ's Object Lessons* (Mountain View, Calif., 1900), pp. 226-228.
[67] *Idem, The Great Controversy*, p. 302.
[68] *Ibid.*, p. x.
[69] *Ibid.*, p. 637.
[70] *Ibid.*, pp. 640, 641.
[71] Ralph E. Neall, *The Nearness and the Delay of the Parousia in the Writings of Ellen G. White* (doctoral dissertation, quoted with the permission of the author).
[72] *Ibid.*, p. 2.
[73] *Ibid.*, pp. 2-4.
[74] *Ibid.*, p. 144. Quotation from *Review and Herald*, July 23, 1970, p. 3, quoting from a letter from W. C. White to the editor of the *Pacific Union Recorder*, April 23, 1915.
[75] *Ibid.*, p. 144.
[76] *Ibid.*, p. 236.
[77] *Ibid.*, pp. 244-246.
[78] *Idem, The Desire of Ages*, p. 36.
[79] Edward Heppenstall, *Our High Priest* (Washington, D.C., 1972), p. 227.

CHAPTER 10

The Advent Hope
in Contemporary Thought

Richard Rice

THE purpose of this chapter is to describe the nature of the advent hope in contemporary Christian thought. Its general procedure will be to examine a number of current eschatological views and indicate the important similarities and differences between them. The magnitude of the subject and the limited space available to consider it impose several specific requirements upon this endeavor.

One is the obvious need to be selective. Since Christian eschatology has probably never generated more interest than during the past few decades, and the eschatological views of different Christians have probably never been more numerous, only a small fraction of them can be considered in a study of this length. Instead of attempting a comprehensive survey of contemporary Christian eschatology, therefore, the most this chapter can provide is a brief review of several representative positions.

Besides their large number, prevalent eschatological views are also extremely diverse. So this study will achieve its objective, in the second place, only if the spectrum of views considered, however limited, somehow reflects the wide divergency of eschatological opinion within the Christian world. This calls for a consideration of sharply contrasting points of view. Both "conservative" and "liberal" theologians must be represented, and it will be necessary also to select among the various contemporary views some of those prevalent among large groups of people, as well as among professional theologians, even though the study is based upon published, and in most cases scholarly, expressions of Christian eschatology, not upon surveys of what various groups of Christians "really believe." Each of the individual theologians mentioned either represents an important position quite clearly or exercises considerable scholarly influence.

This study seeks not merely to describe various eschatological viewpoints but to provide, or at least allow for, a critical comparison of them. Therefore, its analysis of different positions must meet two further requirements. First, each view represented must be described in sufficient detail to permit its basic thrust to be clearly visible. In most cases this requires attending to the general doctrinal or methodological framework of which the specific eschatological view is a part, since eschatology is never held in abstraction from one's theology, or understanding of the Christian faith, as a whole.

Finally, to make critical comparison of the various positions possible, it will be necessary to present them in a way that allows their crucial differences to emerge. One such method is to formulate certain questions that are pertinent to all the positions examined and to which each position provides distinctive answers. Consequently, throughout the following analysis, several "guiding" questions will be kept in mind: According to each interpretation of Christian eschatology, precisely what does Christian hope anticipate? Is it oriented primarily toward future, or toward present, realities? And how should the traditional elements of Christian eschatology be understood—the parousia, the resurrection, the final judgment, and the restoration of the earth? What purpose do they serve? Do they, for example, provide factual information about literal future events? And if so, what is the scope and content of this information?

With these considerations in mind, let us begin our analysis of contemporary Christian eschatologies.

Schubert M. Ogden

The work of Schubert M. Ogden demonstrates how the problem of Christian eschatology is approached by one liberal American theologian. Currently professor of theology at Perkins School of Theology, Southern Methodist University, Ogden is sometimes described as a "left-wing Bultmannian" because of his relation to the theological position of Rudolf Bultmann, whose writings in the areas of theology and New Testament have exerted enormous influence in the scholarly religious world for most of this century.

In the classic statement of his theological program, "New Testament and Mythology,"[1] Bultmann argues that the language of the New Testament is fundamentally mythological in character, depicting spiritual realities in terms and concepts drawn from the distant, prescientific worldview of the first century. The New Testament must therefore be "demythologized" in order to be understood by the modern mind, and this Bultmann attempts to do by translating the gospel into concepts provided by contemporary philosophy, specifically, the existential-ism of Martin Heidegger. When thus demythologized, the gospel presents man, not with a description of a God located somewhere in the physical universe who enters world history from time to time with remarkable manifestations of supernatural power, but with the radical claim of a God who infinitely transcends this world and calls man to live in freedom, in openness to the future rather than in slavery to the past.

Although Ogden feels that Bultmann himself has not demythologized the New Testament message consistently or extensively enough, he fully supports Bultmann's assessment of New Testament language and thought, along with his formulation of the central task confronting Christian theology. Consequently, when Ogden addresses himself to the question of eschatology, his first substantive move is to assert that the "terms in which Christian hope is classically attested are through and through mythological and must be interpreted as such."[2] According to Ogden, the meaning of all myths is "existential," rather than scientific, in character.[3] This means that instead of providing information in the manner of science about the details of reality or factual states of affairs, the intention of myths, regardless of their appearance, is to express "our own most basic understanding of ourselves in relation to reality as such," or "reality as a whole."[4] Since the traditional elements in Christian eschatology are essentially mythological, then, their basic intention is not to provide factual information about future states of affairs. They do not represent a forecast of the closing events of earth's history or of some final stage of cosmic process. Rather, their basic intention is "to illumine the essential structure and meaning of our life in the present." It is true that these elements do have reference to the future, "but this is so because their real reference is to the essential constitution of every present moment."[5] Because the language of Christian hope is mythological, then, it must be "demythologized, or interpreted in terms of its understanding of existence in relation to reality as a whole."[6]

The key to Ogden's approach to eschatology is his concept of God, for having identified the basic task of formulating a Christian eschatology as that of demythologizing the traditional language of Christian hope, he proceeds to interpret this language in light of the "specifically Christian understanding of man's relation to God."[7] Ogden conceives of God as the supreme individual, both distinct from and more than the world, yet intimately involved in the world. Not only does God affect all reality, as the Ground of all that is, but He is Himself affected by every aspect of reality. Every creaturely experience makes a genuine contribution to His own life. His intimate relation to the world of creaturely experience is such that each aspect of finite reality, as it comes into being, is incorporated into His experience in all its detail, there to be retained forever. For Ogden, then, divine love consists in perfect memory, infallible and everlasting. Such love provides the appropriate object—indeed, the only appropriate object—of Christian hope, for it and it alone provides an adequate solution to the problem of death.

As Ogden interprets it, the problem posed by death, the final loss of experience, is nothing other than the problem posed by the loss of being involved in every moment of life. For at any given time a man retains in his fallible memory only a fragment of his past; most of it is swept away. Since all fragmentary, creaturely experience involves some such loss, the notion that human life continues or resumes after death does not provide a solution to this fundamental problem. The problem posed by my death is solved not by the hope that I will personally survive death, but only by the confidence that every aspect of my life will be retained by God without loss forever. According to Ogden, then, confidence in God, not expectations for oneself, lies at the center of Christian hope. And since it focuses upon God and the love that constitutes His essential character, rather than upon man and his self-centered hopes for a future of bliss, Ogden argues that the understanding of hope he proposes is "not merely theologically acceptable but is far more appropriate to the essence of Christianity than more conventional interpretations."[8]

In summary, Ogden approaches Christian eschatology by interpreting the traditional language of Christian hope as mythological in character and by attempting to place God rather than man at the center.

Wolfhart Pannenberg

Wolfhart Pannenberg is the foremost proponent of the "theology of hope," a line of theological reflection developed within Germany in the 1960s that has attracted considerable attention both in Europe and in the United States. As described by Langdon Gilkey, an American theologian, the theology of hope is characterized by the view that "eschatology is the key to theology." The idea of the future is taken to have central theological importance, and the other elements of Christian doctrine—God, man, and Christ, for example—are all interpreted by means of this fundamental concept. Thus, God is described as "the power of the future"; man's distinguishing characteristics of self-transcendence and freedom are determined by his openness to the future and his hope for it;[9] and Jesus Christ is described as an "eschatological occurrence." [10] Moreover, in the theology of hope the priority of the future is emphasized to such an extent that the conventional view of temporal reality, which regards the future as arising from the past and present, is reversed, and present reality is viewed as determined by the future.

The central concept in Pannenberg's eschatology is that of a "final future " a notion he develops in connection with the problem of meaning in history and in human life.[11] Existentialism applies the question of history's meaning not to historical process as a whole but to individual moments within history. According to existentialist thought, the idea of universal or comprehensive history is meaningless, since no one can stand outside history, and history's meaning is realized only in the isolated moment of concrete personal decision. In reaction to this position, which has the effect of removing from eschatology its focus on the future, Pannenberg argues that the idea of universal history is inescapable. The reason for this conclusion is provided by Wilhelm Dilthey, the nineteenth-century German philosopher. Dilthey observes that in history as in literature the meaning of the part and the meaning of the whole are interdependent. Just as a single word acquires its meaning from the sentence in which it appears, so each individual event and experience has its meaning only in connection with history as a whole. and unless history as a whole is meaningful, it is useless to attribute significance to the individual events within it. The meaning of history as a whole requires the termination of history, however, for such a whole exists only when the end occurs. In order for history to be meaningful, therefore, it must have a conclusion, for meaning requires a totality and history acquires wholeness only with its concluding event. Since the events within history are thus meaningful only in light of the end of history, the concept of a "final future" is of fundamental importance.

What is true of history is also true of human life; namely, that individual events and experiences acquire significance only in relation to a comprehensive whole that includes them. But since at any given moment the totality of life is incomplete, the final significance of life's experiences is decided in life's "final future," or "true or essential future," which constitutes the totality of life. However, the essential future of life, which constitutes it a totality and determines its ultimate significance, cannot be identified with death, for death reduces the structure of life's meaning to fragments. Moreover, the meaning of an individual's life depends in part upon its interpretation by society, and this is something subject to further development long after the individual's death. Consequently, "the anticipation of the totality of the individual life . . . always extends, therefore, to the social unity in the context of which the individual lives, and looks beyond his own particular society to its place in the life of mankind." As a result, the essential future of the individual cannot be separated from the essential future of mankind as a whole.[12] The final future thus determines the ultimate significance not only of history as a whole but of every individual human life.

Pannenberg interprets the significance of Jesus by means of this concept of the final future with which history concludes and in light of which its ultimate meaning, and that of each human life, becomes apparent. According to Pennenberg, the ministry of Jesus is appropriately understood as a proleptic disclosure of the ultimate meaning of history. Jesus' mission is that of an "eschatological herald," through whom "the divine future becomes present reality."[13] In other words, the final future is already present in the ministry of Jesus, though it does not, of course, cease to be future.

For Pannenberg, Jesus' resurrection from the dead is central to His disclosure of the final future and also provides an indication of what the final future involves. From an examination of the way Jesus' resurrection is regarded in the New Testament, Pannenberg concludes that the historicity of Jesus' resurrection is inseparable from the significance of His ministry. While acknowledging that Jesus' resurrection is permanently controversial, "because it cuts so deeply into fundamental questions of the understanding of reality," he maintains nevertheless that the claim "Jesus is risen" represents a responsible historical judgment, "even in the context of our present experience of reality."[14]

From his interpretation of the resurrection of Jesus as an eschatological and proleptic event, it seems that Pannenberg conceives the "final future" of which he speaks as involving the resumption of human life beyond death. Apparent support for this conclusion can also be found in his "anthropological interpretation of the traditional eschatological conceptions," namely, the kingdom of God, the final judgment, the resurrection, and the end of the world. While Pannenberg describes these conceptions as essential conditions for the final realization of human nature, the extent to which they correspond to actual future events in his view is not entirely clear.

On the one hand, Pennenberg is careful to qualify their future reference by insisting that they do not represent "prophecies of particular individual happenings which are to come about at some time in the course of events" or "forecasts of political developments," and that they tell us nothing of "the happenings by which, in the material course of events, this essential future of human nature is to be realized.[15] And he also insists that "every . . . idea that reaches out beyond death," "everything we now say and think about a future life," is merely a metaphor, especially the hope of resurrection, which is "only an image, an earthly metaphor, for a future that is still inconceivable in its reality."[16] On the other hand, however, Pannenberg insists that the openness of the question as to precisely how the ultimate destiny of human nature is to be realized should not lead one to conclude that the eschatological future is not a real future, or does not have any connection with real time, or does not differ from the present and the past.[17]

It is apparently Pannenberg's position, then, that Christian hope anticipates a literal future, whose essential historical and anthropological meaning can be identified, but whose specific content can only be metaphorically referred to and whose arrival cannot be predicted on the basis of the traditional elements of Christian eschatology.

Even so, the elusiveness of Pannenberg's language renders problematic any attempt to summarize his position succinctly. For in spite of his emphasis on eschatology, for example, and his insistence that the object of Christian hope is yet future, the distinction between present and future that this emphasis manifestly requires seems to collapse when Pannenberg speaks of "the eternal concurrence of all events" and announces, "Seen from beyond the flow of time, all events coincide in an eternal present." [18]

John A. T. Robinson

John A. T. Robinson, British scholar and churchman, is most widely known as the author of *Honest to God*, a book that evoked immediate controversy upon its publication in 1963.[19] With its author appealing extensively to so familiar themes within the writings of such figures as Paul Tillich and Dietrich Bonhoeffer, the book contains relatively little in the way of original material. But the fact that an ecclesiastical leader of considerable influence was calling for a "radical recasting" of the Christian tradition in a form other than the supernaturalistic framework of Biblical thought generated heated debate.

Robinson is a respected New Testament scholar, and to a certain extent the discussion in *Honest to God* was anticipated by *In the End God,* a study of Christian eschatology devoted largely to an examination of pertinent Biblical concepts, which was first published in 1950 and then reissued in 1968. The thesis of this earlier work is that the various elements in Biblical eschatology concern Christian existence as a present reality and actually provide no information about literal future events. To support this thesis, Robinson distinguishes between and analyzes the essential content of eschatological statements and the characteristic form in which they are expressed in the Bible.

As for their essential content, eschatological statements exhibit two basic characteristics. The first is that "all statements about the End (whether of the individual or of history) are fundamentally affirmations about God," and *vice versa,* "every statement about God is *ipso facto* an assertion about the end, a truth about eschatology." [20] The principle that all eschatological statements express a certain understanding of God, Robinson maintains, provides the ground and the criterion for every Christian statement about Last Things. This implies that the Christian doctrine of Last Things is essentially an extrapolation of the Christian doctrine of God, specifically, "the explication of what must be true of the end, both of history and of the individual, if God is to be the god of the Biblical faith." [21] And the principle also suggests that fundamental differences in eschatology, such as the shift from cosmic to individualistic eschatology in early to medieval Christian thought, are a result, at bottom, of basically divergent views of God.[22]

According to Robinson, it is distinctly characteristic of the Judeo-Christian religion that every statement about God is also an eschatological statement, a statement about the end. This stems from the basic Hebraic understanding of God as a God of history, whose purpose must be realized at the end of history. This conviction that "the ultimate character of God must be expressed by the final state of history" [23] established in the Hebrew mind a close correlation between the end of history and the realization of divine purpose in history. This correlation appears in the way the prophets interpreted every event that fulfilled God's purpose as eschatological in nature—that is, as a "final" event. And it is particularly evident in the claim of the New Testament that in Jesus the end of history, the *eschaton*, has already arrived. Since this means that Jesus is "the infallible revelation of the divine nature, the last word of God and about God," [24] and not, obviously, that history terminated with Him, it appears that Biblical eschatology is fundamentally concerned with the purpose, the *telos*, of history, rather than the termination of historical process.

Besides its theistic focus, then, the content of Biblical eschatology is also characterized by a primary concern with the present rather than the future. In other words, all eschatological statements have their ground in present experience; they derive from "present awareness of the living God." [25] Christian eschatology has to do not with the last things—what happens after everything else—but with the "lastness of all things." It is "the lighting up of a new dimension of life now." [26] This does not mean that eschatology is not in any way concerned with the future. But it does mean that the "last events" of Scripture pertain primarily to present reality and are not predictions of literal future events. That they appear as such is due, according to Robinson, to their essential character as "myths."

As Robinson describes them, the Biblical myths express "an understanding of God given and verified in present experience" by describing events that lie beyond historical investigation, whether in the primeval past, as in Genesis, or in the ultimate future, as in Revelation. Myths thus employ the language of historical events to depict realities that do not literally correspond to these events. The truth of such myths, he contends, depends not upon their accuracy as historical or scientific descriptions but upon the validity of their assertions about God. The various elements in the eschatological myths of Scripture—the second coming of Christ, the resurrection of the dead, the final judgment, the Messianic banquet, the millennium, and so forth—do not, therefore, provide information about actual future events. To interpret them literally is to miss their point, for "they are neither inerrant prophecies of the future nor pious guesswork, [but] necessary transpositions into the key of the hereafter of knowledge of God and his relation to men given in the revelatory encounter of present historical event." [27]

While thus referring to "present realities within the life of the New Age" ushered in by Jesus, the eschatological myths nevertheless emphasize a particular aspect of these realities, namely, that they point to the future for their ultimate fulfillment. In other words, the situation inaugurated by God's act in Christ is both final and yet to be finalized, both present and future. True, the future dimension of these realities is mythically depicted as future *events*, but an accurate understanding of the eschatological statements of Scripture distinguishes this from their essential content concerning the present experience of salvation as something to be ultimately fulfilled in the future and avoids construing the myths as historical predictions. [28]

As Robinson interprets Biblical eschatology, then, what Christian hope anticipates can be stated only in very general terms. It anticipates that the salvation graciously offered to men by God in Christ will find ultimate fulfillment beyond the present situation. Indeed, it anticipates that there is no aspect of reality that will not be ultimately reconciled to God.[29] But it does not include advance information as to how human history will actually terminate. On his view, any such scenario, whether Biblically derived or otherwise, is, strictly speaking, irrelevant to the content of this hope.

Paul Minear

Another approach to Christian eschatology, yielding a conclusion similar to Robinson's, is presented in *Christian Hope and the Second Coming,*[30] by Paul S. Minear. Minear served as Winkley professor of Biblical theology at Yale University, president of the Society of New Testament Studies and the American Theological Society, and director of the faith and order department of the World Council of Churches. In this work Minear analyzes the nature of Biblical hope in general and then examines the expectation of Christ's return within the context of this larger theme.

The outstanding effect of Minear's "quest for a more adequate conception of Christian hope"[31] is to illuminate its distinctive and comprehensive character. For one thing, Christian hope is not simply one of the many forms naturally assumed by man's incorrigible optimism for the future. Nor is it a mere facet of the Christian life, just one of several cardinal virtues. Instead, it is the very mode of Christian existence, intrinsically related to all dimensions of salvation. "Life in Christ without hope," Minear insists, "is unthinkable."[32] Similarly, Christian hope must be viewed in the context of the gospel as a whole. For God Himself, or God in Christ, not the fulfillment of personal wishes and desires, is the all-inclusive object of this hope.[33] Such hope has its sole basis in the promise of God, who "alone is absolutely dependable in doing what he says He will do."[34] Broadly understood, this promise encompasses all of God's saving activity, all His covenants with His people, from the call of Abraham to the charismatic gifts to the church.[35]

Now how does the expectation of Christ's return relate to this broad understanding of hope as the source and substance of the Christian life? To answer this question, Minear examines a number of Biblical images associated with the second coming, including "the clouds of heaven," "the thief," "the earthquake," "the trumpet," and others, and attempts to understand the Biblical terminology as a whole.

The most striking feature of Biblical imagery is the fact that it expresses a world of thought extremely remote from ours today. Whereas modern thought tends to be abstractly conceptual, prosaic, and static, Biblical thought is characteristically imaginative, poetic, and dramatic.[36] Furthermore, the suggestiveness, or evocative richness, of the Biblical symbols, particularly of the second coming of Christ, imbues them with unique "power to convey living truth concerning the depths of reality." This feature demands that the Biblical images be interpreted with great care and precludes the possibility of construing them either in flatly literal or in purely metaphorical terms.

Rejecting both literalism and pure symbolism, then, Minear attempts "to press behind the words to the meanings which they originally carried to men of the Bible."[37] Doing so, he discovers, for example, that the clouds associated with the return of Christ are reminiscent of numerous instances in the history of God's dealings with men where clouds serve an important purpose, such as the covenant with Israel at Sinai, the divine presence in the tabernacle, and the transfiguration and ascension of Jesus. In light of this colorful and complex tradition, it is apparent that the association of clouds with the return of Christ does not provide meteorological information but conveys a theological message. It signifies that Christ's return will mark a decisive event in God's dealings with men, that Christ's return coincides with the revelation of the sins of all men, and so forth.[38]

By thus exploring the original connotations of the Biblical symbols associated with the return of Christ, it is possible to delineate the theological content they express. But this does not mean that the essential meaning of the images can be neatly abstracted from the forms of their original expression and translated into precise conceptual terms any more than it can be simplistically reduced to the symbols' most obvious literal referents. Because of their flexible and complex nature, therefore, the Biblical images associated with the return of Christ defy exact definition. They cannot be neatly integrated into an abstract eschatological statement on the one hand, nor can they be all reduced to a single flat phrase—"literal return"—on the other.[39]

The richness and flexibility of the eschatological images of Scripture also render inconclusive the attempt to determine the precise relation of the expectation of Christ's return to Christian hope in general, and Minear's resolution of this problem is carefully qualified. The expectation of Christ's return is "intrinsic" to Christian hope, he says, but it is not itself "constitutive" of Christian hope as a whole.[40] In other words, it is neither exclusively central nor merely peripheral to hope, properly understood. Instead, the return of Christ is but one way of describing the goal of Christian hope, not its sole object.[41] Consequently, one can say, as Minear does, "we look forward to the coming of Christ," but one cannot identify this with a percise forecast of coming events, nor argue that this expresses precisely the content of Christian hope.

In response to the question, then, what does Christian hope anticipate? Minear would emphasize that hope is the substance of Christian existence as a whole, as a forward orientation toward God and toward the consummation of salvation in all its dimensions. In his view, this hope includes the expectation of Christ's return, but it does not depend on any single conception of that return.[42]

Karl Rahner

The late Karl Rahner represents, and in many respects exemplifies what is best in, contemporary Roman Catholic theology. As professor of theology at the University of Münster, Rahner's scholarly output was prodigious. His voluminous writings encompass a wide variety of themes, from philosophical to dogmatic theology, and the work of no living Catholic scholar commands greater academic respect today. While Rahner is certainly an innovative Catholic thinker, he is no longer "ecclesiastically suspect," as one of his interpreters puts it,[43] and may, therefore, for the purposes of this brief survey, provide an ideal representative of contemporary Catholic thought on eschatology. It must be emphasized, however, that the enormous diversity of thought within the largest Christian communion precludes suggesting anything like *the* contemporary Roman Catholic position on the second coming of Christ."

One of the noticeable features of Rahner's discussions of eschatology is the comparatively small space they occupy within his writings as a whole. Apparently this corresponds to a general lack of emphasis on eschatology in Catholic thought, for Rahner observes that eschatology is relatively underdeveloped as a theological doctrine. Rahner himself provides an agenda for eschatological reflection, rather than actually formulating a constructive doctrine of last things. Rahner's approach to the subject seems to be: (1) to suggest general categories for considering the various elements of traditional eschatology, such as "the final destiny of the individual" and "the cosmic fulfillment of mankind";[44] (2) to formulate principles for the correct interpretation of eschatological assertions; and, (3) to call for the constructive relation of the doctrine of last things to other fundamental Christian doctrines.

When Rahner does address himself to the task of presenting a constructive doctrine of last things, a tension between two elements in his theology seems to emerge. On the one hand, his accounts of what actually constitutes the eschatological future are extremely tentative. The definition of relationships between the last things, he remarks, is "difficult to attain." The items variously described in traditional eschatology cannot be clearly distinguished from one another, nor can they be simply reduced to one and the same "demythologized" meaning.[45] On the other hand, however, despite this tentativeness, it seems apparent that Rahner is willing to affirm all aspects of official Roman Catholic dogma pertaining to eschatology, however problematic they may appear. His article "The Life of the Dead," for example, includes a defense of the doctrine of purgatory, on the grounds that "there can be no decisive objection to the notion that man reaches personal maturity in this 'intermediate state.'"[46] In view of the rather predictable character of Rahner's dogmatic affirmations in the area of eschatology, and in view of the major concentration of his work in this area, it will be most helpful to focus here on his discussion of "the hermeneutics of eschatological assertions."[47]

To understand the essential meaning of eschatological statements, Rahner proposes as the single basic principle of their correct interpretation the view that such assertions represent "not an anticipatory report of future events, but the extrapolation of our present salvation, the situation experienced in faith, into the mode of its completeness."[48] In other words, the traditional Christian descriptions of the ultimate destiny of man and the end of this world's history are essentially projections of the present experience of salvation in Christ into its ultimate future fulfillment.[49] This means that Christian eschatology is concerned primarily with the present, rather than the future. Or, as Rahner variously puts it, "eschatology concerns redeemed man as he now is";[50] "there can be no eschatological assertions that cannot be reduced to the assertion concerned with Christian existence as it now is";[51] "eschatology is the assertion about present salvation as it tends to the future fulfillment."[52] The future to which eschatological statements refer, then, is precisely the fulfillment of the salvation experienced in the present, and the purpose served by eschatological statements is to illuminate the nature of present Christian existence, rather than to provide an advance report of events yet to come.

Rahner's view of eschatological statements excludes both "a false apocalyptic understanding of eschatology," on the one hand, and "a totally existential 'de-mythizing' interpretation," on the other.[53] False apocalyptic, as Rahner describes it, attempts to construct detailed accounts of coming events from the eschatological statements of Scripture. It construes eschatology as "an advance report of events taking place 'later' " [54] or as "the anticipated report of a spectator of the future event." [55] Such eschatologies ignore the facts, in Rahner's view, that "Scripture has no intention of describing the actual phenomena of the eschata themselves" and that "the imaginative portrayals of Scripture" really cannot be harmonized with each other.[56] Moreover, the effect of false apocalyptic is actually to "de-eschatologize" man by removing from the future its character of mystery and hiddenness and regarding it as something that is merely yet to come and not intrinsically "at hand in its futurity." [57]

While the eschatological statements of Scripture do not represent an anticipatory spectator's account of what is to come, Rahner argues, they do indeed refer to literal future events. So a thoroughgoing "demythizing" of eschatological statements that exhaustively accounts for their significance in terms of man's experience here and now is theologically unacceptable.[58]

In summary, Rahner interprets the traditional elements of Christian eschatology as referring to the literal future, not, however, to provide advance information about what will happen, but to affirm the imminent fulfillment of the Christian salvation already being experienced.

G. C. Berkouwer

G. C. Berkouwer, for many years professor of systematic theology at the Free University of Amsterdam, assumes a conservative theological position within the Reformed tradition of Protestant thought. More than a dozen volumes of his ambitious series Studies in Dogmatics have appeared in English, and one of them, *The Return of Christ,* is devoted to the study of eschatology.

In his approach to eschatology, Berkouwer emphasizes both the reality of the future towards which Christian hope is directed and the relevance of this future to present Christian experience. In so doing, he places himself in opposition to the view that the object of Christian hope is fully realized in the present, as well as to the view that the content of Christian hope consists in future events essentially unrelated to the present. The eschaton, he insists, is neither "exclusively present" nor "exclusively futuristic," [59] and the recognition of such tension is indispensable to an adequate grasp of the nature of Christian hope. For just as there is a sense in which the object of Christian hope is already realized and a sense in which it is not yet realized, so there are aspects of the anticipated future that are known and others that remain unknown. According to Berkouwer, then, a properly formulated understanding of Christian hope is one in which its essential elements are held in tension and carefully balanced. Specifically, it is one in which the relation between present experience and the anticipated future is precisely defined in harmony with the New Testament.

Berkouwer emphasizes the future aspect of Christian hope in opposition to the existentialist approach of Rudolf Bultmann, whose "realized eschatology" concentrates upon the present reality of the eschaton in such a way that any future eschatology is precluded. According to Bultmann, all "end-historical eschatology," such as "the expectation of the coming of Christ in glory at the end of time," represents nothing more than "the product of the mythical world-view of the New Testament." [60] Berkouwer insists that such an approach is nothing less than a form of "de-eschatologizing" and argues that the traditional elements of Biblical eschatology, such as the return of Christ, the final judgment, the resurrection of the dead, and the restoration of the earth, have reference to real future events. In short, he maintains that Christian hope anticipates "a fulfilling, supernatural intervention by God."[61]

The fact that Christian hope anticipates actual future events, however, does not justify either a "futuristic eschatology," which divorces the object of Christian hope from present experience, or a "Biblicistic eschatology," which misconstrues the basic intention of apocalyptic imagery. Berkouwer repeatedly emphasizes "the relevance and relation" to the present of the future that Christian hope anticipates. "Eschatology is not a projection into the distant future," he insists at the outset of his study; "it bursts forth into our present existence, and structures life today in the light of the last things."[62] And when discussing each facet of the eschatological future, he is careful to indicate the present impact of its expectation. He insists, for example, that the message of the parousia "can never make one indifferent towards earthly existence, for it places a heavy responsibility on this life."[63] For Berkouwer, then, Christian hope includes a present as well as a future aspect, and it is just as fatal to Christian eschatology to emphasize the future at the expense of the present as to emphasize the present at the expense of the future.

Consequently, while he insists that Christian hope anticipates actual future events, Berkouwer qualifies the extent to which the Biblical descriptions of these events can be interpreted literally. He holds the end to be real, but the language used to describe the end to be figurative. He objects to attempts to harmonize systematically the scriptural images and concepts that bear on the end, particularly those of the book of Revelation, in order to demonstrate "how everything is going to come out." Because such attempts misunderstand the nature of apocalyptic language, which is necessarily "inadequate" to the parousia and whose basic intention is not to provide "a literal, chronological description of future events," or "'history' of the future," not only do they "invariably end in confusion and contradictions" but their ultimate effect is to divorce the future from the present and thus to violate the essential structure of Christian hope. The solution is not, of course, to deny the future perspective of Christian hope, but to recognize the figurative way in which the end is described and to emphasize its intrinsic relation to the present.[64]

For Berkouwer, then, the traditional elements in Christian eschatology have reference to actual future events, and a denial of this future leads to the collapse of Christian hope. However, the Biblical accounts of the future do not provide an exhaustive, literal description of what is to come, as if their purpose were to satisfy curiosity, and their essential orientation to the present must be constantly kept in mind. Only in this way can the real concern of Christian eschatology be preserved, namely, to ascertain the significance of present history and present experience as inherently related to the future.

Dispensationalism

Large numbers of Christians believe not only that the traditional elements in Christian eschatology refer to literal future events, but that, properly interpreted, various portions of the Bible actually chart the course of these events in considerable detail and indicate just how their development is related to present world conditions. Among those holding such views are proponents of dispensationalism. The origin of dispensationalism is generally associated with J. N. Darby (1800-1882), an early leader of the Plymouth Brethren. It spread through the publication of C. I. Scofield's notes to the Bible and received its definitive expression in the eight-volume *Systematic Theology* of Lewis Sperry Chafer (1871-1952), founder of Dallas Theological Seminary. Dispensationalist views have received widespread popular attention in the form of Hal Lindsey's book *The Late Great Planet Earth.*

Dispensationalism is characterized by the view that God's dealings with men move through various distinct phases, or "dispensations"—according to Scofield, seven in number—in each of which "God's governmental relationship with man" and, consequently, man's specific responsibility to God, are different.[65] This view of history presupposes a method of Biblical interpretation, described as "consistent literalism," according to which certain passages of Scripture have exclusive reference to a particular dispensation and cannot be applied to another. The most important consequence of these convictions for eschatology is the sharp distinction made by dispensationalists between the Kingdom and the Church.[66] According to dispensationalism, a central theme of Jesus' preaching was the "Davidic theocratic kingdom," in which all of Israel's prophecies would find literal fulfillment. Because the Jews rejected Jesus as the Messiah, the establishment of this kingdom and the fulfillment of God's promises to Israel are postponed until the millennium, "the thousand-year reign of Christ upon the earth."[67] Hence, the church is not the present form of the kingdom and is not the recipient of Israel's promises.

Inasmuch as God's promises to ancient Israel will yet be literally fulfilled, the Jewish people have an important part to play in eschatological events. Dispensationalists therefore attribute profound theological significance to the establishment of a Jewish state in the Middle East in modern times. Indeed, "the most important sign of all . . . is the Jew returning to the land of Israel after thousands of years of being dispersed," Hal Lindsey states. "The Jew is the most important sign to this generation."[68] What this event presages is a startling series of international political and religious developments that, according to Lindsey, fall into "the specific pattern" "clearly forecasted" by various prophetic passages of the Bible.[69]

As Lindsey interprets it, Biblical prophecy portrays not only the establishment of a Jewish state in Palestine but the repossession of Jerusalem and the resumption of cultic worship on the exact site of the ancient Temple. On a wider scale, Russia will enter into a confederacy with the Arabic nations and the countries of black Africa, and the Roman Empire will be revived, to be headed by "a completely godless, diabolically evil 'future fuehrer,'" who becomes "absolute dictator of the whole world" and "will be worshiped as Satan is worshiped."[70] A seven-year period of tribulation begins with the signing of a pact between this Roman dictator and the head of the Jewish nation at the time. Just prior to the Tribulation all genuine Christians depart the earth—the dead are resurrected and the living raptured—to meet Christ, who has come invisibly to receive them.

During the Tribulation, Russia invades Israel and is destroyed by a miraculous act; 144,000 Jews confess Jesus to be the Messiah, initiating a great period of Jewish conversion; and the forces of the West led by the Roman dictator met the "vast hordes of the Orient" in a cataclysmic battle centered at the Valley of Megiddo in Palestine. Just before the battle of Armageddon completely destroys the human race, and precisely at the end of the seven years of tribulation, Christ will personally and visibly return to earth and establish the Davidic kingdom, which lasts a thousand years. At the close of the millennium the earth will be re-created, to remain the eternal home of all redeemed by Christ.

Several features stand out in this brief review of dispensationalist eschatology. First, the nation of Israel, rather than the Christian church, plays the central role in the final events of world history. Second, specific eschatological significance is assigned to current international developments, particularly those concerning the Middle East. Third, the central eschatological event concerning Christians, or the specific hope of the church, is not the visible return of Christ, or the parousia described in the New Testament, but the secret rapture that enables the church to avoid the Tribulation. According to dispensationalism, then, Christian hope anticipates a complex series of literal events, foretold in detail by Biblical prophecies concerned primarily with the nation of Israel, and highlighted by the rapture of the church at the beginning of a seven-year tribulation and the return of Christ at the end to establish and reign over the Davidic kingdom for a thousand years.

George Eldon Ladd

Pretribulationism—belief in the rapture of the church before the tribulation—is not the only form of premillennialism, the view that Christ's return precedes His millennial reign. Within conservative Christianity an extensive critique of dispensationalist eschatology has been developed by George Eldon Ladd, who served as professor of New Testament exegesis and theology at Fuller Theological Seminary, Pasadena, California. An evangelical Christian thoroughly conversant with contemporary Biblical scholarship, Ladd espouses a "conservative, premillennial position," in harmony with "the Christian worldview found in the Scriptures."[71] He maintains that an "outline of future events" can be derived from the Biblical descriptions of last things and that "the Son of God who lived on earth is to appear again on earth to bring history to a victorious and glorious consummation."[72]

Ladd develops his understanding of eschatology by examining the concept of the kingdom of God as it appears in the Old Testament, in intertestamental literature, and in the Gospels. From this examination he concludes, most fundamentally, that the kingdom is both future and present—"both a present spiritual reign of Christ within the lives of God's people, and a future glorious reign on earth."[73] Thus he divorces himself on the one hand from the dispensationalist view that the kingdom is exclusively future and on the other from the view that the kingdom is purely present and does not include a future aspect.

Although the kingdom involves two temporal aspects, Biblical literature places primary emphasis upon a future eschatological blessing,[74] so the crucial question is precisely how the future eschatological kingdom can be a present reality.[75] The answer to this question, Ladd suggests, lies in "the dynamic meaning of the Kingdom of God," "if . . . the Kingdom is the reign of God, not merely in the human but dynamically active in the person of Jesus and in human history."[76] "The eschatological kingdom has invaded history in advance," so the present age is one of fulfillment; but "the same God who is now acting in historical events to bring about a fulfillment of the Messianic salvation will act at the end of history to bring His Kingdom to its consummation," so the present age is one of "fulfillment without consummation." [77]

According to Ladd, the consummation of salvation at the end of the age involves the "personal, visible, glorious return of Christ to bring the kingdom of God," and His literal millennial reign on earth.[78] Ladd agrees with the dispensationalist outline of prophetic teaching, to the extent that it involves the concentration of evil in the person of the antichrist, a period of great tribulation, a distinctive role played by the Jewish people, many of whom recognize Jesus as the Messiah, the visible, personal return of Christ to punish the antichrist and his followers, "to deliver His people from . . . tribulation, and to establish His millennial kingdom upon the earth."[79] However, he takes exception to the fundamental tenet of dispensationalism, namely, the postponement of the kingdom to the millennium, and disputes the separation of the rapture of the church from the glorious return of Christ to establish His kingdom. Ladd argues that these views cannot be supported by sound rules of Biblical interpretation and that "the expectation of an any-moment secret coming of Christ for the purpose of rapturing the Church" is inconsistent with the Biblical view of the blessed hope of the Bible, which is "the second coming of Jesus Christ and not a pretribulation rapture."[80]

Instead of separating the rapture of the church from the return of Christ, Ladd argues that the return of Christ, the resurrection of the dead in Christ, and the rapture of the living saints are a single, indivisible event followed immediately by the punishment of antichrist and the inauguration of the kingdom.[81] According to this outline of the future, the church will survive the tribulation, rather than being rescued beforehand by the rapture. In its expectation of an any-moment rapture to save the church from the tribulation, Ladd believes dispensationalism slights the "dialectic," or twofold emphasis of Scripture, which comprises both expectancy and perspective, both constant watchfulness for the Lord's return and a theological understanding of history, which the recognition of the presence of the kingdom of God provides.

Jehovah's Witnesses

The unique eschatology of Jehovah's Witnesses, which also involves an outline of literal events, is achieved by placing a remarkable construction of various Biblical passages, whose eschatological import is, in certain cases, far from evident. The central theme in their eschatology is the establishment of God's heavenly kingdom, which occurs in the "time of the end," or "the end of the world," and their essential purpose as a religious group is defined as bearing witness to this event.[82] According to their calculation of prophetic time periods, these two phenomena—the establishment of God's kingdom and the end of the world—began simultaneously in 1914 when Christ was given the heavenly kingdom. Because it took place in heaven, the parousia, or second coming of Christ in glory, though literal, was unseen by human eyes, but the outbreak of World War I provides a visible earthly sign that it had taken place and that the time of the end had begun.[83]

The destiny of human beings in God's kingdom assumes two radically different forms for Jehovah's Witnesses, providing two quite different objects of

Christian hope. A select group, limited to just 144,000 people, will reign with Christ in heaven, where they enjoy everlasting life.[84] These constitute God's "spiritual nation," or "spiritual Israel," and because of their relatively small number are referred to scripturally as "the little flock."[85] Members of the little flock, who reign with Christ in heaven, are selected by God from among individuals who put faith in God, repent of their sins, accept Jesus Christ as their Redeemer, experience conversion and undergo baptism to express their dedication. According to Jehovah's Witnesses, these are all things that an individual can do on his own. God's part in making one a member of the spiritual nation is, if He chooses, to declare such an individual righteous, give him His holy spirit, and adopt him as a spiritual son.[86] Only 144,000 of all earth's inhabitants, then, will be justified, adopted as God's children, born again, and have any hope of eternal life in heaven with Christ. Since the time of Christ God has been selecting the members of this group, and a "remnant" of less than 20,000 is now left on earth.[87] In 1918 the members of God's spiritual nation who had died before that time were raised to life in heaven with Christ in an "invisible resurrection," and since then when members of the little flock die, God immediately raises them to life in heaven.[88]

Besides the 144,000 spiritual Israelites, there is a "great crowd," not limited in number, made up of "other sheep," or "men of good will," who hope not for eternal life in heaven but to "live through the battle of Armageddon" and "gain everlasting life on a paradise earth."[89] The "battle of Armageddon" symbolically refers to the great conflict that ends in the destruction of this wicked world and the "abyssing" of the devil and his demons.[90] The survivors of Armageddon will help renovate the earth and will live without death in a perfect natural and social environment.[91] Over a period of time the "earthly resurrection"—not to be confused with the "spiritual resurrection" of the 144,000 who rule with Christ in heaven—will occur, bringing forth in the "resurrection of life" faithful witnesses of Jehovah who died before Christ did and "men of good will" who died before Armageddon, and in the "resurrection of judgment" billions of others who died without a real opportunity to hear of God's purposes or learn what He expects of men.[92] The "final test" will occur at the end of the thousand years when Satan and his demons are permitted to tempt the earth's inhabitants to turn away from God. In the last judgment all who have succumbed will be destroyed with Satan and his demons, while those who remain loyal to God will be declared righteous, have their names recorded in the book of life, and be given the right to perfect life on the paradise earth forever.[93]

For Jehovah's Witnesses, then, the Bible provides an elaborate scheme of events, already well under way, with which world history ends, and the hope of God's people assumes two forms—"earthly" and "heavenly"—corresponding to the different destinies of the two groups into which they are divided: the 144,000 who reign with Christ in the heavens, and the unnumbered throng who live forever in the earthly paradise.[94] For the vast majority of the saved, therefore, the object of hope is not the return of Christ, or eternal fellowship with Him, but a life of endless material delights following the climactic battle of Armageddon.

Conclusion

The foregoing analyses illustrate the wide diversity of forms that the advent hope assumes in contemporary Christian thought. This study will conclude by calling attention to some significant points of comparison.

Contemporary eschatological views differ most fundamentally with respect to the kind of question that concerns their proponents. As in other areas of Christian theology, most notably its doctrine of God, questions concerning eschatology are currently being raised about the basic meaning of its statements. Ogden, for example, seems to regard this as the most important kind of question for contemporary Christian eschatology. And Rahner devotes considerable attention to it, as do Robinson and Minear. In contrast, more popular eschatologies, such as those of Jehovah's Witnesses and dispensationalists, appear to rest on the tacit assumption that the meaning of eschatological statements is quite obvious, having to do with literal events, and so consist largely of efforts to construct precise descriptions of these events.

Many students of Biblical eschatology, especially those explicitly concerned with the meaning of eschatological statements, agree that its elements have reference to present realities and in various ways illuminate dimensions of Christian existence here and now. The resurrection of the body, for example, might be construed as describing the believer's new life in Christ in this present world. This understanding of eschatological statements is supported by appeals to such factors as the conviction of early Christians that in Jesus Christ the last days arrived, and in particular, the intimate relation of eschatological imagery to the prescientific conceptual world of the first century A.D. Adherents to the general view that the realities referred to by traditional eschatological statements are, in an important sense, present realities would include practically all the individual scholars mentioned above—Berkouwer, Ladd, Minear, Ogden, Pannenberg, Rahner, and Robinson.

There is some difference of opinion among those affirming the present significance of eschatological statements as to whether they refer *also* to realities that are yet future. Ogden, for example, insists that their reference to present realities exhaustively accounts for the significance of eschatological statements, but his view is definitely in the minority.

According to all the other theologians mentioned, Christian hope apparently includes the anticipation of realities that are yet future. Their views differ widely, however, as to whether the anticipated future can be described with any degree of definiteness and, if so, what its precise content will be. Ladd perceives an "outline of future events" in the eschatological statements of Scripture, but other scholars, including Berkouwer, Pannenberg, Minear, Rahner, and Robinson, cite the metaphorical or symbolic nature of the Biblical descriptions of last things as evidence that a precise forecast of the future is not the intention of these statements. Robinson leaves open the possibility of some correspondence between the traditional elements of Christian eschatology and actual future events, but he denies the necessity of such correspondence, insisting that the actual way human history ends is quite irrelevant to the concerns of Christian hope. And Minear seems to argue that the flexibility of the eschatological images of Scripture makes it impossible to affirm or deny unequivocally their correspondence to future events or states of affairs.

Others, however, believe that while the metaphorical nature of Scriptural eschatology precludes the possibility of charting the end of history in great detail, its major elements—the resurrection of the dead, the parousia, the final judgment, and the restoration of the earth—do correspond to actual future events. Thus, Berkouwer maintains that the return of Christ and the accompanying occurrences will indeed be literal events. And it is apparently Pannenberg's position that the resurrection of the dead, at least, refers to the actual resumption of human life after death at some future time.

Also large groups of Christians, including Jehovah's Witnesses and dispensationalists, among the positions reviewed, believe that the eschatological portions of Scripture provide a factual account of how human history will conclude and attempt to chart the course of last-day events from the study of various Bible prophecies. The differences between the resulting descriptions of the end are, of course, far too numerous to mention here. Opinions differ, for example, on such matters as whether the church will be rescued, or "raptured," before the final tribulation and whether the modern state of Israel has a specific role to play in the fulfillment of Biblical prophecies.

On the other hand, there seems to be widespread agreement that we are now living in the last days of earth's history and that the essential elements in Biblical eschatology pertain to events that will transpire in the very near future. And current political, social, and scientific developments are widely appealed to as evidence that we are now living in the time of the end. In addition, most of those who find in the Bible a factual account of history's climax regard its major events, such as the return of Christ and the resurrection of the dead, as yet future. Jehovah's Witnesses are apparently unique in regarding the parousia as having already occurred, although they place other eschatological events—the battle of Armageddon, for example—in the future.

In summary, it is apparent, first of all, that traditional eschatological views are very much alive within contemporary Christianity. Many assume today, as Christians have for centuries, that the Biblical accounts of the end indeed describe the final events of human history. At the same time, there have been important new developments in several directions. A number of relatively recent interpretations of Biblical eschatology extend this traditional conviction into elaborate schemes demonstrating a direct relation between the last days of which Scripture speaks and contemporary social and political phenomena. And others, in contrast, seriously question the assumption that the Bible factually describes the climax of human history, appealing to the radical difference between our modern outlook and the ancient perspective in which the Biblical writers expressed themselves. In short, there seems to be no dominant view of eschatology within Christianity today. The variety of forms that the advent hope now assumes seems to reflect the diversity within Christian thought in general and, perhaps, the widespread religious pluralism of modern times.

NOTES

[1] Rudolf Bultmann, "New Testament and Mythology," in *Kerygma and Myth*, ed. Hans Werner Bartsch, trans. Reginald H. Fuller (New York, 1961), pp. 1-44.
[2] Schubert M. Ogden, "The Meaning of Christian Hope," *Union Seminary Quarterly Review* 30 (Winter-Summer, 1975): 157.
[3] *Idem, The Reality of God and Other Essays* (New York, 1966), 214.
[4] *Idem,* "The Meaning of Christian Hope," p. 158.
[5] *Idem, The Reality of God,* p. 214.
[6] *Idem,* "The Meaning of Christian Hope," p. 158.

[7] *Ibid.*, p. 153.

[8] *Ibid.*, p. 163.

[9] Langdon Gilkey, "Reinhold Niebuhr's Theology of History," *Journal of Religion* 54 (October 1974): 363.

[10] Carl E. Braaten, "The New Theology of the Future," in Carl Braaten and Robert Jenson, *The Futurist Option* (New York, 1970), p. 17.

[11] Wolfhart Pannenberg, *Basic Questions in Theology*, trans. George H. Kehm (Philadelphia, 1971), vol. 2, p. 62.

[12] *Idem, The Idea of God and Human Freedom* (Philadelphia, 1973), pp. 201, 202.

[13] *Idem, The Apostles' Creed in the Light of Today's Questions* (Philadelphia, 1972), pp. 68, 69.

[14] *Ibid.*, pp. 114, 115.

[15] *Idem, The Idea of God*, pp. 197-200.

[16] *Idem, What Is Man? Contemporary Anthropology in Theological Perspective*, trans. Duane A. Priebe (Philadelphia, 1970), pp. 80, 50, 52.

[17] *Idem, The Idea of God*, p. 199.

[18] *Idem, What Is Man?* p. 81.

[19] John A. T. Robinson, *Honest to God* (Philadelphia, 1963).

[20] *Idem, In the End God* (New York, 1968), pp. 22, 47.

[21] *Ibid.*, p. 41.

[22] *Ibid.*, p. 43.

[23] *Ibid.*, p. 47.

[24] *Ibid.*, p. 68.

[25] *Ibid.*, pp. 24, 44.

[26] *Ibid.*, pp. 134, 135.

[27] *Ibid.*, pp. 45, 46.

[28] *Ibid.*, pp. 77, 78.

[29] *Ibid.*, pp. 119-133.

[30] Paul S. Minear, *Christian Hope and the Second Coming* (Philadelphia, 1954).

[31] *Ibid.*, p. 70.

[32] *Ibid.*, p. 28.

[33] *Ibid.*, p. 81.

[34] *Ibid.*, p. 37.

[35] *Ibid.*, p. 204.

[36] *Ibid.*, p. 97.

[37] *Ibid.*, pp. 127, 164.

[38] *Ibid.*, pp. 116-126.

[39] *Ibid.*, pp. 114, 118.

[40] *Ibid.*, pp. 203, 97.

[41] *Ibid.*, p. 81, 82.

[42] *Ibid.*, p. 203.

[43] J. B. Metz, "Foreword: An Essay on Karl Rahner," in Karl Rahner, *Spirit in the World*, trans. William Dych (New York, 1968), p. xiii.

[44] Karl Rahner, "Last Things," in *Sacramentum Mundi: An Encyclopedia of Theology*, ed. Karl Rahner et al. (New York, 1968), vol. 3, p. 275.

[45] *Ibid.*

[46] *Idem, Theological Investigations*, trans. Kevin Smith (London, 1966), vol. 4, p. 353.

[47] *Ibid.*, p. 47.

[48] *Idem*, "Parousia: Theological Doctrine," in *Sacramentum Mundi*, vol. 4, p. 346.

[49] *Idem, Theological Investigations*, vol. 4, p. 333.

[50] *Idem*, "Eschatology," in *Sacramentum Mundi*, vol. 2, p. 244.

[51] *Idem, Theological Investigations*, vol. 4, p. 337.

[52] *Ibid.*, p. 342.

[53] *Ibid.*, p. 336.

[54] *Idem*, "Eschatology," in *Sacramentum Mundi*, vol. 2, p. 244.

[55] *Idem, Theological Investigations*, vol. 4, p. 330.

[56] *Ibid.*, pp. 335, 336, note.

[57] *Ibid.*, pp. 328, 329.

[58] *Ibid.*, p. 326.

[59] G. C. Berkouwer, *The Return of Christ*, trans. James Van Oosterom, ed. Marlin J. Van Elderen (Grand Rapids, 1972), p. 113.

[60] *Ibid.*, pp. 107, 108.

[61] *Ibid.*, p. 233.

[62] *Ibid.*, p. 19.

[63] *Ibid.*, p. 157.

[64] *Ibid.*, pp. 166, 216.

[65] Charles Caldwell Ryrie, *Dispensationalism Today* (Chicago, 1965), p. 37.

[66] *Ibid.*, pp. 159, 176.

[67] *Ibid.*, pp. 171, 160.

[68] Hal Lindsey, *The Late Great Planet Earth* (Grand Rapids, 1970), p. ii.

[69] *Ibid.*, pp. 41, 59.

[70] *Ibid.*, pp. 97, 111, 107.

[71] George Eldon Ladd, *Crucial Questions About the Kingdom of God* (Grand Rapids, 1952), pp. 59, 43.

[72] *Ibid.*, pp. 149, 46.

[73] *Ibid.*, p. 60.

[74] *Ibid.*, pp. 73, 74.

[75] *Idem, The Presence of the Future: The Eschatology of Biblical Realism* (Grand Rapids, 1974), pp. 120, 121.

[76] *Ibid.*, pp. 121, 42.

[77] *Ibid.,* pp. 326, 322, 105.
[78] *Idem, The Blessed Hope* (Grand Rapids, 1956), p. 137; *Crucial Questions About the Kingdom of God*, p. 149.
[79] *Idem, The Blessed Hope*, pp. 8, 7.
[80] *Ibid.,* p. 11.
[81] *Ibid.,* p. 166.
[82] *From Paradise Lost to Paradise Regained* (Brooklyn, 1958), p. 169.
[83] *Ibid.,* pp. 173, 174, 179.
[84] *Ibid.,* pp. 186, 194.
[85] *Ibid.,* pp. 152, 186, 216.
[86] *Ibid.,* p. 152.
[87] *Ibid.,* pp. 231, 190.
[88] *Ibid.,* p. 192.
[89] *Ibid.,* pp. 216, 195.
[90] *Ibid.,* pp. 203, 211.
[91] *Ibid.,* pp. 220-226.
[92] *Ibid.,* pp. 232, 229.
[93] *Ibid.,* pp. 239, 240.
[94] *Ibid.,* p. 216.

CHAPTER 11

The Future and the Present:
The Meaning of the Advent Hope

Fritz Guy

IN GIVING a detailed exposition of the advent hope in Scripture and history, the preceding chapters of this book have explored the content and validity of Adventist eschatology by presenting its Biblical foundation, historical background, denominational formulation, and contemporary theological context. What remains to be done in this final chapter is to illuminate the *meaning* of Adventist eschatology—that is, to consider its principal themes, their importance, and their implications. So the intention of this chapter is to answer the questions What is the advent hope all about? And what difference does it make? In other words, how does (or should) this particular view of the future affect a person's beliefs, attitudes, and actions in the present?

The Place of Eschatology Within Adventist Theology

According to an Adventist understanding of the Biblical revelation, the second advent—the second appearance of God in the concrete form of Jesus the Messiah—is the event that marks the end of the present age of human history. Even more important, it is the event that opens the final act in God's solution to the problem of sin, not only in human history on the Planet Earth, but also in the whole created moral universe. As the primary content of the advent hope, this event naturally occupies a major place in Adventist life and thought.

But the final act in the total process of redemption is not by any means to be regarded as the heart and center of that process. Hence eschatology is not (and must never become) the heart or center of a Christian theology. Even an *Advent*-ist theology, which is by definition interested in the future consummation, is built necessarily and explicitly on the composite event of the incarnation, life, death, and resurrection of Jesus Christ. For it is only because of *this* event, *this* act of God, that there is any reason at all to be interested in a future, final event that is to be another, complementary act of God. Any Christian eschatology must in every respect be both understood and formulated in relation to the authentic theological center—the mission of Jesus the incarnate God. An eschatology with any other center is, quite literally, *eccentric*. Genuine Adventism is therefore not a species of contemporary "futurism"; it is not a religious counterpart of the various secular scenarios (either optimistic or pessimistic) that fascinate (and alternately reassure and distress) the late-twentieth-century mind.

At the same time, however, eschatology is no mere epilogue to theology. While it is not the first word of the Christian gospel, neither is it an optional last chapter; it is not merely the frosting on the theological cake. To the contary, it is the necessary conclusion to the basic Christian affirmation of salvation offered in Christ. On the one hand, the fact that the creation of the world and humanity is the deliberate intention of God demands an ultimate restoration after the shattering and distortion that are the consequence of sin. And on the other hand, the fact that in Christ humanity is to be completely liberated from sin also requires the renewal of the whole world. Thus, as the doctrine of Creation and the doctrine of redemption claim, if God is indeed God, and if Jesus Christ is indeed Lord, then the "kingdom of this world" must become, in fact as well as in principle, His own kingdom—the concrete reality in which His will is fully and irrevocably actualized.

As an essential part of the Christian gospel, eschatology is first of all good news *(euaggelion)*. It is primarily concerned with "our blessed hope"—the confident anticipation and exciting expectation of the final fulfillment of humanity by means of "the appearing of the glory of our great God and Saviour Jesus Christ" (Titus 2:13).* It is the ultimate hope for individuals, who recall the words of their Lord: "When I go and prepare a place for you, I will come again and will take you to myself, that where I am you may be also" (John 14:3). It is also the ultimate hope for humanity as a whole, because "the God of heaven will set up a kingdom which shall never be destroyed" (Dan. 2:44). And it is the ultimate hope for the natural world, inasmuch as "the creation itself will be set free from its bondage to decay" (Rom. 8:21).

Second, eschatology is proclamation *(kerygma)*, and thus exhortation and appeal. It is an invitation to look for and identify the current issues (along with the ultimate principles) in the intensifying conflict between transcendent good and evil in the world; and it is a call to prepare for and participate in the final, unprecedented witness to the infinite love and absolute integrity of God. When Jesus answered His disciples' question about the destruction of the Jerusalem Temple, the end of the world, and the signs of His reappearance, the thesis of His reply was, "You . . . must be ready; for the Son of man is coming at an hour you do not expect" (Matt. 24:44). In three vivid parables He explained what he meant by "being ready": having the ability to handle both unexpected delay and sudden development in eschatological events (the ten bridesmaids, Matt. 25:1-13); making diligent and creative use of one's personal resources, including the knowledge of the gospel (the three servants, verses 14-30); and being responsive to various dimensions of fundamental human need (the sheep and the goats, verses 31-46).

Only thirdly is eschatology a matter of divine warning *(chrematisis)*. And even then the announcement that "the hour of [God's] judgment has come" is introduced as "an eternal gospel" that is destined to be proclaimed "to every

---

* All Bible texts in this chapter are from the Revised Standard Version.

nation and tribe and tongue and people" (Rev. 14:6, 7). The entire Revelation to John is, with all of its pictures of terrifying beasts and horrendous calamities, a powerful reminder of the certainty of the ultimate triumph of God and His righteousness, a triumph that entails (as the other side of the coin) the ultimate doom of the adversary and those who participate in his rebellion. The very words of warning that this outcome is sure and that the end is imminent are at the same time words of assurance and hope.

To the extent that there is a genuine note of warning in Adventist eschatology, there is a need to beware of its possible distortion into expressions of unwarranted, inappropriate, and self-destructive attitudes or feelings. There is, for example, the possibility of a spiritual elitism—an assumed religious superiority based on the self-assurance that "we are God's people; we have the truth and we know all about the future," in contrast to all the other, benighted, second-class Christians in the world. There is also the possibility of a religious paranoia that imagines demonic conspirators and persecutors everywhere, and sees in every social, political, or religious development the ominous specter of supernatural evil. Yet another possibility, derived from either of the first two, is an attitude of hostility toward theological (and even political) opponents, resulting from a premature assumption that all of humanity has already opted deliberately and finally for good or evil, so that whoever does not share "our" understanding and beliefs is by definition allied with the forces of darkness and destruction.

The antidote for these kinds of feelings is a recognition of the proper function of eschatology. It is not intended to satisfy human curiosity about the future—as if Biblical apocalyptic were a crystal ball, and eschatology a kind of theological/historical fortunetelling. Neither is it intended to encourage (much less to produce) self-appointed prophets or judges. Rather, the function of eschatology is to provide Christian assurance and hope, a sensitivity to contemporary religious issues, and an eagerness to communicate to others both the good news and the insight of the gospel.

Furthermore, in the context of Adventist theology, eschatology (like the soteriology that it complements) has a yet broader and deeper significance than the final destiny of humanity. For Adventist thought, the problem of sin is not merely a matter of humanity in rebellion against God, although that rebellion is indeed serious as both the existential context and the fundamental issue for every individual human being. The problem of sin is cosmic conflict, a "great controversy" over the fundamental nature of God as ultimate reality (and, consequently, over the nature of all reality). The crucial question is whether God exists and acts solely for His own interest and benefit, or also for the interest and benefit of His creation—in other words, whether Ultimate Reality is self-serving or self-giving (and, consequently, whether it is the essential nature of all things to coexist in competition with each other for reality, or in complementarity and mutual actualization). This issue transcends humanity and its planetary environment; it originated before humanity and extends beyond it, and it involves angelic and whatever other moral beings God has created. So God's response to the problem has similar cosmic dimensions. It is the divine intention in Christ "to reconcile to himself all things, whether on earth or in heaven" (Col. 1:20). The mission of Jesus thus means more than the possibility of eternal life for those who accept God's gift of forgiveness; and the "last things" mean more than the end of present human history and the inauguration of a new world for redeemed and restored humanity. For the totality of creation, there is an end to the actualization of sin; and this end marks a significantly new beginning.

Although it is by no means unique, this "cosmic dimension" of Adventist theology in general and eschatology in particular is distinctive within contemporary Christian thought; and it is significant for an understanding of the ultimate importance of the salvation and final destiny of humanity. To see humanity as not the only (or even the primary) focus of God's concern in relation to the problem of sin, but as part of an infinitely larger horizon, is both to *relativize* and to *universalize* its importance. What happens to humanity is only one part of a far greater drama; yet just because it is part of a greater drama, it has more extensive consequences. Thus there is no lessening of the ultimate importance of human sin, salvation, and destiny; but there is a change in the way that importance is understood.

The Theological Implications of the Advent Hope

Adventist eschatology combines four major themes for theological reflection, each based on a particular event or element involved in the "last things": (1) the end of the present age; (2) the consummation of God's presence; (3) the determination of individual destiny; and (4) the ultimate fulfillment of human existence.

The end of the present age. The very word *eschatology* (meaning literally the doctrine of the *eschaton,* the end) implies the termination of the present age and its civilization, and the cessation of human existence as we know it: the literal end of our world. The familiar Biblical descriptions are typically brief and dramatic; and they suggest that the end of this era of history is to be catastrophic: "The heavens will pass away with a loud noise, and the elements will be dissolved with fire, and the earth and the works that are upon it will be burned up" (2 Peter 3:10). The picture here is clear enough: on the one hand there is a complete devastation of the apparatus of civilization, an absolute disorganization of the social, economic, and political order; on the other hand there is a radical disruption of natural processes, a total ecological destruction that makes the continuation of human life utterly impossible.

From this picture and the conviction that history is destined to a sudden end, there arise two important theological questions. One of these asks how the present course of history is related to its end: does what happens in the world or the church have any effect on the nature or the timing of its conclusion? If so, what kind of effect is it, and how is it produced? In short, how is history connected to the *eschaton?* The answer to this question must begin with the recognition that the relationship between the present course of history and its culmination is complex. It may be illustrated by a series of four analogies taken from common educational experience.

1. The relationship between history and its end may, for example, be compared to the relationship between a school term and the subsequent vacation period. The end of the term signals a welcome liberation from the pressures of academic life. According to this analogy, the end of history is regarded as a release from the various evils—anxieties, failures, tragedies, bereavements, injustices, frustrations, et cetera, ad infinitum—of our present existence. Further, this analogy reflects the fact that the end comes "from the outside"; whatever the

character or direction of the preceding historical events or developments, they are not in themselves the "cause" of the *eschaton*. That is to say, the end of human history, like its beginning, is to be understood as an act of God.

2. Another analogy is based on the relationship between an academic program and its final, comprehensive examinations, which show whether or not the course study has been sucessful in achieving its objectives. Here the overall course of history is seen primarily as the context for the moral and religious choices by which individual human destiny is determined; and the end of history is seen as the disclosure of the quality and meaning of personal lives. History as a whole has ultimate theological meaning to the extent that particular social, political, or economic events, as well as the character of govenments, nations, and cultures, facilitate or inhibit the kind of personal choices that contribute to the positive future of eternal life. Thus the *eschaton* is a disclosure of the ultimate significance of human beings in history, both individually and collectively.

3. Still another useful analogy draws on the relationship between the educational experience and the event of graduation, which is (in a certain sense) the outcome of a person's own activity as a student (as in the previous analogy), but which at the same time requires an additional, external agency—namely, an educational institution with the power to confer degrees and issue diplomas. Similarly, the *eschaton* can be regarded to some extent as the outcome of events within history, and yet also dependent on the intervention of God. Moreover, just as the educational institution is necessary not only for the event of graduation but also for the possibility of the educational experience that culminates in graduation, so the reality and activity of God are a necessary condition for the very existence of history as well as for its end. The graduation analogy also points to the fact that just as the completion of an educational experience is regarded as the "commencement" of a new phase of a person's life, so the "end" of the present age is properly regarded as the "beginning" of the new age that is to come.

4. A final analogy comes from the relationship between a person's education and his professional life, the fulfillment toward which the education points and for which it is an essential preparation. It is this fulfilment that provides the final, true meaning of the whole educational process. This analogy indicates more clearly than any of the others the continuity between the course of history and the ultimate future of humanity. Just as the quality of a person's total educational experience greatly affects the competence that characterizes his entire career, so the content of present history contributes to the quality of the ultimate human future. For individuals the future is a continuation and development of the positive interpersonal relationships, the self-giving love, and the knowledge of God that give meaning to the present. For humanity collectively, and for history as a whole, the influence of the present on the ultimate future is most easily seen in the fact that human history demonstrates (for the eternal benefit of the entire moral universe) the existential implications of "the great controversy." Because of the intensity and pervasiveness of human sinfulness, the demonstration shows chiefly the destructive consequences of self-interest and competition: hostility, injustice, and violence. At the same time, however, it is part of the mission of the church, as a community of faith, integrity, and love, to demonstrate (on a numerically smaller scale, to be sure, but with equal clarity and power) the magnificent possibilities of grace: ever increasing understanding, sharing,

helping, and mutual fulfillment.

Of course, none of these various analogies is adequate to illustrate the total relationship between the present course of history and its end, for along with its particular emphasis and usefulness, each has its own limitations. But all of them together help to indicate the importance, the nature, and the complexity of this relationship.

The second question that arises here in connection with the idea of the end of the present age asks how it is possible to affirm *both* the openness of history to the exercise of human freedom *and* the effectiveness of God's providence in achieving His own historical objectives. Each of these elements seems absolutely essential to Adventist eschatology as well as to any other Christian thought about the ultimate future of human beings. For without real freedom, human existence is meaningless; humanity is merely a pawn of cosmic forces in conflict. But without God's effective guidance of history, there is no historical security; there can be no assurance that humanity will not destroy itself (for example, by a worldwide nuclear or biochemical disaster). Since Adventist eschatology insists that the end of the present age is to be the result of an intervention of God rather than a human blunder, the questionable part is the reality of human freedom and the openness of history.

Fortunately, the question is not as difficult as it appears at first. Indeed, there are at least three possible answers. In the first place, because the infinite resourcefulness of God enables Him to respond creatively and constructively to every situation and every event, He can leave humanity free to choose its future—the results of every choice can be incorporated into the ultimate actualization of God's intention. Since God is omniscient and omnipotent, He cannot be caught by surprise, much less finally frustrated, by human freedom.

In the second place, while the reality of human freedom requires a *general* possibility of carrying out decisions by effective action (since otherwise there would be no reason for decisions of any kind), it does not require this possibility in *every* case. One of the points in Jesus' sermon on the mount is that sin can occur by intention, even when there is no opportunity to translate the intention into action (cf. Matt. 5:27-30). Furthermore, such things as physical limitations and social, legal, and economic pressures seriously restrict the range of possible actions, without thereby negating the reality of human freedom. For the essence of freedom is not the ability to always accomplish whatever a person wills, but the ability to determine the values by which a person lives (that is to say, the values according to which he does whatever he can actually do). So the fact that the actual openness of human history may be to some extent limited by boundaries set by God is no more a restriction of human freedom than is its limitation by other, this-worldly factors.

In the third place, the eschatological limitation imposed by God on the openness of history is in fact minimal. The very fact that the end of the present age is the result of divine initiative—and therefore not simply a product of the course of history, and not finally dependent on human action of any particular kind—means that the future remains almost wholly open. The principal exclusion is the premature self-destruction of humanity; for on the basis of Jesus' own words, the present age is envisioned to continue until the "gospel of the kingdom" is "preached throughout the whole world, as a testimony to all nations; and then the end will come" (Matt. 24:14). But this is primarily a matter of the relative timing of events. Even a nuclear holocaust is not unthinkable as a possible event to be incorporated into the fulfillment of the eschatological purposes of God. And the communication of the gospel to the world might well take unexpected forms that would surprise even the most enthusiastic members of the community of faith. It is useful to remember that throughout Judeo-Christian history the fulfillment of a divine promise has never been precisely what was anticipated (with the nature and mission of the Messiah standing out as the supreme instance). The God of history is a God of the unexpected. So there may well be some major surprises in the way the present age actually comes to its end.

The consummation of God's presence. The advent hope is focused primarily on the reappearance of God in the form of Jesus, the second coming of God to humanity in this particular way. Here several of the relevant New Testament sayings come immediately to mind. We hear Jesus in the upper room reassuring His disciples: "When I go and prepare a place for you, I will come again and will take you to myself, that where I am you may be also" (John 14:3). We hear the messengers at the time of the ascension: "This Jesus, who was taken up from you into heaven, will come in the same way as you saw him go into heaven" (Acts 1:11). We hear the repeated affirmation of the glorified Lord speaking in the Revelation to John: "Behold, I am coming soon" (chap. 22:12; cf. chaps. 3:11; 22:7, 20). And we hear the prophet's simple but existentially-powerful response, "Come, Lord Jesus!" (chap. 22:20), echoing the early Christian greeting in Aramaic, *Maranatha,* "Our Lord, come!" (1 Cor. 16:22).[1] Thus the advent hope is focused on a *parousia*—a coming and a presence of God that is as objective and specific as the historical presence of God in Jesus of Nazareth, as real as the presence of God in the crucifixion and the resurrection.

This second major theme of Adventist eschatology raises its own theological question: How is this final coming of God to human existence related to His other "comings"? An answer to this question must be begin with the fact that God's presence in and to the world is a permanent reality: God is never in fact *absent* from human existence, or from any part or process of the created universe. And this permanent presence has two dimensions. On the one hand, it has to do with the fundamental reality of things: it is God's *self-involvement* in the world, not only originating it in the past but also maintaining its existence and its processes in the present. On the other hand, the presence of God also results in our awareness of this fundamental reality: it is God's *self-revelation* to the world, making Himself known in such a way that His presence is felt, although it is not always acknowledged.

In both of these dimensions, the presence of God occurs in many different "modes" in the history of human beings. In other words, God "comes" to the world in various ways that may be grouped into three categories. First are modes of God's general, continuing, and universal presence. These include the continuation of the so-called natural order of the world: the physical, chemical, and biological processes of nature, as well as the psychological and rational processes of human existence. They also include the omnipresent ministry of the Holy Spirit, which prompted the rhetorical question from the Hebrew psalmist, "Whither shall I go from thy Spirit? Or whither shall I flee from thy presence?" (Ps. 139:7). Jesus promised His continuing presence with His disciples, emphasizing both its permanence ("I am with you always, to the close of the age" [Matt. 28:20]) and its relation to corporate religious experience ("Where two or three are gathered in my name, there am I in the midst of them" [chap. 18:20]).

In addition to these modes of God's general presence in and to the totality of created being, there are various modes of God's special, particular presence. In these God "comes" in unusual, impressive, and sometimes disturbing ways. God comes in particular events: for example, in Biblical history in the Exodus, Exile, and Restoration of Israel; and in Christian history, in the Reformation and in the Advent Awakening of the nineteenth century. God sometimes comes to particular places, which are thereby made "holy"—especially the Hebrew sanctuaries (the tabernacle in the wilderness, and the successive temples on Mount Zion). God also comes in many comparatively private moments of miracle—healing, protection, and deliverance—both physical and spiritual.

Finally, there is the absolutely unique mode of God's coming to the world by means of incarnation, in the mission (life and death) and end (resurrection) of Jesus of Nazareth as *Emmanuel,* "God with us" (chap. 1:23). This is a surprising, almost unbelievable mode of God's presence—"in the likeness of sinful flesh" (Rom. 8:3), "in every respect . . . tempted as we are" (Heb. 4:15), "reconciling the world to himself" (2 Cor. 5:19). It is the most direct and complete mode, and it is the most profound. Yet it remains the same presence; for it is the same God who thus comes, and who is thus revealed.

What is to be involved in the *eschaton* is yet another, new mode of this presence of God. It is not merely a continuation or a recurrence of the other modes; it is a genuine arrival of that which is not yet here—a true "coming." It constitutes a final, irreversible transcending of the separation between God and human beings that resulted from sin—the separation first experienced in the dread of God's presence and in the subsequent departure from Eden (see Gen. 3:8, 23, 24). In relation to the previous modes of God's presence in the world, it is, literally, their consummation; for it is characterized by the permanence and pervasiveness of the general modes, by the immediacy and impact of the special modes, and by the personal concreteness of the incarnational mode. This is the ultimate presence of God.

This new mode of God's presence is a true "coming" also, in the sense that it comes to the world "from the outside." It is God's own act; it is neither the result of historical developments (as we have already noted) nor the outcome of natural forces, either terrestrial or astronomic. While God may, of course, use such factors as means to the fulfillment of His own intentions, there is no possibility of explaining the *eschaton* in terms of them. For its essential cause is external to the created universe. This fact has two important theological consequences. For one thing, it means that our notions of "hastening" or "delaying" the arrival of the final future must be carefully qualified. They must be understood in terms of God's intention to relate His own actions to human events; thus the relation is not, strictly speaking, a causal or "necessary" one. A parent may agree to take his/her children to the beach after they have washed the breakfast dishes, thus making the parent's action contingent on that of the children; but washing the breakfast dishes does not in itself entail a trip to the beach as a necessary outcome. For another thing, the external causality of the *eschaton* means that its arrival is not strictly predictable. Neither its timing nor its preliminary scenario can be precisely foreseen. Thus it is not a matter of prediction, as if it were concerned with a solar eclipse or an economic recession. It is, rather, a matter of expectation and hope.

Eschatology is not advance information about what is going to happen, but confidence in the God who is Lord of the future. Indeed, it was to emphasize precisely the element of chronological surprise that Jesus used the metaphor of a thief: "If the householder had known in what part of the night the thief was coming, he would have watched and would not have let his house be broken into. Therefore you also must be ready; for the Son of man is coming at an hour you do not expect" (Matt. 24:43, 44). And in regard to the precise form of the events connected with the *eschaton*, we may well learn from a monumental theological blunder of the past: the ancient anticipation of the Messiah distorted its authentic hope into so rigid a prediction that when He turned out to be something quite different from what was expected, He was unrecognized.

Yet for all of its genuine newness, the final presence of God is not absolutely new; for only its continuity with previous modes makes it possible for human beings to identify it and experience it for what it is. The eschatological mode is, not surprisingly, essentially similar to the incarnational mode: it is a personal presence of God in the concrete form of Jesus Christ, the historical Messiah. It is "this Jesus" (Acts 1:11) through whom God is to be ultimately and eternally present to human beings. This is the theological basis of the term *second coming*.[2] Not only does the same form of the personal presence of God "return," but it comes again in a way that is in important respects like the "first coming." The fundamental mission is the same: to be "God with us" as a saving, transforming presence. The first, intrahistorical coming made the ultimate salvation of human beings possible; the second, posthistorical coming is to make that salvation complete. The motivation of the second coming is the same as that of the first: gracious, creative love *(agape)*. And there is the same sort of objective reality and perceptibility—in distinction, for example, from the power of God that is the ground of all created being and process, and from the presence of God in the Spirit. All of this means that our interest in the final future is necessarily interest in Christ; the advent hope is nothing else than hope in Christ.

The determination of individual destiny. From the beginning of Christian theological reflection, eschatology has included an affirmation of final, irrevocable judgment that signifies the ultimate destiny of each individual human being. And this judgment is essentially a binary situation: there are only two possibilities. In the Sermon on the Mount and in the conversation with Nicodemus, Jesus characterized these possibilities as "destruction" versus "life" (Matt. 7:13, 14; John 3:16). In talking to His disciples about the end of the world, He contrasted "eternal life" with "eternal punishment" (Matt. 25:46). The vivid imagery of the Apocalypse pictures those who are "tormented with fire and brimstone" and those who are "standing beside the sea of glass with harps of God in their hands" (Rev. 14:10; 15:2). For Paul the distinction is the same: between "wrath," "fury," "tribulation," and "distress" on the one hand, and "glory," "honor," "peace," and "eternal life" on the other (Rom. 2:7-10).

Just as certainly as the ultimate division of humanity is attested in Scripture, however, it is necessary to face the question of the relationship of this eschatological judgment to God's unlimited love. To put it bluntly: How can the real possibility of eternal damnation for some members of God's human family be

219

part of the "good news" of Christian (and specifically Adventist) belief? And how does it contribute to the resolution of the "great controversy" regarding the nature of ultimate reality (that is, the character of God)? A short answer to this sort of question is that eschatological judgment is a necessary expression of the justice that is required by love. But more needs to be said by way of explaining the nature and function of this judgment.

God's ultimate judgment of human beings constitutes a final acknowledgment and confirmation of individual human decisions concerning the relation of God and oneself. This, of course, is not to be understood as divine approval of all such decisions, but rather as a willingness to accept them as definitive of the quality of one's being in relation to God, and thus determinative of one's destiny. Thus the final judgment is the greatest possible affirmation of human dignity: The ultimate meaning and nature of individual human beings is determined by the individual's own choice—not by divine intention or predetermination. The final judgment is, furthermore, an affirmation of basic order in the universe: events, including moral decisions, have consequences. This order is a necessary condition if there is to be any meaning in human choices and actions; otherwise, the universe would be moral (as well as ontological) chaos.

Eschatological judgment occurs in two forms, both of which express the justice that love requires. One one side of the coin, the final judgment is the negation of evil. It is God's recognition of the refusal of human beings to acknowledge and live in terms of the reality of divine sovereignty. But God does not merely recognize the fact of this refusal; because it is a denial of the nature of His own reality, He disavows it and rejects it. This negation of evil results in radical, eternal destruction. It occurs as God, the source of all being and all capacity for continuing to be, no longer supports the being that chooses finally to sever itself from the very basis of its own existence. By separating humanity from God, sin inevitably results in increasing disorder, and in the degradation of matter and energy toward a final state of inert uselessness; without the power of God to maintain the natural processes on which human beings depend, they cannot exist. According to the very nature of reality "the wages of sin is death" (Rom. 6:23), that is, nonbeing.

So the end of the present age can properly be described in terms of "the wrath of God" (Rev. 14:10; 15:1, 7; 16:1). The effects of this element of final judgment are both historical and natural, as civilization is devastated and the planetary life-supporting environment is completely disrupted. This is indeed "the close of the age" in connection with which "the powers of the heavens will be shaken" (Matt. 24:3, 29).

But on the other side of the coin, the final divine judgment is also a confirmation and authentication of the good in human existence. It is the ultimate recognition of integrity and self-giving, of acceptance of and identification with God's act of reconciliation in Christ. This is not, of course, in any sense a reward for good works, but rather the eschatological fulfillment of "the free gift of God," which is "eternal life in Christ Jesus our Lord" (Rom. 6:23). It is therefore an eternal deliverance from the ontological consequences of sin that would be otherwise inescapable; and it involves either preservation through the catastrophic eschatological disorder or resurrection to eternal life, depending on a person's particular location in history. Thus judgment can be understood positively as a ratification and final actualization of salvation, as a consequence of

God's love.

Furthermore, the God who acts in judgment at the close of the present age is the same God who at the cross took on Himself all of the experiential consequences of human sin—the God who "is love" (1 John 4:8). Love is the way God is eternally in relation to humanity; love motivates every "coming" of God into human existence—at the beginning of sin in Eden, at Mount Sinai, at Bethlehem, at Golgotha, at Pentecost, and at the end of the age. That is to say, there are no sequential phases (or "dispensations") in God's relation to humanity. Love is never "replaced" by, nor is it the replacement of, something else, such as justice. And love and justice are not equal-but-conflicting attributes that constitute some sort of tension in the reality of God. On the contrary, justice is an element in, and an expression of, God's loving intention and action to save the moral universe from the ultimate consequences of sin. In other words, in the character of God, love is logically prior to justice. And because God is the ultimate reality that determines the fundamental character of all other reality, love is to be regarded as logically prior to justice everywhere and in everything God does.

Because eschatological judgment is an affirmation of human responsibility and metaphysical order, because it is a validation of the good as well as a negation of evil, and because it is the action of the same God who came into human existence in Jesus of Nazareth, it can be understood in a quite straightforward way as an actualization of infinite love.

The fulfillment of human beings. Going along with the positive side of the final judgment is the final actualization of the divine intention in creation of human beings—that is, its fulfillment in the presence of God. And this involves a renewal or re-creation of the world. For the Biblical word is that not only human existence as such, but also its natural environment, has been radically affected by the occurrence and continuing reality of sin (see Gen. 3:17, 18). So the complete deliverance of human beings from the consequences of sin means the reestablishment of the originally created order, or at least the establishment of something very much like it. The apostolic witness insists that "the creation itself will be set free from its bondage to decay and obtain the glorious liberty of the children of God" (Rom. 8:21). Both the Old Testament prophet and the New Testament seer envisioned the creation of a new heaven and a new earth (Isa. 65:17; Rev. 21:1). And yet it is clearly not another place, a different place, that is to be the context for the ultimate fulfillment of the divine intention in creating this world. It will be the same place, the same planetary environment—magnificently transformed—in which the eternal future of human existence will be experienced.

The environment for the new age is envisioned as being in many respects similar to the environment we now know. There are to be, for example, the same basic kinds of created reality: matter, energy, life, consciousness, mind. And the same kinds of being: physical, chemical, vegetable, animal, human. Yet within this essential overall similarity between the present and the ultimate future environment, there is also to be a radical difference, for the re-created and transformed world is to exclude the disruptive processes that are destructive of human values and human existence—for example, the meteorological disturbances that bring drought and flood, the botanical pecularities that produce poisonous plants, the genetic accidents that yield congenital defects, and the geological irregularities that result in earthquakes and tidal waves.

Into this transformed world humanity is to be "translated" (literally "carried across"), or resurrected. It is to retain the same general defining characteristics of present humanity while being liberated from the distortions resulting from sin. This means, in the first place, that human existence in the age to come is to be a *material* existence of tangible, physical being, as opposed to a nonmaterial, disembodied being, which could hardly be defined as *human* existence at all. This again implies interesting and important similarities to present human existence. There is to be, for example, sense perception (sight, sound, taste, smell, touch) for both information and aesthetic enjoyment. And there is to be simple spatial location—existence and experience in one place at one time.

But, as in the case of the natural environment, there are also to be some radical differences between the present and the future human being. The absence of disease and genetic aberration implies an intensified sensory acuity and an expanded intellectual ability—a heightened awareness of the world, and an increased comprehension of it. An even more dramatic difference between the present and the future is to be the absence of death. The present inevitability of death as the outcome of life in human as well as vegetable and animal existence makes it difficult for many modern minds to imagine an infinite future as the destiny of an individual person. This is why the Biblical affirmation of an everlasting future is sometimes understood as a quasi-survival of persons in terms of their posterity, their influence, and their place in the memory of other persons and of God. But in fact there is nothing self-contradictory about the hope of an eternal personal future, provided it involves a material existence. There is no reason in principle why personal human existence should ever be terminated. Indeed, the typical human perception of death as intrinsically "unnatural," "wrong," or "absurd" serves as an experiential confirmation of the Biblical vision and hope.

The continuation of the same basic, defining characteristics of humanity also means that human existence in the ultimate future is to be a *temporal* existence, incorporating the reality and relevance of chronological sequence and the resulting temporal modalities of present, past, and future. Besides being a clear implication of the Biblical view of the ultimate future, this is a necessary conceptual counterpart of material existence in a material world, for temporal sequence is an inevitable consequence of physical process, and process is a constitutive characteristic of matter as we know it, all the way from the activity of subatomic particles to the movements of stellar galaxies. And what is true of matter as such applies all the more to life. The necessary conclusion is that in regard to the ultimate human future "eternity" is best understood as "unending time" rather than as "timelessness." Humanity can no more be "timeless" than it can be "matterless."

The experienced quality of time, however, is to be profoundly different. Because physical and biological processes will no longer lead to the inevitable decay and death of human beings, time will not have its present character as the threat of ever-approaching nonexistence. And because there will be an infinite length of time for persons as well as for humanity as a whole, with no possibility of time "running out," there will be no "deadlines." Time will no longer be felt as the major limitation of human existence.[3] So, in contrast to our present experience, time in the age to come will be entirely positive. It will mean new possibilities, continuing development, and the cumulation of experience. Time in the future is to be the vehicle of continuing development and fulfillment.

The continuation of essential humanity in the age to come also means a genuinely *personal* existence, comprising the self-consciousness and personal identity that are the requisite ingredients of selfhood. Individual selfhood in the ultimate future is to be, as it is now, the unique convergence of distinctive characteristics of temperament, tastes, and abilities, along with memory, interpersonal relationships, and self-determination. For selfhood is, for one thing, the summation of past experiences, some of which are consciously remembered while others are not. In the ultimate future, therefore, the past is not simply wiped out—forgotten in some kind of eschatological amnesia—for that would destroy the individual identity of selfhood. But the meaning and significance of the personal past is in part transformed by the fact of repentance and forgiveness, so that it is no longer the source of guilt, shame, or remorse. For another thing, personal identity is constituted also by relationships with other personally identifiable selves. These relationships presuppose both the distinction of oneself from others and the possibility of mutually enriching interaction. In the present age, these relationships are essential to human existence as such, and give it much of its significance; so it is to be in the final future. And, for a third thing, personal existence requires the freedom of self-determination, the ability and responsibility of choosing the values that are to determine the quality of one's total existence. Theologically speaking, this is the possibility of identifying oneself with, or separating oneself from, the intention and claim of the Creator. If, therefore, the ultimate future is to be a truly human future, it must include this freedom, and with it the theoretical possibility of sin. The absence of actual sin and its consequences does not mean an absence of moral freedom, which would be an end of personhood and human existence. Rather, it reflects a collective recognition and affirmation of self-giving love as the character of God and the fundamental nature of reality.

But, as with the other aspects of the continuation of humanity into the final future, there is to be in personal existence too a radical difference from our present experience. Although the memory of one's personal past will still include the memory of sin, it will be remembered only as sin that belongs wholly to the past and that has no power to tyrannize the present or shadow the future. Whereas the consequences of our sin continue to plague our lives (and the lives of others) in this age, the *eschaton* marks their end—and our liberation. In regard to interpersonal relationships, there is a similar difference. We are now so crippled by sin that in spite of our intentions to love completely and without reservation, we are unable to actualize these intentions perfectly, or to intergrate our lives completely around the values that we have chosen to make supreme. And our experience of true community and mutual fulfillment is stunted by the remnants of our selfishness and insecurity. From this kind of limitation, too, the *eschaton* is to be our liberation.

All of this means that the ultimate fulfillment of human existence cannot be understood as the end of history as such, but only as the end of the kind of history we now know—namely, a pathological history that since its beginning has been a compounding distortion of the essential and potentially fulfilling relationships of individuals and groups. The end of the present age of history is the beginning of a new age with a new quality of history. Individuals will continue to have "biographies": they will have new experiences in interpersonal relationships, they will discover new forms of creative expression, they will grow in their understanding of the structure and processes of the natural universe, and they will expand their comprehension of the providential and redemptive activity of God. And what is true of individuals is also true of groups and of humanity as a whole: Whatever may be the shape and dynamics of groups in the age to come, there surely will be developing patterns of mutually fulfilling interaction that will actualize the intentions of God for humanity.

Now and in the eternal future, human existence is always material, temporal, and personal. But while it is forever the same, it will also be radically transformed. The humanity that is now shriveled in self-centered insecurity will become what it was created to be: the human image of the God who is self-giving love.

The Experiential Significance of Adventist Eschatology

Besides being a vision of the eternal future of human beings, Adventist eschatology—the theology of the advent hope—is a powerful force in shaping the experience of the present. In this sense, the future that is yet-to-come is nevertheless already present in various ways. Indeed, the experiential structure of hope determines a person's attitudes toward the whole of existence, including the unexpected continuation of the present age.

The presence of the future. The impact of the envisioned future on the experienced present is felt in many forms, of which one of the most immediate is *relativization*, for the present is obviously not the final reality. Every particular experience is temporary: "This too shall pass." On the one side, the evil that distorts the present is not the last word; and on the other side, the good fortune that blesses the present carries no guarantee of permanence. Thus is pain made more endurable and joy less intoxicating; each has only relative significance in the light of a future that is incomparably superior to the present because it is both infinite in duration and perfect in quality. In the context of the advent hope, life is not any less conditioned by factors beyond a person's knowledge or power to control; it is still characterized by "givenness." But neither this general fact nor the particularities of the "given" need be overwhelming.

Another form of the impact of the future on the present may be called *eternalization:* the permanent importance that the eternal future gives to the decisions of the transient present. For the quality of the final future—the nature of the ultimate destiny of individual human beings—is profoundly influenced by every person's choices in the present. The decisions of tomorrow are in part the product of those of today; and the totality of specific decisions constitutes an ultimate general decision to affirm and identify with, or to reject and dissociate oneself from, the character and reality of God. Every present moral choice implies an ultimate choice of being or nonbeing, a choice that even divine love does not overrule. And besides this influence of the present on one's own future, the present of an individual may, insofar as it encourages or discourages certain attitudes, values, and decisions of others, exert a significant influence on the eternal future of others.

Furthermore, in addition to the influence of individual decisions, there is the influence of groups of various sorts and sizes—familial, geographic, social, vocational, religious, et cetera. All groups exert an influence on individuals both inside and outside the group. And all persons exist in groups of some sort; to be human is to be related to—and thus to be influenced by—other persons.[4] In some cases the religious (and therefore eternally significant) influence of groups is direct: the church is the most obvious example. In other cases, the religious influence is less direct, but no less effective and often far more extensive. The values of a society, for example, are a powerful factor in the adoption of values by an individual—so powerful, in fact, that they may decisively reduce the number of actually live options. As a result, a principal function of a religious community may be to resurrect some of those options. And within any group the structures of freedom and justice may encourage or inhibit the choice of certain values: an environment of thoroughgoing exploitation and oppression, for example, may generate so much fear and hostility that the ideal of self-giving love is almost invisible and even if seen can hardly be taken seriously.

Perhaps "the hand of God in history" may be seen most clearly here, in the developments that create environments in which His love can be effectively communicated and thus become a viable example for human existence. If this is so, then there is ultimate significance in the whole of history, and not just in the comparatively small portion of history that is directly involved in the events of salvation. For every political or cultural development, every military engagement, has some effect on the shape of freedom and justice somewhere in human existence. History may thus be seen not as exclusively negative and destructive, ultimately to be reversed by the divine interposition of the *eschaton,* and not as merely a meaningless collocation of events surrounding the great "acts of God" on Planet Earth, but as an eternally significant (albeit still morally ambiguous) part of the determination of the ultimate destiny of human beings. In this way, not only the decisions of individuals, but the events of history, may be seen as "eternalized."

A third form of the impact of the future on the present is *vitalization:* the vision of the future is an incentive for present activity. Adventist activism—its sense of world mission, its evangelistic outreach, its medical and educational enterprises, its publications—has developed because of, not in spite of, its conviction of the occurrence of the *eschaton* "in this generation." While to others it may seem paradoxical to work so diligently in this world while expecting a kingdom of God only in the next, to Adventists themselves the connection is really quite straightforward: whatever improvements can be made in the health and/or education of people are likely to facilitate a positive response to God and therefore contribute to the richness of the eternal future of human beings. "Lift up the trumpet, and loud let it ring; Jesus is coming again!" is not just a hymn; it is also an inner motivation to invest oneself in service and witness to the world.

A related form in which the future is effective in the present is *stabilization:* those who are confident of the future can calmly attend to the tasks of the present. Of course, the precise shape of the future remains unknown and unknowable because it is open to human decision and divine creativity, and because the causal factors involved are too complex to be fully accessible to human inquiry. For individuals there is always the compounded uncertainty of health, employment, and personal and family relationships; no one's future is guaranteed, and no amount of faith in providence can function as insurance against disaster. For nations and the world as a whole, the view of the proximate future is not only dim;

even worse, what general outlines can be guessed yield a gloomy picture of a host of problems—political, economic, ecological—whose solutions may well be painful and slow, and perhaps impossible to achieve. Yet certainty regarding the ultimate future of humanity and regarding the presence of God's love in one's own life makes it possible to concentrate on responding positively to today's opportunities and responsibilities without apprehension or insecurity about tomorrow's possibilities.

Finally there is the impact of the future in the form of *organization* and *prioritization:* a conception of the ultimate future can serve as a clue to the nature of present reality and as a guide for present efforts to live constructively and redemptively in the world. For example, the fact that the final future includes the same kinds of reality and being that appear in the present world suggests that each of them has its own legitimacy, purpose, and value. While they may be related in a progression of ontological "levels," with each higher level incorporating the qualities of those "below" it, no kind of being is to be understood as merely a "means" to the existence or the fulfillment of another, supposedly higher kind of reality or being. Although the color, design, and fragrance of a flower may enrich human existence, the value of the flower itself is not exhausted by this instrumental function. Because of its original creation by God and its place in God's future, it is to be understood as having its own reason for existence in the presence of God. Here is one theological ground of ecological concern.

Another example is the materiality of ultimate humanity, which means that the body is in no way a "limitation" from which humanity is to be finally delivered, or a "deficiency" to be finally transcended. Rather, the body is the means by which the rest of the created universe is to be experienced, understood, and enjoyed. For the present, this implies genuine respect for and diligent care of the body, and the development of the abilities of sensory perception. It also implies the enjoyment of sensory experience as part of the divine intention for human beings.

If the ultimate future represents the fulfillment of God's creative purpose, it is surely appropriate to endeavor to make the present as much like the future as possible. This means repairing as far as possible the damage resulting from sin, without ignoring the crucial differences between the present and the future. We are still sinners; but we can try to minimize sin in all of its expressions, and we can try to make up for some of its consequences. Thus it is eschatologically proper to overcome interracial and intercultural estrangement, to work for international peace and good will, to alleviate poverty as far as possible, and to encourage every person to develop his/her full intellectual and creative potential.

The nature of hope. Hope is the authentically Adventist relationship to time, and may therefore be understood in terms of the future, the past, and the present.

Hope is first of all anticipation of a particular future—anticipation that is composed of eagerness and patience. It is eager for the arrival of the future because the future means the liberation and fulfillment of humanity in the presence of God, not its negation and the dissolution of its meaning. In this way theological hope is like the natural eagerness of children, for whom the ring of the telephone is an occasion of expectancy, excitement, and enthusiasm. But hope is not euphoria; its eagerness is complemented by a patience that gives to hope its resilience and durability, so that it can survive delay and disappointment without disillusionment. Thus it can remain alert to the possibilities of grace, and attentive to what is happening—and especially what God is doing—in the world.

If hope were related exclusively to the future, however, it would be merely a free-floating fantasy, an elaborate product of wishful thinking, a pious illusion. To be valid and valuable, hope must be based on a particular understanding of the past and a particular experience of the present. In the case of the advent hope, the relevant past is the historical event of the revelation of God in the birth, life, death, and resurrection of Jesus. Here the outcome of the "great controversy" was determined, even though it is not yet actualized; the decisive battle was fought and won, and the ultimate future ensured. The relevant present is the personal transformation known as the "new birth" (see John 3:3-8), confirmed by the continuing presence of the Holy Spirit in one's own existence (see 2 Cor. 1:22; 5:5; Eph. 1:13, 14). This experiential validation of the historical revelation in Christ provides a confidence that can accommodate the unexpected.

On the basis of this confidence it is possible to respond creatively and constructively to what is often called the "problem of delay." The fact is that the reappearance of God in the form of Jesus the Messiah has *not* occurred, and that the present age of history continues year after year and decade after decade. But how long can Adventism say that "Jesus is coming soon" and that "the end is near"? On the one hand there is the matter of credibility: How long can the message of the advent hope remain believable? When does Adventism come to be regarded like the boy who cried "Wolf!" in the ancient fable, so that its eschatological proclamation is no longer taken seriously? On the other hand, there is the possibility of losing the sense of imminence that has been the incentive for the activism of Adventism. How long can the advent hope itself survive? At what point does it begin to fade? When does Adventism cease to "feel" the imminence of the end, and to talk about it less and less, even if it never consciously denies it?

The answers to these questions depend in part on the way the "problem of delay" is understood. It is essential to recognize that it is not, strictly speaking, a problem to be analyzed and then "solved" in the way that an engineer determines how much steel to put into a bridge, or an agronomist figures out how much food a developing nation can produce. Rather, like its theological cousin, the "problem of evil," this "problem of delay" is a *mystery* to be acknowledged. When this is done, there is no demand for a final answer to the question—Why hasn't the end come by now? For it is remembered that in the Biblical revelation God insists that "my thoughts are not your thoughts, neither are your ways my ways" (Isa. 55:8). That is to say, from the perspective of ultimate reality, there is a quite different evaluation of what is and what ought to be. Furthermore there is a different evaluation of time, so that "with the Lord one day is as a thousand years, and a thousand years as one day (2 Peter 3:8). This suggests that the fact of "delay" is more a matter of human perception (or misperception) than of actual reality—something like our impatience with the time it takes for young trees to bear fruit, or for children to outgrow their childishness.

While no final answer will be available until the *eschaton* actually arrives, in the meantime it is possible to identify several possible elements in a provisional answer. For example, Jesus associated the proclamation of the gospel "throughout the whole world, as a testimony to all nations" with the coming of "the end" (Matt. 24:14), although He did *not* say that this proclamation would "bring about" the *eschaton*. He also described the kingdom of God in terms of maturing grain:

"first the blade, then the ear, then the full grain in the ear"; and "when the grain is ripe," it is harvested immediately (Mark 4:28, 29). This has suggested that the end of the present age is associated with the spiritual maturity of the people of God. Indeed, it is plausible to regard a certain level of spiritual maturity as a necessary condition for the effective proclamation of the gospel. In any case, both the proclamation and the maturation would have to occur in a historical context, and would thus be significantly influenced (though certainly not caused) by historical circumstances, which would in turn be influenced by both natural and supernatural factors. Finally, the fact that the end of the present age of human history is part of a larger, cosmic drama means that there may be other factors that will remain entirely unknown to us (at least until the *eschaton*), even as some of the most important factors in Job's life experience remained unknown to him.

All of this shows, on the one hand, that there are various possible "reasons" that can be given to try to explain the experience of delay in the actualization of the advent hope. But it also shows, on the other hand, that there is no way to ascertain the "cause" (or "causes") of the delay, much less to correct it (or them) in such a manner as to "bring about" the *eschaton*. For the end of present history, like its beginning at creation, and its center in Jesus, is an act of God); and its timing is finally a matter of *His* determination, whatever human factors may be involved.

It is evident, then, that in one sense there is nothing that anyone can "do" about the fact that the reappearance of God in the form of Jesus the Messiah has not yet occurred, and that the present age of history continues. But it is possible to *relate* to the experience of delay creatively and constructively. For one thing, it can be regarded in the light of the love and patience of God, who is "forebearing," "not wishing that any should perish" (2 Peter 3:9). For another thing, it can be seen as an opportunity for further growth "in Christ," and for wider and more effective witnessing to the self-giving love of God. Living in the twentieth-century advent hope is thus like the experience of the first-century apostle who felt himself "pressed between the two"—namely, between the desire to "depart" and experience of the immediate, personal presence of Christ, and the need for him to "remain" and do Christ's work in the world and especially in the church (Phil. 1:23, 24). This, to be sure, is an experience of ambivalence, but it can be a spiritually creative and exciting ambivalence. In spite of the "delay" the advent hope can live and even grow, precisely because God is the God of the future. He is infinitely resourceful, and His Spirit is still operative in the world.

And it is also to be remembered that the advent hope is not the *center* of Adventist theology or experience; that center is always the historical revelation of God in Jesus. Here there is an important and happy paradox: the viability of eschatological hope is assured just to the extent that it is not allowed to become the focus of faith, but remains its spontaneous expression. For the more vivid the awareness of the life and death of Jesus, and the clearer the understanding of its meaning, the more vigorous will be the anticipation of the ultimate future as the fulfillment of human existence and the consummation of God's love.

NOTES

[1] Compare the early-second-century church manual Didache 10:6.
[2] This is not quite a Biblical formulation; the closest approximation is a reference to the fact that Christ "will appear a second time" (Heb. 9:28).

³ It is these predominantly negative qualities in the present experience of time that explain why much Christian theology, unconsciously following the lead of ancient Greek philosophy, has associated temporality with finitude and imperfection, and has defined eternity and perfection as timelessness and changelessness—thereby inviting all sorts of theological misunderstandings and dilemmas.

⁴ The importance of interpersonal environment is the reason Adventist parents are often willing to make a major financial investment to provide an appropriate educational context for their children.

GLOSSARY

Glossary

Note: The following definitions are not intended to include the full range of dictionary definitions of the terms listed, but rather are meant to reflect the specific or special meanings of these terms as used in this volume. An attempt has been made to limit this list to (1) terms that deal directly or indirectly with the second advent and (2) other terms that might be unfamiliar to some readers.

Allegorical interpretation. A type of interpretation that minimizes the literal or obvious meaning of a passage in favor of an alleged and hidden spiritual meaning.

Amillennialism. The denial that an earthly millennium of universal righteousness and peace will either precede or follow the second advent of Christ.

Anabaptist. An adherent of a religious sect that arose in Switzerland and other parts of Europe in the sixteenth century, holding that adults formerly baptized as infants should be rebaptized.

Antichrist. A term used by John the revelator to depict persons or groups who oppose Christ and His people. It is implied that antichrist will be destroyed at the second coming of Christ.

Apocalyptic. Pertaining to any remarkable revelation—specifically, the revelation given to the apostle John.

Apocalyptic literature. A type of literature distinguished principally by its allusions to the signs preceding the events to occur in the last days of world history.

Apocrypha. Fourteen books of the Septuagint in the Vulgate but not in the canonical Hebrew Scriptures nor in the Authorized Version. Also may refer to a similar collection of books known as the New Testament Apocrypha.

Aramaic. The northwestern Semitic language spoken by the Jews after the Babylonian captivity; the language spoken by Christ and His disciples.

Arianism. A theological movement initiated by Arius during the fourth century, based on the following principles: (1) God is separate from every created being, (2) Christ is a created being but may be worshiped as a secondary divinity, (3) Christ was neither truly God nor truly man—He assumed a body but not a human soul.

Armageddon. The final great battle before the second advent of Christ, as described in Revelation 16.

Chiliasm. The doctrine that Christ will reign upon the earth a thousand years. From *chilias,* meaning "thousand."

Christology. The branch of theology that treats of the person and attributes of Christ.

Conditionalism. The belief that eternal life will be bestowed on condition that a person has truly accepted Christ as his Saviour, and that anyone who does not receive eternal life will be annihilated.

Conditional prophecy. The hermeneutical theory that the fulfillment of divine predictions may be modified or delayed by the actions and/or attitudes of people.

Consistent eschatology. Albert Schweitzer's interpretation of Jesus' teaching about the kingdom; he considered eschatology the essential element in Jesus' teaching.

Cosmic. Pertaining to the material universe—especially the portion outside the solar system.

Deism. A philosophical movement, characterized by rationalism, of the seventeenth and eighteenth centuries, whose adherents generally subscribed to a natural religion based on human reason and morality, and on the belief in one God who after creating the world and the laws governing it refrained from interfering with the operation of those laws. Its adherents rejected every kind of supernatural intervention in human affairs.

Demythologizing. Divesting a writing of alleged mythological forms in order to uncover the meaning under such forms. A method of Bibical interpretation proposed by Rudolf Bultmann.

Diaspora. The scattering of the Jews throughout the Old World following the Babylonian exile.

Dispensationalism. The doctrine that God's dealings with mankind move through distinct phases, in each of which God's relationship to man and man's responsibility to God are different. For example: the dispensation of *law,* and the dispensation of *grace.*

Dualism. A term with many definitions, among them the doctrine that the universe is under the dominion of two opposing principles, one of which is good and the other evil; and a view of man as constituted of two original and independent elements, known as matter and spirit.

Ecumenism. A study of the nature and mission of the Christian church as a worldwide Christian fellowship.

Eschatology. The branch of theology that deals with death, resurrection, immortality, and the end of the world, often referred to as the *eschaton,* final judgment, and the future state.

Esoteric. Intended for or understood by only a chosen few, as an inner group of disciples or initiates; said of ideas, doctrines, literature, et cetera.

Existentialism. A philosophical system of thought, adopted by some religionists, that places the primary emphasis on human experience or "existence" rather than on revelation, "essence," or authority. It must be remembered that any attempt at definition is inadequate because existentialism has assumed so many different forms.

Fatidic. Able to prophesy; oracular.

Fifth Monarchy Men. A religious group in mid-seventeenth-century England who sought to establish the fifth monarchy of Daniel 2:44. Accordingly they expected the return of Christ and that the "saints" with Him should rule on the earth for a thousand years.

Futuristic eschatology. An interpretation of Jesus' teaching about the kingdom that places the fulfillment of Jesus' statements at or near the time of His second advent.

Great Disappointment. The experience of Adventist believers in the fall of 1844 who had expected the second advent on October 22.

Great Tribulation. According to the rapture theory, a seven-year period before the coming of Christ and after the saints have been caught up to heaven.

Hegemony. Leadership or supreme command; political ascendancy of a city or state.

Hermeneutics. The art and science of interpretation.

Historicism. An interpretation of Daniel and Revelation as a panorama of successively unfolding events spanning the history of the church until the second advent of Christ.

Humanism. A system of thought in which man and his interests and development are made central and dominant. Humanism exalts the cultural and practical rather than the scientific, speculative, and religious.

Iconography. The science of the description or study of paintings, sculptures, portraits, busts, statues, emblems, and symbolism.

Intertestamental. Of, relating to, or being the period of several centuries between the composition of the last canonical book of the Old Testament and the writing of the books of the New Testament.

Johannine literature. The New Testament books generally considered as having been written by John: the Gospel of John; 1, 2, and 3 John; and Revelation.

Kerygma. A term meaning "proclamation," used in the New Testament to describe the Christian gospel of salvation.

Messiah. The Anointed One; the Christ; the Hebrew name for the promised deliverer of mankind; the name assumed by Jesus and given to Him by Christians.

Millerism. The doctrine of William Miller, who taught that the end of the world and the second coming of Christ would occur sometime in 1843 or 1844.

Ontology. A branch of metaphysics relating to the nature and relations of being. Also, a particular system according to which problems of the nature of being are investigated.

Paraclete. The Holy Spirit as helper and comforter as promised by Christ in His meeting with His disciples in the upper room before His crucifixion.

Parousia. A coming, arrival, advent. Used specifically to describe the second advent of Christ.

Pentateuch. The first five books of the Bible, taken collectively.

Pentecostal. A term referring to the outpouring of the Holy Spirit at the Feast of Pentecost, as described in Acts 2.

Peregrinate. To travel from one country to another or from place to place. To travel through or across.

Postmillennialism. The doctrine that Christ's second coming will follow the millennium.

Premillennialism. The doctrine that the millennium is to be introduced by the personal return of Christ.

Proleptic. Of, relating to, or exemplifying prolepsis, i.e., anticipation of an event. Especially, prolepsis can be the describing of an event as taking place before it could have done so, or the treating of a future event as if it had already happened.

Pseudepigrapha. Spurious religious writings ascribed to scriptural characters or times and not considered as canonical by the Christian church.

Qumran library. Surviving manuscripts of an

ascetic sect of Jews who lived in the Judean desert near the Wadi Qumran on the northwest shore of the Dead Sea roughly between 150 B.C. and A.D. 68.

Realized eschatology. C. H. Dodd's interpretation of Jesus' teaching about the kingdom. Dodd considered the message of the kingdom as being "realized" in the life and teaching of Jesus rather than as being prophetic of future events.

Renaissance. The revival of letters and art in Europe, making the transition from medieval to modern history. It began in Italy in the fourteenth century.

Schematization. To form into a scheme; to arrange in regular order.

Scriptural glosses. Explanatory notes written in the margins or between the lines of ancient scriptural manuscripts.

Secret rapture. The doctrine that the saved will be caught up to heaven before the great tribulation that precedes the second advent of Christ.

Septuagint. An old Greek translation of the Old Testament Scriptures, reputed to have been made by seventy or seventy-two translators between 280 and 130 B.C.

Sibylline Oracles. Predictions of a group of prophetesses of the second century.

Soteriology. The branch of theology that deals with salvation, especially the salvation believed by Christians to have been accomplished through Jesus Christ.

Synoptists. Authors of the three Synoptic Gospels—Matthew, Mark, and Luke.

Theocracy. A state, polity, or group of people that claims to be governed by a god; Biblically, the ancient nation of Israel under the rule of Yahweh.

Theophany. A manifestation, or appearance, of God to man.

Vulgate. Jerome's Latin version of the Bible, now revised and widely used by Roman Catholics. This translation was made between about A.D. 383 and A.D. 405.

SCRIPTURE
INDEX

Scripture Index

GENERAL INDEX

General Index

GENERAL INDEX

Bridge, William, 133
Brightman, Thomas, 121, 125, 126, 133, 142, 143
Brooks, Thomas, 140, 148
Bruce, F. F., 58
Bultmann, Rudolf, 192, 201
Bunch, Taylor Grant, 186
Burton, William, 133
Busher, Leonard, 133

C

Calamy, Edmund, 149
Calculations of end: sequence of kingdoms, 36
seven-thousand-year world week, 36
six ages of world history, 103, 104
ten weeks, 35-37
tiredness of earth, 36
Calvin, John, 119, 121, 126, 128, 129
on imminent return of Christ, 115-117
Canterbury Tales (Chaucer), 107
Carcich, Theodore, 183
Chafer, Lewis Sperry, 203
Channing, William Ellery, 166
Charlemagne, 103
Chiliasm, 68, 70, 71, 73, 85, 86, 97, 110, 112, 120, 122, 127-129
Christ: as apocalyptic Messiah, 38-40
as high priest, 19, 20
as Messiah, 21-25
as Servant of God, 20, 21
His priestly ministry, 140, 141
Christ and Time (Cullmann), 63
Christian Herald, The, 157
Christianismi Restitutio (Servetus), 126
Chronica sive Historia de Duabus Civitatibus (Otto), 103
Chrysostom, 86
City of God (Augustine), 86, 97, 98
influence of, 103
Clavis Apocalyptica (Mede), 126, 143
Clement of Rome, 66, 67, 70
Cleveland, Earl E., 184
Columbus, 118
Commodianus, 81, 82
Communist Manifesto (Marx, Engels), 165
Conditional prophecy, 177, 179, 182
Consistent liberalism, 203
Constantine, 83-85, 121-127
edict of toleration, 81
Copernicus, 118
Cosmic restoration, model of, 34
Cullmann, Oscar, 63
Cyclical view, 104
Cyprian of Carthage, 81-83
Cyril of Alexandria, 86
Cyril of Jerusalem, 85

D

Damascus Document, 40
Dante, 109
Darby, J. N., 203
Day of the Lord, 26, 46, 47, 60, 61, 73

Decius, persecution of Christians, 81
Dent, Arthur, 142, 143
Diaspora, 31, 32
Didymus the Blind, 86
Dies Irae (Thomas of Celano), 105
Dilthey, Wilhelm, 194
Diocletian, 81
Dionysius of Alexandria, 82
Disappointment, the, 168-170
Discovery of the World to Come (Seagar), 134
Dispensationalism, 202-204
Dispensationalists, 207, 208
Dodd, C. H., 49, 57
Domitian, 81, 103
Donne, John, 133
Doomsday (Chester), 106
Douglass, Herbert E., 179, 186
Dowling, John, 158
Dualism: apocalyptic, 36, 60, 61
messianic, 40-42, 61
ontological, 68, 69
Durant, John, 132, 139-142, 147
Durham, James, 133

E

Edict of toleration (Constantine), 81
Edson, Hiram, 168
End, The (Douglass), 179
End of times signs, apocalyptic, 37, 38
Engels, Friedrich, 165
Erigena, John Scotus, 100
Eschatological concepts, final future, 194-196
God-centered, 192, 193
literal future, 199-201
present-future relationship, 201
Eschatological judgment, 220, 221
Eschatology: apostolic, 73
early Christian writers' issues on, 73, 74
futuristic, 49, 51, 55, 61, 62
realized, 49, 51, 55, 62
Seventh-day Adventist themes of, 214-216
significance of, 213
Eschatology, Adventist: experiential significance of, 224-228
four major themes, 214-224
place within Adventist theology, 211-214
Eschaton, 21, 51, 134, 187, 197, 201, 214, 215, 218, 223-228
Etymologiae (Isidore of Seville), 103
Eucharist, 65, 98

F

Fagal, William A., 177
Faraday, Michael, 152
Fatadic year (1843), 161
Ferrer, Vincent, 108
Festial (Mirk), 105
Final future, 194
Finch, Sir Henry, 133
Finney, Charles Gandison, 152, 156
Firmilian of Caesarea, 81
Fitch, Charles, 157, 160